RADIO BROADCASTING FROM 1920 TO 1990
An Annotated Bibliography

Diane Foxhill Carothers

GARLAND PUBLISHING, INC. • NEW YORK & LONDON
1991

© 1991 Diane Foxhill Carothers
All rights reserved

Library of Congress Cataloging-in-Publication Data

Carothers, Diane Foxhill, 1927–
   Radio broadcasting from 1920 to 1990 : an annotated bibliography / Diane Foxhill Carothers.
      p. cm. — (Garland reference library of the humanities ; vol. 967)
   Includes index.
   ISBN 0-8240-1209-7 (alk. paper)
   1. Radio broadcasting—Bibliography. I Title. II. Series.
Z7221.C37   1991
[PN1991.5]
016.38454'0904—dc20   90-24352
                                                                        CIP

Printed on acid-free, 250-year-life paper
Manufactured in the United States of America

For the three main men in my life--

Zane, Bruce, and Bob

CONTENTS

Acknowledgments ix

Introduction xi

Chapter 1. **Background of Radio Broadcasting** 1
Includes histories, autobiographies, biographies, anecdotes, information about individual programs and performers.

Chapter 2. **Economic Aspects** 87
Includes advertising, ownership, audience appeal, listening groups, ratings, radio industry, networks, promotion, rates, investing/financing, public relations, and broadcast management.

Chapter 3. **Production Aspects** 179
Includes announcing, writing, directing, editorializing, sound, news production, propaganda, studios, style manuals, standards and codes, speeches, lectures, commentaries, and broadcast journalism.

Chapter 4. **Programming** 257
Includes comedy, music, talk shows, call-ins, children's programs, farm/rural broadcasting, documentaries, drama, sports, political/public affairs, and religious programming.

Chapter 5. **International Broadcasting** 309
  Includes Africa, Asia, Australia, Canada,
  Europe, Great Britain, India, Latin and
  South America, Malaysia, Mexico,
  Scandinavia, the Third World, Radio
  Free Europe, and Radio Liberty.

Chapter 6. **Public Broadcasting** 375
  Includes national public radio,
  community broadcasting, educational
  radio, and the use of radio in education.

Chapter 7. **Regulation and Legal Aspects** 425
  Includes station ownership, radio control,
  licensing, Federal Communications
  Commission rulings, allocation of
  frequencies, copyright, censorship,
  right to access, the Fairness Doctrine,
  and the First Amendment.

Chapter 8. **Amateur/Ham Radio** 463
  Includes history of amateur radio,
  licensing requirements, and station
  operations.

Chapter 9. **Women and Minorities** 471
  Includes ownership and/or management
  of radio stations, career opportunities,
  and station programming.

Chapter 10. **Careers in Broadcasting** 479
  Includes vocational guidance and
  job descriptions.

Chapter 11. **Reference Sources** 489
  Includes handbooks, guidebooks,
  dictionaries, glossaries, directories,
  encyclopedias, and bibliographies.

Author Index 521
Title Index 539

ACKNOWLEDGMENTS

It is indeed a pleasure to express my sincere thanks to the many staff members and student employees in the University Library's circulation, shipping, and interlibrary loan departments for their generous help in acquiring and delivering the many hundreds of books I needed to annotate for this project. Particular appreciation and gratitude are due also to the staff of the Communications Library--Patsy Inskip, Jim Ferguson, and our many student employees--for their cooperation and patience during the preparation of this book. I wish also to thank David Blair, Jacqueline Osby, and especially Tom Galer-Unti, all of the College of Communications, for their help in solving my computer and printing problems.

I am pleased to acknowledge also the University's help given in the form of sabbatical leave. That time and opportunity were indispensable to the research and writing entailed in preparing this book.

Finally, I want to express my thanks for the encouragement, help, and consistent support given throughout by my husband.

INTRODUCTION

Several years ago a University of Illinois faculty researcher came to the Communications Library seeking a printed bibliography listing books about early radio broadcasting. Although we found several related works, none provided the needed information. The absence of such source material led me to create a comprehensive annotated bibliography of radio broadcasting. This book is the result. It is not intended to exhaust the subject but to provide a more extensive source of material than previously available. Obviously not every title published has been included but a good representation of books about radio broadcasting are listed.

In compiling this volume I used the extensive facilities of the University of Illinois Library, the state-wide system of library circulation, and the national interlibrary loan system. Each book cited was examined, the full bibliographic information recorded, and the annotation written with the book in hand. Entries are primarily restricted to published books although a number of periodicals and trade journals are included. Generally, only one edition of a title is annotated while reference is occasionally made to earlier or later ones. Whenever it was available the entries show the International Standard Book Number (ISBN) for monographs or the International Standard Serial Number (ISSN) for serials. Dissertations and theses are excluded.

The book's eleven chapter-categories cover almost the entire range of radio broadcasting. However, radio engineering has been excluded since such extremely technical material was deemed inappropriate for most of the readership to which the book is directed. Some of the historical volumes cited do encompass aspects of engineering and thus provide background material for the general reader.

Radio Broadcasting
from 1920 to 1990

BACKGROUND OF RADIO BROADCASTING

Includes histories, biographies, autobiographies, anecdotes, and information about individual programs and performers.

1. Ace, Goodman. *Ladies and Gentlemen, Easy Aces.* Garden City, NY: Doubleday, 1970. 210 pp.

    The title is a quote from the introduction of the popular radio program of the 1930s and 1940s. This volume is a collection of eight scripts from that period.

2. Adair, James R. *M.R. DeHaan: The Man and His Ministry.* Grand Rapids, MI: Zondervan, 1969. 160 pp.

    DeHaan was the founder of the Radio Bible Class which preached Christianity via the airwaves. In 1939 he broadcast live for the first time on radio station WEXL, a 50-watt outlet in the Detroit suburb of Royal Oak. The program achieved a broad following and in 1968 expanded into television under DeHaan's son.

3. Aitken, Hugh G.J. *Syntony and Spark: The Origins of Radio.* New York: John Wiley & Sons, 1976. 347 pp. (Science, Culture and Society series). ISBN: 0-471-01816-3.

    The foreword states that Aitken "makes us feel that he not only understands the work of Clerk Maxwell and Hertz, but could also have been a pioneer radio operator for Marconi." Two chapters are "intended for the reader with a specialized professional interest" in technology while the others present the non-technical aspects of radio history.

4. Allen, Fred. *Treadmill to Oblivion.* Boston: Little, Brown, 1954. 240 pp.

    One of radio's most popular comedians, Allen devotes most of this autobiography to his years in radio. Included are a number of scripts from actual shows. Al Hirschfeld contributed the drawings that illustrate the text.

2 Radio Broadcasting

5. Allen, Steve. *The Funny Men*. New York: Simon & Schuster, 1956. 279 pp.

    Most of the comedians and humorists profiled in these pages got their start in vaudeville and/or radio and then went on to television. Among them are Fred Allen, Jack Benny, Eddie Cantor, Arthur Godfrey, Bob Hope, Groucho Marx, and Red Skelton.

6. Allighan, Garry. *Sir John Reith*. London: Stanley Paul, 1938. 287 pp.

    The life-story of the Director-General of the British Broadcasting Corporation "is superimposed on the background of the romance of radio itself ... Interesting glimpses are given of those who were creating the new science in readiness for the Reith era and fascinating disclosures are made from inside the BBC itself."

7. Alth, Max. *Collecting Old Radios and Crystal Sets*. Des Moines, IA: Wallace-Homestead, 1977. 74 pp. ISBN: 0-87069-140-6.

    Concerns primarily the equipment used in early radio broadcasting: "the home constructed and assembled crystal sets and radios, and the early, awkward but beautiful, factory constructed equipment." Chapters provide names of manufacturers, operating instructions, repairs, and tips on collecting as well as current (1977) prices.

8. American Advertising Museum. *An Audio History of Commercial Radio*. Portland, OR: Radio Heritage Productions, 1987. 6 cassettes (boxed).

    Written, produced, and narrated by John Salisbury, this is "a compendium from the Beginning through the

Twenties, Thirties, Forties, and Fifties" taken from the permanent collection of the Museum's radio exhibit. Interspersed with Salisbury's narrative are brief, illustrative excerpts from actual programs, including commercials.

9. Andrews, Bart, and Ahrgus Juilliard. *Holy Mackerel! The Amos 'n' Andy Story*. New York: E.P. Dutton, 1986. 188 pp. ISBN: 0-525-24354-2.

    Created as a mid-1920s radio program by Charles J. Correll and Freeman Gosden, the *Amos 'n' Andy Show* successfully made the transition to television in 1951 until criticism concerning racial bigotry helped force it off the air. This book brings back memories for any fan of the show and contains synopses of all 78 TV episodes.

10. Andrews, Robert D. *Just Plain Bill: His Story*. Philadelphia: David McKay, 1935. 249 pp.

    Written in an informal style similiar to that used on the popular radio serial, this presents "the truth about a man millions love." In addition, it contains data and photographs of Elmer and Mrs. Eeps, David Ellis, Kerry, Nancy, and the rest of the "Hartville folks."

11. Archer, Gleason L. *Big Business and Radio*. New York: American Historical Society, 1939. 503 pp.

    Definitely NOT a continuation of Archer's *History of Radio to 1926*, (see item #12) "the bulk of this volume consists of a story based upon records opened for the first time to any historian." It begins with a look behind the scenes at RCA in 1922, continues with compromises and arbitration, and ends with federal anti-trust litigation and the corporation's consent decree. This was reprinted in 1971 as part of the History of Broadcasting: Radio to

Television series published by Arno Press/New York Times.

12. Archer, Gleason L. *History of Radio to 1926*. New York: American Historical Society, 1938. 421 pp.

An outgrowth of a course on radio broadcasting in the College of Journalism of Suffolk University, Boston, Massachusetts. The author begins with what he calls intercommunication of signals in early times, continues with the invention of the electric telegraph, wireless telegraphy, early RCA and Westinghouse companies, and concludes with the struggle for network broadcasting, wave-length allocations and injunctions. The book was reprinted in 1971 by Arno Press/New York Times as part of the History of Broadcasting: Radio to Television series.

13. Arnheim, Rudolf. *Radio*. London: Faber & Faber, 1936. 296 pp.

The World of Sound, Direction and Distance, Spatial Resonance, and The Necessity of Radio-Film are some of the chapter titles. Illustrations show the control room at BBC's Broadcasting House, studios in Konigsberg and Hamburg, a steel tape recording room, a Berlin listening room, and several views of various productions in rehearsal or actually on the air. This book was reprinted in 1971 by Arno Press/New York Times as part of the History of Broadcasting: Radio to Television series.

14. Bacher, William A., ed. *The Treasury Star Parade*. New York: Farrar & Rinehart, 1942. 379 pp.

The *Treasury Hour* and the *Star Parade* were radio programs presented for the benefit of the Treasury Department to raise money through the sale of War

Bonds. This reprints 27 sketches from these programs which were written by leading writers and performed by well-known actors and actresses.

15. Bain, Donald. *Long John Nebel: Radio Talk King, Master Salesman, Magnificent Charlatan*. New York: Macmillan, 1974. 268 pp. ISBN: 0-02-505950-5.

    Nebel was described as "one of the most unique figures to ever sit behind the microphones of a major radio station." For over 18 years he reigned as "king of all-night radio talk in New York." This biography of Jack Knebel who gained fame as Long John Nebel was written while Nebel was still a very active radio personality.

16. Baker, W.J. *A History of the Marconi Company*. London: Methuen, 1970. 413 pp.

    The archives of the Marconi Company were made available to the author who stated that no commercial censorship was exercised by the company during his writing of the book. He was able to record the downs as well as the ups of the firm that pioneered in the fields of radio, television, and electronics.

17. Bannerman, R. LeRoy. *Norman Corwin and Radio: The Golden Years*. University, AL: University of Alabama Press, 1986. 275 pp. ISBN: 0-8173-0274-3.

    More than a biography, this book provides a social history of the period between the mid-1930s and the late 1940s referred to as the "Golden Age of Radio." This is an intimate look at 1940s broadcasting and the man who brought to radio "a spirit of intelligence, integrity, and experimentation"

6 Radio Broadcasting

18. Bannerman, R. LeRoy. *On a Note of Triumph: Norman Corwin and the Golden Years of Radio*. New York: Carol Publishing, 1986. 275 pp. ISBN: 0-8184-0512-0.

    Published originally under the subtitle (see item #17), this tells the story of Norman Corwin who was writer, director, and producer of numerous network radio shows.

19. Banning, William Peck. *Commercial Broadcasting Pioneer: The WEAF Experiment, 1922-1926*. Cambridge, MA: Harvard University Press, 1946. 308 pp.

    The American Telephone and Telegraph Company sponsored experimental work during the early days of radio because it foresaw good prospects in providing telephone subscribers and other users with fresh services such as radio telephony across the ocean, from ship to shore and from moving vehicles. It operated WEAF (formerly WBAY) from 1922 to 1926 and established WCAP as a second experimental station in order to further such research.

20. Bannister, Harry. *The Education of a Broadcaster*. New York: Simon & Schuster, 1965. 351 pp.

    The first half covers the author's experiences in radio while the second part is devoted to television. He was vice-president in charge of station relations for NBC during his 35 years in broadcasting.

21. Barber, Walter L. *The Broadcasters*. New York: Dial Press, 1970. 271 pp.

    Sportscaster Red Barber writes about the pioneers in radio broadcasting: Graham McNamee, Ted Husing, Bill Munday, Harry Wismer, and Bill Stern, and others who are less well known. His main emphasis, however, is on the broadcasting of baseball and football on radio and television, as he looks back over his own 40 years at the microphone.

22. Barman, Thomas. *Diplomatic Correspondent.* New York: Macmillan, 1968. 273 pp.

As a diplomatic correspondent, Barman reported for BBC for more than 20 years. He tells of his world as he traveled and reported from a wide variety of places including Algiers, Cairo, Stockholm, and Moscow.

23. Barnes, Pat. *Sketches of Life.* Chicago: Reilly & Lee, 1932. 119 pp.

Jimmy and Grandad was the radio show on NBC that brought Pat Barnes into prominence. This tells "mainly the story of the program, the characters of Jimmy and Grandad, and their 'Jimtown' friends."

24. Barnouw, Erik. *A History of Broadcasting in the United States.* New York: Oxford University Press, 1966-1970. 3 vols.

A classic in the field, this comprehensive set details the progress of both radio and television from their earliest days to 1970 state-of-the-art. The volumes bear separate titles: *A Tower in Babel, The Golden Web,* and *The Image Builders.*

25. Barnouw, Erik. *Mass Communication: Television, Radio, Film, Press: The Media and Their Practice in the United States of America.* New York: Rinehart, 1956. 280 pp.

Chapters are devoted to the history and psychology of the media, and the sponsors of mass communication. Most of the treatment of radio is given in about 20 pages, but

8 Radio Broadcasting

scattered information about the medium occurs throughout the book.

26. Barson, Michael, ed. *Flywheel, Shyster, and Flywheel*. New York: Pantheon Books, 1988. 330 pp. ISBN: 0-679-72036-7.

    The subtitle states that this is the "Marx Brothers' lost radio show" and contains 26 episodes of the program. Additional contents include "the short, happy life of the Marx Brothers on radio," a conversation with Nat Perrin, their writer, and an interview with Groucho Marx who "tells all."

27. Benny, Mary Livingstone, and Hilliard Marks, with Marcia Borie. *Jack Benny*. Garden City, NY: Doubleday, 1978. 322 pp. ISBN: 0-385-12397-X.

    Written by Benny's widow and brother-in-law, this was actually begun as a collaboration between Jack Benny and Marks. When Benny died the others decided to tell the life story of the man who "took command of a stage and made people love him--because he loved them back (and who was) always the foil for those of his radio and television family who surrounded him."

28. Berg, Gertrude. *The Rise of the Goldbergs*. New York: Barse, 1931. 250 pp.

    Sixteen episodes of the popular radio program are published in narrative form in this volume. They help bring out the personalities of the four main characters: Molly, Jake, Sammy, and Rosie Goldberg.

29. Berg, Gertrude, with Cherney Berg. *Molly and Me*. New York: McGraw-Hill, 1961. 278 pp.

From the opening bars of Toselli's *Serenade* and Molly's "Hello. Is anybody?" *The Goldbergs* were a radio success story. Gertrude Berg's autobiography reads exactly like an episode from the program as she writes about her family, her childhood, and her career as writer-actress-producer.

30. Bergreen, Laurence. *Look Now, Pay Later: The Rise of Network Broadcasting.* Garden City, NY: Doubleday, 1980. 300 pp. ISBN: 0-385-14465-2.

    Both radio and television broadcasting are covered in this history of networks. It begins with a story of corporate rivalry (RCA, NBC, et al.) and ends with "signs of obsolescence" that the author qualifies as "from broadcasting to narrowcasting."

31. Berle, Milton. *B.S. I Love You: Sixty Funny Years with the Famous and the Infamous.* New York: McGraw-Hill, 1987. 286 pp. ISBN: 0-07-004913-0.

    Not principally autobiographical, this book is a collection of anecdotes connected with the Friars Club. Berle tells stories about entertainers, politicians, sports stars, singers, writers, band leaders, gangsters, etc. He includes some of the wit, ad-libs, roasts, and one-liners that have evolved from his association with the organization.

32. Bilby, Kenneth. *The General: David Sarnoff and the Rise of the Communications Industry.* New York: Harper & Row, 1986. 326 pp. ISBN: 0-06-015568-X.

    Intertwined with this biography of David Sarnoff is, of necessity, the history of the Radio Corporation of America and the rise of radio broadcasting itself. The volume covers Sarnoff's life, the creation of RCA, the first network, the subsequent rise of television, and the final years of RCA under his direction.

33. Bittner, John R. *Broadcasting: An Introduction*. Englewood Cliffs, NJ: Prentice-Hall, 1980. 508 pp. ISBN: 0-13-083535-8.

Intended as a textbook for single-semester or introductory broadcasting courses, this treats the historical basis of broadcasting and continues to the contemporary industry. The development of modern radio, data about radio waves and the spectrum, networks, and educational and public broadcasting are covered along with international broadcasting, programming, audiences, ratings, and the FCC.

34. Bittner, John R. *Broadcasting and Telecommunication: An Introduction*. 2nd ed. Englewood Cliffs, NJ: Prentice-Hall, 1985. 526 pp. ISBN: 0-1308-3551-X.

Intended for introductory courses, this presents a total approach to electronic communication from the history of telegraph to the future of personal computers, including traditional topics such as radio and television history, ratings, telecommunications, research, economics, and international broadcasting.

35. Bittner, John R. *Professional Broadcasting: A Brief Introduction*. Englewood Cliffs, NJ: Prentice-Hall, 1981. 255 pp. ISBN: 0-13-725465-2.

This offers information on the field "wrapped in an easily understood, uncomplicated, and non-technical format." Its radio section describes station diversity, characteristics of radio, its beginnings, studios, stations, controls, programming, marketing strategies, and regulations.

36. Black, Peter. *The Biggest Aspidistra in the World: A Personal Celebration of Fifty Years of the BBC*. London: British Broadcasting Corporation, 1972. 243 pp. ISBN: 0-563-12154-8.

Newspaper critic Black writes that he doesn't seek to tell the history of the BBC but intends the book to be a "celebration of the first half-century of the house that Reith built." However, he does present an indirect history as he includes data and anecdotes about the BBC from its creation, through WW II and up to its status as of the publication date.

37. Bliss, Edward, Jr., ed. *In Search of Light: The Broadcasts of Edward R. Murrow, 1938-1961*. New York: Alfred A. Knopf, 1967. 364 pp.

Murrow made more than 5,000 radio broadcasts, beginning with an eyewitness report on Hitler's seizure of Austria and ending 23 years later with his own observations on John F. Kennedy's inaugural address. This volume reprints several hundred of these broadcasts--some as short as a brief paragraph and others four to five pages in length--that were chosen because they add dimension to history by means of Murrow's perspective, or that show development of his unique reporting style and beliefs.

38. Blythe, Cheryl, and Susan Sackett. *Say Good Night, Gracie! The Story of Burns & Allen*. New York: E.P. Dutton, 1986. 304 pp. ISBN: 0-525-24386-0.

In 1950 *The Burns and Allen Show* made a smooth transition from radio to television where it remained a highly rated and popular program for eight years. This tells the story of the team that made the show the success it was and that had one of the more enduring marriage-partnerships in show business.

39. Boyle, Andrew. *Only the Wind Will Listen: Reith of the BBC*. London: Hutchinson, 1972. 368 pp. ISBN: 0-09-113820-5.

   Dedicated as a tribute to the BBC on its 50th birthday, this is the biography of John Reith, known as the father of the British Broadcasting Corporation. It combines the story of Reith's life with that of the BBC, as the two are irrevocably intertwined.

40. Brickhouse, Jack, with Jack Rosenberg and Ned Colletti. *Thanks for Listening*! South Bend, IN: Diamond Communications, 1986. 224 pp. ISBN: 0-912083-16-6.

   This Hall of Fame announcer reminisces about his broadcast beginnings in Peoria, Illinois, his long-time association with the Chicago Cubs, broadcasting White Sox baseball, Big Ten and Notre Dame football, the Chicago Bears, and professional wresting. There are 24 pages of photographs, generally of Brickhouse with one celebrity or another.

41. Briggs, Asa. *The BBC: The First Fifty Years*. Oxford, Eng.: Oxford University Press, 1985. 439 pp. ISBN: 0-19-212971-6.

   After having published a four-volume history of British broadcasting (see item #42), Briggs concentrates on a detailed account of the British Broadcasting Corporation between 1922 and 1972. This book is not an abridgement of the earlier work but incorporates previously unpublished primary source material and covers programming, personalities, and the role of the BBC as an institution.

Background 13

42. Briggs, Asa. *The History of Broadcasting in the United Kingdom*. Oxford, Eng.: Oxford University Press, 1961-1979. 4 vols.

    The titles of the individual volumes of this monumental history of the British Broadcasting Corporation are *The Birth of Broadcasting, The Golden Age of Wireless, The War of Words*, and *Sound and Vision*. The author states that he explored all available primary sources to compile this history. A number of illustrations found in the BBC archives have been incorporated.

43. Briggs, Susan. *Those Radio Times*. London: Weidenfeld & Nicolson, 1981. 232 pp. ISBN: 0-297-77929-X.

    In her introduction to this pictorial survey the author notes that she looked for and discovered pictures relating to the early history of sound broadcasting in the most unlikely places. She has reproduced many photographs from the archives of the British Broadcasting Corporation and utilized sketches, blueprints, cartoons, caricatures, advertisements, and illustrations of various other kinds.

44. British Broadcasting Corporation. *More From Ten to Eight on Radio 4*. London: The Corporation, 1969. 75 pp.

    This is part of a series about BBC Radio 4's *Ten to Eight* program and reflects listener interest in memorable broadcasts of the 1968/69 season. It includes a selection of "Midweek Messages," "Holy Places," "Meditations," and "Reflections."

45. *Broadcasting in Britain*. 2nd ed. London: Her Majesty's Stationery Office, 1975. 47 pp. (Central Office of Information, Reference Pamphlet 111).

14 Radio Broadcasting

Gives a brief history of the growth of British broadcasting and outlines the constitutions and organizations of the two public bodies licensed to provide radio and television broadcasting services--the British Broadcasting Corporation (BBC) and the Independent Broadcasting Authority (IBA). It describes the details of the services provided by each agency.

46. *A Broadcasting Primer: With Notes on the New Technologies.* New York: Television Information Office, 1985. 18 pp.

    Even though this is published by TIO, there is a great deal of information about radio broadcasting contained therein. It offers a history of the medium, information on broadcasting regulation and the FCC, programs, advertising, payola, and both AM and FM broadcasting.

47. Brokenshire, Norman. *This Is Norman Brokenshire: An Unvarnished Self-Portrait.* New York: David McKay, 1954. 307 pp.

    Brokenshire gained his greatest fame on the *Theatre Guild of the Air* program where he interacted with the best-known dramatic stars of the period. He did ten shows a week as a disc jockey and was at one time chief announcer for the Columbia Broadcasting System.

48. Brown, David, and W. Richard Bruner, eds. *I Can Tell It Now.* New York: E.P. Dutton, 1964. 362 pp.

    First person experiences related by members of the Overseas Press Club of America, this is a collection of stories that were never filed or broadcast during WW II. Among those contributing such accounts are broadcasters Robert Sherrod, Cecil Brown, H.V. Kaltenborn, Quentin Reynolds, Bob Considine, Jules Bergman, and Irving R. Levine.

49. Burlingame, Roger. *Don't Let Them Scare You: The Life and Times of Elmer Davis*. Philadelphia: J.B. Lippincott, 1961. 352 pp.

Not a run-of-the-mill biography this chronicle tells the story of Davis's life, but it deals principally with the period of time when Senator Joseph McCarthy was practically a household name and the witch-hunt for communists was at its peak. As a commentator Davis was outspoken on the subject and, as a result, was widely criticized. Burlingame projects a picture of the trials Davis underwent at the time.

50. Burns, Tom. *The BBC: Public Institution and Private World*. London: Macmillan, 1977. 313 pp. ISBN: 0-333-19720-8.

Based primarily on tape recordings and personal notes taken in 1963 and 1973, this describes the BBC as "a working community and an occupational mileu, about the changes which have taken place during the ten years' interval between the two series of interviews and about the continuities observable over the same period." Burns writes about the early days of radio broadcasting and the ensuing problems of providing regular transmission of programs to the huge corporation it has become while controlling all aspects of British radio and television.

51. Burrows, A.R. *The Story of Broadcasting*. London: Cassell, 1924. 182 pp.

The foreword states that "Mr. Burrows ... who has been so intimately associated with this popular application of wireless science, has placed on record the story of broadcasting from its inception, dating back, as he states, to the first S O S at sea." The book includes eight half-tone plates, principally of personnel involved in the medium.

52. Buxton, Frank, and Bill Owen. *The Big Broadcast, 1920-1950.* New York: Viking Press, 1972. 301 pp.

> Described on the title page as "a new, revised and greatly expanded edition of *Radio's Golden Age*, the complete reference work (see item #53)," this appeared five years after the publication of the first title. There are special narrative sections on announcers, comedy and comedians, big band remotes, commercials, interviewers, quiz shows, religion, singers, soap operas, sound effects, sports and sportscasters, women's programs, and "a catch-all titled Animal Imitators, Baby Criers, Doubles, Mimics, and Screamers."

53. Buxton, Frank, and Bill Owen. *Radio's Golden Age: the Programs and the Personalities.* New York: Easton Valley Press, 1966. 417 pp.

> Trivia experts would love this book because it is full of details such as why Prof. Kaltenmeyer's name was changed to Prof. Applegate, who took the part of Jack Benny's telephone operator Mabel, and the real names of the Hoosier Hotshots. Casts, directors, writers, and producers are included along with items such as "The program (*Famous Jury Trials*) began with crowd noises and the sound of a gavel."

54. Campbell, Robert. *The Golden Years of Broadcasting: A Celebration of the First 50 Years of Radio and TV on NBC.* New York: Charles Scribner's Sons, 1976. 256 pp. ISBN: 0-684-14816-1.

> The story of NBC's early history is told through the programs it presented during that time and in the framework of the factors influencing the genre's development. The coverage of radio programming is

presented in the first 48 pages of the book; the remainder is devoted to television.

55. Cantor, Eddie, with Jane Kesner Ardmore. *Take My Life*. Garden City, NY: Doubleday, 1957. 288 pp.

Long a vaudeville personality, Eddie Cantor was also a well-known radio performer, and his program, *The Chase and Sanborn Hour*, was extremely popular during the 1930s. This is his autobiography written after his heart attack when he admitted that his life really did pass in review in his mind.

56. Cantril, Hadley, with the assistance of Hazel Gaudet and Herta Herzog. *The Invasion from Mars*. New York: Harper & Row, 1966. 224 pp.

The subtitle describes this as "as a study in the psychology of panic," and it includes the complete script of the famous Orson Welles radio broadcast. Published originally by Princeton University Press in 1940, this was part of its Researches in the Social, Cultural and Behavioral Sciences series.

57. Carneal, Georgette. *A Conqueror of Space: An Authorized Biography of the Life and Work of Lee De Forest*. New York: Horace Liveright, 1930. 296 pp.

As implied in the subtitle, the author had access to De Forest's own accounts of the evolution of his inventions and this material was supplemented by his diaries and notebooks kept from early boyhood. She based her book on this material as well as her contact with another biographer, William Arvin, who published a lengthy article on De Forest in *Radio News* in 1924.

18 Radio Broadcasting

58. Carroll, Carroll. *None of Your Business, or, My Life with J. Walter Thompson*. New York: Cowles, 1970. 288 pp. ISBN: 0-402-12039-6.

An additional subtitle aptly describes this book: Confessions of a Renegade Radio Writer. Because everybody was ad-libbing on live programs, according to Carroll, the Thompson agency figured the only way to get radio shows that would work as advertising was to have them conceived, written, and produced by an advertising agency. This is what Carroll did during the time span covered in this book.

59. Carter, Alden R. *Radio: From Marconi to the Space Age*. New York: Franklin Watts, 1987. 95 pp. (A First Book). ISBN: 0-531-10310-2.

Written for children by a former radio announcer, this has chapters titled Radio's Mysterious Waves and Fields, Marconi and the Development of Radio, Giving Radio a Voice, Radio Comes of Age, The Golden Age of Radio, The Transistor Revolution, and Radio in the Space Age.

60. Carter, Boake. *I Talk As I Like*. New York: Dodge Publishing, 1937. 232 pp.

The author, a well-known radio commentator, states his belief that a program of news worth listening to is a program that is provocative of thought and argument. That was his philosophy during his broadcasting career, and this autobiographical volume gives him a chance to express his views without concerns of censorship or sponsor retaliation.

61. *The Charlie Grimm Show*. Milwaukee, WI: Radio Station WTMJ, 1956? 14 pp.

Contains "baseball stories as told on *The Charlie Grimm Show*" and broadcast over radio station WTMJ on Sunday afternoons.

62. Chase, Francis, Jr. *Sound and Fury: An Informal History of Broadcasting.* New York: Harper & Brothers, 1942. 303 pp.

    Beginning with an account of the first broadcast by Lee De Forest of Madame Eugenia Farrar singing *I Love You Truly* and *Just A'Wearyin' for You*, Chase tells the story of radio broadcasting as a chatty narrative. He discusses some of radio's "giants" (Milton Cross, Norman Brokenshire, Ted Husing) and ends the book with a look at "the wave of the future--FM and television."

63. Churchill, Allen. *Remember When?* New York: Golden Press, 1967. 286 pp.

    Divided chronologically by five-year intervals from 1900 to 1940, this has data on the Golden Age of radio and includes a number of pictures of performers from that period.

64. Clark, Dick, and Richard Robinson. *Rock, Roll & Remember.* New York: Thomas Y. Crowell, 1976. 276 pp. ISBN: 0-690-01184-9.

    Before he became noted for television's *American Bandstand* program, Dick Clark was an announcer and disc jockey for Philadelphia radio station WFIL. This is his autobiography.

65. Clarkson, R.P. *The Hysterical Background of Radio.* New York: J.H. Sears, 1927. 257 pp.

Written for the general public and intended more for entertainment than instruction, this is actually a series of essays on radio's early history and related topics that form the background of radio broadcasting.

66. Cole, J.A. *Lord Haw-Haw & William Joyce: The Full Story.* New York: Farrar, Straus & Giroux, 1964. 316 pp.

    William Joyce gained notoriety when he broadcast as Lord Haw-Haw over the radio during WW II. He was a former member of British Fascist organizations and on the radio he achieved the largest audience that an English-speaking Fascist ever had. Following the war he was tried for treason and executed. This is his biography.

67. Collins, Philip. *Radios: The Golden Age.* San Francisco: Chronicle Books, 1987. 119 pp. ISBN: 0-87701-419-1.

    This is a volume of colored photographs of radios produced between 1933 and 1957. Each set is identified by brand, model and its present owner. A brief bibliography and a name/address listing of the collectors are included.

68. Correll, Charles J., and Freeman F. Gosden. *All About Amos 'n' Andy and Their Creators Correll and Gosden.* New York: Rand McNally, 1929. 126 pp.

    Written partly in a question-and-answer format, this gives the background of the two men who created the show and their alter egos, Amos Jones and Andrew Brown. The book is illustrated largely by photographs of the two in their character makeup although a few pictures show them as they appeared offstage.

69. Coughlin, Charles E. *Father Coughlin's Radio Sermons, October 1930-April 1931, Complete*. Baltimore: Knox & O'Leary, 1931. 253 pp.

An extremely controversial radio personality, Father Coughlin had a wide following in the early 1930s. His "was a widely discussed name and protestants, jews and those of no religion listened, waiting for the disclosure that this was 'more propaganda' to win converts for the Roman Catholic Church (but many) became believers in the message of this man" who broadcast nationally from a Detroit station.

70. Coulton, Barbara. *Louis MacNeice in the BBC*. London: Faber & Faber, 1980. 215 pp. ISBN: 0-571-11537-3.

Known primarily as a poet, Louis MacNeice worked for the BBC as a radio writer for 20 years. This book describes that part of his life.

71. Cox Broadcasting Corporation. *Welcome South, Brother: Fifty Years of Broadcasting at WSB, Atlanta, Georgia*. Atlanta: Cox Broadcasting, 1974. 112 pp.

WSB became the South's first radio station in 1922--two years after KDKA, Pittsburgh, was given the first "regular" call letters. It was licensed to the *Atlanta Journal* and expanded into WSB-FM and, later, WSB-TV. Here is its story.

72. Crabb, Richard. *Radio's Beautiful Day*. Aberdeen, SD: North Plains Press, 1983. 349 pp. ISBN: 0-87970-163-3.

Based on the experience of Everett Mitchell, the "Voice of American Agriculture," this recalls the first 50 years of American broadcasting as lived by a man whose deeply religious outlook on life created his "beautiful day" philosophy.

73. Crocker, Patti. *Radio Days: A Personal View of Australia's Radio Heyday*. Brookvale, NSW: Simon & Schuster, 1989. 144 pp. ISBN: 0-7318-0098-2.

    Patti Crocker grew up during the period when radio was the main medium that entertained and informed Australians. She was an early childhood performer and she conveys the excitement and drama of this period as she looks at all the important shows and their stars.

74. Crosby, Bing, as told to Pete Martin. *Call Me Lucky*. New York: Simon & Schuster, 1953. 344 pp.

    Bing Crosby got his start in radio with Paul Whiteman and later had his own long-term radio program. This is his autobiography where he talks about his memories of radio days as well as personal matters.

75. Crosley, Powel, Jr. *Simplicity of Radio: The Blue Book of Radio*. Cincinnati: Crosley Publishing, 1924. 80 pp.

    The verso of the title page states "this edition of *The Simplicity* has been completely rewritten, and supercedes edition fifteen." The booklet basically tries to tell as simply as possible just what radio is and how it works. No date is given for its original publication.

76. Cullinan, Howell. *Pardon My Accent*. Norwood, MA: Plimpton Press, 1934. 221 pp.

    The title page describes this as "a radio news announcer apologizes, 'points with pride' and 'views with alarm.'" The book is actually a combination confession and autobiography and relates Cullinan's experiences as a newspaperman, radio news announcer, and public speaker.

77. Cuthbert, Margaret, ed. *Adventures in Radio*. New York: Howell, Soskin, 1945. 288 pp.

The radio scripts in this book show varied techniques of structure and presentation and all were written to be heard, not read. They include Edward R. Murrow's first broadcast on his return to this country in 1944, Bill Stern's 1945 Rose Bowl broadcast, an excerpt from the Charlie McCarthy-Edgar Bergen program, a radio adaptation of *Let's Pretend*, and a section of the late Mayor F.H. LaGuardia's weekly talk to the people of New York.

78. Czitrom, Daniel J. *Media and the American Mind*. Chapel Hill, NC: University of North Carolina Press, 1982. 254 pp. ISBN: 0-8078-1500-4.

The frontispiece has a photograph of early radio being demonstrated at a farmhouse around 1925. This sets the tone for the volume as the author examines various media, including American radio from wireless through broadcasting in the period between 1892 and 1940 and then looks at later aspects of the medium.

79. De Forest, Lee. *Father of Radio: The Autobiography of Lee De Forest*. Chicago: Wilcox & Follett, 1950. 502 pp.

Recollections of early childhood in Waterloo and Muscatine, Iowa, begin this volume as the author writes about his life, family, education, and most of all, his fascination with his "grid Audion," wireless signals, and the growth of radio. He includes technical details of his various inventions and reproduces numerous photographs of himself, his laboratories, equipment, and patent drawings.

80. DeLong, Thomas A. *The Mighty Music Box: The Golden Age of Musical Radio*. Los Angeles: Amber Crest Books, 1980. 335 pp. ISBN: 0-86533-000-X.

This book describes "the power and the magic of radio-- a mighty music box whose songs and stories would create history and enduring legends for many generations."

81. Dimbleby, Jonathan. *Richard Dimbleby: a Biography*. London: Hodder & Stoughton, 1975. 422 pp. ISBN: 0-340-17744-6.

Dimbleby "was the voice of the BBC on thousands of occasions" and was one of the best known and most loved of British radio and later, television, personalities. He began his broadcasting career in 1936 and it lasted nearly 30 years as he played "an intimate and dominant part" in the growth of the British Broadcasting Corporation.

82. Douglas, Alan. *Radio Manufacturers of the 1920's*. Vestal, NY: Vestal Press, 1988. 3 vols.

While there have been many books written on the technical history of radio and its inventors as well as broadcasting stations and personalities, the author states there have been none on the companies that actually built the receivers. This three-volume set is his answer as he attempts to fill the gap and provide a history of both the companies and the radio models they made.

83. Douglas, George H. *The Early Days of Radio Broadcasting*. Jefferson, NC: McFarland, 1987. 248 pp. ISBN: 0-89950-285-7.

Douglas describes the important areas in the development of the radio industry beginning with the creation of KDKA, through the crystal set, the rise of the radio announcer, "wave length wars," radio news, sportscasting, networks, educational stations, classical and pop music, and the expanding broadcast day. He concentrates on the years between 1920 and 1930 when radio was rapidly growing and changing and was not concerned by the competition of TV.

84. Douglas, Susan J. *Inventing American Broadcasting, 1899-1922.* Baltimore: Johns Hopkins University Press, 1987. 363 pp. (Johns Hopkins Studies in the History of Technology). ISBN: 0-8018-3387-6.

The author investigates what she calls broadcasting's "prehistory"--the period before KDKA went on the air. She says that was when "the basic technological, managerial, and cultural template of American broadcasting was cast." She ends her book during the age of "social construction of American broadcasting" which took place in 1922.

85. Drake, Galen. *This Is Galen Drake.* Garden City, NY: Doubleday, 1949. 296 pp.

For a number of years Galen Drake was heard regularly over CBS station WCBS under the auspices of the Housewives' Protective League. He is credited with having "the coziest, coaxingest, convincingest voice on the air" and was voted "the most microgenic personality in radio". This book is a collection of his radio commentaries.

86. Dreher, Carl. *Sarnoff: An American Success.* New York: New York Times Books, 1977. 282 pp. ISBN: 0-8129-0672-1.

26 Radio Broadcasting

This biography of Sarnoff briefly examines his childhood, describes his reception of the Titanic distress message, and goes on to tell of his career with KDKA, RCA, and NBC. The first 18 chapters emphasize Sarnoff's interest in radio while the last dozen or so deal primarily with his involvement with television.

87. Driver, David, compiler. *The Art of Radio Times: The First Sixty Years*. London: British Broadcasting Corporation, 1981. 252 pp. ISBN: 0-563-179-6-6.

Radio Times was founded in September 1923 by John Reith of the BBC "in response to a hostile British press which wanted to charge advertising rates for publishing BBC programmes ... It was founded as 'the official organ of the BBC'" and furnishes a history of British broadcasting. This book is composed solely of the illustrations, along with both new and old captions, taken from the publication.

88. Dryer, Sherman H. *Radio in Wartime*. New York: Greenberg, 1942. 384 pp.

The author states in the preface that it is his "hope that this book will be regarded as a tentative approach to a critical evaluation of radio's new role (in wartime), that it will promote a better understanding of an instrument which poses a tremendous potential for building in society an appreciation of the hazards and obligations of war and the ultimate peace." He defines radio as "the secret weapon" and expands on the roles played by news personnel and commentators, discussion programs, and dramatic shows. Each chapter is followed by a commentary about it by "seven distinguished persons."

89. Duncan, James H., Jr. *American Radio Tenth Anniversary Issue, 1976-1986: a Prose and Statistical History*. Kalamazoo, MI, James Duncan, 1986. 1 vol.

Instead of the usual market and station data of his *American Radio* volumes, Duncan has included a personal history and a section devoted to individual histories. Another section contains contributions by various radio personalities expressing their views on the medium, its financial outlook, sales and management, advertising, services provided, etc.

90. Dunlap, Orrin E., Jr. *Marconi: The Man and His Wireless*. New York: Macmillan, 1937. 360 pp.

"The emphasis in this biography is on the man's work and on his personality ... is the story of Marconi as he came into the news." The book was reprinted in 1971 by Arno Press/New York Times as part of the series History of Broadcasting: Radio to Television.

91. Dunlap, Orrin E., Jr. *Radio's 100 Men of Science: Biographical Narratives of Pathfinders in Electronics and Television*. Freeport, NY: Books for Libraries Press, 1970. 294 pp. (Essay Index Reprint series). ISBN: 0-8369-1916-5.

Published originally in 1944 by Harper & Brothers, this is divided into two parts--pioneers of electricity and pioneers of the radio age. Among the former are William Gilbert, Benjamin Franklin, Luigi Galvani, and Michael Faraday, while some of the latter "pioneers" are Edison, Bell, Tesla, Steinmetz, De Forest, Marconi, DuMont, and Farnsworth.

92. Dunlap, Orrin E., Jr. *The Story of Radio*. New York: Dial Press, 1927. 226 pp.

Chapter titles indicate the scope of this history of the medium: It Speaks for Itself; TransAtlantic Triumphs; Dramatic Moments; Enrolled for War; With Pioneer Birdmen; Secrets of Marconi's Magic; Turning Points; and Looking Through Space!

93. Dunn, William J. *Pacific Microphone.* College Station: Texas A&M University Press, 1988. 399 pp. (Texas A&M University Military History series, 8). ISBN: 0-89096-339-8.

Written by a radio reporter who covered WW II in the Pacific, this is his story of that war. He based it on memories, diaries, notes, and transcripts of field broadcasts and offers some different viewpoints on aspects of the Pacific war as it happened.

94. Dunning, John. *Tune In Yesterday: The Ultimate Encyclopedia of Old-Time Radio, 1925-1976.* Englewood Cliffs, NJ: Prentice-Hall, 1976. 703 pp. ISBN: 0-13-932616-2.

"It all began November 15, 1926, with the opening of the National Broadcasting Company (and) ended September 30, 1962, when the last two dramatic shows were canceled by CBS. The final struggle between radio and television for the affections of the American people ended with TV the total victor." This book is an account of the radio programs that were aired during that period, all of which are arranged alphabetically for easy reference.

95. Edwards, Frank. *My First 10,000,000 Sponsors.* New York: Ballantine Books, 1956. 185 pp.

The author was a commentator for the American Federation of Labor and broadcast over the Mutual

Network. This is a description of his more than 30 years in radio broadcasting.

96. Eichberg, Robert. *Radio Stars of Today, or, Behind the Scenes in Broadcasting*. Boston: L.C. Page, 1937. 218 pp.

    More than 275 illustrations are included in this volume that features programs such as Fred Allen's *Town Hall Tonight, Lux Radio Theatre,* and *Believe It or Not* as well as personalities (Fred Waring, Boake Carter, Edgar Guest, Ted Husing, etc.). Additional chapters discuss amateur broadcasting, radio police, radio at sea, and some large broadcasting stations.

97. Elkin, Stanley. *The Dick Gibson Show*. New York: Random House, 1970. 335 pp.

    This is a novel about an itinerant radio personality and his career in the medium. Portions of this work originally appeared in several magazines.

98. Elliott, Bob, and Ray Goulding. *From Approximately Coast to Coast: It's the Bob and Ray Show*. New York: Penguin, 1985. 214 pp. ISBN: 0-1400-7561-5.

    A paperback reprint of the original book published in 1983 has lost none of its appeal. Numerous radio routines of these two comedians are printed along with a series of serious (?) photographs.

99. Elliott, Bob, and Ray Goulding. *Write If You Get Work: The Best of Bob and Ray*. New York: Random House, 1975. 177 pp. ISBN: 0-394-49668-X.

    An assortment of the familiar Bob and Ray sketches are included in this anthology. They feature characters dreamed up by the two humorists: Wally Ballou, Elmer

W. Litzinger, Spy, Captain Parker Gibbes, Wanda Stapp, Mug Mellish, Calvin Hoogevin, Stuffy Hodgson, Mary Backstayge, and the prototype of sportscasters, Biff Burns.

100. Evans, James F. *Prairie Farmer and WLS: The Burridge D. Butler Years*. Urbana: University of Illinois Press, 1969. 329 pp.

Written by a University of Illinois College of Agriculture professor, this describes the influence of early radio on Midwest farmers and the influence of the *Prairie Farmer* newspaper on broadcasting. The paper acquired station WLS from Sears, Roebuck in 1928 at a cost of $250,000 with the intention of making it "a living, breathing, human influence in the million farm homes of those states surrounding Chicago."

101. Evans, Richard L. *From the Crossroads....* New York: Harper & Brothers, 1955. 256 pp.

One of a number of titles by Evans, this contains the texts written and read by the author for the Sunday morning CBS broadcast "with the Tabernacle Choir and organ from Temple Square in Salt Lake City."

102. Fang, Irving E. *Those Radio Commentators!* Ames: Iowa State University Press, 1977. 341 pp. ISBN: 0-8138-1500-2.

Fifteen "excess prophets" (as categorized by Quincy Howe) are profiled in this volume that offers biographical data, career information, an illustration, and a bibliography of books and articles by and about each. In addition, there are four sides of 33⅓ monaural records that reproduce their voices recorded during live broadcasts.

103. Fein, Irving A. *Jack Benny: An Intimate Biography*. New York: G.P. Putnam's Sons, 1976. 319 pp. ISBN: 0-399-11640-0.

Jack Benny got his start in radio and eventually captured the early Sunday evening audience for nearly two decades and made a successful transition to television. His close friend and publicist tells the story of Jack's childhood, his ups and downs in show business, and finally the worldwide fame he enjoyed as a man of 39 even when he turned 80.

104. Ferguson, Max. *And Now, Here's Max: A Funny Kind of Autobiography*. Toronto: McGraw-Hill of Canada, 1967. 167 pp.

The subject of this autobiography is a popular Canadian broadcaster who called himself Rawhide and played country music. Instead of photographs, this is illustrated by a series of humorous pen-and-ink drawings.

105. Fessenden, Helen May. *Fessenden: Builder of Tomorrow*. New York: Coward-McCann, 1940. 362 pp.

The subject of this biography, Reginald Aubrey Fessenden, the author's husband, is credited by her with having "the mind which conceived the correct theory of wireless transmission, which invented the wireless telephone and with it accomplished the first broadcasting, which invented and developed the fathometer and all it implied (and) that this mind failed to defend itself against commercial assault, whether financial or scientific...."

106. Field, Charles Kellog. *The Story of Cheerio by Himself*. Garden City, NY: Garden City Publishing, 1936. 382 pp.

Cheerio was a program designed to help listeners, particularly shut-ins, face each new day with a brighter outlook and was presented without any commercial elements. It was based on a definite series of personal experiences of the broadcaster, the narrator of this story.

107. Fink, John. *WGN: A Pictorial History.* Chicago: Chicago Tribune, 1961. 109 pp.

    Expanding an earlier company history compiled by Francis Coughlin, this tells the story of station WGN whose call letters stand for the "World's Greatest Newspaper"--the station is owned by the Chicago Tribune Company. The text is illustrated by both photographs and drawings.

108. *The First 50 Years of Broadcasting: The Running Story of the Fifth Estate.* New York: Broadcasting Publications, 1982. 297 pp.

    Articles from *Broadcasting* reproduced in this volume are arranged chronologically. In addition, there is an interview with the late Sol Taishoff, *Broadcasting* Chairman and Editor, titled "The First 50 Years Were the Hardest."

109. Fitelson, H. William, ed. *Theatre Guild on the Air.* New York: Rinehart, 1947. 430 pp. (Rinehart Radio series).

    The purpose of this volume, according to the foreword, is to give the interested public an opportunity to study the actual technique employed in transposing a dramatic play from stage form into radio form. A number of texts are included.

110. Floherty, John J. *Behind the Microphone.* Philadelphia: J.B. Lippincott, 1944. 207 pp.

Floherty writes about radio's early history and its progress through the years. He has a chapter on bloopers that he calls Slips Behind the Mike and others on the Heralds of Industry, News Hunters, and Come In, London.

111. Floherty, John J. *On the Air: The Story of Radio.* Garden City, NY: Doubleday, Doran, 1937. 99 pp.

   The author writes what he calls a homely story of what he saw, heard and felt as he made his way through "mazes of ... the most modern of industries." He relates some history of the medium, talks about rehearsals and sound effects, and describes various types of broadcasts, including marine communication, television, and aviation radio.

112. Ford, Ed, Harry Hershfield, and Joe Laurie, Jr. *Can You Top This?* Garden City, NY: Blue Ribbon Books, 1945. 237 pp.

   The radio program *Can You Top This?* was the brainchild of "Senator" Ed Ford, who not only created, produced, and owned the show, but also appeared in it. It was an audience-participation program in which the listening audience sent in stories and jokes that were edited and presented by an actor in the role of the people's representative. The three authors then tried to top the submitted story with a joke on the same subject. The visible audience was the judge, and the program was extremely popular during radio's golden age.

113. Fornatale, Peter, and Joshua E. Mills. *Radio in the Television Age.* Woodstock, NY: Overlook Press, 1980. 212 pp. ISBN: 0-87951-106-0.

The authors state this is, first and foremost, a history of radio in the 1950s, 60s, and 70s, told in chronological order. Two major facets--radio news and non-commercial radio--are treated separately within the text.

114. Friedersdorf, Burk. *From Crystal to Color: WFBM*. Indianapolis: The WFBM Stations, 1964. 189 pp.

"Contained in these pages are some of the people and places, the times and the events that have made memorable the forty-plus years that broadcasting has been a lively part of Hoosier life." The station began as 9ZJ in the garage of radio pioneer Francis F. Hamilton in Indianapolis, became WLK in 1922, and WFBM in 1924.

115. Friendly, Fred W. *Due to Circumstances Beyond Our Control....* New York: Random House, 1967. 325 pp.

"This book is a series of interconnected essays about broadcast journalism and an occupational memoir of its author." Friendly was president of CBS's news division and writes about his nearly 20 years with that network.

116. Furlaud, Alice. *Air Fair: Alice Furlaud's Dispatches from Paris*. Layton, UT: Gibbs Smith, 1989. 190 pp. ISBN: 0-87905-304-6.

Alice Furlaud has been creating radio documentaries from Paris for seven years and is heard over National Public Radio (primarily on *All Things Considered*), the BBC and the Canadian Broadcasting Corporation. This is a collection of her work on a variety of topics.

117. Garis, Roger. *My Father Was Uncle Wiggily*. New York: McGraw-Hill, 1966. 217 pp.

Howard R. Garis was a newspaper man, an author of numerous children's books, and the inventor of the Uncle Wiggily game. He wrote the Uncle Wiggily stories for children and read them over station WJZ, making Uncle Wiggily a household word for young listeners and their parents. This is his biography.

118. Gaver, Jack, and Dave Stanley. *There's Laughter in the Air! Radio's Top Comedians and Their Best Shows*. New York: Greenberg, 1945. 291 pp.

Selections from the programs of Fred Allen, Bob Hope, Jack Benny, Ed Gardner, Eddie Cantor, Abbott and Costello, Ed Wynn, Fanny Brice, Milton Berle, Colonel Stoopnagle, Fibber McGee and Molly, Burns and Allen, Phil Baker, Durante and Moore, Joan Davis, Raymond Knight, and others are reprinted.

119. Gibbons, Edward. *Floyd Gibbons: Your Headline Hunter*. New York: Exposition Press, 1953. 350 pp.

Written by Floyd Gibbons's brother, this is the biography of the war correspondent, author, globe-trotter, and radio broadcaster. He was "one of radio's super-salesmen of products, world's fairs and new ideas" and had an estimated audience of thirty million listeners to his radio network commentaries.

120. Gielgud, Val. *One Year of Grace: A Fragment of Autobiography*. London: Longmans, Green, 1950. 168 pp.

This is an account of the radio writer's attempt to "get away from it all" as he left Great Britain for a little over a year. It is based on his own recollections and diary entries. On a genealogical note, Gielgud is the older brother of the well-known British actor, John Gielgud.

121. Gielgud, Val. *Years in a Mirror*. London: The Bodley Head, 1965. 224 pp.

> This is the third volume of "autobiographical reminiscences" by the author who was associated with the British Broadcasting Corporation for 35 years. He states in the foreword that a considerable amount of personal material has been omitted, but he does include a considerable amount of material about the BBC and, in particular, the development of its drama presentations.

122. Gielgud, Val. *Years of the Locust*. London: Nicholson & Watson, 1945.

> "A collection of personal opinions, of personal prejudices, and of personal reminiscences" of the author, a longtime British Broadcasting Corporation writer. He writes about Broadcasting House, the growth of the BBC, and broadcasting in wartime.

123. Gilbert, Douglas. Burton Rascoe, ed. *Floyd Gibbons: Knight of the Air*. New York: Robert M. McBride, 1930. 96 pp.

> Gibbons began his career as a reporter for the *Chicago Tribune* in 1912 but gained his fame as a radio broadcaster, earning the nickname of "radio's knight errant." This book is a series of anecdotes about Gibbons and his experiences as a reporter, broadcaster, and world traveler.

124. Goldmark, Peter C., with Lee Edson. *Maverick Inventor: My Turbulent Years at CBS*. New York: Saturday Review Press/E.P. Dutton, 1973. 278 pp. ISBN: 0-8415-0046-0.

> The author writes that he uses an autobiographical form for this book because he feels that was the best way to share his ideas and to provide his own view of how things

actually developed. It is actually a recounting of the inventions Goldmark was involved in during the 35 years he worked in technological development at CBS.

125. Goldsmith, Alfred N., and Austin C. Lescarboura. *This Thing Called Broadcasting*. New York: Henry Holt, 1930. 362 pp.

The description on the title page states this is "a simple tale of an idea, an experiment, a mighty industry, a daily habit, and a basic influence in our modern civilization."

126. Gray, Barry. *My Night People*. New York: Simon & Schuster, 1975. 191 pp. ISBN: 0-671-22090-X.

The author's career in radio began when he was hired by WOR to do staff announcing right after WW II. From there he announced quarter-hour and half-hour broadcasts of music performed live at various New York night spots and eventually had his own late-night/early morning program. In this autobiography he relates how it all came about.

127. Grisewood, Frederick. *The World Goes By*. London: Secker & Warburg, 1952. 256 pp.

The author was a radio broadcaster for the British Broadcasting Corporation for 20 years and after his retirement from there he continued his career as a freelance public speaker and lecturer. He writes about his own experiences on and off the air.

128. Gross, Ben. *I Looked and I Listened: Informal Recollections of Radio and TV*. New York: Random House, 1954. 344 pp.

After spending 30 years in broadcasting, Gross reminisces about his first experience in the radio room of the *New*

York Daily News, early programs that featured a stock company of comics and emcees, the beginning of the networks, and the Orson Welles infamous 1938 Halloween broadcast. In between are anecdotes about Ted Husing, Graham McNamee, Jan Peerce, and one of radio's pioneer announcers, John S. Young, who later became American ambassador to Haiti. This book was reprinted by Arlington House in 1970.

129. Guest, Edgar A. *Edgar A. Guest Broadcasting*. Chicago: Reilly & Lee, 1935. 123 pp.

Edgar A. Guest had a radio program in the 1930s that consisted of commentaries and readings from his own poetry. This volume is a compilation of "certain verses exactly as (he) gave them over the air."

130. Gunston, David. *Marconi: Father of Radio*. New York: Crowell-Collier Press, 1965. 128 pp. (World in the Making series).

"This account of Marconi concentrates on the scientific and practical aspects of his work, relating it sympathetically to his strange, aloof, not always happy life, and puts his once much publicized and disputed achievements in true perspective."

131. Gurman, Joseph, and Myron Slager. *Radio Round-Ups: Intimate Glimpses of the Radio Stars*. Boston: Lothrop, Lee & Shepard, 1932. 109 pp.

Material dealing with many of the country's outstanding radio personalities has been gathered together in order to familiarize listeners with the background and lives of popular performers. The authors "attempted to describe, by means of over 150 drawings, the personal appearance of most of those unseen entertainers about whom the multitude of radio listeners are curious."

132. Harden, Frank, and Jackson Weaver, with Ed Meyer. *On the Road with Harden and Weaver.* New York: William Morrow, 1983. 224 pp. ISBN: 0-688-02032-1.

Harden and Weaver were both successful radio announcers before they combined as a morning radio team that was number one for 25 years on a 5,000 watt Washington, D.C., station. They had a successful format of talking about 80 percent of the time and playing non-rock music the rest. This is their account of their experiences as talk-show hosts and disc jockeys.

133. Harlow, Alvin F. *Old Wires and New Waves: The History of the Telegraph, Telephone, and Wireless.* New York: D. Appleton-Century Company, 1936. 548 pp.

Numerous photographs and drawings illustrate this history in which the author states "America may with equal pride boast of having originated the wireless telephone, and of having as citizens the two or three men who did most to develop it; and wireless telephony, be it remembered, means radio broadcasting, a thing which has become so fundamental a part of our lives that the world now would seem chaos to us without it." This was reprinted by Arno Press/New York Times as part of the History of Broadcasting: Radio to Television series of 1971.

134. Harmon, Jim. *The Great Radio Comedians.* Garden City, NY: Doubleday, 1970. 195 pp.

Harmon divides comedy programs into 13 categories such as So Many Voices, Suds in Your Eye, Those Brats We Loved but Could Never Be, and Songs and Laughter. He discusses the more famous--Hope, Allen, Benny, Wynn, Groucho--as well as not-quite-so-famous Joe Penner, the Great Gildersleeve, Henry Aldridge, Baron Munchausen, and others.

135. Harmon, Jim. *The Great Radio Heroes*. Garden City, NY: Doubleday, 1967. 263 pp.

A companion volume to his *Great Radio Comedians* (see item #134), Harmon states that "everybody in the United States of America over 25 years of age must have listened intently to the radio at that hour (five o'clock) during some period of their lives." That was when dramatized stories were most popular, and he writes about Jack, Doc, and Reggie (*I Love a Mystery*), *Gangbusters*, *The Shadow*, Tom Mix, and *Jack Armstrong, the All-American Boy*.

136. Harris, Credo Fitch. *Microphone Memoirs of the Horse and Buggy Days of Radio*. Indianapolis: Bobbs-Merrill, 1937. 281 pp.

In 1922 the author was invited by Judge Robert W. Bingham, then publisher of two newspapers and later American ambassador to England, to organize the building of "a radio telephone broadcasting station." That station began as WHAS, and Harris recalls its very early days as well as those of radio broadcasting in general.

137. Harwell, Ernie. *Tuned to Baseball*. South Bend, IN: Diamond Communications, 1985. 229 pp. ISBN: 0-912083-10-7.

While this is partly about Harwell's playing days, most of it is about his broadcasting experiences when he did play-by-play on the radio for 20 years for the Brooklyn

Dodgers, New York Giants, Baltimore Orioles, and Detroit Tigers.

138. Hasty, Jack. *Done with Mirrors: Admissions of a Free-Lance Writer.* New York: Ives Washburn, 1943. 337 pp.

The author was involved with a number of radio shows including *The Time of Your Life* (before that title was made better known by author William Saroyan). In this volume Hasty looks back on both the good times and the bad as he provides information on radio's Golden Age.

139. Hawks, Ellison. *Pioneers of Wireless.* New York: Arno Press, 1974. 304 pp. (Telecommunications series). ISBN: 0-405-06049-1.

A reprint of the 1927 edition published by Methuen in London, this discusses the research of William Gilbert, Benjamin Franklin, Luigi Galvani, Alessandro Volta, Dominic Francois Arago, William Sturgeon, Joseph Henry, Michael Faraday, Alexander Graham Bell, Thomas Alva Edison, Willoughby Smith, David Edward Hughes, Gugielmo Marconi, Heinrich Rudolf Hertz, Lee De Forest, and others who contributed to the early development of radio.

140. Henderson, Amy. *On the Air: Pioneers of American Broadcasting.* Washington: Smithsonian Institution Press, 1988. 198 pp. ISBN: 0-87474-499-7.

Published for the National Portrait Gallery and the Museum of Broadcasting, this is the catalog of an exhibition at the National Portrait Gallery held between October 7, 1988, and January 2, 1989. Among those featured are Ed Wynn, Jack Benny, Bob and Ray, Red Barber, Lowell Thomas, Huntley and Brinkley, Milton

Cross, Kate Smith, Amos 'n' Andy, President Franklin Roosevelt, Father Coughlin, and Dick Clark.

141. Hickman, Ron. *Touching the Stars*. Tallahassee, FL: Loiry, 1986. 151 pp. ISBN: 0-933703-21-X.

A former member of the Presidential Press Corps, Hickman was involved in an eight-year legal struggle to become the founder of WOTB-FM in Rhode Island. In this book he shares his experiences in gaining FCC approval for the station as well as telling numerous anecdotes of the great and near-great he has known during his more than 30 years as a broadcaster.

142. Higby, Mary Jane. *Tune In Tomorrow, or, How I Found the Right to Happiness with Our Gal Sunday, Stella Dallas, John's Other Wife, and Other Sudsy Radio Serials*. New York: Cowles, 1968. 226 pp.

The subtitle indicates the type of humorous book this is. It was written by "a daytime serial star in what is now nostalgically called the Golden Age of Radio" and most of the material "has been taken from memory--my own and that of friends."

143. Hilbrink, W.R. *Who Really Invented Radio?* New York: G.P. Putnam's Sons, 1972. 107 pp.

The author puts together an account of the invention of radio and makes "use of the writings of many and has drawn from the memories of a few old-timers in this radio game." He writes about Guglielmo Marconi, Ambrose Fleming, Lee De Forest, Edwin Armstrong, James Clerk Maxwell, Heinrich Hertz, and other pioneers of the medium.

144. Hill, Jonathan. *The Cat's Whisker: 50 Years of Wireless Design*. London: Oresko Books, 1978. 96 pp. ISBN: 0-905368-46-0.

The author follows the development of wireless from its beginning as an 1890s laboratory experiment to the foundation of the broadcasting industry in 1922. He traces the various changes in the appearance of wireless sets, the different cabinet styles, and the way in which art and social events influenced their design.

145. Hill, Jonathan. *Radio! Radio!* Bampton, Eng.: Sunrise Press, 1986. 244 pp. ISBN: 0-9511448-1-2.

The development of the wireless set from its experimental beginnings in Victorian England, through the foundation of a domestic manufacturing industry and the inception of broadcasting in the early 1920s is described in this book. It continues until after the introduction of the first transistor in the late 1950s and contains illustrations of radio sets and various accessories.

146. Hope, Bob. *Have Tux, Will Travel*. New York: Simon & Schuster, 1954. 308 pp.

The title page describes this as Bob Hope's own story, as told to Pete Martin. It tells about Hope's life, his career in radio, screen and television, plus his well-known and well-publicized jaunts to entertain servicemen and women during WW II and later.

147. Hosley, David H. *As Good As Any: Foreign Correspondence on American Radio, 1930-1940*. Westport, CT: Greenwood Press, 1984. 165 pp. (Contributions to the Study of Mass Media and Communications, 2).

The author chronicles a special moment in radio history when radio journalism was preeminent and America's window to the world was acoustic--and the likes of Edward R. Murrow, Howard K. Smith, Winston Burdett, and Charles Collingwood gave us the news of a world bound for war.

148. Howe, Russell Warren. *The Hunt for 'Tokyo Rose'*. Lanham, NY: Madison Books, 1990. 354 pp. ISBN: 0-8191-7456-4.

During WW II a sultry-voiced Japanese radio announcer known as "Tokyo Rose" amused, entertained and angered Allied troops with a mixture of propaganda, popular music, and imperialistic taunts. Though commonly assumed that there was only one Tokyo Rose, there were actually at least 27 Japanese-American broadcasters who played the role. This is the story of Iva Toguri, the only one who had refused to renounce her American citizenship, and so was able to be tried for treason. She was found guilty on a minor charge, served more than eight years in prison, and eventually pardoned by President Gerald Ford in 1977.

149. Hurst, Jack. *Nashville's Grand Ole Opry: The First Fifty Years, 1925-1975*. New York: Abradale Press, 1989. 364 pp. ISBN: 0-8109-8094-0.

This is a complete and unabridged reprint of the 1975 book published by Harry N. Abrams. Even though changes have occurred in the lives of the musicians featured and new stars have risen in the country music scene, the book still stands as a complete history of the first half-century of a great American institution and a well-loved radio (and later, television) program.

150. Husing, Ted. *Ten Years Before the Mike*. New York: Farrar & Rinehart, 1935. 298 pp.

This autobiographical account details Husing's entry into radio announcing with WJZ in September 1924, and provides both facts and pictures of his career for the ensuing ten years. He began with news and later became one of the best-known sports announcers on the air.

151. Husing, Ted, with Cy Rice. *My Eyes Are in My Heart*. New York: Bernard Geis Associates, 1959. 287 pp.

"Good afternoon, everyone, everywhere" was the standard radio greeting of one of radio's most famous announcers who "probably covered a greater variety of events than any other commentator in broadcasting history." This is the story of his rising career, his life as a top announcer, and his later years as a mostly blind, semi-invalid.

152. Jolly, W.P. *Marconi*. New York: Stein & Day, 1972. 291 pp. ISBN: 0-8128-1507-6,

Guglielmo Marconi, the "father of radio," was born the second child of an Italian widower and an Irish mother and was comfortably well-off with a privileged early childhood. This book relates the story from the elopement of his parents to his becoming the famous pioneer of wireless communication, a Nobel laureate, and the founder of rich and powerful companies for the development and exploitation of radio systems.

153. Jones, Louis M., with Charles K. Wolfe. *Everybody's Grandpa: Fifty Years Behind the Mike*. Knoxville: University of Tennessee Press, 1984. 288 pp. ISBN: 0-87049-439-2.

Most recently known for his participation on television's long-running *Hee Haw*, Grandpa Jones actually was a star performer at the Grand Ole Opry on the stage and radio. In this autobiography he recalls his days on

WWVA (Wheeling), WTIC (Hartford), WCHS (Charleston), and WLW (Cincinnati), as well as his childhood, WW II military service, and rise as a country musician.

154. Josefsberg, Milt. *The Jack Benny Show*. New Rochelle, NY: Arlington House, 1977. 496 pp. ISBN: 0-87000-347-X.

One of the team of writers for the *Jack Benny Show*, Josefsberg has written "not so much a formal statistical biography, but a personal portrait as I remember him." He writes about "Benny the *man* and Benny the *comedian*" and includes much information about Benny's radio career.

155. Julian, Joseph. *This Was Radio: A Personal Memoir*. New York: Viking Press, 1975. 238 pp. ISBN: 0-670-70299-4.

The introduction by Harold Clurman states that Julian accomplishes a triple task in this book: there is a great deal of information about the medium, the atmosphere and moral landscape of the times during which radio came into being and flourished are described, and the issues reported are "not only truthful but pure." Julian was an actor who became prominent because of his association with Norman Corwin's plays and documentary broadcasts and later became "one of Joseph McCarthy's many victims."

156. Kaltenborn, H.V. *Fifty Fabulous Years, 1900-1950: A Personal Review*. New York: G.P. Putnam's Sons, 1950. 312 pp.

Shortly after his 71st birthday, news broadcaster Kaltenborn decided it was time to write the story of his life and times. This autobiography is the result.

157. Kaltenborn, H.V. *I Broadcast the Crisis*. New York: Random House, 1938. 359 pp.

Dedicated to his co-workers at the Columbia Broadcasting System who made his broadcasts possible, this covers the period of September 12 to October 2, 1939. It contains excerpts from Kaltenborn's *Headlines and Bylines* programs, international news broadcasts, special bulletins, and daily news reports. Appendices contain the texts of speeches by Hitler and Prime Minister Chamberlain, the text of a British White Paper on the Czech-German crisis, the text of the Four-Power Accord, and the Anglo-German Peace Pact.

158. Kaltenborn, H.V. *Kaltenborn Edits the News*. New York: Modern Age Books, 1937. 183 pp.

Having virtually been in on the ground floor as a radio commentator, H.V. Kaltenborn earned his reputation in broadcasting news. This book concentrates on his news broadcasts from Europe, Asia, and America prior to the advent of WW II.

159. Kaufman, Murray. *Murray the K Tells It Like It Is, Baby*. New York: Holt, Rinehart & Winston, 1966. 127 pp.

In show business since he was nine years old, the nation's then-leading disc jockey and radio/TV personality talks primarily to teenagers in this book. It combines anecdotes, photographs, and advice, provides a background on popular music on radio, and includes a glimpse of Superman's experience at Wapshire Broadcasting.

160. Keiller, Garrison. *Lake Wobegon Days*. New York: Viking Press, 1985. 337 pp. ISBN: 0-670-80514-9.

Minnesota's most famous hometown is the setting for these reminiscences of growing up in a quieter time and at a slower pace than most of us follow today. The book has detailed anecdotes about the "town that time forgot and the ages can't improve" which will be familiar to listeners of PBS radio because they were all broadcast on its program titled *Prairie Home Companion*. Although imaginary, Lake Wobegon is listed in the *AAA Minesota Tour Book*--an accomplishment few, if any other, make-believe places have achieved.

161. Keliher, Alice V., ed. *Radio Workers*. New York: Johnson Publishing, 1946. 55 pp. (Picture Fact Books).

Intended for grade-school children, this explains radio's early history through modern (1946) times. It is illustrated and concentrates on the various jobs done by radio station personnel.

162. Kendrick, Alexander. *Prime Time: The Life of Edward R. Murrow*. Boston: Little, Brown, 1969. 548 pp.

The author based this biography on his own 20 years in broadcasting and his association with Murrow that provided the background against which this book was written. He incorporated information gathered in interviews with Murrow's family, college friends, and associates both in England and the United States.

163. King, Larry, with Emily Yoffe. *Larry King*. New York: Simon & Schuster, 1982. 207 pp. ISBN: 0-671-41138-1.

In this autobiography's opening chapter radio/television personality King details his "fall" when he was accused of stealing $5,000 from financier Louis Wolfson. In the chapters that follow he describes his childhood, early years in radio, and finally the success of *The Larry King Show*.

164. Kirby, Edward M., and Jack W. Harris. *Star-Spangled Radio*. Chicago: Ziff-Davis Publishing, 1948. 278 pp.

The authors are Edward Kirby who was named in 1941 as adviser for radio to the Secretary of War and who was Public Relations Chief for the National Association of Broadcasters, and his executive officer, Jack W. Harris. The acknowledgments state that this book "is more than the recollections of two individuals; it is a mirror held against the vast panorama of American radio through the war years, its people in uniform and out, their headaches and heartaches in every part of the world."

165. Kneitel, Tom. *Radio Station Treasury, 1900-1946*. Commack, NY: CRB Research, 1986. 176 pp. ISBN: 0-939780-04-6.

Based on a number of rare and historic archive publications, this volume offers an overview of wireless as it evolved from its early beginning, through the Golden Age of radio broadcasting to the start of the television era. It lists call letters, spark gap coastal telegraph stations, longwave stations, AM-band and shortwave broadcasters, and police, fire and aeronautical stations.

166. Koch, Howard. *The Panic Broadcast: Portrait of an Event*. Boston: Little, Brown, 1970. 163 pp.

This version of the Orson Welles 1938 broadcast is illustrated by drawings, photographs, newspaper reproductions, and maps. There is also the complete text of the radio play, *Invasion from Mars*, as it was actually broadcast that Halloween night.

167. Lackmann, Ron. *Remember Radio*. New York: G.P. Putnam's Sons, 1970. 128 pp.

The author has tried to "construct a radio and fill it with the lost memories and lost art of a less complicated time." He includes photographs, polls, advertisements, quizzes, summaries, and introductory material of dozens of programs primarily from radio's Golden Age.

168. Landry, Robert J. *This Fascinating Radio Business*. Indianapolis: Bobbs-Merrill, 1946. 343 pp.

"Prior to radio, or 'wireless,' there were three successive and successful media of telecommunication--telegraphy, cables, and telephony, each of which represented a major conquest by man of time and distance." The author shares his own enthusiasm and awe as he describes the background and history of the newer medium of radio.

169. Lane, Daryl, William Vernon, and David Carson. *The Sound of Wonder: Interviews from "The Science Fiction Radio Show."* Phoenix, AZ: Oryx Press, 1985. 2 vols. ISBN: 0-89774-175-7; 0-89774-223-8.

These two volumes constitute a collection of interviews with authors, artists, movie critics, editors, and others in the field. Originally broadcast on a nationally syndicated radio show, they have been transcribed, compiled, and supplemented with additional material written by the authors.

170. Larsen, Egon. *Radio and Television: The Everyday Miracle*. London: J.M. Dent, 1976. 96 pp. ISBN: 0-460-06685-4.

A brief history of radio development is presented along with a chapter titled Radio Today which takes the reader

Background 51

behind the broadcasting scene at BBC radio. Illustrations show the recording of a radio play, the BBC pop-music studio, the BBC Monitoring Service, and various other activities within the British Broadcasting Corporation.

171. Leaming, Barbara. *Orson Welles*. New York: Viking Press, 1985. 562 pp. ISBN: 0-670-52895-1.

   This biography was written with the cooperation of Welles who was interviewed over a period of time by the author. It describes his childhood as a prodigy, his young-manhood as a recognized genius, and his later years when critics claimed he never reached the fullness of his earlier potential. Photographs from Welles' own collection and RKO studies are included and depict his life before and after radio.

172. Lean, E. Tangye. *Voices in the Darkness: The Story of the European Radio War*. London: Secker & Warburg, 1943. 243 pp.

   The author writes "This is not a guidebook, handbook or Official History of the War ... I wanted as far as possible to write only of what I had heard with my own ears, choosing Germany's offensive against France instead of her attack on Jugoslavia, reporting speakers on whom I had my own notes, and where my languages gave out and my ignorance of different audiences set in; it did not worry me that the treatment became sketchy."

173. Leinwoll, Stanley. Fred Shunaman, ed. *From Spark to Satellite: A History of Radio Communication*. New York: Charles Scribner's Sons, 1979. 242 pp. ISBN: 0-684-16048-X.

   The introduction states that the development of wireless communication was uneven, with the first 20 years showing painstakingly slow progress. This was followed by a rapid expansion, then another period of slow development, followed by a period of unprecedented progress. The story of these ups and downs is told in this volume.

174. Lessing, Lawrence. *Man of High Fidelity: Edwin Howard Armstrong*. New York: Bantam, 1969. 272 pp.

    Lessing writes that "Edwin Howard Armstrong was the last--and perhaps least known--of the great American inventors ... the man who discovered and developed high fidelity and channeled it to speak its mighty tones through FM radio." The book was originally published in 1956 by J.B. Lippincott.

175. Lichty, Lawrence W., and Malachi C. Topping. *American Broadcasting: A Source Book on the History of Radio and Television*. New York: Hastings House, 1975. 723 pp. (Studies in Public Communication). ISBN: 0-8038-0362-1.

    Divided into eight parts, this volume covers technical aspects, stations, networks, economics, employment, programming, audiences, and regulation. The authors tried to acquire essays that would balance scholarly articles with the journalism of the time.

176. Lucas, Peter. *The Constant Voice*. Lyndhurst, Aust.: Australian Broadcasting Commission, 1965. 46 pp.

    Published to commemorate Radio Australia's 25th anniversary, this presents its history from 1939 to 1964. Well illustrated, it relates "how Radio Australia has won the ears of the world" and created its own chapter in the history of international broadcasting.

177. Lujack, Larry, with Daniel A. Jedlicka. *Superjock*. Chicago, Henry Regnery, 1975. 200 pp. ISBN: 0-8092-8302-6.

An extremely popular Chicago radio disc jockey tells in his own unique fashion what life is like in "the loud, frantic, nonstop world of a rock radio DJ." In addition, he writes about his early childhood in Iowa and Idaho, his college days, the early broadcasting jobs, and finally being hired in Chicago where he made achieved great success.

178. Lyons, Eugene. *David Sarnoff: A Biography*. New York: Harper & Row, 1966. 372 pp.

The first chapter begins with the statement that "the life of David Sarnoff has been cited times without number as a great--and typical--American success story ... because it relates to the quintessential stuffs of our 20th-century world--radio, television, communication satellites, the gadgetry of the electronic age." This story is told here as the author writes of Sarnoff's first 60 years.

179. MacDonald, J. Fred, ed. *Richard Durham's Destination Freedom: Scripts from Radio's Black Legacy, 1948-50*. Westport, CT: Praeger, 1989. 263 pp. (Media and Society series). ISBN: 0-275-93139-2. ISSN: 0890-7161.

Destination Freedom was a half-hour Sunday evening program broadcast over WMAQ in the late 1940s that recounted the achievements and careers of eminent blacks. This volume contains 15 of the scripts "deemed most important," and each is introduced "with a short history of the subject matter and consideration of the play within Durham's intellectual world view."

180. Maclaurin, W. Rupert, with the technical assistance of R. Joyce Harman. *Invention & Innovation in the Radio Industry*. New York: Macmillan, 1949. 304 pp. (MIT Studies of Innovation series).

Maclaurin includes chapters on the scientific pioneers of radio, the impact of new scientific advances, the process of invention and innovation, the role of the large electrical firms in early wireless, the struggle over patents in the 1920s, and rising competition. He discusses industrial research, government regulation, and technical progress, and includes data on FM and television before 1941. This was reprinted in 1971 by Arno Press/New York Times as part of the History of Broadcasting: Radio to Television series.

181. MacVane, John. *On the Air in World War II*. New York: William Morrow, 1979. 384 pp. ISBN: 0-688-03558-2.

The author was an eyewitness radio reporter in Europe and North Africa for six years during WW II. He talked with millions of Americans every day from the London blitz, the Dieppe Raid, the North African landings, in Normandy on D-Day, during the liberation of Paris, and the meeting of American and Russian soldiers on the Elbe River. This is his firsthand account of these times and broadcasts.

182. Maier, Irwin. *A Career in Newspapers & Broadcasting*. Milwaukee: The Journal Company, 1981. 116 pp.

The author looks back on his 60 years in the newspaper and radio broadcasting businesses, his activities in professional organizations, and in civic affairs.

183. Marconi, Degna. *My Father, Marconi*. New York: McGraw-Hill, 1962. 320 pp.

Written by the daughter of the inventor of the wireless, this is the biography of Guglielmo Marconi and offers a different insight into his life as well as her own early years in his home.

184. Matheson, Hilda. *Broadcasting*. London: Thornton Butterworth, 1933. 253 pp. (The Home University Library of Modern Knowledge).

Basing this book on her six years of experience with the British Broadcasting Corporation, the author provides a brief background of broadcasting's history. She recalls various facets of radio broadcasting including literature and drama, music, entertainment, education, and broadcasting and the state.

185. Mayes, Thorn L. *Wireless Communication in the United States: The Early Development of American Radio Operating Companies*. East Greenwich, RI: New England Wireless and Steam Museum, 1990. 242 pp. ISBN: 0-9625170-0-3.

This book is about the inventors, engineers, and promoters who brought about wireless and its first use for marine radio communication. The book was written by an engineer who knew many of these pioneers, and it was prepared for publication by a Westinghouse Radio engineer and historian, Arthur C. Goodnow.

186. McBride, Mary Margaret. *Here's Martha Deane*. Garden City, NY: Garden City Publishing, 1936. 294 pp.

Mary Margaret McBride writes that she feels she is a dual personality with her other half being radio's "Martha Deane." This book is less an autobiography than it is the story of Martha Deane and the popular radio interview program she conducted.

187. McBride, Mary Margaret. *Out of the Air*. Garden City, NY: Doubleday, 1960. 384 pp.

The focus of this autobiography is on the radio years of Miss McBride's life. She was able to use recordings of most of her broadcasts to jog her memory.

188. McLuhan, Marshall. *Understanding Media.* New York: McGraw-Hill, 1964. 359 pp.

The man who coined the phrase "the medium is the message" examines the different types of media in this volume. He includes radio in the chapter he calls The Tribal Drum as he writes of its history and the effect it has had on its audience.

189. McMahon, Morgan E. *A Flick of the Switch: 1930-1950.* Palos Verdes Peninsula, CA: Vintage Radio, 1976. 311 pp. ISBN: 0-914126-09-1.

This picks up in 1930 where the author's original pictorial history book, *Vintage Radio* (see item #191), leaves off. The author discusses the personalities and broadcast programs of the era and then goes on to "record the times and hardware of the radio amateur" as well as early radio sets, all accompanied by numerous illustrations.

190. McMahon, Morgan E., ed. *Radio Collector's Guide, 1921-1932.* Palos Verdes Peninsula, CA: Vintage Radio, 1973. 264 pp. ISBN: 0-914126-03-2.

Ralph H. Langley's *Set Catalog and Index* published in 1933 is the basis for this volume that is intended to provide information for collectors, historians, and dealers. It tabulates manufacturers, model numbers and names, years introduced, original prices, cabinet types, and technical information.

191. McMahon, Morgan E. *Vintage Radio*. 2nd ed. Palos Verdes Peninsula, CA: Vintage Radio, 1973. 263 pp.

The notation on the title page says it all: "Harold Greenwood's historical album expanded with many old ads, illustrations, and many photos of wireless and radio equipment."

192. McNamee, Graham, in collaboration with Robert Gordon Anderson. *You're on the Air*. New York: Harper & Brothers, 1926. 207 pp.

Beginning with his first job at WEAF in New York, McNamee combined a career of music and broadcasting and rose to become one of radio's premier announcers. His diverse assignments ranged from concerts to political conventions and sessions of Congress, but he gained most fame for sports announcing (boxing, baseball, football), and his closing phrase, "Good night all."

193. McNicol, Donald. *Radio's Conquest of Space: The Experimental Rise in Radio Communication*. New York: Murray Hill Books, 1946. 374 pp.

Without using mathematics, this book is intended to help a layperson learn how radio operates and acquire a knowledge of radio's history. It is helpful to readers who have little or no background in the field.

194. Metz, Robert. *CBS: Reflections in a Bloodshot Eye*. New York: Signet, 1976. 427 pp. (New American Library).

The cover of this paperback reprint states this is "the anecdote-packed, uncensored inside story of America's greatest entertainment factory and communications empire." The first third of the book deals with the "salad days," the Second World War, and the postwar years of radio while the balance covers television.

195. Miller, Joseph L., ed. *Working for Radio*. Washington: National Association of Broadcasters, 1942. 23 pp.

Among the first-person accounts are short articles written by Bing Crosby, Cecil B. DeMille, Gertrude Berg, and Edward G. Robinson. Topics covered are acting, staging a radio show, announcing, play writing, singers and musicians in radio, operators and technicians, small stations, and advertising.

196. Milligan, Spike. *The Goon Show Scripts*. New York: St. Martin's Press, 1972. 189 pp.

The Goon Show was one of the British Broadcasting Corporation's most popular programs in the early 1950s. This volume reprints scripts of some of the broadcasts between October 1954 and January 1956. A number of photographs and drawings depict the cast and the main characters plus several articles describing The Goons-- then and now.

197. Mitchell, Curtis. *Cavalcade of Broadcasting*. Chicago: Follett Publishing, 1970. 256 pp. ISBN: 0-695-80209-7.

As Mitchell relates the history of radio and television broadcasting, he uses some unusual chapter titles: Crackpots, Kooks and Geniuses; Enterprisers and Amateurs, 1911-1918; The Admirals and Generals Take Over; Patent, Patent, Who's Got the Patent; Growing Pains; That's How Networks Were Born; Broadcasting Goes to War; and, with the advent of television, To Serve a Nation.

198. Morrow, Bruce, and Laura Baudo. *Cousin Brucie! My Life in Rock 'n' Roll Radio*. New York: William Morrow, 1987. 255 pp. ISBN: 0-688-06615-1.

One of the foremost radio personalities of the 1960s, Cousin Brucie joined New York's WABC in 1961 and helped it become the highest rated station in the country. This autobiography provides anecdotes about many of the stars he helped popularize and includes photographs of his appearances with them.

199. Moseley, Sydney. *Broadcasting in My Time*. London: Rich & Cowan, 1935. 244 pp.

Part of a career series written in the first person, this is written by "an independent critic" who bases it on his experience of daily listening "for some twelve years ... sometimes *all* day and far into the night." This is his report of British Broadcasting from an angle of complete independence that reports the picture as he sees it.

200. Murrow, Edward R. *This Is London!* New York: Simon & Schuster, 1941. 237 pp.

Edited and with an introduction, commentary, and footnotes by Elmer Davis, this book is a compilation of Murrow's broadcasts in the first 16 months of WW II. The selection was made by F.W. Mordaunt Hall of CBS and might not have been the same ones chosen by Murrow himself, but they do paint a realistic picture of events early in the war as they were broadcast to the American people at a time when the United States was not yet in the war.

201. National Association of Broadcasters. *Portrait of a "Protector."* New York: The Association, 1941. 16 pp.

This volume "presents the facts behind the rumor that an organization called ASCAP (American Society of Composers, Authors and Publishers) intends to bar from the air some of the popular music (people) have been listening to--unless radio agrees to pay $9,000,000 a year for its use." As history notes, ASCAP did call a boycott, the case was eventually settled, and radio broadcasting of music did not cease.

202. Nelson, Lindsey. *Hello Everybody, I'm Lindsey Nelson*. New York: William Morrow, 1985. 430 pp. ISBN: 0-688-04186-8.

Nelson, an elected member of the Sportscasters and Sportswriters Hall of Fame, describes events in his personal and professional life as he covered major league baseball for 25 years and football for 33. He offers an in-depth look at life both in and out of the broadcast booth.

203. Nelson, Lindsey, with Al Hirshberg. *Backstage at the Mets*. New York: Viking Press, 1966. 180 pp.

Nelson had been broadcasting NCAA football games for many years before he was hired to do the radio play-by-play for the brand- new New York Mets in 1962. This is his account of the first few years of the team and his broadcasting of its games.

204. O'Brien, P.J. *Will Rogers: Ambassador of Good Will, Prince of Wit and Wisdom*. Philadelphia: J.C. Winston, 1935. 288 pp.

One of radio's superstars in the 1930s was Will Rogers who gained fame as a folksy, down-home type of humorist. This biography recalls his early life in Oklahoma, his rise to world renown, and his untimely death in a plane crash in 1933.

205. O'Connell, Mary C. *Connections: Reflections of Sixty Years of Broadcasting*. New York: National Broadcasting Company, 1986. 267 pp.

   Personal recollections of people who were part of the 60-year history of NBC are assembled in this volume. Among those contributing are affiliate broadcasters, NBC executives, network news personnel, sports commentators, and network entertainers.

206. Osborn, Lynn R. *Commercial Radio in Kansas, 1908-1945*. Lawrence: University of Kansas, 1963. 41 leaves.

   This history of Kansas commercial radio was prepared as part of the University's Radio-Television Research project. It covers the pioneering era, early growth and expansion, the establishment of the commercial era, the coming of age of Kansas radio, and the war years.

207. Osgood, Dick. *Wyxie Wonderland: An Unauthorized 50-Year Diary of WXYZ Detroit*. Bowling Green, OH: Bowling Green University Popular Press, 1981. 537 pp. ISBN: 0-87972-186-3.

   Not purely a local story, this reflects national radio and television history from 1925 to 1975 through a single broadcasting station--WXYZ Detroit--AM, FM, and TV. Osgood covers the payola scandal, how the Top 40 format materialized from a bar in Omaha, the rise and decline of radio network programming, and the emergence and rise of disc jockey status to sometime national prominence.

208. Overstreet, Harry A., and Bonaro W. Overstreet. *Town Meeting Comes to Town*. New York: Harper & Brothers, 1938. 268 pp.

62 Radio Broadcasting

This book is about a particular institution in a particular American city. It describes Town Hall in New York and its creation, *America's Town Meeting of the Air*, which was a highly successful radio program in the 1930s.

209. Paley, William S. *As It Happened: A Memoir*. Garden City, NY: Doubleday, 1979. 418 pp.

    Bill Paley speaks for himself in this story of his life before and after CBS. He writes about his early childhood in Chicago, living in post-WW I New York, his connections with CBS-Paramount, and the great success of both CBS radio and television.

210. Paper, Lewis J. *Empire: William S. Paley and the Making of CBS*. New York: St. Martin's Press, 1987. 384 pp. ISBN: 0-312-00591-1.

    The names Paley and CBS are almost synonymous because the two have been connected so closely since the beginning of the network. This is the biography of the man who has been the principal force behind CBS and, as a result, has had extensive influence on the American public and contemporary popular culture.

211. Parker, Derek. *Radio: The Great Years*. Newton Abbot, Eng.: David & Charles, 1977. 160 pp. ISBN: 0-7153-7430-3.

    Accompanied by a large number of illustrations, this is the author's personal tribute to "Auntie"--the British Broadcasting Corporation that brought him so much pleasure all his life. He relates the history of the company and concentrates on its programming and the performers who became part of the radio listeners' families.

212. Pawley, Edward. *BBC Engineering, 1922-1972*. London: British Broadcasting Corporation, 1972. 569 pp. ISBN: 0-563-12127-0.

While some parts of this volume are relatively technical, other sections are purely historical as they describe the early steps and the first broadcasts of the Broadcasting Company in the 1920s. The early years of the Corporation are detailed as are the World War II years and post-war reconstruction. A final chapter covers the years of expansion from 1956 to 1972.

213. Poindexter, Ray. *Arkansas Airwaves*. North Little Rock, AR: Ray Poindexter, 1974. 421 pp.

Arkansas' first station, WOK (Workers of Kilowatts) was licensed in February 1922 and was quickly followed by WCAC the following May. Poindexter traces the history of broadcasting in the state from those humble beginnings to a 1974 total of 82 AM and 45 FM commercial stations, 6 educational FMs, 8 commercial TV stations, and 1 educational TV station.

214. Post, Steve. *Playing in the FM Band: A Personal Account of Free Radio*. New York: Viking Press, 1974. 230 pp. ISBN: 0-670-55927-X.

The foreword states this is "the story of a radio station (WBAI-FM) whose programming is a constant adventure, and whose day-to-day fight for survival is often one as well." WBAI-FM is the flagship station for the Pacifica Foundation that also operates stations in California, Texas, and Washington, DC, and receives its sole support from listeners.

215. Pringle, John, ed. *The Radio Listener's Week-end Book*. London: Odhams Press, 1950. 288 pp.

A selection of broadcasts between 1945 and 1950 are classified into the following groups titled: Strange Experiences; Memories of the Great; They Were There; Personal Document; Travel and Adventure; Home and Family; All That's Past; Beauty and Fashion; Books and Their Writers; The World Around Us; Sporting Pleasures; Short Stories; and First and Last Things.

216. Quinlan, Sterling. *Inside ABC: American Broadcasting Company's Rise to Power*. New York: Hastings House, 1979. 290 pp. ISBN: 0-8038-6765-4.

ABC's past, according to the author, is as fascinating as its present: it is a star-crossed tale, the roots of which go back, not only to the origins of radio, but to the beginnings of the motion picture industry. Quinlan describes those beginnings and roots as he writes about the company's progression to become a major media force.

217. Radio Corporation of America. *The First 25 Years of RCA: A Quarter-Century of Radio Progress*. New York: The Corporation, 1944. 87 pp.

In addition to providing an actual history of the company, this lists 25 historic advances in radio as achieved by RCA in its first 25 years.

218. *The Radio Industry: The Story of Its Development as Told by Leaders of the Industry*. New York: Arno Press, 1974. 330 pp. ISBN: 0-505-06055-6.

A reprint of the original book on the history of the industry published by A.W. Shaw Company in 1928, this consists of a series of lectures to the students of the Graduate School of Business Administration, George F. Baker Foundation, Harvard University. The first edition included an introduction by David Sarnoff and a foreword by Dr. Anton de Haas.

219. Reith, John C.W. *Into the Wind*. London: Hodder & Stoughton, 1949. 536 pp.

This consists of the author's memoirs of events that occurred during World War I, the early struggles of the British Broadcasting Corporation, his career in coalition politics during WW II, and in Commonwealth communications. He includes bits and pieces of correspondence with British prime ministers, ambassadors, and American presidents.

220. Rhymer, Mary Frances, ed. *The Small House Half-Way Up in the Next Block: Paul Rhymer's Vic and Sade*. New York: McGraw-Hill, 1972. 301 pp. ISBN: 0-07-073792-4.

One of the most popular programs during radio's Golden Age, *Vic and Sade* was a unique comedy series that had millions of listeners. Each program was a complete episode and told the story of the small family, their relatives, and their friends. This book contains the scripts of a number of the shows broadcast between 1933 and 1940.

221. Richardson, David. *Puget Sounds: A Nostalgic Review of Radio and TV in the Great Northwest*. Seattle: Superior Publishers, 1981. 192 pp. ISBN: 0-87564-636-0.

The author invites the reader to "return with us to those exciting days of yesteryear (and) to remember the half-forgotten voices and images that thrilled us years ago." He writes about specific programs, stations, and locals who made good--Bing Crosby, Art Gilmore, Wendell Niles, Trevor Evans, Frances Farmer, Mary Livingston, Howard Duff, "Major" Edward Bowes, Norma Zimmer, and Paul Rhymer, the author of the radio soap *Vic and Sade*.

222. Rockwell, Don, ed. *Radio Personalities: A Pictorial and Biographical Annual*. New York: Press Bureau.

An annual publication, this was divided into classifications with each containing an editorial on the subject (Silver Tongues, Jesters, Monarchs of Melody, On Wings of Song, etc.). These essays were followed by photographs and biographical information about the performers and/or personnel working in those categories. The initial issue published in 1935 was 268 pages.

223. Rogers, Will. *Wit and Philosophy from the Radio Talks of America's Humorist, Will Rogers*. New York: E.R. Squibb & Sons, 1930. 46 pp.

The text of 12 radio talks delivered by Will Rogers during the spring of 1930 are reproduced in this volume. They cover the Arms Conference, Charles Lindbergh, President Herbert Hoover, Alfred E. Smith, and several other personalities.

224. Rolo, Charles J. *Radio Goes to War: the "Fourth Front."* New York: G.P. Putnam's Sons, 1942. 293 pp.

A New York radio station interrupted its football game broadcast on December 7, 1941, at 2:26 p.m. to announce the attack on Pearl Harbor. From then on radio networks mobilized into action and went on a 24-hour-a-day basis. This signalled the start of U.S. radio going to war, and the author details the short period of American history from then until his own publication date the next year.

225. Rothel, David. *Who Was That Masked Man? The Story of the Lone Ranger.* South Brunswick, NJ: A.S. Barnes, 1976. 256 pp. ISBN: 0-498-01914-4.

With a hearty "heigh-ho, Silver," the Lone Ranger and his faithful Indian companion, Tonto, rode into the hearts of listeners everywhere beginning in 1933. One of radio's most popular programs, *The Lone Ranger* successfully made the transition to television. This is the story behind the stories and includes several photographs of the different actors who were in one version or the other.

226. Saerchinger, Cesar. *Hello America! Radio Adventures in Europe.* Boston: Houghton Mifflin, 1938. 393 pp.

Describing himself as the first foreign radio representative, Saerchinger writes about his years of overseas broadcasting to the United States. He divides his book into people, events, atmospheres, and systems and policies.

227. Sanger, Elliott M. *Rebel in Radio: The Story of WQXR.* New York: Hastings House, 1973. 190 pp. ISBN: 0-8038-6329-8.

Radio station WQXR in New York "was and still is different and which despite great odds made a place for itself in the history of radio ... It blazed a trail in the then-wilderness of broadcasting." The author tells the story of the "effect it had upon the musical life of New York and its influence elsewhere" as it became a station that emphasized the best in music.

228. Sarnoff, David. *Looking Ahead.* New York: McGraw-Hill, 1968. 313 pp.

Excerpts from the major documents and papers during Sarnoff's career with RCA are assembled in this volume that is intended "for the convenience of researchers and for young people interested in careers in electronics." Most of this collection of letters, public statements, and speeches (some 1,000 volumes) cover technical and commercial activities, and are housed near the RCA laboratories in Princeton, New Jersey.

229. Schechter, A.A., with Edward Anthony. *I Live on Air.* New York: Frederick A. Stokes, 1941. 454 pp.

In addition to his own recollections and various anecdotes about the industry, Schechter includes 64 reproductions of photographs on a variety of subjects more or less related to early radio broadcasting.

230. Schmeckebier, Laurence F. *The Federal Radio Commission: Its History, Activities, and Organization.* Washington: Brookings Institution, 1932. 162 pp. (Institute for Government Research, Service Monographs of the U.S. Government, 65).

The Federal Radio Commission was an independent establishment of the national government dealing with the licensing of radio stations of every character, including the assignment of frequencies, the fixing of power to be used in transmission, and the determination of hours of operation. This is the story of the agency that was created in 1927 and subsequently became the Federal Communications Commission.

231. Schroeder, Peter B. *Contact at Sea.* Ridgewood, NJ: Gregg Press, 1967. 139 pp.

Schroeder has written a history of maritime radio communications from the point of view of both a historian and a technological authority. He tries to use as little jargon as possible and emphasizes maritime radio communications' application to the safety of life at sea.

232. Schubert, Paul. *The Electric Word: The Rise of Radio*. New York: Macmillan, 1928. 311 pp.

Reprinted in 1971 as part of the History of Broadcasting: Radio to Television series by Arno Press/New York Times, this divides the history of radio into three eras: maritime adoption, military use, and popular use. Schubert begins with Marconi's wireless and ends with the radio boom of the 1920s.

233. Settel, Irving. *A Pictorial History of Radio*. 2nd ed. New York: Grosset & Dunlap, 1967. 188 pp. ISBN: 0-448-01913-2.

Following "a lament for old-time radio," this volume provides a flow chart that "shows why no one man can be credited with having 'invented' radio or television" along with photographs of Morse, Marconi, and Bell. Pictures taken from 1960s programs complete the history.

234. Sevareid, Eric. *Not So Wild a Dream*. New York: Alfred A. Knopf, 1947. 516 pp.

Eric Sevareid gained fame as a political and war reporter, as a writer and commentator, and finally as a television "elder statesman." He reports "on himself" in this volume as he writes of growing up in a North Dakota village, serving as a foreign correspondent in France, England, China, Italy, Germany, and Burma, and comments on the moral and social problems facing the modern world.

235. Shirer, William L. *Berlin Diary: The Journal of a Foreign Correspondent, 1934-1941.* New York: Alfred A. Knopf, 1941. 605 pp.

During his years as a foreign correspondent and radio broadcaster, Shirer jotted down notes in his diary. Although not all of these notes left Germany when he did, he was able to piece together the missing material. He combined his own recollections with copies of all his radio broadcasts so that he could present a full picture of the events of the early war years in Germany from an insider's view.

236. Shurick, E.P.J., ed. *The First Quarter-Century of American Broadcasting.* Kansas City, MO: Midland Publishing, 1946. 371 pp.

According to the preface, this book was compiled from the writings of "several hundred qualified authorities" and was based on research from the *Broadcasting Yearbooks* and a questionnaire that was widely distributed. The editor was Director of Advertising and Promotion for station KMBC of Kansas City.

237. Singular, Stephen. *Talked to Death: The Life and Murder of Alan Berg.* New York: William Morrow, 1987. 320 pp. ISBN: 0-688-06154-0.

This recounts the shooting of Denver's KOA radio talk show host, Alan Berg, and the subsequent trial of those arrested for his murder.

238. Sklar, Rick. *Rocking America: An Insider's Story: How the All-Hit Radio Stations Took Over.* New York: St. Martin's Press, 1984. 220 pp.

Thirty years of you-are-there anecdotes and analysis of the rock radio revolution are presented by a man who was intimately involved in the phenomenon. This is his own history of the era.

239. Slate, Sam J., and Joe Cook. *It Sounds Impossible*. New York: Macmillan, 1963. 270 pp.

Illustrated by photographs from "radio's infancy" and teenage years, this offers "an amusing, interesting commentary that will give a better understanding and appreciation of this amazing business." Written by two radio writers with a combined experience of over 50 years in the field, this describes the invention of radio, its early ups and downs, the success it enjoyed for so many years, and finally its shared popularity with the new medium--television.

240. Slater, Robert. *This Is CBS: A Chronicle of 60 Years*. Englewood Cliffs, NJ: Prentice-Hall, 1988. 354 pp. ISBN: 0-13-919234-4.

Behind the scenes interviews and excerpts from memoirs of personalities Walter Cronkite, Dan Rather, and Edward R. Murrow contribute to this history of the CBS network from its 1920s inception to the present time. Special emphasis is placed on television broadcasting although there is much history of radio included.

241. Slide, Anthony. *Great Radio Personalities in Historic Photographs*. New York: Dover, 1982. 117 pp. ISBN: 0-486-24298-6.

Two hundred and thirty-nine photographs are included in this gallery of familiar and unfamiliar faces along with full biographical captions for each. Included are Rudy Vallee, Walter Winchell, Ben Bernie, Whispering Jack

Smith, Edward R. Murrow, Arthur Godfrey, Edgar Bergen, the Andrews Sisters, and Gertrude Berg and others to create a virtual who's who of the medium.

242. Smart, Samuel Chipman. *The Outlet Story, 1894-1984*. Providence, RI: Outlet Communications, 1984. 223 pp.

In addition to being the history of one of Providence's leading department stores, this is also the history of radio station WJAR, established in 1922, and its sister station, WJAR-TV. Photographs enhance the account of the development of the stations, and television buffs will be surprised to see several pictures of a much younger Ted Knight, long before he became TV's Ted Baxter.

243. Smith, R. Franklin. *Edward R. Murrow: The War Years*. Kalamazoo, MI: New Issues Press, 1978. 156 pp.

This is a chronicle of the early career of Murrow and includes an evaluation of his character, values and professional approach to broadcasting. It is based on interviews with prominent media-world individuals (Eric Sevareid and Charles Collingwood, for example) as well as wartime BBC personnel who worked with Murrow.

244. Snagge, John, and Michael Barsley. *Those Vintage Years of Radio*. London: Pitman Publishing, 1972. 247 pp. ISBN: 0-273-31663-X.

The scope of this book covers the years 1935 to 1953, chosen because that was the time the British Broadcasting Corporation accepted the challenges of events of world-wide importance and, according to the authors, produced the greatest achievement in broadcasting the world has ever known. Thus they have created a collection of reminiscences about people and programs from those years.

245. Sobel, Robert. *RCA*. New York: Stein & Day, 1986. 282 pp. ISBN: 0-8128-3084-9.

In his preface the author states that the history of RCA has been one of high drama and, in recent years, of unexpected developments. He tells the story of the company from its creation to the planned but never materialized merger with MCA in late December 1985.

246. Sperber, A.M. *Murrow, His Life and Times*. New York: Freundlich Books, 1986. 795 pp. ISBN: 0-88191-008-2.

Telling it like it was, the author recounts Murrow's life from childhood through his death at the age of 57. She paints vivid pictures of the wartime radio broadcasts that brought Murrow instant fame, the success and struggles with CBS, his collaboration with Fred Friendly, later government service, and finally, his losing battle with lung cancer.

247. Stamberg, Susan. *Every Night at Five: Susan Stamberg's All Things Considered Book*. New York: Pantheon, 1982. 212 pp. ISBN: 0-394-70652-8.

Here is an inside look behind the scenes of National Public Radio's popular late afternoon-early evening program, *All Things Considered*, which began broadcasting in 1971. Stamberg writes about taping and editing sessions, staff meetings, reporting the news, and some of the interesting, exciting, or mundane episodes and events during that decade.

248. Sterling, Christopher H., and John M. Kittross. *Stay Tuned: A Concise History of American Broadcasting*. Belmont, CA: Wadsworth, 1978. 562 pp. ISBN: 0-534-00514-4.

The goal of the authors, as described in their preface, is to tell how American broadcasting got where it is today and, by analyzing principles, events, and trends, suggest what directions it may take in the future. They emphasize trends rather than incidents and trivia, key individuals rather than random examples, and basic principles rather than isolated facts. A second edition was published in 1989.

249. *The Story of WWJ Radio One: Where It All Began.* Detroit, MI: Radio Station WWJ, 1970. 16 pp.

This history of radio station WWJ was published in commemoration of its 50th anniversary and is credited on the title page as being the first station in the world to broadcast regularly scheduled daily programs.

250. Stuart, Charles, ed. *The Reith Diaries.* London: Collins, 1975. 541 pp. ISBN: 0-00-211174-8.

British Broadcasting Corporation Director-General Sir John Reith maintained a diary throughout his life and was concerned with the possibility of it being used for publication. He finally entrusted it to Stuart to edit. This book, based on the diaries, covers primarily the years between 1922 and 1970.

251. Stumpf, Charles K. *Ma Perkins, Little Orphan Annie, and Heigh Ho, Silver!* New York: Carlton Press, 1971. 127 pp.

After a brief autobiographical sketch of the author's childhood imaginary station, WCKS, he writes about the soaps, musical programs, comedians, dramatic programs, mysteries, on-air gossip columnists, quiz shows, children's programs, and regular series that were broadcast on radio. He concludes with a chapter on his apparent first love, radio sound effects, as he describes how so many of them were generated and the ways they helped certain shows become standards (Benny's Maxwell, Fibber McGee's closet, Silver's hoofbeats, etc.)

252. Stursberg, Peter. *Mister Broadcasting: The Ernie Bushnell Story*. Toronto: Peter Martin Associates, 1971. 292 pp. ISBN: 0-88778-061-X.

    Ernie Bushnell was in on the early days of Canadian broadcasting, and this biography tells of not only his life but the growth of Canadian broadcasting. It is based on Bushnell's own memoirs and numerous tapes and conversations with the author who had access to Bushnell's files and those of the CBC.

253. Summers, Harrison B., ed. *A Thirty-Year History of Programs Carried on National Radio Networks in the United States, 1926-1956*. New York: Arno Press/New York Times, 1971. 228 pp. ISBN: 0-405-03572-1.

    This compilation provides a year-by-year record of the programs carried from the season of 1926-27, the first season of formally organized networks, through that of 1955-56. Omitted are programs that were broadcast only as summer replacements unless they were picked up subsequently by a network. The compilation was finished in January 1958 and published by the Department of Speech of Ohio State University.

254. Summers, Harrison B., Robert E. Summers, and John H. Pennybacker. *Broadcasting and the Public*. 2nd ed. Belmont, CA: Wadsworth, 1978. 467 pp. ISBN: 0-534-00532-2.

Beginning with the development of American radio, this continues with the introduction and success of television as an entertainment medium. The radio sections cover both non-commercial and commercial radio, radio during WW II, public and educational radio, ratings, programming, and regulation. The first edition was published in 1966 under the authorship of Robert E. and Harrison B. Summers.

255. Swing, Raymond Gram. *"Good Evening": A Professional Memoir*. New York: Harcourt, Brace & World, 1964. 311 pp.

The author was raised in the college town of Oberlin, Ohio, and his first newspaper job was as night man for the afternoon paper, *Toledo Blade*. He became a writer and radio broadcaster, starting with WOR and the Mutual Network, and eventually working with the Voice of America, U.S. Information Service, and Edward R. Murrow.

256. Swing, Raymond Gram. *How War Came*. New York: W.W. Norton, 1939. 266 pp.

The author disclaims that this volume is in any sense a brief history of the outbreak of WW II, but it is simply the presentation in book form of his radio commentaries on the situation. The text of the broadcasts have been retained except for an occasional alteration from the spoken to the written word.

257. Swing, Raymond Gram. *In the Name of Sanity*. New York: Harper & Brothers, 1946. 116 pp.

Early in the morning of August 24, 1945, after the dropping of the atomic bomb ending WW II, the author made a decision to announce during his regular radio broadcast that night that he would devote each Friday's program to the influence of the release of atomic energy on the world. This book contains the texts of some of these Friday evening talks.

258. Taylor, Glenhall. *Before Television: The Radio Years*. Cranbury, NJ: A.S. Barnes, 1979. 169 pp. ISBN: 0-498-02204-8.

The various sections of this book are titled Tuning in at the Beginning; Crashing the Hollywood Scene; The Big Time; Other Favorite Characters; Onward and Upward?; and It's Come a Long Way, Baby! Photographs of radio performers illustrate the book.

259. Taylor, Marion Sayle. *"The Voice of Experience."* New York: Dodd, Mead, 1933. 367 pp.

"The Voice of Experience" began dispensing advice over the CBS network in 1933 after broadcasting on local stations for several years previously. This book contains the replies to 50 of the most frequently asked questions submitted to Dr. Taylor during her years of broadcasting.

260. Taylor, Robert. *Fred Allen: His Life and Wit*. Boston: Little, Brown, 1989. 340 pp. ISBN: 0-316-83388-6.

Allen was "propelled to superstardom" by radio in the 1930s and 40s on such programs as *Town Hall Tonight* and *The Fred Allen Show*. This biography, while it, of course, describes Allen's life, also "is an informed and entertaining vision of 20th century comedy, seen through vaudeville, Broadway, Hollywood, radio, and early television."

261. Tebbel, John. *David Sarnoff: Putting Electronics to Work*. Chicago: Encyclopaedia Britannica Press, 1973. 191 pp. (Britannica Bookshelf--Great Lives).

"Superficially the Sarnoff story is based on the old conventional rags-to-riches theme, the rise of a poor immigrant boy from the lower East Side of New York to success by dint of hard work and virtue." This book does tell that story as Sarnoff rose to become the Chairman of the Board of Radio Corporation of America and one of the most powerful men in the history of communications.

262. Terrace, Vincent. *Radio's Golden Years: the Encyclopedia of Radio Programs, 1930-1960*. San Diego: A.S. Barnes, 1981. 308 pp. ISBN: 0-498-02393-1.

Fifteen hundred nationally broadcast network and syndicated entertainment programs are included in this alphabetical listing. In addition to the many types of programming, there are 90 photographs, an index, and a list of first-run programs broadcast during the 1970s.

263. *Thirty Years of Pioneering and Progress in Radio and Television*. New York: Radio Corporation of America, 1949. 79 pp.

"Through research and engineering over the past 30 years, RCA has pioneered and put into practical use many of the outstanding developments in the field of radio science; it leads the way in electronics and television." This is the story of the history of RCA and its accomplishments.

264. Thomas, Alan. *Broadcast and Be Damned: The ABC's First Two Decades*. Melbourne, Aust.: Melbourne University Press, 1980. 230 pp. ISBN: 0-522-84198-8.

This book is concerned with the Australian Broadcasting Commission's policies and practices between 1932 and 1948. The ABC began in 1932 with six state branches and a head office in Sydney, and the author describes this start along with information about radio programs and personalities of the period and concludes with the return of peace in 1945 and the advent of television.

265. Thomas, Bob. *Winchell*. Garden City, NY: Doubleday, 1971. 288 pp.

Broadcasting to "Mr. and Mrs. America and all the ships at sea," Walter Winchell was famous for his rapid-fire delivery after he added radio to his endeavors as a newspaper columnist. This is the biography that was written with the cooperation of the Winchell family.

266. Thomas, Lowell. *Fan Mail*. New York: Dodge Publishing, 1935. 171 pp.

As indicated in the title, this is a collection of letters received by Thomas through the National Broadcasting Company. They contain both praise and criticism, suggestions for future commentaries, and other suggestions in general; each writer is identified by name or initials and city or town.

267. Thomas, Lowell. *Good Evening Everybody: From Cripple Creek to Samarkand*. New York: William Morrow, 1976. 349 pp. ISBN: 0-688-03068-8.

Thomas approached his "rambling reminiscences" by trying to explain how, "having long resisted some misguided urgings to write something about my life, I now find myself doing it (and) going off in all directions." The book covers his childhood, schooling, early jobs, his career as a reporter and as a radio commentator but, most of all, as a world traveler. He continued his autobiography by writing *So Long Until Tomorrow: From Quaker Hill to Kathmandu* which began after the Japanese attack on Pearl Harbor in 1941 and continues up to the age of 85, his age at the time it was published in 1977.

268. Thomas, Lowell. *History As You Heard It.* New York: Garden City, NY: Doubleday, 1957. 486 pp.

Arranged chronologically from 1930 to 1955, Thomas recounts the major events that happened in each year. Each entry was taken from one of Thomas's own radio broadcasts.

269. Thomas, Lowell. *Magic Dials: The Story of Radio and Television.* New York: Lee Furman, 1939. 142 pp.

The introduction states "This is a story combining the features of the maddest myths and legends--mingling magic carpets, seven league boots and slaves of the lamp with weird brews in beakers and test tubes, and uncanny filaments that generate the thunderbolts of Jove." That about sums up the contents of this book describing radio's history, technology, personnel, and future.

270. Tracey, Michael. *A Variety of Lives: A Biography of Sir Hugh Greene.* London: The Bodley Head, 1983. 343 pp. ISBN: 0-3703-0026-2.

Greene, British Broadcasting Corporation Director-General from 1960 to 1969, was a *Daily Telegraph* correspondent, served in RAF Intelligence, helped create a new German broadcasting system after World War II, and was head of the Emergency Information Services in Malaya. This is an unusual biography of an active and sometimes controversial figure still living at the time of publication because the author was able to research Greene's life and then talk over the particular events with him.

271. Treadwell, Bill. *Head, Heart and Heel.* New York: Mayfair Books, 1958. 212 pp.

"Uncle Don" of WOR and the Mutual Network was a legendary character in the early days of radio and influenced not only the millions of children who listened to his daily programs but also their parents and grandparents. This is the biography of the man who "lived five lives in one: he was a businessman, a theatrical performer, a Beau Brummel, educator, and a public benefactor" as well as one of children's radio's first stars.

272. Trethowan, Ian. *Split Screen.* London: Hamish Hamilton, 1984. 222 pp. ISBN: 0-2411-1258-3.

Motivated by a 1979 heart attack, a former British Broadcasting Corporation Director-General recounts events in his life leading to his career as a prominent political commentator before switching to senior management of the BBC.

273. Ulanov, Barry. *The Incredible Crosby.* New York: McGraw-Hill, 1948. 336 pp.

Bing Crosby gained fame in radio before he became so famous as a movie actor. His *Kraft Music Hall* was a long-time favorite program, and this book describes his broadcasting years as well as events concerning the rest of his life.

274. Vallee, Rudy, with Gil McKean. *My Time Is Your Time: The Story of Rudy Vallee*. New York: Ivan Obolensky, 1952. 244 pp.

Vallee became a big radio star when he aired *The Fleishmann Hour* in 1929 and followed it with a series of other popular shows. This is his autobiography, and he reminisces about his days in radio as well as on the stage and in the movies.

275. Velia, Ann M. *KOB: Goddard's Magic Mast: Fifty Years of Pioneer Broadcasting*. Las Cruces: New Mexico State University, 1972. 195 pp.

Ralph Goddard was the founder of radio station KOB that emerged from a campus radio club. It went on the air in 1920, and Goddard was its director until he was killed in the KOB transmitter room in 1929. This book, however, does not end with the story of Goddard's death, but is continued until KOB celebrates its 50th anniversary as an AM station and the creation of the college's stereo FM station with the call letters KRWG, after Ralph Willis Goddard.

276. Vyvyan, Richard N. *Wireless Over Thirty Years*. London: George Routledge & Sons, 1933. 256 pp.

Containing 16 plates and 12 diagrams, this tells about the early pioneers; transocean wireless; modern commercial wireless stations in England; at war on land, at sea, and in the air; the British post office's contribution to wireless development; wireless as a career; commercial wireless telegraph development; and suggestions for research problems.

277. Waters, James F. *The Court of Missing Heirs*. New York: Modern Age Books, 1941. 281 pp.

Broadcast over CBS in 1939 and the early 1940s, *The Court of Missing Heirs* attempted to find the beneficiaries to large and small fortunes. This book recounts case histories of discovered recipients and includes an alphabetical list of unclaimed estates.

278. Wedlake, G.E.C. *SOS: The Story of Radio-Communication.* New York: Crane, Russak, 1973. 240 pp. ISBN: 0-8448-0270-0.

After describing the experimental and very early stages of radio communication, the author writes about its use during WW I and WW II and the uses it was put to both during wartime and peacetime.

279. Wentworth, Brandon. *The Fabulous Radio NBD.* Southwest Harbor, ME: Beech Hill Publishing, 1984. 34 pp. ISBN: 0-933786-07-7.

This booklet tells the story of the old Otter Cliffs Naval Radio Station in Acadia National Park, Maine, which began operations in 1917 and was razed in 1935. Its founder received the Navy Cross from President Wilson at the end of World War I.

280. Westfield, Ernie. *So You Want to Be a "Dee Jay" After All This?* Urbana, IL: Ernie Westfield, 1978. 61 pp.

Written by Champaign-Urbana's "Mr. E," this contains a collection of quoted phone calls from his show, parts of letters he received, and a section titled "Meeting the DJ" about personal appearances. The book is illustrated with cartoons and a list of "DJ expressions."

281. Whetmore, Edward Jay. *The Magic Medium: An Introduction to Radio in America.* Belmont, CA: Wadsworth Publishing, 1981. 246 pp. ISBN: 0-534-00922-0.

This paperback furnishes a history of radio and goes on to describe radio production in detail. Radio as a profession is discussed, and there is a chapter about the future of the medium.

282. Winchell, Walter. *Winchell Exclusive: "Things That Happened to Me--and Me to Them."* Englewood Cliffs, NJ: Prentice-Hall, 1975. 332 pp. ISBN: 0-13-960286-0.

Photographs from the author's personal collection illustrate this autobiography of the man who started out as a vaudeville hoofer and ended up as one of the most famous radio/television/newspaper reporters in the world.

283. Wood, Clement. *The Life of a Man: A Biography of John R. Brinkley.* Kansas City: Goshorn Publishing, 1934. 332 pp.

Brinkley was "a graduate of distinguished medical universities in the U.S. and Europe, one of the leading surgeons and distinguished scientists of today, owned a millionaire's estate in Texas, an airplane, and two yachts, had been twice elected governor of a state and was a candidate for the governorship for the third time." He was also the owner of Milford, Kansas, radio station KFKB that was closed by order of the Federal Radio Commission in February 1931 He established XER the same year, and later "voluntarily closes XER to prevent civil war between the government and the local government which sides with him."

284. Woodfin, Jane. *Of Mikes and Men.* New York: McGraw-Hill, 1951. 275 pp.

The author was a radio continuity writer and based this book on her own experiences in broadcasting.

285. *WTIC: Radio to Remember.* Hartford, CT: Ten Eighty Corp., 1985. 62 pp.

Published to celebrate 60 years of service of the AM and FM stations, this summarizes the history of the stations that were owned and developed by Travelers Insurance Company executives who chose the call letters from their own name--WTIC.

286. Wyatt, Frederick. *The Lone Ranger: Some Psychological Observations.* Columbus: Ohio State University, 1941. 7 leaves. (Evaluation of School Broadcasts Bulletin, 27).

The Lone Ranger was an extremely popular radio program for children during the 1930s and 40s. This is a psychological interpretation of its content in terms of its appeal to children and the role it plays in children's lives.

287. Wylie, Max, ed. *Best Broadcasts of 1938-39.* New York: McGraw-Hill, 1939. 576 pp.

In this first volume of a series, the editor states it is his "intention to offer to the public for the first time a collection of superior programs representing all the major subdivisions in which the written word and the spoken word express themselves over the air." Subsequent volumes have appeared annually since this first one.

288. Young, Filson. *Shall I Listen: Studies in the Adventure and Technique of Broadcasting.* London: Constable, 1933. 287 pp.

Broadcasting in England, according to the author, was launched in the year 1923 by one or two men with an extremely practical vision. This volume consists of a series of essays written on the history of the medium, the listeners, music and the open air, the spoken word, radio drama, humor, and mass-production and individuality.

ECONOMIC ASPECTS

Includes advertising, ownership, audience appeal, listening groups, ratings, radio industry, networks, promotion, investing/financing, rates, public relations, and broadcast management.

289. Abel, John D., Richard V. Ducey, and Mark R. Fratrik. *Radioutlook: Forces Shaping the Radio Industry.* Washington: National Association of Broadcasters, 1988. 164 pp. ISBN: 0-89324-049-4.

    The various forces cited include the health of the economy, demographic changes, consumer electronics, technological trends, radio programming, the radio industry, station operations, total advertising revenues and radio's share, and audience research developments. An appendix presents the results of 1986 and 1987 NAB radio technology surveys.

290. *Advertising on Radio and Television.* Geneva: European Broadcasting Union, 1966. 37 pp. (EBU Legal and Administrative Monograph, 4).

    Intended to provide only a general introduction to the subject of commercial broadcasting, this examines basic concepts, the types of advertisements and their positioning, timing and format, and content and form.

291. Advertising Research Foundation. *National Survey of Radio and Television Sets Associated with U.S. Households, May 1954.* New York: The Foundation, 1954. 120 pp.

Conducted by Alfred Politz Research, this presents data on total radio and/or television sets in working order as well as the room location of such sets. The study was conducted in cooperation with ABC, Broadcast Advertising Bureau, CBS Radio, Mutual Broadcasting System, and NBC.

292. Advertising Research Foundation. *Recommended Standards for Radio and Television Program Audience Size Measurements.* New York, The Foundation, 1954. 70 pp.

Because different program audience-size measurement services have often reported widely divergent measurements for the same broadcast, the Foundation developed these standards to produce more uniform measurements. They cover information standards, procedures, and accuracy standards.

293. Agnew, Hugh E., and Warren B. Dygert. *Advertising Media.* New York: McGraw-Hill, 1938. 465 pp.

While this is a general overview of advertising in the media, there is a lengthy chapter devoted to radio as an advertising medium. It describes the chief characteristics of radio, radio circulation, coverage, equipment, rates, spot announcements, networks, electrical transcriptions, broadcasting time sales, foreign-language stations, classifications, terms of use, and production services.

294. American Research Bureau. *Understanding and Using Radio Audience Estimates: A Quick Reference Guide.* New York: Arbitron, 1976. 24 pp.

Arbitron Radio offered this guide to both new and experienced users of radio. It attempts to "strip away some of the mysteries of what audience estimates mean, how they are calculated, and how they can be used."

295. Arbitron Radio. *Research Guidelines for Programming Decision Makers: A Programmer's Guide to the Dynamics of Radio.* New York: Arbitron, 1977. 48 pp.

The three sections of this booklet are (1) understanding the marketing factors that influence your audience; (2) definitions of basic research terms and solving programming problems using the Arbitron Radio Market Reports; and (3) how Arbitron measures radio and how to calculate the reliability of the estimates.

296. Arbitron Ratings Company. *A Guide to Understanding and Using Radio Audience Estimates.* New York: Arbitron, 1987. 40 pp.

This Arbitron Radio Market Report contains over one hundred thousand numbers termed audience estimates, each one capable of contributing valuable information to the picture of radio listening in a market. It is intended to help the reader use such reports.

* Archer, Gleason L. *Big Business and Radio.* Cited above as item 11.

297. Arnold, Frank A. *Broadcast Advertising: The Fourth Dimension.* New York: John Wiley & Sons, 1931. 275 pp.

After spending 25 years in the field of advertising, the author joined the executive staff of the National Broadcasting Company in 1926 as its Director of Development. Consequently, he taught a course in 1930 at the College of the City of New York on radio broadcast advertising. This book includes the subject matter of that course and presents the same background, history, facts, and miscellaneous categories it covered.

298. Avery, Lewis H. *The Elements of a Successful Radio Program.* Washington: National Association of Broadcasters, 1943. 37 pp.

Written in collaboration with the Advisory Committee of Program Managers of NAB, this approaches the subject of radio from a new angle. It explains why people listen to radio, offers guidelines for selecting the program to use, and defines the consumers' attitude toward retailers' radio programs as well as public attitudes toward commercials.

299. Avery, Lewis H., in collaboration with Walter Johnson. *How to Buy Radio Time.* Washington: National Association of Broadcasters, 1943. 38 pp.

Information and suggestions in this booklet were prepared in collaboration with experienced time-buyers of leading advertising agencies in New York and Chicago. It offers certain basic, common-sense rules to aid the reader in buying radio time.

300. Avery, Lewis H., and Robert H. Leding. *Radio and Retailing in 1943.* Washington: National Association of Broadcasters, 1943. 31 pp.

Prepared by the Retail Promotion Committee for the Broadcasting Industry, this discusses what retailers are actually doing with radio, why, and with what kind of success. The Committee conducted a survey on the use of local broadcast advertising and has combined its results with other surveys to produce this pamphlet.

301. Avery, Lewis H., and Charles Harriman Smith. *How to Measure Radio Audiences.* Washington: National Association of Broadcasters, 1943. 21 pp.

This booklet describes what has been done, what is being done, and what can be done in the future to measure radio audiences and the effect broadcast advertising has on listeners.

302. Aylesworth, Merlin Hall. *The Modern Stentor: Radio Broadcasting in the United States.* Princeton, NJ: Princeton University, 1928. 35 pp.

The text of a Cyrus Fogg Brackett Lecture delivered before the engineering faculty and students of Princeton University is reprinted in this booklet. An appendix lists the stations owned and associated with the National Broadcasting Company.

303. Balon, Robert E. *Rules of the Radio Ratings Game.* Washington: National Association of Broadcasters, 1988. 131 pp. ISBN: 0-89324-042-7.

The author has drawn on seven years of research in every radio format to combine the critical elements which must be isolated and controlled in order to win at the ratings game. He states "the rules are meant to embellish the overall effect of good-sounding radio, but not to replace it ... the station must sound its very best to derive maximum benefit from the rules."

304. Barnett, Steven, and David Morrison. *The Listener Speaks: The Radio Audience and the Future of Radio.* London: Her Majesty's Stationery Office, 1989. 138 pp. ISBN: 0-11-340901-X.

In February 1987 a Green Paper was published in London titled *Radio: Choices and Opportunities* which raised many questions about the demands and needs of the radio audience, the adequacy of existing provisions, the appeal of more local or national services, and audience requirements for greater range and quality of content. This volume is a result of a detailed investigation of the questions raised in that earlier report.

305. Barrass, Bob, ed. *Cellular Radio Markets*. London: Financial Times Media Intelligence Unit, 1984. 31 pp. (Key Issue Briefs).

Background information, major companies in the field, market size and trends, advertising and distribution are analyzed for both the U.S. and the U.K. Other markets in Japan, Europe, and Canada are examined briefly.

306. Bergendorff, Fred L., Charles H. Smith, and Lance Webster. *Broadcast Advertising & Promotion!* New York: Hastings House, 1983. 449 pp. ISBN: 0-8038-0801-1.

Subtitled "A Handbook for Students and Professionals," this textbook was initiated by the Broadcasters Promotion Association to assist colleges and universities in training students in the basics of radio and TV advertising, promotion, and publicity. It describes the duties of the broadcast promotion director, suggests special promotion challenges, and offers case studies.

307. Beville, Hugh Malcolm, Jr. *Audience Ratings: Radio, Television, and Cable*. Rev. ed. Hillsdale, NJ: Lawrence Erlbaum Associates, 1988. 381 pp. (Communication series). ISBN: 0-8058-0175-8.

The historical development of radio and radio ratings is followed by the history of TV ratings which directly drew on radio experience. A comparative analysis of methodologies, qualitative audience measurements, utilization of ratings, and future trends comprise the balance of this revised edition of a book first published in 1985.

308. Beville, Hugh Malcolm, Jr. *Social Stratification of the Radio Audience*. Princeton, NJ: Princeton Radio Research Project, 1940. 91 pp.

Reproduced from typewritten copy, the results of this study are intended to acquaint a larger public with the vast fund of material on radio listening that commercial agencies collected for years and to show the sort of social information that could be gained in order to assist radio advertising sales.

309. Bogue, Donald J. *The Radio Audience for Classical Music: The Case of Station WEFM, Chicago*. Chicago: University of Chicago, 1973. 212 pp. (CFSC Communication Laboratory Monographs).

After 32 years of continuous broadcasting of classical music, radio station WEFM was sold on March 2, 1972, to the General Cinema Corporation which proposed to change the station's call letters and to cease the broadcasting of fine arts programming. This is a report of a survey taken to measure the loss that would result if such changes were implemented.

310. Book, Albert C., Norman D. Cary, and Stanley I. Tannenbaum. *The Radio & Television Commercial*. 2nd ed. Lincolnwood, IL: NTC Business Books, 1984. 222 pp. ISBN-0-8442-3097-9.

This is intended to show how to create and produce powerful advertisements for the broadcast media. It illustrates the importance of beginning with a solid creative strategy and then tells how to write that strategy. The second section concentrates on radio commercials.

311. Bortz, Paul I., and Harold Mendelsohn. *Radio Today--and Tomorrow*. Washington: Washington: National Association of Broadcasters, 1982. 75 pp.

Prepared for NAB, this report summarizes the uses of radio both at the time of publication and in the future. One segment examines changing demographics and popular taste while the other forecasts technical, market, and economic factors affecting radio's future.

312. Broadcast Advertising Bureau. *Radio: America's Star Reporter and Super Salesman*. New York: National Association of Broadcasters, 1950. 1 vol.

This presents a "selling job" for the medium of radio as it attempts to convince advertisers that radio is the preferred means to increase profit. Its emphasis is on radio news as it offers statistics concerning the number of listeners to radio news programs, describes locally sponsored news broadcasts, and tells the effect on the audience that a "human voice" has reporting radio news.

313. Broadcast Advertising Bureau. *Radio's Feminine Touch*. New York: National Association of Broadcasters, 1950. 1 vol.

The opening lines of this large-format book call for attention: "You can't take a WOMAN for granted--not if you're in business and have something to sell. She's the one who buys the lion's share of everything ... from food to clothing to home furnishings." The whole point of the piece is the need to attract women's interest in a product if it is to be a good seller.

314. *Broadcast Financial Journal*. Des Plaines, IL: Broadcast Financial Management Association.

This periodical is the official publication of The Broadcast Financial Management Association. It has been published since 1972, appears six times a year, and contains articles in the areas of economics and finance. There is a special section on BFM member news.

315. Broadcast Financial Management Association. Operational Guidelines Committee. *Accounting Manual for Broadcasters*. Chicago: The Association, 1981. 1 vol.

    In a loose-leaf format, this was created originally in October 1963 and has been updated and completely revised since then. It provides account descriptions, financial statement forms, trade agreements, etc.

316. *Broadcast Investor*. Carmel, CA: Paul Kagan Associates. ISSN: 0146-0110.

    A monthly newsletter, this periodical offers information on investment data for radio and television. It began publication in 1972.

317. Broadcast Measurement Bureau. *Radio Families USA 1949*. New York: The Bureau, 1949. 1 vol.

    Published annually, this profiles listeners by geographic areas, states, counties, cities of 25,000 or more population in metropolitan districts, cities of 10,000 or more population outside metropolitan districts, radio station cities regardless of size, and metropolitian districts.

318. *Broadcast Stats*. Carmel, CA: Paul Kagan Associates. ISSN: 0749-2936.

    While the emphasis is on television, this monthly newsletter that began in 1984 summarizes statistical data on station sales and transfers of both radio and television.

319. *Broadcaster.* Toronto: Northern Miner Press. ISSN: 0008-3038.

The subtitle of this monthly publication is "Canada's Communications Magazine." First published in 1942, it covers the Canadian broadcasting industry.

320. *Broadcasting.* Washington: Broadcasting Publications. ISSN: 0007-2028.

Founded in 1931 as "Broadcasting, the News Magazine of the Fifth Estate," this publication now incorporates several other periodicals--"Broadcasting-Telecasting," "Television," and "Cablecasting." It is published every Monday and has recently had its format updated. Regular features are titled Changing Hands; Closed Circuit; Datebook; Fates and Fortunes; Fifth Estater; For the Record; Open Mike; Programming; Radio; Stock Index; Top of the Week; and Washington.

321. *Broadcasting and the Law.* Miami, FL: Broadcasting and the Law, Inc. ISSN: 0161-5823.

The front cover of this twice-monthly periodical publication states it is "a report on broadcast rules and regulations." It began publication in 1970 and features coverage and interpretation of current court and FCC rulings affecting broadcast practice and operation.

322. Brotman, Stuart N. *Broadcasters Can Negotiate Anything.* Washington: National Association of Broadcasters, 1988. 127 pp. ISBN: 0-89324-044-3.

The introduction states that this is the first book of its kind on negotiation planning, strategies, and tactics for radio and television station managers. It covers negotiations with employees and unions, citizen groups, program suppliers/networks, hardware vendors, professional service vendors, a corporate parent, research and ratings services, joint venture partnerships, and potential station buyers or sellers.

323. Brown, Ray. *Characteristics of Local Media Audiences.* Farnborough, Eng.: Saxon House, 1978. 130 pp. ISBN: 0-566-00218-3.

This survey was conducted among residents of Oxford, Hull, Liverpool, Bristol, and Nottingham. The results provide city characteristics, exposure to local media, reactions to the content of local media, images of local radio, gratifications associated with listening to radio, and summary scores of local satisfactions.

324. Bryson, Lyman. *Time for Reason--About Radio.* New York: George W. Stewart, 1948. 127 pp. (Radio House series).

On December 1, 1946, the Columbia Broadcasting System began a series of informal talks to inform listeners of the problems and possibilities of radio in America as broadcasters themselves saw them. This book was edited for publication from the 27 broadcasts that constituted the series.

325. Bryson, Lyman. *The Use of the Radio in Leisure Time.* New York: Radio Institute of the Audible Arts, 1936. 4 pp.

One of a series of publications of the Radio Institute on various phases of radio, this brochure is aimed primarily at "every mother (who) is an educator to her family" and suggests ways she "can help build character and knowledge into the personalities of her sons and daughters by studying carefully the whole range of radio programs in order that she may find those things which will be most valuable to them."

326. Buehler, E.C., compiler. *American vs. British System of Radio Control*. New York: H.W. Wilson, 1933. 361 pp. (The Reference Shelf, Vol. 8, No. 10).

Prepared primarily for students in the field of debate, according to the introduction, this volume presents "a wealth of material on the general subject of the radio, particularly on the problems of technical operation and on the legal aspects of radio broadcasting."

327. Buono, Thomas J. *1984 Broadcast Financial/Legal Service Guide*. Fairfax, VA: Broadcast Investment Analysts, 1984. 160 pp.

Included in this informational directory are profiles of brokerage firms, lending institutions, and attorney firms.

328. Bureau of Labor Statistics. U.S. Dept. of Labor. *Employment and Earnings of Radio Artists*. Washington: Government Printing Office, 1949. 1 vol.

Consisting of three reports, this presents data on employment and unemployment, earnings from radio performing between 1946 and 1948, and total earnings for 1947.

329. Burns, George A. *Radio Imagery: Strategies in Station Positioning*. Studio City, CA: Burns Media Consultants, 1980. 101 pp.

Not a text on radio programming, this "probes instead the issues concerning how well programmed stations can be marketed ... (it) asserts that the skills and points on which radio stations will win and lose during the '80s do not essentially involve the intricacies of programming itself ... the details of music programming or audience research, for instance, are viewed from the marketing and positioning perspective, not a how-to context."

330. Canadian Association of Broadcasters. *Broadcast Code for Advertising to Children*. Rev. ed. Ottawa: The Association, 1982. 12 pp.

Designed to complement the general principles for ethical advertising outlined in the *Canadian Code of Advertising Standards* which applies to all advertising, this is intended for both radio and television broadcasting.

331. Canadian Radio-Television and Telecommunications Commission. *Broadcast Advertising Handbook*. Ottawa: The Commission, 1978. 1 vol. ISBN: 0-660-01825-X.

A summary of federal government legislation, regulations, and guidelines relating to broadcast advertising. It does not include all government legislation pertaining to advertising but is limited to those regulations which apply specifically to radio and television commercial messages.

332. Canadian Radio-Television and Telecommunications Commission. *Ownership of Private Broadcasting: An Economic Analysis of Structure, Performance and Behaviour*. Ottawa: The Commission, 1978. 46 pp.

Written in both English and French, this is the report of the Ownership Study Group made to CRTC and is presented strictly as a working paper to the public. It concentrates on ownership, groups vs. singles economic and financial performance, effects of concentration on advertising results, activity and selling prices of major transfers, and quantitative effects of concentration on programming.

333. Canadian Radio-Television Commission. *Canadian Ownership in Broadcasting: A Report on the Foreign Divestiture Process*. Ottawa: The Commission, 1974. 44 pp.

When Canada's first radio station, XWA, went on the air in Montreal in 1919, the ownership of Canadian broadcasting was in Canadian hands, but the problem of foreign ownership was a matter for concern even at that early time. The situation has become more serious as time has passed and the medium has grown so this report was prepared to summarize foreign divestitures and the interests foreign firms have in Canadian broadcasting, both from a financial standpoint and as a source of programs.

334. Canadian Radio-Television Commission. *Lists Showing the Ownership of Radio and Television Stations Licensed by the Canadian-Radio-Television Commission*. Ottawa: The Commission, 1970. 1 vol.

Arranged in a loose-leaf format so that amendments and revisions can be easily inserted, this is divided alphabetically by major corporation and lists each subsidiary in that organization. Entries show directors, executive officers, their citizenship, and number of shares held.

335. Cantril, Hadley, and Gordon W. Allport. *The Psychology of Radio*. New York: Harper & Brothers, 1935. 276 pp.

Reprinted in 1971 by Arno Press/New York Times as part of the History of Broadcasting: Radio to Television series, this "is the first attempt on the part of psychologists to map out from their own point of view the new mental world created by radio." It describes the mental setting of radio and offers practical interpretations of the medium.

336. *Capital: Local Radio & Private Profit*. London: Comedia, 1983. 128 pp. (Comedia series, 15). ISBN: 0-906-890-19-5.

Chapter titles are The Origins of Commercial Radio; Capital Radio Ltd.; Programming for Profit; Building a Public Image: Capital's Off-air Services; Government Printing Office; Public Relations: Capital's Publicity Language; and Local Radio and Private Profit.

* Carroll, Carroll. *None of Your Business, or, My Life with J. Walter Thompson*. Cited above as item 58.

337. Chappell, Matthew N., and C.E. Hooper. *Radio Audience Measurement*. New York: Stephen Daye, 1944. 246 pp.

Chappell and Hooper state that it is fundamental to commerce that the vendor be able to demonstrate how much he is offering and it is necessary that both buyer and seller use the same measuring standard. This book is intended to help supply that standard by reviewing the various audience measurements developed thus far.

338. Cheen, Bruce Bishop. *Fair Market Value of Radio Stations: A Buyer's Guide*. Washington: National Association of Broadcasters, 1986. 193 pp. ISBN: 0-89324-017-6.

The first part of this volume offers an overview of radio broadcasting describing radio ownership and regulation, technical aspects of radio signals, the competitive economy, the audio marketplace, radio revenue sources, and positioning. The other two sections cover station acquisition and evaluation/fair market value appraisal.

339. Chester, Giraud, Garnet R. Garrison, and Edgar E. Willis. *Television and Radio.* 5th ed. Englewood Cliffs, NJ: Prentice-Hall, 1978. 543 pp. ISBN: 0-13-90281-8.

Originally published in 1950 by Appleton Century Crofts as *Radio and Television* by Chester and Garrison, this book has undergone a transformation since then as its emphasis has shifted from radio to television. It continues to describe the growth of American radio, programming, the FCC, networks, stations, advertisers, agencies, and the audience, but now includes cable TV, more technical aspects of television, and fewer radio scripts.

340. Clearinghouse on Development Communication. *A Sourcebook on Radio's Role in Development.* Washington: CDC, 1976. 85 pp.

This bibliography attempts to portray the breadth of past experience in applying radio to problems of education and development along with complete access information. It includes project reports, country surveys, research and evaluation studies, discussions, and bibliographies on a variety of issues such as policy and planning, costs, innovation, software, materials, and training.

341. Codel, Martin, ed. *Radio and Its Future.* New York: Harper & Brothers, 1930. 349 pp.

This anthology is divided into Broadcasting, Communications, Industry, Regulation, and Some Scientific and Other Considerations. Articles were written by experts in these fields including William S. Paley, William S. Hedges, David Sarnoff, Clarence C. Dill, and Lee De Forest. The title page states there is a foreword by Guglielmo Marconi but it does not appear in this edition. This was reprinted in 1971 by Arno Press/New

York Times as part of the History of Broadcasting: Radio to Television series.

342. Coleman, Howard W. *Case Studies in Broadcast Management*. New York: Hastings House, 1970. 95 pp. ISBN: 0-8038-1150-0.

Among the authentic problems dealt with are: the radio audience, station revenue and the station manager, going on the air, program rating weaknesses, and costs. Coleman offers case study profiles of marketing, potential lawsuits, editorializing, in-fighting among local media, good public service, and controversial programming. A second edition was published in 1978 with the added subtitle "Radio and Television."

343. Columbia Broadcasting System. *Broadcasting and the American Public*. New York: CBS, 1936. 28 pp.

Report of a forum on radio conducted over the facilities of CBS and broadcast during February 1936.

344. Columbia Broadcasting System *Exact Measurements of the Spoken Word, 1902-1936*. New York: CBS, 1936. 32 pp.

The purpose of this little book, according to the foreword, is not nearly so much to "sell" radio broadcasting as it is to help explain why radio is what it is. Seventeen psychological investigations have been abridged to suggest just how important the matter of the ear vs. the eye is, and, of course, this provides impetus for radio listening.

345. Columbia Broadcasting System. *Radio in 1937*. New York: CBS, 1937. 53 pp.

Described on the front cover as a book for executives who want to know the number and quality of families in the radio audience, this presents those data. It is one of the very early Starch studies on radio audiences, and it recounts radio distribution in homes by income levels, city size, and time zones, and the listening habits of these radio owners based on "the 95,500,000-hour radio day."

346. Columbia Broadcasting System. Research Dept. *An Analysis of Radio-Listening in Autos*. New York: CBS, 1936. 22 pp.

The detailed findings of this survey reveal that the average listening is 2.6 hours per day, the average Sunday listening is 3.2 hours, and the average number of listeners is 2.7. More than 1,000 personal interviews were conducted as a check to the questionnaires mailed or distributed to approximately 20,000 names of people in 46 states.

347. Committee on Interstate and Foreign Commerce. U.S. House of Representatives. *Network Broadcasting*. Washington: Government Printing Office, 1958. 737 pp.

This is the Committee report required under the Legislative Reorganization Act of 1946, Public Law 601, 79th Congress, and House Resolution 99, 85th Congress.

348. Committee on Interstate and Foreign Commerce. U.S. House of Representatives. *Regulation of Radio and Television Cigarette Advertisements*. Washington: Government Printing Office, 1969. 266 pp.

The hearing in this publication was held on June 10, 1969, on self-regulation by the broadcasting industry of radio and television cigarette advertisements.

349. Committee on the Merchant Marine and Fisheries. U.S. House of Representatives. *National Radio Broadcasting.* Washington: United States Daily, 1929. 93 pp.

The text is primarily a statement by Merlin Hall Aylesworth, President of the National Broadcasting Company, at hearings held in January 1929.

350. Compaine, Benjamin M., et al. *Who Owns the Media?* White Plains, NY: Knowledge Industry Publications, 1979. 370 pp. (Communications Library series). ISBN: 0-914236-36-9.

The concentration of ownership in the mass communications industry is the main subject of this volume. Christopher Sterling wrote the 66 page essay on television and radio broadcasting.

351. Connah, Douglas Duff. *How to Build the Radio Audience.* New York: Harper & Brothers, 1938. 271 pp.

The greatest part of this volume is written from the viewpoint of those concerned with nationally broadcast programs while only a single chapter concerns local stations and programming. It provides opportunities to build audiences along with techniques of exploitation in order to generate more effective listener circulation.

352. *Controversy on Radio and TV.* New York: Civil Liberties Educational Foundation, 1958. 37 pp.

Undertaken on behalf of the Foundation by the Department of Communications in Education of New York University, this is a pilot study of network radio and television coverage of controversial issues and many-sided discussions.

353. Coons, John E., ed. *Freedom and Responsibility in Broadcasting*. Evanston, IL: Northwestern University Press, 1961. 252 pp.

This publication contains the entire proceedings of a conference held at Northwestern in 1961 on the state of the broadcasting industry and the divergent proposals for its repair. Addresses were made by LeRoy Collins, President of the National Association of Broadcasters, and Newton N. Minow, Chairman of the Federal Communications Commission.

354. Corporation for Public Broadcasting. *Audience 88: A Comprehensive Analysis of Public Radio Listeners*. Washington: The Corporation, 1988. 6 vols.

Cataloged individually under the Dewey classification of 302.2344, each volume has a separate title, covers a specific area of public radio, and runs around 35 to 40 pages with many charts and tables. The titles are: *Issues & Implications*, *Advertising & Promotion*, *Underwriting*, *Membership*, *Programming*, and *Terms & Concepts*.

355. Crozier, Mary. *Broadcasting (Sound and Television)*. London: Oxford University Press, 1958. 236 pp. (Home University Library of Modern Knowledge).

Following an introduction, the first chapter is titled What Radio Does as the author explains the way the medium works. She discusses broadcasting in Britain and elsewhere in the world and has individual chapters titled Politics in Broadcasting, Education and Religion, and Machine and Poet.

356. David, Miles. *Making Money with Co-Op: The Complete Radio Co-Op Course*. New York: Radio Advertising Bureau, 1986. 215 pp.

The foreword states that this is the first-ever book for media salespeople about co-op advertising, and it is a unique collaboration--of 300 co-authors. Several sections present a management overview, explain the basics of the field, define the co-op plan, and examine goals and expectations, law and ethics, strategy, sales presentation, sales, operations and case histories.

357. Day, Enid. *Radio Broadcasting for Retailers*. New York: Fairchild Publishing, 1947, 194 pp.

The preface states "the purpose of this book is to set down in detail a formula for successful radio program planning, writing, and broadcasting for retailers; hence the title. The basic principles may be applied to all broadcasting designed to sell, as well as institutional advertising over the radio."

358. Dominick, Joseph R., and James E. Fletcher. *Broadcasting Research Methods*. Boston: Allyn & Bacon, 1985. 330 pp. ISBN: 0-205-08307-2.

Techniques for Conducting Research and Theoretical and Applied Research Problems are the the titles of the two main sections of this textbook. Individual essays were contributed by Alan Wurtzel, Fay C. Schreibman, Raymond L. Carroll, Linda J. Busby, Roger D. Wimmer, John R. Bittner, and several others active in the field.

* Duncan, James H., Jr. *American Radio Tenth Anniversary Issue, 1976-1986: A Prose and Statistical History*. Cited above as item 89.

359. Duncan, James H., Jr. *Duncan's Radio Market Guide*. Kalamazoo, MI: James Duncan, 1987. 1 vol.

The first edition of this appeared in 1984 and was intended to be a companion to *Duncan's American Radio* with very little overlap. It discusses histories, projections, and the condition of each market; it is published biannually.

360. Duncan, James H., Jr. *The Relationship Between Radio Audience Shares and Revenue Shares*. Indianapolis: James Duncan, 1989. 1 vol.

    Data on different-sized markets are provided along with an arrangement of stations alphabetically by format categories. The book is published annually in April. This edition is based on 1988 revenue and ratings.

361. Duncan, James H., Jr., and Christine Woodward, eds. *American Radio: Small Market Edition*. 2nd ed. Kalamazoo, MI: James Duncan, 1985. 1 vol.

    Now published every September, this annual provides expanded coverage of the smaller radio markets in the United States and Canada. Section A offers Arbitron condensed radio market reports while Section B lists Birch non-monthly reports, and Section C the Birch Canadian markets.

362. Dunlap, Orrin E., Jr. *Advertising By Radio*. New York: Ronald Press, 1929. 186 pp.

    The advertising value of radio lies in the creation of good will or what Dunlap calls "that indispensable factor in the foundation of successful sales promotion." He writes about the mutual benefit between the broadcaster and the advertiser and suggests ways each can improve the medium.

363. Dunlap, Orrin E., Jr. *Radio in Advertising.* New York: Harper & Brothers, 1931. 383 pp.

Intended to aid the advertisers, especially those interested in reaching the consumer by radio, this is written as a handbook for every advertising agency and all advertisement departments of industry, according to the preface. Dunlap covers the evolution of radio as an advertising medium, describes numbers of listeners and what they think and do, tells how to plan a radio program from an advertiser's view, and relates the best ways to merchandise such a program.

364. Dygert, Warren B. *Radio As an Advertising Medium.* New York: McGraw-Hill, 1939. 261 pp.

Written primarily to give businessmen and advertising executives enough fundamental data about radio to evaluate it as a medium for advertising, this covers what they should know in order to get the most out of their advertising. The author's viewpoint is strictly that of the advertiser although he concedes "there are, of course, other worthy (many might say *more* worthy) viewpoints from which to study radio."

365. Eastman, Susan Tyler, Sydney W. Head, and Lewis Klein. *Broadcast/Cable Programming: Strategies and Practices.* 2nd ed. Belmont, CA: Wadsworth Publishing, 1985. 529 pp. (Wadsworth series in Mass Communication). ISBN: 0-534-03353-9.

Chapters on program and audience research, radio networks and format syndication, systems, networks, and local origination have been added to the 1981 edition as well as revised and expanded material on group-ownership, public radio and television, and cable. The title of the earlier edition is *Broadcast Programming: Strategies for Winning Television and Radio Audiences.*

366. Eicoff, Al. *Eicoff on Broadcast Direct Marketing.* Lincolnwood, IL: NTC Business Books, 1988. 191 pp. ISBN: 0-8442-3144-4.

   Some of the tips offered in this book are ways to select a product or service for direct response advertising, how to buy media effectively, how to create television and radio advertisements that sell, and how to organize and evaluate a successful direct response campaign. The author is Chairman of the Board of an agency he founded and that now has become an Ogilvy & Mather subsidiary specializing in broadcast advertising.

367. *Electronic Media.* Chicago: Crain Communications. ISSN: 0745-0311.

   A weekly publication, this periodical contains news and features of the entire electronic media industry. It began publication in 1982.

368. *The Empire of the Air.* Ventura, CA: Ventura Free Press, 1932. 106 pp.

   The title page describes this as "the story of the exploitation of radio for private profit, with a plan for the reorganization of broadcasting." It is actually a discussion of the early history of technical radio with an emphasis on its economic and social implications, the work of early radio pioneers, and the creation of NBC.

369. Eoyang, Thomas T. *An Economic Study of the Radio Industry in the United States of America.* New York: Arno Press, 1974. 218 pp. (Telecommunications series). ISBN: 0-405-06041-6.

A reprint of the author's 1936 Columbia University Ph.D. dissertation, this examines the technical aspects of radio science in general and the economics of both the radio manufacturing industry and the radio broadcasting industry in particular.

370. European Broadcasting Union. *Advertising on Radio and Television*. Geneva: The Union, 1966. 37 pp. (EBU Legal and Administrative Monograph, 4).

The preface states this does not seek to do more than provide a general introduction to the subject of commercial broadcasting. It examines the types of advertisements, timing and format, regulation of content and form, and rates.

371. European Broadcasting Union. *Medium and Long-range Economic Planning in Broadcasting Organizations*. Geneva: The Union, 1975. 152 pp.

The contents of this volume were taken from the IXth Symposium for the Study of Problems of Economic Organization and Associated Matters, held in Vienna in October 1973. It covers reports from the BBC Great Britain, NOS Netherlands, ORF Austria, RAI Italy, RNE-TVE Spain, RTB/BRT Belgium, RTE Ireland, SR Sweden, SSR Switzerland, YLE Finland, and ZDF Federal Republic of Germany.

372. Evans, Jacob A. *Selling and Promoting Radio and Television*. New York: Printers' Ink Publishing, 1954. 348 pp.

The gist of this book is to train salesmen in selling the medium of radio more effectively. The author, NBC Director of National Advertising and Promotion, discusses ways to service accounts, retrieve lost business, prepare for and close a sales call, and to train personnel.

373. Felix, Edgar H. *Using Radio in Sales Promotion*. New York: McGraw-Hill, 1927. 386 pp.

In an effort to take advantage of the new market opened by radio, this volume is described in a subtitle as "A Book for Advertisers, Station Managers, and Broadcasting Artists."

374. Fisk, George. *Defining and Measuring Radio Audiences*. Pullman, WA: State College of Washington, 1949. 40 pp. (Economic and Business Studies Bulletin, 10).

A survey guide for radio stations, this appraises the claims of various radio-rating services and shows small and independent station operators how to plan their own surveys with a minimum of outside help.

375. Fletcher, James E., ed. *Handbook of Radio and TV Broadcasting: Research Procedures in Audience, Program and Revenues*. New York: Van Nostrand Reinhold, 1981. 336 pp. ISBN: 0-442-22417-6.

Beginning as CASH (a Comprehensive Assessment Handbook), a project of the Research Committee of the Broadcast Education Association, this was originally intended to be a research manual for broadcasters to assist them in reducing the risks of their operations while improving revenue. It has been expanded to include reading market reports, sampling, measuring station audiences by phone, message and program testing, and rating reports.

376. Fletcher, James E. *Profiting from Radio Ratings: A Manual for Radio Managers, Sales Managers and Programmers*. Washington: National Association of Broadcasters, 1989. 1 vol. ISBN: 0-89324-065-6.

Economic Aspects 113

This volume replaces the author's *Squeezing Profits Out of Ratings* that was published by the Association in 1985. This version addresses the many changes and improvements in the audience measurement reports available to radio stations.

377. Fratrik, Mark R., and Mark Cunningham. *Radio Financial Report 1985.* Washington: National Association of Broadcasters, 1985. 95 pp.

The results of the NAB Annual Financial Survey of all commercial radio stations of 1984 revenues and expenses are published in this report. There are 90 detailed tables for various station types, market sizes, and station sizes so that broadcasters can compare individual station performance.

378. Frazier, Gross & Clay, Inc. *Radio in 1985.* Washington: National Association of Broadcasters, 1977. 88 pp.

This report was prepared "to assist radio broadcasters in their long-range business planning" and information was collected "about a variety of factors--economic, technical, regulatory, and competitive--that will affect radio in 1985." Readers are invited to join the NAB Research Department "in looking ahead to radio, 1985."

379. Garver, Robert I. *Successful Radio Advertising with Sponsor Participation Programs.* New York: Prentice-Hall, 1949. 329 pp.

Portions of this book are based on data gathered by the author in a national survey on participation programs. He describes the most popular programs (disc jockeys, musical clock or wake-up programs, women's service, farm shows) and explains how to go about selecting a format.

380. Gaudet, Hazel, and Cuthbert Daniel. *Radio Listener Panels.* Washington: Federal Radio Education Committee, 1941. 46 pp.

Prepared with the cooperation of the U.S. Office of Education, Federal Security Agency, this pamphlet presents the collective observations of the Office of Radio Research on listener panels. They offer a general evaluation of repeated interviews, discuss the technical aspects of panel operation, describe practical applications of the panel technique, and provide examples of actual questions which could be used.

381. Goode, Kenneth M. *What About Radio?* New York: Harper & Brothers, 1937. 255 pp.

In order to present a picture of radio's place in the American home, the author examined reports of more than 700 separate inquiries by at least 600 different investigators who were in personal contact with the daily habits of at least 10,000,000 different people (according to the introduction). He looks at radio's universal audience, asks how many listen, for how long, how often, and when and why they do so.

382. Gross, Lynne Schafer. *Telecommunications: An Introduction to Electronic Media.* 3rd ed. Dubuque, IA: Wm. C. Brown, 1989. 497 pp. ISBN: 0-697-03037-7.

The importance of electronic media in the international arena and the continuing growth of corporate telecommunications has led to the addition of two new chapters in this textbook revision. Other updating is in the areas of network management changes, the use of peoplemeters, deregulation, and variances in audience viewership.

383. Gruenberg, Sidonie Matsner. *The Use of the Radio in Parent Education*. Chicago: University of Chicago Press, 1939. 94 pp.

The report spells out what is being offered in the name of parent education, who the listeners are, listening groups, registered listeners, the limitations of one-way communication, the most effective form of presentation, radio content for parents, recording, competition for time on the air, commercial sponsorship, and evaluation of broadcasts.

384. Gunter, Barrie, and Michael Svennevig. *Attitudes to Broadcasting Over the Years*. London: John Libbey, 1988. 77 pp. (IBA Television Research Monograph). ISBN: 0-86196-173-0.

Almost every year since 1970 the Independent Broadcasting Authority has undertaken a large national survey to assess public attitudes toward British broadcasting. This book summarizes the results and reflects the rapid development and growth in both the availability and use of mass media as well as the attitudes of the viewing public toward the medium.

385. Harding, Alfred. *The Pay and Conditions of Work of Radio Performers*. New York: Actors' Equity Association, 1934. 19 pp.

This describes the general situation extant at the time of publication when there were no standard minimum contracts, conditions, or rates of pay in radio. It suggests such standards for auditions, rehearsals, actual work, and pay scales.

386. Head, Sydney W., and Christopher H. Sterling. *Broadcasting in America: A Survey of Electronic Media*. 5th ed. Boston: Houghton Mifflin, 1987. 604 pp. ISBN: 0-395-35936-8.

Thirty years after its original publication, this revised edition has been restructured to accommodate the substantial changes going on in the field. It treats the electronic media within a broad academic perspective and emphasizes the newer technological advances, programming processes and trends, and its economic aspects. A 6th edition is being prepared for publication in 1990.

387. Heighton, Elizabeth J., and Don R. Cunningham. *Advertising in the Broadcast and Cable Media*. 2nd ed. Belmont, CA: Wadsworth Publishing, 1984. 368 pp. ISBN: 0-534-02914-0.

The first part of this book traces the history of broadcast advertising and the structure of the modern-day industry. Other sections cover specific procedures for developing campaigns, buying and selling time in radio and television, and the controversies surrounding broadcast advertising.

388. Herring, James M., and Gerald C. Gross. *Telecommunications: Economics and Regulation*. New York: Arno Press, 1974. 544 pp.

First published in 1936 by McGraw-Hill, this was reprinted as part of Arno's Telecommunications Series of reprints. The first four chapters deal with the development of the industries with special emphasis on the development and history of radio communication, broadcasting, and federal regulations affecting both.

389. Herzog, Herta. *Survey of Research on Children's Radio Listening.* New York: Columbia University, 1941. 1 vol.

This is a survey of the literature in the field of children and their leisure time listening to the radio. It covers children between the ages of 6 and 10 and deals with the programs actually listened to by children and is not limited to programs designed for a child audience.

390. Hettinger, Herman S. *A Decade of Radio Advertising.* Chicago: University of Chicago Press, 1933. 354 pp.

The psychological and economic bases of broadcast advertising are discussed in the first part of this book while the use of broadcasting by advertisers and the then-current practice in the field constitute the balance. This volume was reprinted in 1971 by Arno Press/New York Times as part of the series History of Broadcasting: Radio to Television.

391. Hettinger, Herman S., ed. *New Horizons in Radio.* Philadelphia: American Academy of Political and Social Science, 1941. 253 pp.

This book is a separate issue of *The Annals of the American Academy of Political and Social Science* that was published as Volume 213 in January 1941. The articles are categorized into sections: Broadcasting As a Social Force Today, Current Problems in Radio, and Coming Developments in Radio. (See also item 511.)

392. Hettinger, Herman S., ed. *Radio: The Fifth Estate.* Philadelphia: American Academy of Political and Social Science, 1935. 301 pp.

This monograph is actually Volume 177 of *The Annals of the American Academy of Political and Social Science* for

January 1935. It is concerned only with radio and evaluates "this new social force in terms of the services which it renders and the problems it has raised." (See also item 511.)

393. Hettinger, Herman S., and Walter J. Neff. *Practical Radio Advertising*. New York: Prentice-Hall, 1938. 372 pp.

The emphasis in this book is upon planning and sales strategy in connection with radio and there is a repeated use of examples. Hettinger was on the faculty of the University of Pennsylvania's Wharton School as a professor of marketing and Neff was president of his own advertising agency and former sales manager for radio station WOR.

394. Hiber, Jhan. *Hibernetics: A Guide to Radio Ratings and Research*. Los Angeles: R & R Books, 1984. 251 pp. ISBN: 0-931183-00-6.

Issued in both paperback and hard cover, this examines the history and foundation of market research and the ratings services. It provides in-depth treatment of Arbitron methods, diary analysis, the Birch radio methodology, and summarizes sales-oriented research.

395. Hiber, Jhan. *Winning Radio Research: Turning Research into Ratings & Revenues*. Washington: National Association of Broadcasters, 1987, 302 pp. ISBN: 0-89324-034-6.

The first major section looks at the audience, the second focuses on ratings, while the third offers information about "winning on the street." Hiber has updated material from his previous book, *Hibernetics* (see item 394), for this one and now covers new techniques and new areas for research.

396. Hill, Frank Ernest. *The Groups Tune In*. Washington: Federal Radio Education Committee, 1940. 35 pp.

Published with the cooperation of the U.S. Office of Education, this pamphlet is a comprehensive survey of the listening group field.

397. Hill, Frank Ernest, and W.E. Williams. *Radio's Listening Groups: The United States and Great Britain*. New York: Columbia University Press, 1941. 270 pp.

A comparison of listening habits between Americans and the British is presented in this study. Among the findings are that experimentation was the order of the day in America, and there was little development of group listening in rural areas in Britain.

398. Hilmes, Michele. *Hollywood and Broadcasting: From Radio to Cable*. Urbana: University of Illinois Press, 1990. 221 pp. (Illinois Studies in Communication). ISBN: 0-252-01709-9.

The complex and mutually dependent relationship between Hollywood and broadcasting is documented from the days before network radio to contemporary times. The film industry has played a central role in the evolution of the economic structures, program forms and patterns of distribution of broadcasting, according to the book jacket, and the author details the part each industry has played in the development of the other.

399. Hoffer, Jay. *Managing Today's Radio Station*. Blue Ridge Summit, PA: Tab Books, 1968. 288 pp.

This book is a series of essays divided into categories titled Management Thinking, Programming, and Sales. The individual articles cover everything from handling "the boozer" and personal telephone calls to selection of music, editorializing, house accounts, and sales presentations.

400. Hoffer, Jay. *Organization & Operation of Broadcast Stations.* Blue Ridge Summit, PA: Tab Books, 1971. 251 pp.

    Separate sections are devoted to the nature of the business, program director, public relations, announcers, news director, music director, traffic manager, copy writers, sales manager, account executives, promotion manager, merchandising director, station manager, and office staff.

401. Hoffer, Jay, and John McRae. *The Complete Broadcast Sales Guide for Stations, Reps & Ad Agencies.* Blue Ridge Summit, PA: Tab Books, 1981. 252 pp. ISBN: 0-8306-9775-6.

    The main divisions in this volume are titled Radio Stations, Advertising Agencies, and Station Rpresentatives. Each contains chapters pertinent to that area and covers sales training, sales aids and tools, account executives, time-buying behavior, personal involvement, and future outlooks.

402. Hooker, Jim. *Radio Station Turnaround Strategies That Work.* Washington: National Association of Broadcasters, 1987. 120 pp. ISBN: 0-89324-035-4.

    Based on data acquired from a study of successful turnaround stations, this offers both concrete techniques that have been used and useful insights into the attitudes and interactions which contributed to such success. The focus of this book is primarily on newly acquired radio station properties which have been turned around.

403. Hopf, Howard E., and Raymond T. Bedwell, Jr. *Listener Availability and Types of News and Music Preferred by Radio Listeners.* Columbus: Ohio State University, Department of Speech, 1959. 9 leaves. (Radio-Television Audience Studies, New Series, 1).

Data include average minutes per day spent listening to the radio in and out of the home by individuals of various sex and/or age groups, daytime listening by women 19 to 70 years of age, and type of music indicated as "liked" or "disliked."

404. Hunn, Peter. *Starting and Operating Your Own FM Radio Station: From License Application to Program Management.* Blue Ridge Summit, PA: Tab Books, 1988. 155 pp. ISBN: 0-8306-2933-5.

The history behind the licensing of broadcast stations, the start of FM broadcasting, the significance of call letters, and ways to locate a good site for a new FM station are covered. There are chapters on station permit applications, equipment and construction specifics, advertising, operating costs, and buying or selling existing stations.

405. Hyers, Faith Holmes. *The Library and the Radio.* Chicago: University of Chicago Press, 1938. 100 pp.

This pamphlet, prepared at the request of the American Library Association by the Chair of its Library Radio Broadcasting Committee, reports on the experiences of librarians working with broadcasting and discusses the problems concerned with such interaction.

406. *The Importance of Radio in Television Areas Today.* New York: Thorndike, Jensen & Parton, 1953. 34 pp.

The results of a nationwide survey conducted by Alfred Politz Research are presented in this volume. It examines the reasons people have radio, their attitudes toward it, and the benefit advertisers can draw from such analysis.

407. *Inside Radio*. Cherry Hill, NJ: Inside Radio Co.

    Published weekly since 1975, this newletter provides "the hot news in ratings and sales." It has news briefs, current Arbitron ratings, and sales and management tips.

408. Institute of Radio Engineers. *Radio Markets After the War*. New York: The Institute, 1944. 26 pp.

    The purpose of this analysis that was sent to the membership of the Institute is "to stimulate early planning toward the further expansion and success of the field and a widening of the service of that field to the public."

409. Joint Communications Corporation, Toronto. *Public Attitudes and Preferences to Radio Programming in the Windsor-Detroit Area*. Toronto: Ministry of Transportation and Communication, 1984. 66 pp.

    Using *The Radio Reality of Windsor* as a cover title, this presents a summary of major findings and implications of the extent to which Windsor, Ontario, residents tune in Detroit radio, how radio programming in Windsor can improve, and the implications for CRTC regulations of the situation.

410. Jome, Hiram L. *Economics of the Radio Industry*. Chicago: A.W. Shaw, 1925. 332 pp.

    In his preface the author writes: "Scientists have so perfected this new agency of communication that its future organization and uses have become a matter of public concern ... it behooves us to mold this instrument of service according to our desires (and) to accomplish this purpose, however, knowledge of the economic problems raised by wireless communication is a prerequisite." He then proceeds to spell out these "economic problems" and offer his solutions. This was reprinted in 1971 by Arno Press/New York Times as part of the History of Broadcasting: Radio to Television series.

411. Jones, William K. *Cases and Materials on Electronic Mass Media: Radio, Television and Cable*. 2nd ed. Mineola, NY: Foundation Press, 1979. 545 pp. (University Casebook series).

Following an introduction and overview, this covers selection of a broadcaster for an available frequency, challenges to incumbent broadcasters, concentration of control of mass media, network practices, regulation of programming, cable television, subscription services, and public broadcasting.

412. Joske Brothers Company. *Radio for Retailers*. San Antonio, TX: Joske, 1947. 1 vol.

Loose-leaf in format, this is a report of the radio advertising study conducted in San Antonio in cooperation with the National Association of Broadcasters. Individual sections cover planning, results, copy, programs, and promotion ideas.

413. *Journal of Broadcasting & Electronic Media*. Washington: Broadcast Education Association. ISSN: 0883-8151.

Published since 1956, this periodical was formerly titled *Journal of Broadcasting*. It is published quarterly and includes research articles, essays about research in brief, book reviews, and criticisms.

414. Karshner, Roger. *The Music Machine*. Los Angeles: Nash Publishing, 1971. 196 pp. ISBN: 0-8402-1242-9.

Primarily a book about the record business, this describes the excitement, hype, and enthusiasm that is generated by the industry. There is a lengthy chapter on top-40 radio which the author has subtitled "The Rock of Ages," that covers the ins and outs, trials, and tribulations of the broadcasting station and, in particular, the disc jockey who spins the records and creates the incessant patter between records.

415. Keith, Michael C., and Joseph M. Krause. *The Radio Station*. 2nd ed. Boston: Focal Press, 1989. 273 pp. ISBN: 0-240-80028-1.

Published first in 1986, this updates information on the vital departments and functions of every radio station, including station management, programming, sales, news, research, promotion, traffic and billing, production, engineering, consultants, and syndication. Expanded coverage is provided on buying and selling stations, noncommercial and digital radio, satellite and syndication programming, and AM improvements.

416. Kirkley, Donald H., Jr. *Station Policy and Procedures: A Guide for Radio*. Washington: National Association of Broadcasters, 1985. 83 pp. ISBN: 0-89324-003-6.

The intention of this book is "to suggest language for policies and operational procedures to be incorporated in ... a station manual for employees ... (It) will take a 'how-to' approach, but only as a rationale for certain station policies." A second edition was published in 1989.

417. Kirkpatrick, Clifford. *Report of a Research into the Attitudes and Habits of Radio Listeners.* St. Paul, MN: Webb Publishing, 1933. 63 pp.

This book specifically looks at the volume and trends of radio listening, program preferences, reactions to advertising, radio's influence on recreation outside the home, and listeners' reactions to the broadcasting source. There is a section on feelings about broadcasting content and suggestions for improvement.

418. Knitel, H.G. *Advertising in Radio and Television Broadcasts.* Strasbourg: Council of Europe, 1982. 45 pp. (Mass Media Files, 1). ISBN: 92-871-0014-4.

This reveals a considerable diversity in the relevant rules applying in Council of Europe member states although nearly all have some restrictions on radio and television advertising. This report compares the current situation within member states and offers prospects for harmonization of the regulations.

419. Koening, Allen E., ed. *Broadcasting and Bargaining: Labor Relations in Radio and Television.* Madison: University of Wisconsin Press, 1970. 344 pp. ISBN: 0-299-05521-3.

Four major areas are covered in this collection of articles: radio and television unionism, federal action and arbitration in broadcasting, problems in labor and broadcasting, and the future of broadcasting/labor relations. An appendix contains the text of the Report and Order of the FCC and the Further Notice of Proposed Rulemaking, FCC, both of June 4, 1969.

420. Konecky, Eugene. *Monopoly Steals FM from the People.* New York: Provisional Committee for Democracy in Radio, 1946. 48 pp.

The author is the Chairman of the committee that published this pamphlet, a founder of the People's Radio Foundation of New York, and an activist for FM organization. He presents a documented study of the technical, social, and economic aspects of FM broadcasting and airs facts about the industry that have not been presented previously.

421. Krasnow, Erwin G., J. Geoffrey Bentley, and Robin B. Martin. *Buying or Building A Broadcast Station: Everything You Want--and Need--to Know, But Didn't Know Who to Ask*. 2nd ed. Washington: National Association of Broadcasters, 1988. 129 pp.

The authors provide a step-by-step guide to becoming an owner of a radio or television station as they describe the process involved in applying for a new station or acquiring an existing facility. Included is information on financing, FCC authorizations, legal aspects, etc.

422. Krieger, Susan. *Hip Capitalism*. Beverly Hills: Sage, 1979. 304 pp. (Sage Library of Social Research, 81). ISBN: 0-8039-1262-5.

The front cover describes this book as "the incredible story of a San Francisco rock music radio station and its transformation from underground, hippie origins to commercial success. Flower children and corporations clash in this account of chaos in the sixties."

423. Landry, Robert J. *Who, What, Why Is Radio?* 2nd ed. New York: George W. Stewart, 1942. 127 pp. (Radio House series).

Writing from his experience as Director of the Division of Program Writing of CBS and the New York University Summer Radio Workshop, this former radio editor of

Variety discusses the regulators, broadcasters, and advertisers (who), folkways, techniques, and attitudes (what), and problems, neighbors, critics, and prophets (why) of radio broadcasting.

424. Lange, Mark R. *Radio Station Operations.* 3rd ed. Vincennes, IN: The Original Company, 1989. 129 pp. ISBN: 0-943987-04-0.

   In his foreword the author writes "There seems to be a feeling out there that educators can't handle commercial broadcasting successfully and that commercial broadcasters can't educate." As an operator of a small chain of commercial radio stations and full time teacher of broadcasting, he takes "a stab at it" as he delineates the basics required for success in the field.

425. Lazarsfeld, Paul F. *Psychological Impact of Newspaper and Radio Advertisements.* New York: Columbia University Bureau of Applied Social Research, 1949. 74 leaves.

   This study was undertaken to ascertain what goes on in people's minds when they see an advertising message in a newspaper, and when they hear the same message in the form of a radio commercial. It also investigates how people come to pay attention to newspaper or radio advertisements and seeks further information on the attitudes people have developed toward radio and newspaper advertising in general.

426. Lazarsfeld, Paul F. *Radio and the Printed Page: An Introduction to the Study of Radio and Its Role in the Communication of Ideas.* New York: Duell, Sloan & Pearce, 1940. 354 pp.

   This volume grew out of discussions of a 1937 report of the Princeton Radio Project that studied the role played by radio for different groups of listeners in the United States. It looks at the educational aspects of radio, the conditions under which people choose to read or to listen, news broadcasting, and some of the effects that radio has or could have, upon the reading of newspapers and books. It was reprinted in 1970 by Arno Press/New York Times as part of the History of Broadcasting: Radio to Television series.

427. Lazarsfeld, Paul F., and Harry Field. *The People Look at Radio*. Chapel Hill: University of North Carolina Press, 1946. 158 pp.

The object of this survey was to assess the strengths and weaknesses of the radio industry and to ascertain where radio stands with the public in order to create a sound plan of action for the future of the medium.

428. Lazarsfeld, Paul F., and Patricia L. Kendall. *Radio Listening in America: The People Look at Radio--Again*. New York: Prentice-Hall, 1948. 178 pp.

Following an earlier survey conducted in 1946 (see item #427), this examines the communications behavior of American programs and their listeners, an over-all appraisal of radio, and some observations on advertising. This was reprinted by Arno Press in 1979 as part of its Perennial Works in Sociology series.

429. Lazarsfeld, Paul F., and Frank N. Stanton, eds. *Radio Research 1941*. New York: Duell, Sloan & Pearce, 1941. 333 pp.

The first in a series of findings from Columbia University's Office of Radio Research, this book includes six papers presenting the relationship of listeners to broadcasts. Three deal with actual radio programs while the other three investigate listener reactions and the influence radio has on such listeners. The book was reprinted in 1979 by Arno Press as part of its Perennial Works in Sociology series.

430. Lazarsfeld, Paul F., and Frank N. Stanton, eds. *Radio Research 1942-1943*. New York: Essential Books; distributed by Duell, Sloan & Pearce, 1944. 599 pp.

The Radio Research series was begun in 1941 and expanded greatly the area in which communication research had become important. This book, as part of that series, publishes a summary of the early efforts of the Radio Bureau, a division of the Office of War Information. The main topics covered are daytime serials, radio in wartime, radio in operation, progress in listener research, and a section called "The Good Neighbors" dealing with films and magazines. The volume was reprinted in 1979 by Arno Press as part of its Perennial Works in Sociology series.

431. Levin, Harvey J. *Broadcast Regulation and Joint Ownership of Media*. New York: New York University Press, 1960. 219 pp.

Areas covered include the character of intermedia competition, the pattern and trend of joint media ownership, the case for separate ownership, economies of joint ownership, the impact of new media on the old, competition in price and quality, and broadcast regulatory policy.

432. Lewis, Dorothy. *Radio and Public Service: A Guidebook for Radio Chairmen*. Washington: National Association of Broadcasters, 1944. 96 pp.

The author, Coordinator of Listener Activity for the National Association of Broadcasters, suggests ways that radio chairpersons (national, state or local) can develop various fields of activity. The aim is to increase radio listenership, and she offers suggestions and procedures that have been based on the experience of others throughout the country.

433. *Listening Habits of Greater Milwaukee, 1947.* Milwaukee, WI: Radio Station WTMJ, 1947. 16 pp.

Based on more than 74,400 completed calls, this was compiled and published by WTMJ, the *Milwaukee Journal* radio station. It depicts on an hourly basis the number of sets on and the stations they were tuned to during the two weeks of the survey.

434. *Little Books on Broadcasting.* New York: National Broadcasting Company, 1927-1932. 12 vols.

These are exactly what the title says--little (3' by 6' inch) books on a variety of broadcasting subjects. Among the titles are *Commercial Broadcasting, The Technique of Broadcast Advertising,* and *Popular Reactions to Radio Broadcasting* all by Frank A. Arnold; *The Listener Rules Broadcasting,* and *Who Pays for Broadcasting* by Merlin Hall Aylesworth; *Legal Aspects of Radio Broadcasting* by A.L. Ashby; *Radio Broadcasting* by Don E. Gilman; and *The Advertising Agency and the Broadcasting Medium* by James O'Shaughnessy.

435. Logan, John S., and Erwin G. Krasnow. *Radio Retention Guide for Radio and Television Stations.* Washington: National Association of Broadcasters, 1988. 57 pp.

The format and design of this handbook are in the form of a workbook. It describes how to develop a system for record retention, access to records, FCC records, tax data, employer/employee records, and corporate or other business records.

436. Lumley, Frederick H. *Measurement in Radio.* New York: Arno Press/New York Times, 1971. 318 pp. (History of Broadcasting: Radio to Television series). ISBN: 0-405-03576-4.

A reprint edition, this was originally published in 1934 by the Ohio State University. It is a report of a study made by the Bureau of Educational Research to show how broadcasting investigators have attempted to discover what programs appeal to listeners, what ones they actually hear, when they find time to listen, how much listening they do, and how radio affects their daily activities.

437. Macdonald, Jack. *The Handbook of Radio Publicity and Promotion.* 2nd ed. Blue Ridge Summit, PA: Tab Books, 1970. 371 pp. ISBN: 0-8306-0213-5.

Suggestions are made about planning local and national publicity, various types of promotions, sales presentation material, and good publicity releases. The table of contents lists contests, outside stunts, promotions for special days, weeks or months, on-air themes, quickie humor material, personality promos, and station ID's.

438. Marek, George R. *How to Listen to Music Over the Radio.* New York: Pictorial Review, 1937. 31 pp.

This is a series of essays on the general topic of broadcast music and includes a week's schedule of CBS music programs. Marek offers hints for enjoying classical music, describes the sections of a symphony orchestra, writes about the various forms of orchestral music, and discusses what he calls "unseen opera."

439. Market Facts, Inc. *The Images of WGN Radio and Its Competitors in Metropolitan Chicago.* Chicago: WGN Radio, 1960. 31 pp.

WGN Radio commissioned Market Facts to investigate the roles of WGN Radio and its chief competitors--the first major qualitative study to exclusively measure Chicago audiences and stations. This booklet reports the findings of that research.

440. Martin, Robin B. *Broadcast Lending: A Lender's Guide to the Radio Industry.* Washington: National Association of Broadcasters, 1984. 14 pp.

This booklet is intended to familiarize financial consultants with the radio industry and the investment concepts within it. It defines the value of a radio station and its ability to compete in the media marketplace so that potential lenders can be assisted in making sound investments,

441. Marx, Herbert L., Jr., ed. *Television and Radio in American Life.* New York: H.W. Wilson, 1953. 198 pp. (The Reference Shelf, Vol. 25, No. 2).

The focus of this book deals primarily with the impact television has had on radio, the motion picture industry, the theatre, and spectator sports. The author explains why and how radio has been hard hit by television and the ways radio stations and networks have changed their emphasis from one medium to another.

442. Mayer, Martin. *The Intelligent Man's Guide to Broadcast Ratings*. New York: Advertising Research Foundation, 1962. 26 pp.

Underwritten by ABC, CBS, and NBC, this is a condensed version of the report made by the firm of Madow, Hyman and Jessen to the House Committee on Interstate and Foreign Commerce. The original report contains a lengthy evaluation of broadcast rating methods, both as originally started by Archibald Crossley for radio, and expanded by C.E. Hooper, A.C. Nielsen, and Arbitron for radio and television.

443. McCavitt, William E., and Peter K. Pringle. *Electronic Media Management*. Boston: Focal Press, 1986. 325 pp. ISBN: 0-240-51733-4.

Management principles in general and those involving radio and television stations in particular are the main topics covered. The authors look at personnel development, programming, promotion, sales, and regulation as well as community relations, and the media's responsibilities to society.

444. McFadyen, Stuart, Colin Hoskins, and David Gillen. *Canadian Broadcasting: Market Structure and Economic Performance*. Montreal: Institute for Research on Public Policy, 1980. 277 pp. ISBN: 0-920380-68-9.

The authors examine and attempt to answer the following questions: What are the ownership patterns in the TV, radio, and cable-TV industries? What are the effects of ownership and cross-ownership on the conduct of firms in areas such as pricing and programming? What effects do the ownership patterns have on various performance measures such as profitability, audience size, and program choice and diversity?

445. McGee, William L. *A What, When and How Guide to Broadcast Co-Op: The Untapped Goldmine*. San Francisco: Broadcast Marketing, 1975. 88 pp.

The author's summary describes several varieties of cooperative advertising involving three parties--the seller, the customer, and the media--all with legal responsibilities. He views co-op "as a means of reaching more precise market segments by pooling the manufacturer's national selling skills with the merchandising expertise of local retailers."

446. McNair, W.A. *Radio Advertising in Australia*. Sydney: Angus & Robertson, 1937. 461 pp.

Divided into several parts, this provides an outline of the principles of advertising, a description of the broadcasting structure, the measurement of the radio audience, and two short chapters summarizing the position of commercial broadcasting in Australia and its future prospects.

447. Meany, Anthony B. *America Handcuffed by Radio C-h-a-i-n-s: Our Radio Revolution; Prosperity's Flight Through the Air*. New York: Daniel Ryerson, 1942. 132 pp.

The title page states this is "A sales manual to increase general business and prevent inevitable post-war economic distress, exonerating the G.O.P. of Depression's Guilt." It is accompanied by a number of satirical drawings on the effect radio has on its public.

448. Meany, Anthony B. *Radio-TV: Perils to Prosperity*. New York: Pageant Press, 1954. 167 pp.

The author has been interested in what he calls "economic disturbance or disorder" ever since the "magnetic environment that keeps people indoors" was created. He believes that the two media are causing under-consumption of products because they generate mass inactivity.

449. *MegaRate$: How to Get Top Dollar for Your Spots.* National Association of Broadcasters, 1986. 162 pp. ISBN: 0-89324-013-3.

Prepared by The Research Group of Seattle for the National Association of Broadcasters, this is aimed at advertising sales directors of radio stations. It describes the best ways to convince potential clients to use a particular station.

450. Merrill Lynch, Pierce, Fenner and Beane. *Radio, Television and Motion Pictures.* New York: Merrill Lynch, 1950. 28 pp.

A selected group of companies in the entertainment business are analyzed regarding their financial standing (earnings, expenditures, etc.). Those most involved in the radio industry include ABC, Emerson, RCA, and Philco Corp.

451. Midgley, Ned. *The Advertising and Business Side of Radio.* New York: Prentice-Hall, 1948. 363 pp.

Midgley felt that the business principles, ethics, and practices in broadcasting differ from any other business and that it was time that these factors of radio advertising were drawn together into a complete framework. He hopes that this book would "chart the course and show not only what broadcasting has to sell, but also how to sell it."

452. Miller, Justin. *The Blue Book*. Washington: National Association of Broadcasters, 1947. 21 pp.

The Blue Book is the popular title of a booklet issued on March 7, 1946, by the FCC as "Public Service Responsibility of Broadcast Licensees" (see item 1529). This piece is an analysis of the booklet by National Association of Broadcasters President Miller and reprints in full an exchange of letters between him and Oregon Congressman Harris Ellsworth.

453. Miller, Neville. *Let's Keep Radio Free*. Washington: National Association of Broadcasters, 1942. 51 pp.

This is the text of Miller's testimony before the House Interstate and Foreign Commerce Committee that took place on April 16, 1942, at a hearing on the Sanders Bill (HR 5497) to amend the Federal Communications Act of 1934. It includes three NAB proposals and several appendices analyzing broadcast stations and listing NAB members.

454. Morell, Peter. *Poisons, Potions and Profits: the Antidote to Radio Advertising*. New York: Knight Publishers, 1937. 327 pp.

In his acknowledgments section the author states "this study could have been carried out much more effectively had the officials of network radio been somewhat more cooperative." Nevertheless, he tries to prove that "radio advertisers have made a consistent record of exploiting radio solely for profits at the expense of the consumer" as he concentrates on cosmetics, dental products, cough medicines, and some foods.

455. Murphy, Jonne. *Handbook of Radio Advertising*. Radnor, PA: Chilton, 1980. 240 pp. ISBN: 0-8019-6890-9.

Intended to be light and easy to read, with a minimum of statistics, this book is designed to answer the need for a basic reference in planning, buying, and selling radio. The author states he hopes that retailers, advertising agencies, and marketing personnel will find such a text useful in planning and using radio.

456. Mutual Broadcasting System, Inc. *Mutual's Second White Paper.* New York: The System, 1941. 20 pp.

Prepared for the stockholders and affiliates of the corporation, this is the follow-up to Mutual's White Paper published in May 1941 (see item 457). It analyzes the FCC's revision of its chain broadcasting regulations and is dated October 20, 1941.

457. Mutual Broadcasting System, Inc. *Mutual's White Paper.* New York: The System, 1941. 15 pp.

This analyzes the causes and effects of the Federal Communications Commission report on chain broadcasting and the Mutual-ASCAP agreement. It was prepared for the stockholders and affiliates of the corporation.

458. Myrick, Howard A., and Carol Keegan. *Review of 1980 CPB Communication Research Findings.* Washington: Corporation for Public Broadcasting, 1981. 123 pp. ISBN: 0-89776-063-8.

The main categories are titled Research on Programming and Audience Trends, Minority and Special Interest Audience Research, Formative and Diagnostic Research, Development of Improved Methodologies for Measuring Audience Interests and Needs, Local Station and System Support, Special Studies, and Implications for Future Research.

459. National Advisory Council on Radio in Education. *Four Years of Network Broadcasting.* New York: The Council, 1937. 77 pp.

   The text is a report by the Council's Committee on Civic Education by Radio and the American Political Science Association. Its primary subject is the series, *You and Your Government,* which concluded on June 9, 1936, with its 210th individual broadcast.

460. National Association for Better Radio and Television. *Look and Listen: Radio and Television Guide to Better Programs.* Los Angeles: The Association.

   The programs listed in this serial publication were the result of work and study by the Association's evaluation committee, based on their standards of production, writing, performance, commercial arrangements, acceptability as home entertainment, etc. It is interesting to note that no crime programs are recommended if they are broadcast before 9 p.m. because of the large audience of children in the early evening hours. Publication began in 1956.

461. National Association of Broadcasters. *The ABC of Radio.* 2nd ed. Washington: The Association, 1941. 34 pp.

   The purpose of this book is to teach listeners more about radio. Section titles include That "Thing," the Microphone; We Tune In; Across the Dial; and Pathways of the Air. Individual chapters enlarge upon these subjects.

462. National Association of Broadcasters. *Accounting Manual for Broadcast Stations.* Washington: The Association, 1945. 23 pp.

Economic Aspects 139

This particular manual is a revision of the previous system prepared in 1935 by the Association's Accounting Committee. It is designed to provide a simple, workable system to meet the daily needs of station management. The revision was brought about in part by the FCC annual financial report required of all stations.

463. National Association of Broadcasters. *A Broadcast Research Primer*. Washington: The Association, 1971. 62 pp.

This booklet is intended to provide station management with a basic manual on research. It discusses in non-technical language how research can help in formulating policy, identifies the types of research that require outside professional help, and offers step-by-step information on how to conduct simple surveys.

464. National Association of Broadcasters. *NAB Employee-Employer Relations Bulletin*. Washington: The Association, 1946. 1 vol.

In a loose-leaf form, this is a collection of pamphlets on a variety of subjects affecting employee-employer relations. Among them are such titles as The Wage and Hour Act, When You First Face Unionization, and Broadcasting: a Gilt-Edged Field of Employment.

465. National Association of Broadcasters. *NAB Member Service*. Washington: The Association.

A weekly report published since 1949 by the Association for its membership, this serial publication provides information on station management, FCC docket and actions, engineering, employee-employer relations, legal aspects, government relations, broadcast advertising, programs, etc.

466. National Association of Broadcasters. *NAB Radio Code Roster.* Washington: The Association, 1971. 56 leaves.

    Published on a regular basis, this lists alphabetically by state the individual stations who are radio code subscribers. Also included are radio networks.

467. National Association of Broadcasters. *Purchasing a Broadcast Station: A Buyer's Guide.* Washington: The Association, 1978. 38 pp.

    An overview of broadcasting as an investment is presented in the first chapter, and information on mounting a successful search is described in the second. Other chapters cover the evaluation of the worth of a station and setting a price, financing the purchase, creating the legal contract, and dealing with the FCC.

468. National Association of Broadcasters. *Radio Financial Report, 1989.* Washington: The Association, 1989. 225 pp. ISBN: 0-89324-070-2.

    An annual publication, this summarizes results from the NAB Radio Financial Survey and contains a wealth of financial information on radio stations across the country. Standard statistical techniques are employed in order to maintain the logic and representation of the data presented.

469. National Association of Broadcasters. *Radio in Search of Excellence: Lessons from America's Best-Run Radio Stations.* Washington: The Association, 1985. 150 pp. ISBN: 0-89324-006-0.

    The management firm of McKinsey and Company analyzed the management practices of radio stations and has consolidated in this volume its findings on 11 top-performing stations. Also included are chapters written by other consultants describing ways for stations to attain and maintain high performance records.

470. National Association of Broadcasters. *Radio Station Management: News Survey Report*. Washington: The Association, 1960. 1 vol.

A number of topics are covered in this volume: the amount of news programming; its importance; news sources; newsroom facilities; personnel; charges; sponsored news programs; classification by kind of news; editing and rewriting wire service copy; location of commercials; broadcasting of editorials; editorial patterns; and editorials invoking issues.

471. National Association of Broadcasters. *Successful Radio Promotions: From Ideas to Dollars*. Washington: The Association, 1988. 137 pp. ISBN: 0-89324-048-6.

Client events/incentives, contests, listener events, holidays and seasonal promotions, and sports are some of the subject areas covered in this book. It offers suggestions on merchandising, on-air promotions and station services, and provides some new twists on old ideas.

472. National Association of Broadcasters. Research Committee. *Radio Audience Measurement*. Washington: The Association, 1946. 15 pp.

Asked on several occasions to prepare a definitive statement regarding the relative merits and demerits of the various audience rating methods and agencies operating in the field, the Research Committee has created this brief statement of general principles.

473. National Broadcasting Company. *NBC and You.* New York: The Company, 1945. 139 pp.

> This is "an account of the Organization, Operation and Employee-Company Policies of the National Broadcasting Company designed as a Handbook to aid you in your daily work." It is intended for all employees so that they can learn about its past, its policies, practices, and various departments.

474. National Broadcasting Company. *NBC Markets.* New York: The Company, 1931. 1 vol.

> Originally published in a loose-leaf format, the subtitle describes this as "a presentation of basic market facts on the key sales territories of the United States--the trading areas served by NBC associated stations."

475. National Broadcasting Company. *Straight Across the Board.* New York: The Company, 1936. 65 pp. (General Edition 2).

> This is the second of a series of survey reports dealing with essential information about radio. It is intended to be "a contribution to mutual understanding of matters in which advertisers, advertising agencies and NBC have a common interest."

476. National Broadcasting Company. *They Listen by the Millions.* New York: The Company, 1949. 6 pp.

> Prepared for national advertisers by NBC, this brochure describes how many millions of listeners there are, where they are located, and to what station or network they listen as determined by the Broadcast Measurement Bureau.

477. National Retail Dry Goods Association. *A Survey on the Use of Radio As a Retail Advertising Medium*. New York: The Association, 1946. 6 pp.

The results of a survey conducted by the Association are presented in this booklet. Its intent was to find out to what extent members were using radio, for how long, with what success, and their future plans for continuing advertising in that manner.

478. O'Donnell, Lewis B., Carl Hausman, and Philip Benoit. *Radio Station Operations: Management and Employee Perspectives*. Belmont, CA: Wadsworth Publishing, 1989. 409 pp. (Wadsworth series in Mass Communication). ISBN: 0-534-09540-2.

The focus is on the day-to-day workings of radio as a business. The authors look at the history and development of the medium, programs and programming, sales, advertising, promotion, engineering, automation, facility planning and management, and regulation and control.

479. O'Neill, Neville, ed. *The Advertising Agency Looks at Radio*. New York: D. Appleton, 1932. 232 pp.

Written from the point of view of an advertising agency, the essays in this volume were contributed by various members of the radio departments of agencies such as McCann-Erickson, Young & Rubicam, and Batten Barton, Durstine & Osborn. They examine results, relations between stations and agencies, women's programs, copy, selection of stations, and production.

480. Palmer, B.J. *Radio Salesmanship: How Its Potential Sales Percentage Can Be Increased*. 4th ed. Davenport, IA: PSC Press, 1943. 83 pp.

First published in July 1942 by the President of WOC (Basic Blue Network) and WHO (NBC Basic Red Network), this provides information for radio sponsors, agencies, copy writers, broadcasters, station managers, program managers, and announcers.

481. *Paperwork Control in Broadcasting Stations.* Washington: National Association of Broadcasters, 1962. 20 pp.

    This is intended to provide a system for handling sales contracts and billing, traffic, and availabilities. It is based on the system used at WMAL AM-FM-TV in Washington, D.C.

482. Parker, Bruce, and Nigel Farrell. *TV & Radio: Everybody's Soapbox.* Poole, Eng.: Blandford, 1983. 192 pp. ISBN: 0-7137-1306-2.

    A detailed and humorous account of how to get on the air and what to do after you are on is presented in this informative text. Advice is offered especially for the first-timers along with explanations of techniques and jargon.

483. Peatman, John Gray, and Tore Hallonquist. *The Patterning of Listener Attitudes Toward Radio Broadcasts.* Stanford University, CA: Stanford University Press, 1945. 58 pp. (Applied Psychology Monographs, 4).

    Published for the American Association for Applied Psychology, this study presents methods developed for the analysis of the patterning of listeners' attitudes toward radio broadcasts. The research can ascertain whether a radio broadcast elicits a single general pattern of attitudes or a number of different ones.

484. Peck, William A. *Radio Promotion Handbook.* Blue Ridge Summit, PA: Tab Books, 1968. 191 pp.

Suggestions are provided for contests in general, treasure hunts, number games, "drop us a card or letter" offers, and various publicity stunts. Other chapters describe still different methods of promotion: programming, public service, news, sales, and off-air ideas.

485. Pegg, Mark. *Broadcasting and Society, 1918-1939*. London: Croom Helm, 1983. 263 pp. ISBN: 0-7099-2039-3.

The introduction reads: "As the basis for a regular broadcasting system, established in 1922, radio soon consolidated its position in British society, so that by 1935, 98% of the British population could hear broadcast programmes if they possessed a receiver and the audience consisted of some thirty million people." This book describes listening patterns, the means of listening, wireless organizations, the broadcasters, and listener research of this period.

486. Peigh, Terry D., et al. *The Use of Radio in Social Development*. Chicago: University of Chicago, Communication Laboratory, 1979. 172 pp. (Media Monograph, 5). ISBN: 0-89836-005-6.

The focus is on techniques for imparting essential information, motivation, and legitimization for new ideas and practices to an audience which, generally speaking, can be described as below the poverty line or is otherwise socially disadvantaged, according to the preface.

487. Pellegrin, Frank E. *Manual of Radio Advertising*. Washington: National Association of Broadcasters, 1941. 1 vol.

A loose-leaf publication, this is a series of articles on various facets of radio advertising. Included is material on circulation, dealer's preference, social forces, and comparative costs.

488. *People in Broadcasting*. Washington: National Association of Broadcasters, 1962. 94 pp.

Prepared jointly by NAB and the Association for Professional Broadcasting Education, this research study provides basic information on the background of those who work in broadcasting and sheds light on the current employment, educational needs, and problems in the industry. Questionnaires from over 2300 managers, employees, and former employees provided the data.

489. *The People Speak: Public Attitudes Towards Radio and Television Broadcasting*. Ottawa: Canadian Association of Radio and Television Broadcasters, 1958. 15 pp.

A Canadian Cross-Section Report through the Canadian Institute of Public Opinion (The Gallup Poll) and the Canadian Association of Radio and Television Broadcasters, asked (1) whether Canadians preferred the existing CBC regulation or regulation by a separate non-government body, (2) if they thought broadcasting should be controlled in a manner similar to airline and railway regulation, and (3) if they approved or disapproved the regulations restricting private stations in six major Canadian cities.

490. Powell, Jon T., and Wally Gair, eds. *Public Interest and the Business of Broadcasting: The Broadcast Industry Looks at Itself*. Westport, CT: Quorum Books, 1988. 193 pp. ISBN: 0-89930-198-3.

Divided into three parts, the articles are classified as The Broad View, In the Marketplace, and Other Views. Among the contributors are Newton Minow, Edward O.

Fritts, Arthur C. Nielsen, Jr., Gene F. Jankowski, Charles E. Wright, Ward L. Quaal, and Edgar A. Vovsi.

491. Power, Leonard. *Radio Advisory Committees and Audience Preparation.* Washington: Federal Radio Education Committee, 1940. 43 leaves (American Cooperative Broadcasting, Supplementary series, Bulletin 3).

The text is a survey of local radio committees that cooperate with radio stations to determine methods used by stations and committees to build audiences for programs resulting from such station-committee cooperation.

492. Price, Tom. *Radio Program Timelines, 1920-1980.* Salinas, CA: Tom Price, 1980. 57 leaves.

A research/graphics project, this is described on the title page as "a charted cross-reference of American radio broadcasting displaying program titles, broadcasting timelines sponsorship, and network affiliation." It evolved out of a collection of old-time radio programs Price used in his social science classes at the junior high school and community college levels.

493. Prowitt, Marsha O'Bannon. *Guide to Citizen Action in Radio and Television.* New York: United Church of Christ. Office of Communication, 1971. 44 pp.

This guide is designed to show the public how to deal with broadcaster violations concerning extreme propaganda, commercials, personal attacks, lack of public affairs or news programming, children's programming, bias in news programming, and discrimination in programming and employment.

494. *Public Broadcasting Report.* Washington: Warren Publishing. ISSN: 0193-3663.

Warren Publishing states that for 45 years it has been the authoritative news service for broadcasting and allied fields. This publication began in 1978 and is published every two weeks.

495. *Pulse of Radio: Radio's Management Weekly.* North Palm Beach, FL: Streamline Communications. ISSN: 1044-1603.

This periodical is published 50 times a year. It has interviews, a cover story, and several articles in each issue. Regular departments are Editorial, News, Radio Ink, Radio Calendar, and DC Databank describing "who's buying, who's selling, who's getting ready to move."

496. *Purchasing a Broadcast Station: A Buyer's Guide.* Washington: National Association of Broadcasters, 1979. 38 pp.

Helpful information is provided for anyone wishing to buy into broadcasting as an investment. This reprinted pamphlet describes the search for a station, evaluating its worth and setting a price, financing, and finally, the contract to be arranged between buyer and seller.

497. Pusateri, C. Joseph. *Enterprise in Radio: WWL and the Business of Broadcasting in America.* Washington: University Press of America, 1980. 366 pp. ISBN: 0-8191-0955-X.

This book concerns WWL in New Orleans, a radio station licensed to Loyola University since March 1922. The ownership of WWL by a church-related university and, at the same time, its operation as a fully commercial enterprise is an exceptional situation in broadcasting; its story is told here.

498. Quaal, Ward L., and James A. Brown. *Broadcast Management: Radio--Television*. 2nd ed. New York: Hastings House, 1976. 464 pp. (Studies in Media Management). ISBN: 0-8038-0763-5.

    This book offers representative patterns of practical management procedures. According to the preface, it not only attempts to set down minutely detailed and standardized practices for managing a radio or television station, it suggests areas for improved managerial leadership. This revision contains considerable statistical documentation as well as excerpts from and references to other commentators on media management. The first edition was published in 1968.

499. *Radio & Records*. Los Angeles: Radio & Records.

    Published weekly (except Christmas week) since 1973, this periodical is the trade newspaper of the radio industry. It features news about records and play lists.

500. *Radio and Television*. Prague: Administrative Council of the International Radio and Television Organization (OIRT).

    Published six times a year in English, Russian, and German, this periodical is the official *OIRT Review*.

501. *Radio Business Report*. Springfield, VA: Radio Business Report, Inc. ISSN: 0741-8469.

    A weekly publication, this periodical calls itself the "voice of the radio broadcasting industry." It has been published since 1983 and has sections titled Radio News: The Breaking News of the Radio Industry and Media

Trends: News and Views from the Editors among other features.

502. *Radio Communications Report*. Denver: RCR Publications. ISSN: 0744-0618.

Published biweekly, this serial publication is "the newspaper for the mobile communications industry." It began publication in 1981 and supercedes a publication titled *Two-Way Radio Dealer*.

503. *Radio Enters the Home*. New York: Radio Corporation of America, 1922. 128 pp.

The title page states: "How to enjoy popular radio broadcasting. With complete instructions and description of apparatus. For those who desire to be entertained with radio concerts, lectures, dance music, and for the radio amateur and experimenter."

504. *Radio Listening Throughout Non-TV America*. New York: J.A. Ward, 1952. 1 vol.

Prepared by the audience measurement firm of J.A. Ward, Inc., this incorporates the Second Nationwide Audit of Radio Listening in Home Town America. It covers listening habits during home-town periods, programs, radio listening during non-TV periods, and specific programs.

505. *Radio Market Guide: A Service for Radio Advertising, Marketing, Promotion, Merchandising*. Chicago: Radio Marketing Guide Publishing.

Published monthly since 1945, this magazine offers articles to help those involved in radio advertising and its related fields. The market data section is arranged by state and lists station representatives, networks, frequency, ownership, and coverage.

506. *Radio Market Trends*. Washington: National Association of Broadcasters/Radio Advertising Bureau, 1988. 47 pp. ISBN: 0-89324-050-8.

The data were collected by several CPA firms to cover 1987 revenues for radio stations in 82 markets. The reported values are based on Arbitron market rankings and include gross revenues for the sale of station time to national advertisers or sponsors, gross revenues from the sale of station time to local and regional advertisers, and total time sales along with a list of the stations reporting. This is published annually.

507. *Radio Only*. Cherry Hill, NJ: Inside Radio, Inc. ISSN: 0731-8294.

A monthly publication, this periodical has news and features about radio broadcasting. There are articles on sales, programming, ratings, promotions, and management. Departments feature the latest business leads, personal marketing plans, anti-print articles, and strategic listening tips.

508. *Radio Ownership and Set Use*. Chicago: A.C. Nielsen, 1962. 1 vol.

The Nielsen organization presents this supplementary report based on their coverage service providing an analysis of total radio circulation, county by county, in the United States. Data include total homes and total radio homes and radio usage broken down into weekly, daytime and nighttime listening.

509. *Radio Programming Profile*. Farmingale, NY: BF/Communication Services. 2 vols.

Published three times a year since 1967, these volumes contain information supplied by the radio stations directly or, in a few instances, from materials supplied by their national representatives. Arranged alphabetically by city or area, data include call letters, addresses, ownership and key personnel, frequency, power, network affiliation, daily programming, sales representatives, and, in many cases, rate information.

510. *Radio Reaches People*. Lexington, KY: Radio Station WLAP, 1940. 39 pp.

Actually a brochure to attract advertisers, this shows in visual form radio's influence and compares radio commercial advertising with other media. Several pages are devoted to WLAP itself and summarize its position in the Bluegrass Market. It gives facts and figures about audience, income of listeners, and the amount of retail sales in the area.

511. *Radio: Selected A.A.P.S.S. Surveys, 1929-1941*. New York: Arno Press/New York Times, 1971. 679 pp. (History of Broadcasting: Radio to Television series). ISBN: 0-405-03556-X.

Irwin Stewart, former Assistant Solicitor of the Texas Department of State edited the first account, *Radio*; Herman S. Hettinger of the University of Pennsylvania edited the other two, *Radio: The Fifth Estate* and *New Horizons in Radio*. All three reports were reprinted from *The Annals of the American Academy of Political and Social Science* and appeared in 1929, 1935, and 1941.

512. *Radio Today: The Black Listener.* New York: Arbitron, 1984. 8 pp. (Radio Today series).

This special edition examines exclusively, for the first time, the listening patterns and preferences of today's black audience. Arbitron surveyed black listeners to all stations in 10 metropolitan markets with significant black populations to offer a reasonably good representation of how metropolitan black listeners use radio.

513. *Radio Today: The Hispanic Listener.* New York: Arbitron, 1985. 14 pp. (Radio Today series).

Written in English and Spanish, this examines the listening patterns and preferences of today's Hispanic radio audience. It identifies which stations, where, when, and how often Hispanics listen to radio today so that advertisers, marketers, and programmers can gain insight into how the Hispanic marketplace uses radio.

514. *Radio Week: A Resource for Managers.* Washington: National Association of Broadcasters.

Actually the NAB radio member's newsletter, this weekly publication has articles on radio-related subjects, such as programming, promotion, engineering, regulation, station transfers, and station sales. Published since 1933, it was formerly titled *NAB Highlights and Radioactive.*

515. *Radio World.* Falls Church, VA: Industrial Marketing Advisory Services. ISSN: 0274-8541.

Beginning publishing in 1977, this semi-monthly calls itself "radio's best read newspaper." It serves technical and management personnel responsible for the operation of radio stations.

516. *Radio Year-Round: The Medium for All Seasons.* New York: Arbitron, 1987. 23 pp. (Radio Today series).

The focus of this study is on how audiences vary their listening habits seasonally. It is arranged, as are the others in the series, by time of day, demographic groups, and formats.

517. Reid, Seerley. *Radio Preferences of Tenth-Grade Students.* Columbus: Ohio State University, 1941. 24 leaves (Evaluation of School Broadcasts Bulletin 26).

In 1937 students of Rochester, New York, were surveyed to determine their favorite radio programs, the types of programming they preferred, and how many programs they listened to each week. This report interprets the results of this survey and examines the differences in radio listening between sexes, between students of various intellectual abilities, and between students from homes of various economic levels.

518. Reinsch, J. Leonard, and Elmo Israel Ellis. *Radio Station Management.* 2nd ed. New York: Harper & Brothers, 1960. 337 pp.

The first edition of this book was published in 1948 and this revision expands on "the profound changes that have taken place in listening habits, programming concepts, production techniques, sales methods--in virtually every phase of radio broadcasting." The foreword to this edition was written by Sol Taishoff, late editor and publisher of *Broadcasting*.

519. *Religious Broadcasting.* Parsippany, NJ: National Religious Broadcasters. ISSN: 0034-4079.

This is the official magazine of the NRB and is distributed eleven months of the year. The July and August issues are combined. It began publication in 1969.

520. Reymer & Gersin Associates. *Radio W.A.R.S.: A Study of the Needs, Motivations, and Attitudes of Today's Radio Listeners.* Washington: National Association of Broadcasters, 1983. 34 pp.

Telephone interviews with 1300 radio listeners were conducted to find out what they needed and wanted out of radio. The psychology of the fans of the major formats were compared to create key data tables and a guide to apply a "segmentation" approach to marketing.

521. Reymer & Gersin Associates. *Radio W.A.R.S.: An In-Depth Look at Full Service Fans.* Washington: National Association of Broadcasters, 1983. 10 vols.

Supplemental volumes to the original Radio W.A.R.S. Study, these are titled How to Survive in the '80s; A Look at Beautiful/Easy Music; A Look at AOR; A Look at Adult Contemporary; A Look at CHR; A Look at Country; A Look at Full Service; A Look at News/Talk; A Look at Nostalgia; and a Look at Urban Contemporary.

522. Reymer & Gersin Associates. *Radio W.A.R.S. II: How to Push Listeners' "Hot Buttons."* Washington: National Association of Broadcasters, 1985. 18 pp.

Similar to the earlier volumes of *Radio W.A.R.S.*, this reveals seven basic types of radio listeners as groups cutting across format boundaries. Sharing common attitudes they are classified as cheer-me escapists, info-maniacs, friend-seekers, radio junkies, social followers, rabble-rousers, and "good ole music onlies."

523. Robinson, Sol. *Broadcast Station Operating Guide*. Blue Ridge Summit, PA: Tab Books, 1969. 256 pp. ISBN: 0-306-9467-6.

Written mainly for those involved in the operation of radio stations in small to medium-sized markets, this tries to define the most essential factors for successful station operation and explains how these factors can be evolved into operating practices which would improve the bottom line--the station profit picture.

524. Robinson, Thomas Porter. *Radio Networks and the Federal Government*. New York: Columbia University Press, 1943. 278 pp.

Chapters discuss the early history of broadcasting, the national networks, networks and advertising, federal regulation, radio censorship and free speech, artist contracts and transcriptions, network control of station rates and length of contracts, exclusivity, station ownership, rejection of programs, option time, and a look forward for the medium.

525. Rose, C.B., Jr. *National Policy for Radio Broadcasting*. New York: Harper & Brothers, 1940. 289 pp.

This volume began as a report of a committee of the National Economic and Social Planning Association and was subsequently reprinted by Arno Press/New York Times as part of the 1971 series History of Broadcasting: Radio to Television. It examines the problems of a national policy for radio broadcasting, its technical structure, its commercial structure, program content, and those regarding freedom of the air.

526. Rosen, Philip T. *The Modern Stentors: Radio Broadcasters and the Federal Government, 1920-1934*. Westport, CT:

Greenwood Press, 1980. 267 pp. (Contributions in Economics and Economic History series). ISBN: 0-313-21231-7. ISSN: 0084-9235.

Rosen states that American radio broadcasting might have been very different than it is today but for the particular interplay during the crucial years 1920 to 1934 among businessmen in the infant industry, the prospective market, politics, and bureaucrats. What happened--and the results--are the story he relates in this book.

527. Rosenbloom, Richard S. *The Continuing Revolution in Communications Technology: Implications for the Broadcasting Business*. Cambridge, MA: Harvard University Program on Information Resources Policy, 1981. 30 pp.

This report was adapted from a seminar presentation sponsored by McGavren Guild Radio at the National Radio Broadcasters Association's American Radio Expo '80 held in Los Angeles in October 1980.

528. Ross, Wallace A. *Best TV & Radio Commercials*. New York: Hastings House, 1968. 191 pp.

A serial publication, this summarizes the purpose and ceremonies of the American TV and Radio Commercial Festival that meets to determine the winners in the various categories of its competition. The scene is set verbally for each winner and excerpts from the dialogue are included, along with data about agency production credits, first air date, and length.

529. Rothafel, Samuel L., and Raymond Francis Yates. *Broadcasting: Its New Day*. New York: Arno Press/New

York Times, 1971. 316 pp. (History of Broadcasting: Radio to Television series). ISBN: 0-405-03571-3.

This title was originally published by The Century Company of New York in 1925. At that time its foreword states the authors "tried to present the bigger and more vital issues of broadcasting and commercial radio in as practical a manner as possible. No attempt has been made to embellish the treatment with fanciful prognostications or dreamy outlines of the future."

530. Routt, Edd. *The Business of Radio Broadcasting*. Blue Ridge Summit, PA: Tab Books, 1972. 400 pp. ISBN: 0-8306-2587-9.

The preface states that the purpose of this book is to integrate the concepts of management principles, public relations, policies, legal interpretations, and federal politics, and to interpret everyday operating problems of commercial radio stations, regardless of operational or programming format, market size, or appeal.

531. Sandage, Charles H. *Building Audiences for Educational Radio Programs*. Urbana: University of Illinois. Institute of Communications Research, 1951. 40 pp.

This booklet describes an experiment in audience promotion that was conducted in Champaign County, Illinois, using selected programs broadcast by station WILL, the University of Illinois radio station. The results helped determine whether listenership could be increased and which promotions were most effective.

532. Sandage, Charles H. *Qualitative Analysis of Radio Listening in Two Central Illinois Counties*. Urbana: University of Illinois, 1949. 57 pp. (Bureau of Economic and Business Research Bulletin, 68).

Champaign and McLean Counties were the two areas studied for this report that was begun to assist several University of Illinois groups in their educational operations. Both quality and quantity of radio listening were measured, and this report summarizes some of the information resulting from the two different studies.

533. Sandage, Charles H. *Radio Advertising for Retailers.* Cambridge, MA: Harvard University Press, 1948. 280 pp.

Very specialized, this is a report based on a national study of the actual use of radio advertising by retail stores and services and by regional manufacturers.

534. Sandage, Charles H. *A Survey of Radio Listening in Champaign County, Illinois.* Urbana: University of Illinois, 1954. 71 pp.

Covering the week of November 21-27, 1954, this was a diary-type survey, with listening diaries distributed throughout the entire county to 1,200 families. The survey results are published herein.

535. Sarnoff, David. *Principles and Practices of Network Radio Broadcasting.* New York: RCA Institutes Technical Press, 1939. 111 pp.

This contains the text of Sarnoff's testimony before the FCC in Washington on November 14, 1938, and May 17, 1939. At the time Sarnoff was President of RCA and Chairman of the Board of NBC.

536. Schulberg, Bob. *Radio Advertising: The Authoritative Handbook.* Lincolnwood, IL: NTC Business Books, 1989. 204 pp. ISBN: 0-8442-3130-4.

Charles Osgood wrote the foreword to this book that describes the way advertisers spend over $7.5 billion each year to promote their products and services on the radio. It covers format, market segmentation, buying and selling time, creative advertising, direct response, and other related subjects.

537. Schuler, Edgar A. *Survey of Radio Listeners in Louisiana.* Baton Rouge: Louisiana State University, 1943. 77 pp.

Prepared for LSU's General Extension Division, this study was designed to secure data for use in connection with the planning and scheduling of educational radio programs for Louisiana. No attempt was made to present general conclusions or to develop the implications suggested by the findings. It deals only with the information needed to implement the educational radio program.

538. Schutz, David E., ed. *Radio Station Transfers, 1987.* New York: ComCapital Group, 1987. 1 vol.

This book is Volume 1, Number 1, of an annual publication. It is intended to provide the most detailed information possible regarding recent station sales and information about other individual station sales. It includes statistical inferences which can be drawn from these data.

539. Schwartz, Tony. *The Responsive Chord.* Garden City, NY: Anchor Press/Doubleday, 1974. 173 pp. ISBN: 0-385-08895-7.

Schwartz created more than 5,000 radio and television spot advertisements and had a regular program for more than 25 years on WNYC in New York City. He offers advice on the new communication environment; hard sell, soft sell, deep sell; education in the global village; and sounds in the city.

540. Schwoch, James. *The American Radio Industry and Its Latin American Activities, 1900-1939*. Urbana: University of Illinois Press, 1990. 184 pp. (Illinois Studies in Communication). ISBN: 0-252-01690-4.

This is a historical analysis of the development of radio concurrent with the rise of the United States as a world power. It discusses the similarities between the global radio-based media culture of the past and the global video-based media of the present.

541. Seehafer, Gene F., and Jack W. Laemmar. *Successful Television and Radio Advertising*. New York: McGraw-Hill, 1959. 648 pp. (McGraw-Hill series in Marketing and Advertising).

Originally published in 1951 under the title of *Successful Radio and Television Advertising*, this has changed its name and scope as television grew in size, scope and influence and radio found new programming and sales patterns to reposition itself as a valuable advertising medium. The authors discuss both media and examine elements of the entire commercial broadcasting system, creation of commercials, research, campaigns, and station management.

542. Seldes, Gilbert. *The Great Audience*. New York: Viking Press, 1951. 299 pp.

Chapters are devoted to various entertainment media: movies, radio, television, and the stage. Fifty-four pages are devoted to "Oracle: Radio" wherein Seldes discusses licensing, broadcast coverage, programming, sponsors, and writing.

543. Seldes, Gilbert. *The Public Arts*. New York: Simon & Schuster, 1956. 303 pp.

Seldes states that this book is fundamentally the story of a revolution--one that began in the late summer of 1929 when millions of Americans stayed home to be entertained by the *Amos 'n' Andy* radio program. He discusses the popularity of radio and what happened after the advent of television in American homes.

544. Seymour, Craig. *Developing an Effective Business Plan: A Working Guide for Radio Stations*. Washington: National Association of Broadcasters, 1987. 55 leaves. ISBN: 0-89324-028-1.

This manual serves as an introduction to business planning and provides the radio station owner and/or manager with the tools to begin creating an actual business plan. The appendix contains several worksheets developed specifically for that purpose.

545. Sill, Jerome. *The Radio Station: Management, Functions, Future*. New York: George W. Stewart, 1946. 127 pp. (Radio House series).

The introduction states that Mr. Sill "examines the interplay of advertising and entertainment elements well behind the outer facade which the layman recognizes as 'radio.' His point of view is starkly professional. He deals with competition and profits. He reveals basic attitudes ... photographs the local station manager in characteristic pose--the best foot carefully forward."

546. Silvey, Robert. *Who's Listening? The Story of BBC Audience Research*. London: Allen & Unwin, 1974. 219 pp. ISBN: 0-04-384001-9.

"This is the story of one specialised BBC activity--part of its housekeeping--seen through the eyes of one who had the good fortune to be closely associated with it for longer than anyone else. It is told chronologically, although not slavishly so, and it includes reflections as well as facts."

547. Smith, Anthony. *The Shadow in the Cave: The Broadcaster, His Audience, and the State*. Urbana: University of Illinois Press, 1973. 351 pp. ISBN: 0-252-00442-6.

Although the major focus is on television, sections of this book describe the history of broadcasting in general and radio in particular, and the influence the two media have had on public affairs.

548. Smith, F. Leslie. *Perspectives on Radio and Television: Telecommunication in the United States*. 3rd ed. New York: Harper & Row, 1990. 597 pp. ISBN: 0-06-046301-5.

The author looks at radio and television from a variety of perspectives: historical, creative/informational, physical, legal/ethical, economical, comparative, and sociopsychological. He examines networks, non-commercial broadcasting, media careers, non-electronic media, and research trends in this broad overview.

549. Smith, Marvin. *Radio, TV & Cable: A Telecommunications Approach*. New York: Holt, Rinehart & Winston, 1985. 386 pp. ISBN: 0-03-060567-9.

Divided into five sections, this textbook depicts the nature of mass communication and the communications revolution, technology and development, the effects of broadcasting and cable, law/regulation/policy, and economics/programming/advertising.

550. Spingarn, Jerome H. *Radio Is Yours*. New York: Public Affairs Committee, 1946. 31 pp. (Public Affairs Pamphlet, 121).

The gist of this pamphlet is that the public owns the air waves and has, therefore, certain prerogatives; "....radio is no gift horse, and (the listener has) every right to look into the mouth of the loudspeaker." There are listeners' groups and radio councils and if something isn't satisfactory, it should be changed by these means or through FCC hearings.

551. Standard Rate & Data Service. Research Department. *Spot Radio Promotion Handbook*. Chicago: SRDS, 1949. 63 pp.

Research specialists for SRDS have explored "the thinking and the time-buying methods of spot radio users ... (to learn) *who* buys and influences buying, *why* they buy, *when* they buy, *what* they buy, and *how* they buy."

552. Standard Rate & Data Service. Research Department. *A Survey of Advertiser and Agency Buying Practices and Patterns for Spot Radio*. Chicago: SRDS, 1949. 155 pp.

The President of SRDS writes in his foreword that this is a study of functions that are common to any spot radio advertising problem. The study presents the survey sample, method, conclusions and findings, along with samples of the accompanying letter and questionnaire.

553. Stanley, Robert H. *The Broadcast Industry: An Examination of Major Issues*. New York: Hastings House, 1975. 256 pp. ISBN: 0-8038-0768-6.

The views of prominent broadcasting practitioners and teachers on the problems facing broadcasters are presented. Several major issues are examined including license renewal, the impact of new technology, political broadcasting, fairness, news management, and short- and long-term economic questions.

554. Starch, Daniel. *Revised Study of Radio Broadcasting: Covering the Entire United States and Including a Special Survey of the Pacific Coast.* New York: National Broadcasting Company, 1930. 1 vol.

Prepared for NBC, this is a study of radio broadcasting consisting of a revision of the author's original report, dated April 1, 1928, together with an original survey of the Pacific Coast territory, both as of January 1, 1930.

555. Statistics Canada. *Radio and Television Broadcasting.* Ottawa: Canadian Government Publishing Centre. ISSN: 0575-9560.

An annual publication, this provides data on operating revenues, number of licensed and operating business organizations of the media, air time sales, classification of the radio universe, and international payments and receipts of the broadcasting industry. Information is presented both in text format and in tables.

556. Steiner, Peter O. *Workable Competition in the Radio Broadcasting Industry.* New York: Arno Press, 1979. 223 pp. (Dissertations in Broadcasting series). ISBN: 0-405-11777-9.

Reprinted from the author's Ph.D. thesis at Harvard University in 1949, "This study is concerned with the question of whether the present network system of radio broadcasting is the best of the feasible alternatives in serving the public interest ... (it) accepts as given and unchangeable the American system of commercial radio broadcasting operating within a free-enterprise system, which is subject to regulation but not control by the federal government."

557. *Study of Listening Habits.* Kansas City: Robert S. Conlan, 1949. 90 pp.

This contains the findings of a KFRM area survey conducted by the Robert S. Conlan and Associates firm concentrating on central and western Kansas with adjacent Nebraska and Oklahoma counties within the Kansas City primary trade area. The initial question asked was "This is a radio survey; are you listening to your radio?" and additional questions were subsequently asked if the first answer was in the affirmative.

558. Sturmey, S.G. *The Economic Development of Radio.* London: Gerald Duckworth, 1958. 284 pp.

Three areas of radio--marine radio, point-to-point communications, and broadcasting--were studied. The way in which the use of radio developed in each field is described, and the emphasis is on the process of change within each sphere.

559. Subcommittee of the Committee on Interstate and Foreign Commerce. U.S. House of Representatives. *Broadcast Ratings.* Washington: Government Printing Office, 1964. 759 pp.

The hearings were on the methodology, accuracy, and use of ratings in broadcasting and were held in March and April 1963.

560. Subcommittee of the Committee on Interstate and Foreign Commerce. U.S. House of Representatives. *Broadcast*

Ratings. Washington: Government Printing Office, 1965. 1932 pp.

The hearings described in this publication were held in May and June 1963, and January and September 1964. They dealt with the methodology, accuracy, and use of ratings in broadcasting.

561. Subcommittee on Communications. Committee on Commerce, Science, and Transportation. U.S. Senate. *Minority Ownership of Broadcast Stations.* Washington: Government Printing Office, 1989. 188 pp.

Because minority ownership was virtually nonexistent prior to the 1970s, minorities throughout the country were in effect denied service directed toward their needs and interests so the FCC adopted its minority ownership policy some 15 years ago. It is this policy which is being reviewed here.

562. Subcommittee on Telecommunications and Finance. Committee on Energy and Commerce. U.S. House of Representatives. *Radio Broadcasting Issues.* Washington: Government Printing Office, 1990. 97 pp.

This hearing began an inquiry into the overall state of the radio broadcasting industry. Specific concerns were the problems brought about after the 1982 repeal by the FCC of the antitrafficking rules and new opportunities in the field for women and minorities as employees and owners of radio properties.

563. Subcommittee on Telecommunications, Consumer Protection, and Finance. Committee on Energy and Commerce. U.S. House of Representatives. *Broadcast Regulation and Station Ownership.* Washington: Government Printing Office, 1985. 403 pp.

Two bills to amend the Communications Act of 1934 to reform the requirements applicable to commercial broadcasting station licensees and to assure the diversity of ownership of broadcasting stations were the subject of this hearing held in September 1984.

564. Summers, Leda P. *Daytime Serials and Iowa Women.* Des Moines, IA: Radio Station WHO, 1943. 47 pp.

Among the findings of a study of daytime serial listening in Iowa were the facts that approximately one-half of all women living in radio homes are regular listeners to daytime radio serials, and there is no recognizable "daytime serial listening type" of woman. There are minor differences between regular listeners and non-listeners to serials in the proportions of women in various age, educational, and place-of-residence groups, but there is evidence of a closer relationship between the amount of serial listening and the amount of magazine reading.

565. Swaziland Government. *Survey of Radio Listenership, 1977.* Mbabane, Swaziland: Central Statistical Office, 1977. 35 pp.

This is a report of a survey conducted by the Central Statistical Office on behalf of the Swaziland Broadcasting Service. It offers data, tables, and graphs regarding general listening patterns, times of listening, listenership by age and sex, and listenership to different stations by area.

566. Taylor, Laurie, and Bob Mullan. *Uninvited Guests: The Intimate Secrets of Television and Radio.* London: Chatto & Windus, 1986. 218 pp. ISBN: 0-7011-2973-5.

Working with a London research business, the authors questioned viewers and listeners about their feelings regarding particular programs. They examined attitudes toward performers, knowledge of "media's tricks" and the programs that evoked the strongest reactions.

567. Tebbel, John. *The Media in America*. New York: Thomas Y. Crowell, 1974. 422 pp. ISBN: 0-690-00500-8.

While Tebbel writes about all media in this book, he has one section devoted to the media in the 20th century. In this he describes the "great transformation" in society and writes about radio and television as "the new dimension."

568. Ted Bolton Associates. *The Critical Issues Report: Radio from 1984-1990*. Philadelphia: Ted Bolton Associates, 1984. 29 pp.

Prepared for McGavren Guild Radio, New York, this research report describes the prevailing attitudes in the radio industry, current market strategies, and future aspirations. It explores issues involving radio programming, sales, and technology.

570. Ted Bolton Associates. *The Re-Marketing of AM Radio: A Research Report*. Philadelphia: Ted Bolton Associates, 1984. 16 pp.

From research sponsored by McGavren Guild Radio, New York, this recommends what must be done to maintain and increase audience share over one year, five years, and ten years.

570. *Television/Radio Age*. New York: Television Editorial Corp. ISSN: 0040-277X.

Coverage of the broadcast business for both buyers and sellers of radio and television time is provided in this bimonthly publication that began in 1953.

571. Thomas, Denis. *Competition in Radio.* London: Institute of Economic Affairs, 1965. 27 pp. (Occasional Paper, 5).

Mr. Thomas's general theme is that the efforts to prevent competition in broadcasting have been unsuccessful and that the future of local or "community" radio lies with companies operating under the competitive conditions of free enterprise.

572. Tolleris, Beatrice K. *Radio: How, When and Why to Use It.* New York: National Publicity Council, 1946. 47 pp.

Among the topics covered are assessing radio as a medium, choices of format, ready-made opportunities in radio, joining forces for radio education, building a radio audience, and a checklist on station relations.

573. Tyler, I. Keith. *The Listening Habits of Oakland (California) Pupils.* Chicago: The English Journal, 1936. 10 pp.

This was originally a convention paper presented at the Indianapolis meeting of the National Council of Teachers of English held in November 1935. It is reprinted from the March 1936 issue of *The English Journal.*

574. Unesco. Division of Statistics on Culture and Communication. Office of Statistics. *Latest Statistics on Radio and Television Broadcasting.* Paris: Unesco, 1987. 132 pp. (Statistical Reports and Studies, 29). ISBN: 92-3-102468-X.

Organized a little differently from earlier statistical reports, this still provides information on broadcasting facilities, receivers, and programs. There is an opening chapter on organization that discusses broadcasting institutions, personnel employed in broadcasting, and some economic aspects of the field.

575. Unesco. Division of Statistics on Culture and Communication. Office of Statistics. *Statistics on Radio and Television 1960-1976*. Paris: Unesco, 1979. 124 pp. (Statistical Reports and Studies, 23). ISBN: 92-3-101681-4.

Part one covers the organization of radio broadcasting, audio transmitters, and audio receivers while part two describes the present statistics for television. A third part provides data on radio and television programs.

576. U.S. Department of Commerce. *Radio Activities of the Department of Commerce*. Washington: Government Printing Office, 1931. 34 pp.

The origin and organization of the Radio Division are explained along with information on marine radio inspection, regulation of radio communication, monitoring, radio test cars, examination and licensing of radio operators, and the radio activities of the Bureau of Standards and the Lighthouse Service.

577. U.S. Federal Communications Commission. *Broadcast Primer*. Washington: Government Printing Office, 1961. 25 pp.

This pamphlet is actually INF Bulletin No. 2-B published July 1961. It provides information on the evolution of broadcasting, the history of broadcast regulation, and AM and FM broadcast operations. It is updated on a regular basis.

172 Radio Broadcasting

578. U.S. Federal Communications Commission. *An Economic Study of Standard Broadcasting.* Washington: The Commission, 1947. 111 pp.

This report explores factors raised by the expansion of the industry as they affect standard broadcasting. It examines geographical distribution, size of community, first-time stations in communities, problem areas for stations, costs of entering the broadcast industry, revenues required to meet operating expenses, and total volume of advertising necessary to realize a profit.

579. U.S. Federal Trade Commission. *Radio and Phonograph Manufacturing Corporations.* Washington: Government Printing Office, 1941. 19 pp.

This is a report in the FTC's project for the collection of annual financial reports from a large number of industrial corporations operating in many of the principal industries of the country. This one provides financial statistics for seven corporations in the standard industrial classification #3661.

580. *Urban Radio Listening in the United States.* Washington: National Association of Broadcasters, 1941. 40 pp.

Prepared jointly on behalf of the broadcasting industry by the NAB in cooperation with CBS and NBC, this offers basic data on urban radio to date. It measures the impact of radio on the 20,000,000 families who live in American cities and shows how many of them listen to the radio every day, how much, and when.

581. Waller, Judith C. *Radio: The Fifth Estate.* Boston: Houghton Mifflin, 1946. 483 pp.

Written by NBC's Director of Public Service for the Central Division, this concentrates on the different national forms for the administration of radio and the organization of American radio stations. The author tells how networks are put together and operated, programs are planned, and the work of the various members of the staff along with information on sales, station contracts, promotion, listener groups, etc. A second edition was also published by Houghton Mifflin in 1950.

582. Watson, K., A. Sunter, and F. Ermuth. *A Financial Analysis of the Private Radio Broadcasting Sector in Canada and the United States.* Ottawa: Department of Communications. Social Policy and Programs Branch, 1978. 1 vol.

An executive summary describes the principal regulatory and industry differences of the private radio broadcasting sector in Canada and the United States, and some tentative conclusions are presented. Subsequent chapters detail the regulatory environments, economic trends in radio broadcasting in both countries and the profitability of AM and FM radio stations related to the regulatory contexts in each country.

583. Weaver, Luther. *How to Listen to the Radio.* Washington: National Association of Broadcasters, 1942. 15 pp.

This is the text of a speech presented before the 11th NAB District Meeting and the Minnesota Radio Council on November 24, 1942.

584. Wedell, E.G. *Broadcasting and Public Policy.* London: Michael Joseph, 1968. 370 pp.

The first chapter places the broadcasting system within the context of the whole range of mass media and the public stake in them while chapter two covers the British system of broadcasting. Subsequent chapters deal with the forces that determine broadcasting output and some of the choices open to broadcasters, particularly with reference to radio's problems and competition with the television industry.

585. Whan, Forest L. *The Boston Trade and Distribution Area: Radio-Television Audience of 1952*. Boston: Westinghouse Radio Stations, 1952. 70 pp.

The results of a study of adult radio-television listening habits are presented in this volume. It discusses listener classification, radio set ownership and use, automobile radio use, simultaneous use of more than one radio in the home, and radio vs. television.

586. Whan, Forest L. *The 1957 Iowa Radio-Television Audience Survey*. Des Moines: Central Broadcasting Company, 1957. 46 pp.

Similar to the Boston area study, this is the 20th consecutive annual study of listening/viewing habits in the state of Iowa and was conducted in March-April 1957. The first Iowa study dealt with listeners in small towns and on farms, but all of the subsequent ones covered both urban and rural areas in every county of the state.

587. *What Every Student of Radio Should Know*. Lexington: University of Kentucky. Department of Radio Arts, 1955. 11 leaves.

Twenty-nine radio stations are represented in the questionnaire sent out to Kentucky broadcasters to solicit their opinions. The first part regarded the programs and tape distribution of the University of Kentucky

Broadcasting Service while the second asked advice on its training program; the results are included in this booklet.

588. White, Barton C., and N. Doyle Satterthwaite. *But First, These Messages: The Selling of Broadcast Advertising.* 2nd ed. Boston: Allyn & Bacon, 1989. 389 pp. ISBN: 0-205-11687-6.

The authors evolved a step-by-step approach that points out the similarities of selling different kinds of electronic media as well as adapting techniques in order to accommodate the differences among these media.

589. White, Llewellyn. *The American Radio: A Report on the Broadcasting Industry in the United States from The Commission on Freedom of the Press.* Chicago: University of Chicago Press, 1947. 259 pp.

The problems and opportunities of the "new medium" are explored in chapters titled Marconi's Marvel, Ragtime to Riches, Toward Self-regulation, The Government's Role, Conclusions and Proposals, and What Do the Listeners Say? This was reprinted in 1971 by Arno Press/New York Times as part of the History of Broadcasting: Radio to Television series.

590. Wiebe, G.D. *Radio Listening and Popular Song Tastes.* Columbus: Ohio State University, 1941. 9 leaves (Evaluation of School Broadcasts Bulletin, 28).

In 1941 some 300,000 pieces of music controlled by the American Society of Composers, Authors and Publishers (ASCAP) were prevented from being broadcast on the radio, and there was much discussion about the effect of not being able to broadcast familiar and popular music. This study examines the influence such music had on listeners and the effect the ASCAP restriction had on radio listening and tastes in music.

591. Willey, Malcolm M., and Stuart A. Rice. *Communication Agencies and Social Life*. New York: McGraw-Hill, 1933. 229 pp.

While this deals with several aspects of communication, there is a lengthy chapter on radio broadcasting. It discusses the distribution of radio sets, trends in broadcasting facilities, chain broadcasting, the audience, radio advertising, and problems of radio control.

592. Williams, Albert N. *Listening: A Collection of Critical Articles on Radio*. Freeport, NY: Books for Libraries Press, 1948. 152 pp. (Essay Index Reprint series).

Originally published by the University of Denver Press in 1948 and reprinted as this edition the same year, this contains essays about networks, programs, "the artisans," and advertising. The last chapter contains reviews of radio books by Norman Corwin, Max Wylie, Arch Oboler, and Sherman Dryer published in the *Saturday Review of Literature* when Williams was that magazine's radio columnist.

593. Willing, Si. *How to Sell Radio Advertising*. Blue Ridge Summit, PA: Tab Books, 1970. 315 pp. ISBN: 0-8306-0511-8.

The author "charts the course of progressive steps that a salesman of broadcast advertising must take in order to develop expertise." The book is based on his "carefully documented chronicle of experience on the firing line from Main Street right up on to Madison Avenue ... it is an account of personal confrontations with merchants and time buyers."

594. Wilson, Charles Morrow. *Money at the Crossroads*. New York: National Broadcasting Company, 1937. 21 pp.

This brochure is described as "an intimate study of radio's influence upon a great market of 60,000,000 people." Wilson has undertaken to provide a more comprehensive picture of radio's place in the rural market and to interpret the farm market to potential advertisers.

595. Wilson, David. *Broadcasting: Vision and Sound*. London: Pergamon Press, 1968. 84 pp.

The contents of this book are described on the back cover as: Broadcasting is information transmission; Broadcasting organisations in Britain; Producing a programme; News and current affairs; School programmes; Adult education; Science broadcasting; Technical information; Feedback information; Training for broadcasting; Careers and who has them; and A special example.

596. Wober, J.M. *Teens and Taste in Music and Radio*. London: Independent Broadcasting Authority, 1984. 22 pp.

A London survey among teenagers assessed their preferences for radio stations, styles of music, and of sensory imagery along with some contextual aspects of their appreciation of music. The findings are presented here.

597. Wolfe, Charles Hull. *Modern Radio Advertising*. 2nd ed. New York: Funk & Wagnalls, in association with Printers' Ink, 1953. 738 pp.

Originally published in 1949, this book is a basic overview of the radio advertising industry, and each article is preceded by a foreword written by an executive in the field. The areas covered are the basic fundamentals; techniques; network advertising; spot radio for national, regional and local sponsors; commercial announcements; the past, present and future of the genre; and opportunities in radio.

598. *World Broadcast Advertising: Four Reports.* New York: Arno Press/New York Times, 1971. 177 pp. ISBN: 0-405-03586-1.

The reports reprinted here are *Radio Markets of the World* (1930) by Lawrence D. Batson, and three edited by E. D. Schutrumpf: *Broadcast Advertising in Asia, Africa, Australia, and Oceania* (1932), *Broadcast Advertising in Europe* (1932), and *Broadcast Advertising in Latin America* (1931).

599. Zeigler, Sherilyn K., and Herbert H. Howard. *Broadcast Advertising.* 2nd ed. Ames: Iowa State University Press, 1984. 391 pp. ISBN: 0-8138-0073-0.

A comprehensive working textbook, this encompasses broadcast stations and networks, coverage, circulation and facilities, programming, advertising regulation, writing and producing commercials, and selling TV time. Examples of advertising plans and campaigns are provided along with data on audience research. A new edition is in preparation.

PRODUCTION ASPECTS

Includes announcing, writing, directing, editorializing, sound, news production, propaganda, studios, style manuals, standards and codes, speeches, lectures, commentaries, and broadcast journalism.

600. Aldington, Toby Low. *The Task of Broadcasting News.* London: British Broadcasting Corporation, 1976. 34 pp. ISBN: 0-563-17175-8.

    Prepared as a study for the BBC General Advisory Council, this describes the points raised and argued in the general controversy over broadcast news. It then describes the principles and practices followed by BBC news journalists. Both radio and television news broadcasts are covered.

601. Allen, Louise C., Audre B. Lipscomb, and Joan C. Prigmore. *Radio and Television Continuity Writing.* New York: Pitman Publishing, 1962. 261 pp.

    The first few chapters cover the beginning and development of radio, station environment, and radio personnel. The balance tell how to collect copy data, write copy, stylize it, and finally evaluate it.

602. Anderson, Virgil A. *Training the Speaking Voice.* New York: Oxford University Press, 1942. 387 pp.

    A good speaking voice is essential for a career on the air in radio. This guide is intended to help anyone aspiring to a radio career or who wants improvement in diction for whatever reason.

603. Angell, James R. *War Propaganda and the Radio.* Philadelphia: University of Pennsylvania Press, 1940. 19 pp.

This booklet contains the text of the Howard Crawley Memorial Lecture delivered before the faculty and students of the Wharton School of the University of Pennsylvania on March 18, 1940, by Angell who was then educational counselor of the National Broadcasting Company.

604. Aspinall, Richard. *Radio Programme Production: A Manual for Training.* Paris: Unesco, 1971. 151 pp.

Intended primarily for use in the African states, this book nevertheless can be helpful for anyone involved in training radio personnel. It covers technical facilities, radio production, staff development, and training. Appendices provide an audition report sheet and script layout samples.

605. Association of the Junior Leagues of America. *Radio, Your Station and You.* New York: The Association, 1942. 98 pp.

Prepared as a guide to planning, producing, and promoting local radio programs in the children's and community interpretative fields, this is based on the experiences of the members of more than 90 individual Junior Leagues who have been involved in such activity.

606. Barnhart, Lyle D. *Problems in Announcing for Radio and Television.* Evanston, IL: Student Book Exchange, 1950. 192 pp.

The foreword states this book is designed to be a drill book for the field, calling attention to problems involved in the training of the professional radio or television announcer. It is not a book "about announcing; it is a book in announcing."

607. Barnhart, Lyle D. *Radio and Television Announcing.* Englewood Cliffs, NJ: Prentice-Hall, 1953. 283 pp.

Very similiar to Barnhart's earlier book (see previous annotation), this is keyed to what the author believes to be the demands made upon the announcer (and) views radio and television announcing as established professions in an established industry."

608. Barnouw, Erik. *Handbook of Radio Production: An Outline of Studio Techniques and Procedures in the United States.* Boston: Little, Brown, 1949. 324 pp.

Intended for people interested in any of the special fields of radio, this looks at the production process from the point of view of co-workers and not just from the director's view. The book takes up where its companion volume, *Handbook of Radio Writing* (see next annotation), leaves off and carries the reader through rehearsals to the actual broadcast.

609. Barnouw, Erik. *Handbook of Radio Writing: An Outline of Techniques and Markets in Radio Writing in the United States.* Rev. ed. Boston: Little, Brown, 1950. 336 pp.

Published originally in 1939, this offers a bird's-eye view of the market and the medium. Chapters on technique discuss sound effects, music, speech, routines, trick devices, and the requirements of various program types.

610. Barrett, Marvin, ed. *Broadcast Journalism, 1979-1981.* New York: Everest House, 1982. 256 pp. ISBN: 0-89696-160-5.

The Eighth Alfred I. duPont/ Columbia University Survey is reported in this volume. Part I describes the state of the art, part II the awards, and part III reports and commentaries.

611. Barrett, Marvin. *The Politics of Broadcasting.* New York: Thomas Y. Crowell, 1973. 247 pp.

Radio and television broadcasting of politics (the primaries, the conventions and the campaign) are a major part of this volume of the Alfred I. duPont/Columbia University Survey of Broadcast Journalism for 1971-1972. In addition, there are reports and commentaries by Sig Mickelson, Michael Novak, Steve Knoll, Dick Schaap, and John Houseman.

612. Barrett, Marvin, ed. *Survey of Broadcast Journalism.* New York: Grosset & Dunlap, 1969-1971. 3 vols.

Published for several years under this title and with varying pagination, these volumes were part of the Alfred I. duPont/Columbia University Surveys of Broadcast Journalism. They cover a variety of topics: how television and radio report the news, how they serve the public, the environmental crisis, the plight of cities, the war in Indochina, the bias of television, women on the air, the *CBS Report*: "The Selling of the Pentagon," and advertisers and the FCC.

613. Beckoff, Samuel. *Radio and Television.* New York: Oxford Book Company, 1952. 92 pp. (Oxford Communication-Arts series).

The whole gamut of radio broadcasting is covered briefly in this guide: advertising, programs for homemakers, sustaining programs, drama, recordings, news, public issues, audiences, sports, and educational programming.

614. Biagi, Shirley. *News Talk II: State-of-the-Art Conversations with Today's Broadcast Journalists*. Belmont, CA: Wadsworth Publishing, 1987. 232 pp. (Wadsworth Media Interview series). ISBN: 0-534-06858-8.

Interviews were conducted with Susan Spencer, Doug Kriegel, Judy Woodruff, David Dow, Sam Donaldson, Byron Harris, Marlene Sanders, David Brinkley, Bill Whitaker, Susan Wornick, Don Oliver, and Charles Osgood. This volume is the second in a series of interviews that discuss the participants' roles in radio and/or television. A sample script or transcript from a story by the interviewee is included at the end of each segment.

615. Bickel, Karl A. *New Empires: The Newspaper and the Radio*. Philadelphia: J.B. Lippincott, 1930. 112 pp.

This volume began as an amplification of an address delivered by Bickel before the Journalism Section of the 10th Educational Conference held at Ohio State University in April 1930. It examines the relationship between radio and the press and includes an international survey of radio broadcasting presented in summary form.

616. Bickford, Leland, in collaboration with Walter Fogg. *News While It Is News: The Real Story of the Radio News*. Boston: G.C. Manthorne, 1935. 127 pp.

The flowery preface states this "takes the host of followers of the Radio News behind the scenes. It affords them the opportunity of sharing in the orderly bustle and tireless endeavor which render it possible for the twelve Yankee Network broadcasting stations in the six Northeastern states to keep them intelligently and promptly informed of the sharply-shifting kaleidoscope of fire and flood, politics and courts, industry and the arts, religion and reform, peace and war, sports and social whims."

617. Bittner, John R., and Denise A. Bittner. *Radio Journalism*. Englewood Cliffs, NJ: Prentice-Hall, 1977. 207 pp. (Prentice-Hall series in Speech Communication). ISBN: 0-13-750463-2.

The chapters are titled: Radio, an Emerging Consciousness; Ethics and Responsibilities; News Sources; Covering Radio News; Gathering Radio News; Writing and Production; Programming; Regulation; Promotion and Sales; and Landing a Job. An appendix includes the RTNDA Code of Broadcast News Ethics, NAB Programming Standards for News, NAB Standards of Conduct for Broadcasting Public Proceedings, and the Society of Professional Journalists, Sigma Delta Chi, Code of Ethics.

618. Bland, Michael. *The Executive's Guide to TV and Radio Appearances*. White Plains, NY: Knowledge Industry Publications, 1980. 138 pp. ISBN: 0-4422-3318-3.

Originally published in England in 1979 under the title *You're On Next*, (see next annotation) this explains the preparation necessary for the interviewee and tells how to get the most publicity out of such opportunities. Sample interviews are included in the do-it-yourself training section.

619. Bland, Michael. *You're On Next! How to Survive on Television and Radio*. London: Kogan Page, 1979. 136 pp. ISBN-0-85038-164-9.

On radio, unlike television, people listen more to the words spoken so radio is an excellent way to communicate ideas, and this book tells the reader the best way to go about reaching the audience. Only a few chapters are devoted solely to radio, but these cover interview techniques and local radio in particular.

620. Bland, Michael, and Simone Mondesir. *Promoting Yourself on Television & Radio*. 2nd ed. London: Kogan Page, 1987. 121 pp. ISBN: 1-85091-176-2.

First published in 1979 under the title *You're On Next* (see previous annotation), this describes how to promote causes, companies or products on TV and radio--free. It discloses how to contact producers and how to get a message across effectively.

621. Bliss, Edward, Jr., and John M. Patterson. *Writing News for Broadcast*. 2nd ed. New York: Columbia University Press, 1978. 220 pp. ISBN: 0-231-04372-4.

Published first in 1971, this is described in the foreword as a text for the bold investigator and the careful reporter, and the lesson of the book is that you can't be one without the other. This fully revised edition continues the original goal of establishing guidelines for broadcast journalists.

622. Block, Mervin. *Writing Broadcast News--Shorter, Sharper, Stronger: A Professional Handbook*. Chicago: Bonus Books, 1987. 231 pp. ISBN: 0-933893-20-5.

Block writes: "The tips and reminders--or rules--are omnidirectional. They cover radio and television and apply to all kinds of newswriting, from 20-second stories to 2-hour specials, from anchor 'readers' to reporters 'wraps.'"

623. Blu, Susan, and Molly Ann Mullin. *Word of Mouth: A Guide to Commercial Voice-Over Excellence*. Los Angeles: Pomegranate Press, 1987. 156 pp. ISBN: 0-938817-10-8.

    This is a guide to a very specialized facet of the broadcasting industry--the audio portion of a radio or television sales or promotional spot. It tells how to perfect technique as well as how to get hired.

624. Bly, Robert W. *The Copywriter's Handbook: A Step-by-Step Guide to Writing Copy That Sells*. New York: Dodd, Mead, 1985. 353 pp. ISBN: 0-396-08546-6.

    Intended to provide guidelines and advice about how to write effective copy, this offers the basics in the field for the beginner as well as a refresher course for those already established.

625. Boyd, Andrew. *Broadcast Journalism: Techniques of Radio and TV News*. Oxford, Eng.: Heinemann, 1988. 380 pp. ISBN: 0-434-90175-X.

    This presents step-by-step instruction in the essential skills of the trade and lays the foundations for a career in broadcast journalism. Subjects include news writing, news gathering, interviewing, presentation, technology, and available jobs.

626. Braun, Everett C., and Frederick Jackson Stanley. *Let's Broadcast*. Minneapolis: Northwestern Press, 1948. 249 pp.

"A textbook on the use of radio broadcasting as an educational tool in the secondary schools ... It was written to teach students and teachers how to put on actual radio broadcasts."

627. British Broadcasting Corporation. *Broadcast English*. 3rd ed. London: The Corporation, 1935. 2 vols.

The first volume contains "recommendations to announcers regarding certain words of doubtful pronunciation" while the second advises announcers about the pronunciation of some English place-names.

628. Brooks, William F. *Radio News Writing*. New York: McGraw-Hill, 1948. 200 pp. (NBC-Columbia University Broadcasting series).

This is based on a Columbia University extension course in radio news writing that is given in cooperation with the National Broadcasting Company. It is intended to cover the fundamentals and to point out some of the pitfalls in the field.

629. Broughton, Irv. *The Art of Interviewing for Television, Radio and Film*. Blue Ridge Summit, PA: Tab Books, 1981. 266 pp. ISBN: 0-8306-9743-8.

The focus is on problem-solving methods and techniques so that the interviewer can come up with the best interview possible under a variety of circumstances.

630. Broussard, E. Joseph, and Jack F. Holgate. *Writing and Reporting Broadcast News*. New York: Macmillan, 1982. 191 pp. ISBN: 0-02-315270-2.

After relating a history of broadcast news, the authors discuss styles, grammar and sentence construction, common errors, organization of materials, story development, accuracy and balance, writing special stories, rewriting, interviewing, news sources, and the topics of libel, privacy, good taste, and ethics.

631. Brown, Donald E., and John Paul Jones. *Radio and Television News*. New York: Rinehart, 1954. 472 pp.

Although this book appears to be essentially a how-to manual, it uses a different approach than other similar texts. There is a series of exercises accompanied by an informal discussion and explanation, and each unit has a brief introduction by an expert in that particular field.

632. Bulman, David, ed. *Molders of Opinion*. Milwaukee: Bruce Publishing, 1945. 166 pp.

The subjects of this book are the columnists and commentators the author refers to as "the Delphic Oracles of today." The authors of these commentaries are journalists who write in this book about radio personalities H.V. Kaltenborn, Gabriel Heater, Raymond Gram Swing, and Walter Winchell.

633. Burchfield, Robert. *The Spoken Word: A BBC Guide*. New York: Oxford University Press, 1982. 40 pp. ISBN: 0-19-520380-1.

Written by the chief editor of the Oxford English dictionaries, this booklet is referred to as "the last word on the Queen's English." It is actually a guide to pronunciation, diction, and grammar and was published specifically for the BBC network's broadcasters.

634. Busby, Linda, and Donald Parker. *The Art and Science of Radio*. Boston: Allyn & Bacon, 1984. 214 pp. ISBN: 0-205-08049-9.

Every aspect of broadcasting is covered in this basic textbook. The authors provide current information on radio's history, audio production, broadcast copywriting, station ownership and operations, sales and promotion, and broadcast regulations.

635. Campbell, Laurence R., Harry E. Heath, Jr., and Ray V. Johnson. *A Guide to Radio-TV Writing*. Ames: Iowa State College Press, 1950. 407 pp.

The four parts of this spiral-bound volume are Exploring Radio and Television, News on the Airlanes, Radio-TV Entertainment and Opinion, and Specialized Service for the Public. The authors emphasize principles of radio writing and apply these principles in practical and realistic assignments.

636. Carlile, John S. *Production and Direction of Radio Programs*. New York: Prentice-Hall, 1940. 397 pp.

This is intended to "provide a useful volume on radio production for those who are busy performing tasks within the industry and for those who hope to enter radio's gates to create or direct, entertain or inform, or to assist in any capacity."

637. Carmen, Ruth. *Radio Dramatics: Introduction Lectures*. 2nd ed. New York: John C. Yorston Publishing, 1937. 180 pp.

Written from the professional's viewpoint, the author has divided this book into nine different lectures covering topics such as enunciation and pronunciation, voice and breath control, casting, timing, sound effects, scripts, characterization, and cuing.

638. Chappel, G.A. *Radio Stations: Installation, Design and Practice*. New York: Pergamon Press, 1959. 248 pp.

190 Radio Broadcasting

The preface states the purpose of this book is to discuss various methods employed in planning and designing radio stations. Much of the work is applicable to stations irrespective of size or power, since the general conventions remain basically the same.

639. Charnley, Mitchell V. *News by Radio.* New York: Macmillan, 1948. 403 pp.

"Describes the special practices, principles and characteristics developed in the brief life of radio news. It evaluates them in the light of their effectiveness or their failure ... (and) suggests methods of achieving and expanding radio news effectiveness and of avoiding failures."

640. Chernoff, Howard L. *"Anybody Here from West Virginia? "* Charleston, WV: Charleston Printing Company, 1945. 105 pp.

In his introduction to this book Edward R. Morrow states that it isn't the usual war correspondent's book. Chernoff was the first radio war correspondent, aside from those representing national networks, to arrive in the European Theatre of Operations and, according to Murrow, "he used the spoken word as a means of transporting the home folks over there where their boys and girls were." This is a collection of Chernoff's dispatches that were read by those home folks.

641. Chesmore, Stuart. *Behind the Microphone.* London: Thomas Nelson & Sons, 1935. 120 pp. (Discovery books, 11).

Provides a look "through the doors of Broadcasting House." Chesmore discusses British Broadcasting Corporation programming, children's programs, on-location broadcasting, and the broadcasting of time, weather and news.

642. Childs, Harwood L., and John B. Whitton, eds. *Propaganda by Short Wave*. Princeton, NJ: Princeton University Press, 1942. 352 pp.

The Princeton Listening Center was America's eavesdropper on the radio propaganda of the world immediately prior to the start of WW II. This book reports some of the important finds made during the period when the group monitored, transcribed, translated, and analyzed such broadcasts.

643. Cirino, Robert. *Power to Persuade: Mass Media and the News*. New York: Bantam, 1974. 246 pp.

"Over 150 fascinating case studies of newsmakers and newsmaking, illustrating the decisions that vitally affect every American's right to know" is the way this paperback is described on the front cover. "It provides realistic, practical insight into such issues as 'censorship,' 'bias,' and 'public interest.'"

644. Clifford, Martin. *Microphones*. 2nd ed. Blue Ridge Summit, PA: Tab Books, 1982. 256 pp. ISBN: 0-8306-0097-3.

An essential component in successful radio transmission is sound, and good microphone equipment and technique are vital to good sound transmission. This book discusses the world of sound, acoustics and noise, and goes into detail about microphone characteristics, manufacture and use. A third edition was published in 1986.

645. Clifford, Theresa R., ed. *Sourcetap: a Directory of Program Resources for Radio*. 2nd ed. Washington: National Federation of Community Broadcasters, 1978. 1 vol.

In a loose-leaf format, this is one of a series of information manuals for non-commercial radio stations published by NFCB. This provides more than 250 separate listings of production and distribution groups both in this country and internationally.

646. Codding, George A., Jr. *Broadcasting Without Barriers*. Paris: Unesco, 1959. 167 pp.

Unesco has long been concerned with assisting radio broadcasting to play a major part as an instrument for communication between peoples. This book is a survey by independent expert Codding to determine the extent radio broadcasters have succeeded in this goal and what future prospects should be.

647. Coddington, Robert H. *Modern Radio Broadcasting: Management & Operation in Small-to-Medium Markets*. Blue Ridge Summit, PA: Tab Books, 1969. 286 pp. ISBN: 0-8306-9482-X.

Topics covered are the unique requirements of the small market, audiences and profits, choosing markets, selecting facilities, licensing, the FCC, land and building requirements, transmitter plants, control rooms and studio equipment, staffing, programming, program types, program logs, sales and promotion, engineering, microphone basics, construction notes, and operation and maintenance.

648. Cohler, David Keith. *Broadcast Journalism: A Guide for the Presentation of Radio and Television News*. Englewood Cliffs, NJ: Prentice-Hall, 1985. 334 pp. ISBN: 0-13-083155-7.

Expanding the basics of journalism, this describes the specialized techniques of broadcasting news--from the initial stage of news gathering to the finished on-air show. There are chapters on interviewing, editing, field reporting, videotaping, computerization, and job hunting.

649. Cott, Ted. *How to Audition for Radio.* New York: Greenberg, 1946. 142 pp.

   The title page describes this as "a handbook for actors; a workbook for students." It covers "radio actor's tools, radio actor's dictionary (and) radio actor's workshop."

650. Cowgill, Rome. *Fundamentals of Writing for Radio.* New York: Rinehart, 1949. 301 pp. (Rinehart Radio series).

   A former script writer for *Voice of America* explains techniques and terminology involved in writing drama, talks, continuities, and non-dramatic features. He also provides guidance in program planning, production, and marketing.

651. Creamer, Joseph, and William B. Hoffman. *Radio Sound Effects.* New York: Ziff-Davis, 1945. 61 pp.

   The title page states this is "a manual for broadcasting stations, sound effects technicians, students, and all others who use, or are interested in, modern sound effects technique."

652. Crews, Albert, ed. *Professional Radio Writing.* Boston: Houghton Mifflin, 1946. 473 pp. (Houghton Mifflin Radio Broadcasting series).

   Four main sections comprise this textbook on radio writing. They are General Considerations of Writing, including Program Types and Writing Mechanics; General Continuity Writing with Emphasis on Music

Programs, Talk Shows, and Features; Radio Dramatic Writing; and Marketing Radio Writing.

653. Crews, Albert. *Radio Production Directing.* Boston: Houghton Mifflin, 1944. 550 pp. (Houghton Mifflin Radio Broadcasting series).

One of the first in a series of textbooks commissioned by the National Broadcasting Company, this attempts to present the basic concepts on which all sound production work is founded. The author acknowledges help, criticism and contributions from some of NBC's "most capable people."

654. Crosby, John. *Out of the Blue: A Book About Radio and Television.* New York: Simon & Schuster, 1952. 301 pp.

John Crosby began his radio column in 1946, and it eventually evolved into a column about television. This book is a compilation of his columns that cover such diverse subjects as NBC's broadcast of the Easter Parade on Fifth Avenue in 1947, soap operas, Ralph Edwards of *Truth or Consequences* fame, advertising jingles, and the Bickersons.

655. Culbert, David Holbrook. *News for Everyman: Radio and Foreign Affairs in Thirties America.* Westport, CT: Greenwood Press, 1976. 238 pp. ISBN: 0-8371-8260-3.

This examines the part played in foreign affairs by early radio correspondents. Those profiled include Boake Carter, H.V. Kaltenborn, Raymond Gram Swing, Elmer Davis, Fulton Lewis, Jr., and Edward R. Murrow.

656. Daly, John. *The News: Broadcasting's First Responsibility.* Washington: National Association of Radio and Television Broadcasters, 1957. 16 pp.

On July 15, 1957, John Daly, Vice President of ABC in charge of News and Special Events and a Member of the Freedom of Information Committee of NARTB, addressed the convention of the American Bar Association on the subject of Canon 35 which forbids the broadcasting of courtroom proceedings or the taking of photographs during court sessions or recesses. This is the text of Daly's talk.

657. Dary, David. *Radio News Handbook*. Thurmont, MD: Tab Books, 1967. 173 pp.

Recounts the world of radio news from writing to delivery, from remote unit to editorializing, and from the history of the craft to covering the courts. Most of the book is based on the author's experiences as a radio newsman. A second edition appeared in 1970.

658. Dexter, Gerry L. *Muzzled Media: How to Get the News You've Been Missing*. Lake Geneva, WI: Tiare Publications, 1986. 96 pp. ISBN: 0-936653-02-7.

Suggestions are provided on ways to use international radio to go beyond the usual sources in order to open a new world of news and information. Dexter tells how to acquire local news from foreign countries, foreign press opinions, world news unreported in the U.S. as well as financial and business news, human interest items, and feature stories.

659. Dixon, Peter. *Radio Sketches and How to Write Them*. New York: Frederick A. Stokes, 1936. 274 pp.

In a note, the author states this offers examples of radio material that have been used on the most important radio programs in the country and also offers examples of the mechanical construction of a working radio script.

He based this book on his own experience with two major networks and includes 18 sketches.

660. Dixon, Peter. *Radio Writing*. New York: Century, 1931. 324 pp.

In addition to discussing the technique of writing for the medium, the author presents a very short history of radio, discusses the writing system itself, and includes material on taboos, sound effects, and production. Complete texts of "six famous radio scripts" are reproduced.

661. Donahue, Hugh Carter. *The Battle to Control Broadcast News: Who Owns the First Amendment?* Cambridge, MA: MIT Press, 1989. 238 pp. ISBN: 0-262-040999.

This "chronicles the power plays, fights, betrayals, and skirmishes behind the use and misuse of both the Fairness Doctrine ... and the Equal Time Law" in radio and television broadcasting. The author argues that "these restrictions were never justified, that the public lost more than it gained by having them, and that fear of the power of mass communications is a constant theme shaping regulating of broadcast journalism."

662. Drake, Harold L. *Humanistic Radio Production*. Washington: University Press of America, 1982. 116 pp. ISBN: 0-8191-2251-3.

Chapters discuss what the author means by humanistic mass communications, teaching "live" radio by way of "golden age" formats, an audio history of broadcasting, high school broadcast competitions, interviewing, working for Egyptian radio, the NAB radio code, and sample internship and workshop agreements.

663. Dudek, Lee J. *Professional Broadcast Announcing.* Boston: Allyn & Bacon, 1982. 378 pp. ISBN: 0-205-07660-2.

This book is structured as a guidebook for beginning announcers and as a handbook for reference and self-improvement for the more advanced. Among the subjects covered are paraphrasing and copy markups, rehearsals, newscasting, interviewing, commentary and editorializing, talk program hosting, commercials, public service announcements (PSAs), sports, and disc jockeys.

664. Duerr, Edwin. *Radio and Television Acting: Criticism, Theory, and Practice.* New York: Rinehart, 1950. 417 pp. (Rinehart Radio series).

The author states in the preface that "after fifteen years spent in teaching and directing actors in the legitimate theatre ... and after six additional years in New York City working with actors in all manner of top-flight radio and TV shows (he has) managed to squeeze out enough time to examine a vast amount of radio and TV acting, and to read and think and argue about it. The result is this book for actors and directors" that describes the how, why and ways of performing in these media.

665. Dunbar, Janet. *The Radio Talk: A Practical Study of the Art and Craft of Talks Broadcasting.* London: George G. Harrap, 1954. 137 pp.

Because she believes that most people who broadcast a talk are not professional broadcasters, public speakers, or another kind of orator, the author has written this guide to show how to prepare and deliver a talk on the radio. She introduces various types of talks, e.g., factual, specialized, personal, or controversial, and explains how a script should be prepared and then actually presented.

666. Dunlap, Orrin E., Jr. *Talking on the Radio.* New York: Greenberg, 1936. 216 pp.

Subtitled "A Practical Guide for Writing and Broadcasting a Speech," this includes material on laws and ethics, teaching by radio, and some practical do's and don'ts. There is a special section for newscasters and commentators on delivery, preparing copy, handling of flash bulletins, and stories to avoid in broadcasts.

667. Durham, F. Gayle. *News Broadcasting on Soviet Radio and Television.* Cambridge, MA: MIT Press, 1965. 63 pp.

In this paper processed for the Defense Documentation Center, Defense Supply Agency, Ms Durham discusses the Soviet conception of the functional role of broadcasting media and the news. She examines both the mechanics and the content of news broadcasts.

668. Edmonds, Robert. *Scriptwriting for the Audio-Visual Media: Radio, Films, Television, Filmstrips, Slide Films, Multimedia.* 2nd ed. New York: Teachers College Press, 1984. 216 pp. ISBN: 0-8077-2753-9.

Practical advice on creating good scripts is offered along with suggestions for ways they can be sold. The author also discusses basic markets and how to get jobs in the industry.

669. Educational Radio Script and Transcription Exchange. *Radio Program Production Aids.* Washington: U.S. Office of Education, 1948. 50 pp.

Three titles previously published by the Educational Radio Script Exchange are combined in this revised volume. They are *Radio Manual, Radio Glossary* and *Handbook of Sound Effects.*

670. Ethridge, Mark. *A Fair Deal for Radio*. Washington: National Association of Broadcasters, 1941. 17 pp.

This pamphlet contains the text of an address on the state of the radio industry presented before the 19th Annual Convention of the National Association of Broadcasters in St. Louis on May 14, 1941.

671. Etkin, Harry A. *AM/FM Broadcast Station Planning Guide*. Blue Ridge Summit, PA: Tab Books, 1970. 190 pp. ISBN: 0-8306-0500-2.

Intended primarily for those contemplating a new facility or remodeling an existing station, this book covers all the basics--from frequency search or channel allocation to planning and wiring studio and transmitter plants. Separate chapters deal with preventive maintenance and proof-of-performance measurements.

672. Ewbank, Henry L., and Sherman P. Lawton. *Broadcasting Projects: Radio and Television: A Manual for the Student*. New York: Harper & Brothers, 1953. 152 pp.

A workbook, this includes program projects, listening and viewing projects, and writing projects. Radio scripts, continuity and commercial copy exercises are provided along with survey projects for measuring the audience.

673. Ewbank, Henry L., and Sherman P. Lawton. *Broadcasting: Radio and Television*. New York: Harper & Brothers, 1952. 528 pp.

The first seven chapters of this college textbook describe existing radio and television systems, examine the public service responsibilities of these media, and suggest standards for evaluating broadcast programs. The rest of the book discusses planning and promoting the program schedule, preparation of programs, rehearsals and production

674. Ewbank, Henry L., and Sherman P. Lawton. *Projects for Radio Speech: A Manual for the Student.* New York: Harper & Brothers, 1940. 158 pp.

Microphone projects constitute the first half of this volume while the balance is devoted to laboratory or listening projects. They cover such topics as timing the elements of a variety show, listening to a round-table discussion, formulas for newscasts, and personal voice recording.

675. Ewing, Sam. *You're on the Air.* Blue Ridge Summit, PA: Tab Books, 1972. 224 pp. ISBN: 0-8306-2620-4.

Ewing lets the reader in on some of the little tricks of the trade he has learned and observed during his career in radio broadcasting. He provides what he calls "career short-cuts that are time-tested and proven by the pros."

676. Fairbanks, Grant. *Voice and Articulation Drillbook.* 2nd ed. New York: Harper & Brothers, 1960. 196 pp.

A book of practice materials, this stresses auditory discrimination and is organized by the phonetic and acoustic features of speech. It is particularly helpful for those who want to pursue a career in radio, especially as an announcer, news person, talk show host, or interviewer.

677. Fang, Irving. *Television News/Radio News.* 4th ed. rev. St. Paul, MN: Rada Press, 1985. 418 pp. ISBN: 0-9604212-3-8.

Not just a simple guide to broadcast and electronic news gathering and writing, this also identifies the problems affecting television and radio news. Additional chapters on special areas such as weather, sports, editorials, and documentaries are included.

678. Federal Council of the Churches of Christ in America. Department of Research and Education. *Broadcasting and the Public: A Case Study of Social Ethics*. New York: Abingdon Press, 1938. 220 pp.

The purposes of this book, according to the foreword, are (1) to trace the development of the radio broadcasting industry with particular reference to its cultural, social, moral, and spiritual values, (2) to try to achieve a "wholesome balance of liberty and social control in broadcasting," and (3) to offer some guidance to the church group in furthering the development of high standards in radio as a public service.

679. Fisher, Hal. *The Man Behind the Mike: A Guide to Professional Broadcast Announcing*. Blue Ridge Summit, PA: Tab Books, 1967. 288 pp.

The purpose of this book is to provide detailed study methods and drills to develop the talent of individuals just starting as well as offer a review for experienced broadcast personnel. Several chapters discuss advancement and information for succeeding in the business.

680. Fitzpatrick, Leo. *Radio Realities: A Series of Talks Dedicated to American Radio Broadcasting*. Detroit: Radio Station WJR, 1933. 80 pp.

Among the subjects covered are "radio birthdays," radio's financial situation, advertising, differences between American and English broadcasting, the coverage of President Franklin D. Roosevelt's first inauguration, and the Authors, Composers and Publishers Society (ASCAP).

681. Fly, James Lawrence. *Radio in America Today*. New York: Town Hall, Inc., 1940. 22 pp. (Town Hall Pamphlets, Series III, No. 1).

This is a reprint of an original presentation by Mr. Fly on October 17, 1940, at the opening session of Town Hall's short course on American Radio and How to Use It.

682. *FM Radio Station Operations Handbook*. Thurmont, MD: Tab Books, 1986. 196 pp.

Based on articles which appeared in *BM/E Magazine*, this anthology contains information on a variety of subjects from engineering and management to programming and sales. Many are illustrated with photographs, drawings and/or diagrams.

683. *FMedia*. Esko, MN: FM Atlas Publishing. ISSN: 0890-6718.

Published monthly, this is "a newletter of fact and opinion about FM radio and related technologies--from the publishers of the *FM Atlas and Station Directory*." (See item 1645.)

684. Franklin, O. Thomas. *Broadcasting the News*. New York: Pageant Press, 1955. 147 pp.

This explains in detail how to get maximum effectiveness from radio news. The author considers the entire operation--obtaining information, writing, editing, and presenting the news. He also has one chapter devoted to defamation by radio.

685. French, Florence Felten, William B. Levenson, and Vera Cober Rockwell. *Radio English*. New York: McGraw-Hill, 1952. 368 pp.

The essentials of competent writing and speaking are presented in this book written by two former English instructors and a supervisor of radio for the Cleveland (Ohio) Board of Education. It utilizes radio techniques to attract and hold an audience and offers sample scripts for study.

686. *The Future of Broadcasting*. London: Eyre Methuen, 1974. 100 pp. ISBN: 0-413-31140-6.

A report presented to the Social Morality Council in October 1973, this makes interesting and far-reaching recommendations about radio and television broadcasting. It reveals a great deal about the inner processes of the British broadcasting organizations.

687. Gaines, J. Raleigh. *Modern Radio Programming*. Blue Ridge Summit, PA: Tab Books, 1973. 190 pp. ISBN: 0-8306-3623-4.

After describing the job, rating and evaluation of a program director, Gaines writes about the special problems of on-the-air programming, station community involvement, commercial creativity, station promotion, production, and ratings. He identifies the PD's duties as well as those of the usually better known disc jockey.

688. Garvey, Daniel E., and William L. Rivers. *Broadcast Writing*. New York: Longman, 1982. 280 pp. ISBN: 0-582-28173-3.

Intended to teach the basic skills of the genre, this covers the major kinds of writing found in American broadcasting. It is a companion volume to the authors' *The Broadcast Writing Workbook*.

689. Garvey, Daniel E., and William L. Rivers. *Newswriting for the Electronic Media: Principles, Examples, Applications*. Belmont, CA: Wadsworth Publishing, 1982. 250 pp. (Wadsworth series in Mass Communication). ISBN: 0-534-01069-5.

    The authors take the reader through the various elements of writing news and explain the basics of such writing. Chapters discuss editing and reporting as well as actual writing techniques.

690. General Electric. Electronics Department. *The ABC's of Radio*. Bridgeport, CT: General Electric Company, 1943. 68 pp.

    This is intended to help the beginner understand the fundamentals of radio. It is the outgrowth of a training course prepared for sales personnel and others employed in non-technical positions in the radio industry.

691. Giangola, Andrew, ed. and compiler. *Radio Copy Book: Ideas and Inspiration for Radio Copywriters*. New York: Radio Advertising Bureau, 1986. 222 pp.

    This book contains a cross-section of radio scripts including humor, hard sell, image, item, and straight sales copy. All the commercials in the book are written for local accounts and created with specific advertisers in mind.

692. Gifford, F. *Tape: A Radio News Handbook*. 2nd ed. New York: Hastings House, 1977. 224 pp. (Communication Arts Books). ISBN: 0-8038-7161-9.

Presenting his subject from an introductory point of view, the author regards this as a "teach-yourself" course if access is available to common tape equipment. He begins with brief historical and philosophical considerations, defines the fundamentals of tape, explains telephone tape, writes about the various broadcast tape forms and content, tells how to write for the medium, and how to handle tape and tape equipment. A third edition was published in 1987.

693. Gilmore, Art, and Glenn Y. Middleton. *Radio Announcing.* Hollywood: Hollywood Radio Publishers, 1946. 118 pp.

Former announcer Jimmy Wallington wrote the foreword in which he states "This book will supply the crying need for a radio announcer's textbook and will do a world of good to those just starting and to many who need a review of past training." It covers terminology, voice production and speech, microphone technique, staff and free lance announcers, narration, commercial copy, special events, timing and pacing, and how to get a job.

694. Golding, Peter, and Philip Elliott. *Making the News.* London: Longman, 1979. 241 pp. ISBN: 0-582-50460-0.

The authors investigated the production and content of radio and television news in Ireland, Nigeria, and Sweden. They wanted to determine how broadcast news pictures the world and how this relates to the routine demands of news production in broadcasting organizations.

695. Gould, Samuel B., and Sidney A. Dimond. *Training the Local Announcer.* New York: Longmans, Green, 1950. 201 pp.

A number of drills and exercises are included with each chapter offering instruction in microphone technique, improvement of voice quality, ad-libbing ability, and reading of commercials. Other information is provided on job opportunitites, qualifications, and compensation.

696. Hall, Mark W. *Broadcast Journalism: An Introduction to News Writing.* 2nd ed. New York: Hastings House, 1978. 156 pp. (Communication Arts Books). ISBN: 0-8038-0781-3.

Using a "nuts-and-bolts" approach to the topic, the author covers not only radio-television news writing, but also provides information and guidelines for handling the major types of stories broadcast journalists might be expected to cover during their careers. Numerous examples are included along with material that closely reflects what is going on in the "real" world, according to the author. The first edition was published in 1971 and a third in 1986.

697. Hasling, John. *Fundamentals of Radio Broadcasting.* New York: McGraw-Hill, 1980. 205 pp. ISBN: 0-07-026992-0.

The material for this book was gleaned from the author's years of experience working with commercial and non-commercial stations. It is directed to students who plan to work in college or community radio stations and to those who might be considering broadcasting as a career.

698. Hayes, John S., and Horace J. Gardner. *Both Sides of the Microphone: Training for the Radio.* Philadelphia: J.B. Lippincott, 1938. 180 pp.

The two-fold purpose of this book is, first, to enlighten those who are interested in various phases of broadcasting from a vocational standpoint and, second, to detail the fundamentals of radio for those who are the listeners on the other side of the microphone. The treatment given to the broadcasting station emphasizes program staff, engineering, sales, publicity, and office departments.

699. Hayes, Vangie, with Gloria Hainline. *How to Get Into Commercials*. New York: Harper & Row, 1983. 311 pp.

The subtitle describes this work well: "A Complete Guide for Breaking Into and Succeeding in the Lucrative World of TV and Radio Commercials by One of the Nation's Leading Casting Directors". It also includes samples of scripts for practice, résumés, interviews, and self-evaluation checklists.

700. Henneke, Ben G. *The Radio Announcer's Handbook*. New York: Rinehart, 1948. 308 pp. (Rinehart Radio series).

Written by the University of Tulsa Director of Radio, this book "is an outgrowth of my attempts to teach speech students the rudiments of announcing." He includes Announcer Vocabulary Drills to help improve pronunciation as well as other textual material that can be used for additional oral reading drills.

701. Herman, Lewis Helmar, and Marguerite Shalett Herman. *Manual of American Dialects for Radio, Stage, Screen and Television*. Chicago: Ziff-Davis Publishing, 1947. 326 pp.

The authors state that the main purpose of this book is to teach the regional American dialects to actors. Phonetic symbols, characterization, lilt and stress, vowel changes, and consonant changes are some of the areas covered.

702. Herman, Lewis Helmar, and Marguerite Shalett Herman. *Manual of Foreign Dialects for Radio, Stage and Screen*. Chicago: Ziff-Davis Publishing, 1943. 415 pp.

A companion volume to the authors' *Manual of American Dialects* and published first (see previous annotation), this emphasizes that each element (characterization, lilt, etc.) should be attacked by itself and after it has been learned thoroughly, the next one should be studied. The result should be a finished and authentic dialect.

703. Hesse, Jurgen. *The Radio Documentary Handbook: Creating, Producing and Selling for Broadcast.* Vancouver, Can.: International Self-Counsel Press, 1987. 135 pp. ISBN: 0-88908-653-2.

A Canadian Broadcasting Corporation radio writer and documentarist explains how to develop an idea for radio, make a proposal, research it, choose recording equipment, use a microphone, record interviews, create sound effects, select music, dub the original recording, edit the master tape, and assemble the final product.

704. Hill, Edwin C. *The Human Side of the News.* New York: Walter J. Black, 1934. 226 pp.

This is a series of essays by a well-known radio commentator of the 1930s. They cover a variety of subjects including "the grip of the god of gold," Sherlock Holmes, Lloyds of London, and a Pullman porter.

705. Hilliard, Robert L., ed. *Radio Broadcasting: An Introduction to the Sound Medium.* 3rd ed. New York: Longman, 1985. 334 pp. ISBN: 0-532-28422-8.

Following a brief summary of radio's history, the editor presents articles on administration, operations, programming, sales, advertising, studio and operating facilities, format, writing, producing, directing, and performing. The first edition was published in 1967 and a second in 1974.

706. Hilliard, Robert L. *Writing for Television and Radio.* 4th ed. Belmont, CA: Wadsworth Publishing, 1984. 385 pp. (Wadsworth series in Mass Communication).

Not just a how-to book, this demonstrates the potential of the media to affect people's thinking and actions humanistically and to serve the public interest through improved programming. It was first published in 1962 and has been revised several times.

707. Hoffer, Jay. *Radio Production Techniques.* Blue Ridge Summit, PA: Tab Books, 1974. 192 pp. ISBN: 0-8360-3661-7.

Jay Hoffer was associated with KRAK radio in Sacramento and examines "all the myriad elements that go into the production aspects of a good sounding radio station." He emphasizes the "sound" itself and tells how to produce it at its various stages of development.

708. Hoffman, William G., and Ralph L. Rogers. *Effective Radio Speaking.* New York: McGraw-Hill, 1944. 241 pp.

The authors have put together a systematic discussion of what makes a good radio talk good and offer advice to speakers about obtaining the right scripts and then presenting the material effectively.

709. Holsopple, Curtis R. *Skills for Radio Broadcasters.* 3rd ed. Blue Ridge Summit, PA: Tab Books, 1988. 201 pp. ISBN: 0-8306-2930-0.

Inside information to broadcasters at all levels is provided in this book that emphasizes proficiency in learning the skills and responsibilities of a broadcaster. One section deals with the special needs of volunteer operators at non-commercial radio stations affiliated with schools and colleges.

710. Hood, James R., and Brad Kalbfeld, compilers and eds. *The Associated Press Broadcast News Handbook*. New York: Associated Press, 1982. 298 pp. ISBN: 0-917360-49-4.

Intended for radio and television writers and broadcasters, this provides a comprehensive look at the theory and practice of good broadcast news writing and combines text on the basics of good writing with a dictionary-like guide to the specifics of broadcast style. It also incorporates the text of the *AP Libel Manual*.

711. Hotaling, Burton L. *A Manual of Radio News Writing*. Milwaukee, WI: Milwaukee Journal, 1947. 62 pp.

The special problems of preparing radio news broadcasts are addressed in this book intended for those who are interested in radio news and already have some journalistic training. Its three sections are devoted to news style, news selection, and building the newscast. A revised edition was published in 1949.

712. Howe, Quincy. *The News and How to Understand It: in Spite of the Newspapers, in Spite of the Magazines, in Spite of the Radio*. New York: Simon & Schuster, 1940. 250 pp.

The author states "this is a how-to book about the news. It tells no inside story. It proposes no crusade. It has just one purpose--to show how you can get more pleasure and profit from following the news." His main vocation and avocation have been to interpret world news, he asserts.

713. Hulbert, Claude. *Learn to Write for Broadcasting.* London: Denis Archer, 1932. 128 pp.

The author wrote this book in response to requests for information on how to write effectively for broadcasting. He covers various types of writing, how to get ideas and inspiration, the actual writing of the manuscript, and ways to include humor, when appropriate.

714. Hybels, Saundra, and Dana Ulloth. *Broadcasting: An Introduction to Radio and Television.* New York: D. Van Nostrand, 1978. 320 pp. ISBN: 0-442-23625-5.

This textbook is designed for both introductory broadcasting and mass media courses and will also serve those who are seeking a career in broadcasting. It examines broadcast history, public broadcasting, cable, satellites, broadcast industry functions, and many important issues facing broadcasters.

715. Hyde, Stuart W. *Television and Radio Announcing.* 5th ed. Boston: Houghton Mifflin, 1987. 509 pp. ISBN: 0-395-35939-2.

A wide variety of topics are included in this updated textbook: careers, ad-libbing, working with equipment, pronunciation, voice, specialized techniques, news reporting, interviewing, commercials, and sports announcing. There is a special section on foreign pronunciation that includes several news stories featuring names and words in Spanish, German, French, and Italian as well as other languages. Editions were published in 1959, 1971, 1979, and 1983.

716. *INS Radio News Manual.* Rev. ed. New York: International News Service, 1947. 63 pp.

Originally presented as "a tour behind the teletypes to demonstrate how International News Service functions for its vast family of radio clients," this booklet has been revised to bring it up to date. The main sections are titled INS News on the Air, Newscasts and News Staffs, and Preparing the Newscast.

717. *The Job of the Radio Announcer.* Washington: Government Printing Office, 1946. 14 pp. (Occupational Brief, 87).

Spelled out in this pamphlet is what an announcer does, qualifications needed, earnings, and the outlook for employment. It was prepared for the education programs of the Armed Services by the Industrial Services Division, U.S. Employment Service, for returning WW II veterans.

718. Johnson, Joseph S., and Kenneth K. Jones. *Modern Radio Station Practices.* 2nd ed. Belmont, CA: Wadsworth Publishing, 1978. 418 pp. ISBN: 0-534-00550-0.

Approaching programming from a management view, the authors have expanded the section on production in this edition. It was published first in 1972, and its focus and purpose remain the same although the material has been updated.

719. Jordan, Edward C., et al. *Fundamentals of Radio.* New York: Prentice-Hall, 1942. 400 pp.

The purpose of this volume is to present the basic material required for all types of radio work, both civil and military. According to the preface the several authors have covered each topic in such a way as to make clear the functioning of a complete radio system.

720. Karr, Harrison M. *Your Speaking Voice.* Glendale, CA: Griffin-Patterson Publishing, 1938. 320 pp.

This is designed as a guide for those who desire to improve their everyday speaking voices, especially with an aim toward radio broadcasting. Practical advice and favorite exercises are included from "notable artists of the stage, screen, and platform," for example, radio's Kenny Baker, Lowell Thomas, and David Ross.

721. Kaufman, William I., ed. *How to Announce for Radio and Television*. New York: Hastings House, 1956. 95 pp.

Contributors to this volume include network announcers Richard Stark, Bill Cullen, Cy Harrice, John Reed King, Bob Stanton, Ed Herlihy, Joel Chaseman, Bud Collyer, Johnny Olsen, Carl King, and Norman Brokenshire.

722. Keating, Rex. *Grass Roots Radio*. London: International Planned Parenthood Federation, 1977. 67 pp. ISBN: 0-86089-008-2.

This is a manual for field workers in family planning and other areas of social and economic development. Its purpose is to instruct in certain basic elements of radio production and writing.

723. Keith, Alice. *How to Speak and Write for Radio: A Manual of Broadcasting Technique*. New York: Harper & Bros., 1944. 240 pp.

Written by the Director of Washington's National Academy of Broadcasting, this introduces materials for broadcasting, radio talks, interviews, news, sports, quiz shows, advertising commercials, music continuity, variety programs, and radio drama.

724. Keith, Alice, in collaboration with Larry Carl. *The Microphone and You*. New York: Hastings House, 1955. 58 pp.

An instruction manual intended for announcers, writers, speakers, and recording studio personnel, this explains how to write for and speak on radio, television, and the platform.

725. Keith, Michael C. *Production in Format Radio Handbook.* Lanham, MD: University Press of America, 1984. 206 pp. ISBN: 0-8191-3886-X.

The ways that program formats affect preparation of commercials are examined in this text. There is an analysis from a production perspective of ten such formats.

726. Kester, Max, and Edwin Collier. *Writing for the B.B.C.* London: Sir Isaac Pitman & Sons, 1937. 58 pp.

Practical hints are furnished in this handbook on how to write successfully for the Light Entertainment Department of the British Broadcasting Corporation.

727. Kilmer, Bill. *Announcing for Radio.* Des Moines: Sarcone Publishing, 1947. 96 pp.

Kilmer "seeks to point out the factors in effective radio speaking and to indicate the ways in which improvement may be achieved." He was an announcer for Des Moines radio station WHO at the time he wrote this book.

728. Kingston, Walter Krulevitch, and Rome Cowgill. *Radio Drama Acting and Production: A Handbook.* Rev. ed. New York: Rinehart, 1950. 373 pp. (Rinehart Radio series).

The revision of this handbook was generated by suggestions made by a number of radio acting teachers, along with the intent to create a text for radio production workshops. It includes a new section titled Fundamentals of Radio Acting, as well as a short play to provide a variety of acting experiences with a minimum of production.

729. Kirschner, Allen, and Linda Kirschner. *Radio and Television: Readings in the Mass Media.* New York: Odyssey Press, 1971. 301 pp.

The authors warn that there are no experts in the mass media, and this book will not make the reader an expert, but it may, however, help in understanding more fully both radio and television. The articles are divided into categories titled Form and Technique, Audience and Effect, and Critics and Criticism.

730. Kleiser, Grenville, compiler. *Radio Broadcasting: How to Speak Convincingly.* New York: Funk & Wagnalls, 1935. 286 pp.

The five main suggestions the author offers in this volume are (1) open your mouth well when you talk; (2) speak distinctly; (3) do not shout; (4) pronounce your words correctly; and (5) learn to read well.

731. Kris, Ernst, and Hans Speir. *German Radio Propaganda: Report on Home Broadcasts During the War.* London: Oxford University Press, 1944. 529 pp. (Studies of the Institute of World Affairs).

This book reports how German propagandists presented the events of the Second World War to the German people. It grew out of the research of a group of students who, for more than two years, joined in a cooperative effort to obtain these data.

732. Landry, Robert J. *Magazines and Radio Criticism.* Washington: National Association of Broadcasters, 1942. 14 pp.

This is a reprint of an answer to a criticism of American radio written by Curtis Nettels in a *New Republic* article. In his rebuttal which was published in *Variety*, Landry states there is "no bureaucracy in radio" and that the "quasi-independent radio industry of over 900 stations ... is more completely a democracy" and he writes about its controls, values, entertainment capabilities, and advertising policies.

733. Lawrence, Jerome, ed. *Off Mike: Radio Writing by the Nation's Top Radio Writers.* New York: Essential Books, 1944. 195 pp.

The contributors to this book are the people who have been "off mike" seven days and nights a week, pounding the typewriters, making with the words--words by the millions, the editor writes. He told each writer to "take down your back-hair and talk to us. Nothing fancy. Just talk. Let us know what goes on behind that typewriter." They did, and this book is the result.

734. Lawton, Sherman P. *Introduction to Modern Broadcasting: A Manual for Students.* New York: Harper & Row, 1963. 157 pp.

The projects in this volume are divided into activities, laboratory, and discussion, and they are all intended for beginners in radio. They range from demonstrating the use of audio equipment, marking scripts, and producing commercials to local news, interviews, and sports summaries.

735. Lawton, Sherman P. *The Modern Broadcaster: The Station Book.* New York: Harper & Brothers, 1961. 351 pp.

Intended for radio station employees, this describes station (but not network) jobs and emphasizes the work of sales, promotion, advertising, and announcing. It is written with the point of view that the industry must aim toward becoming a profession, and professionals must have a high sense of public responsibility and pride in standards; that is the author's main purpose.

736. Lawton, Sherman P. *Radio Continuity Types.* Boston: Expression Company, 1938. 529 pp.

This collection of radio continuity types was compiled for one purpose: to represent what continuity types were in common use at the time of publication. It offers a large selection of dramatic and talk continuities and fewer examples of "hybrids," novelties and specialties, and variety shows.

737. Lawton, Sherman P. *Radio Speech.* Boston: Expression Company, 1932. 453 pp.

Exercises and questions scattered throughout this textbook are meant to be more suggestive and conceptual rather than exhaustive and detailed. There are specimens of radio writing to assist the student in learning the basics about writing for the medium.

738. Leatherwood, Dowling. *Journalism on the Air.* Minneapolis: Burgess Publishing, 1939. 100 leaves.

The title page states this is an abridged textbook for a course in radio journalism, with laboratory and microphone exercises. It includes suggestions for readings from books and articles on the topic.

739. Levine, Carl R. *Producing Radio and Television Programs.* New York: Richards Rosen Press, 1982. 157 pp. (Student Journalist Guide series). ISBN: 0-8239-0559-4.

Discusses using radio and television to present school news and suggests ways to initiate, prepare, and produce such programs. The book is intended for student journalists and their advisors.

740. Lindsley, Charles Frederick. *Radio and Television Communication*. New York: McGraw-Hill, 1952. 492 pp.

The first purpose of this book is to familiarize the student with the influence which radio has on the thinking and behavior of society. It also aims to discipline the reader in critical and discriminating listening and to explain the various kinds of performances and the skills employed by the performers.

741. Lloyd James, Arthur. *The Broadcast Word*. London: Kegan Paul, Trench, & Trubner, 1935. 207 pp.

This is a compilation of talks, lectures, and essays that were originally written for the British Broadcasting Corporation and primarily for its Advisory Committee on Spoken English. Other chapters include six broadcast talks given in May and June 1932, a public lecture on speech and language in the world today, and a paper on standards in speech read before the Philological Society of Great Britain in December 1932. A reprint edition was published in 1971.

742. Longmate, Norman, compiler and ed. *Writing for the BBC*. 4th ed. London: British Broadcasting Corporation, 1974. 81 pp. ISBN: 0-563-12632-9.

The title page states this is "a guide for professional and part-time free lance writers on possible markets for their work within the British Broadcasting Corporation." In addition to general advice, it provides information on the BBC organization, the network production centers,

English and national regions, BBC external services, educational broadcasting, religious broadcasting, and local radio.

743. Lowell, Maurice. *Listen In: An American Manual of Radio.* New York: Dodge Publishing, 1937. 114 pp.

    Practical suggestions for the organization and operation of community radio groups are offered. The book contains information for script writers, artists, announcers, and directors about techniques applicable to their crafts and hints on seeking employment in the medium.

744. MacDonald, R.H. *A Broadcast News Manual of Style.* New York: Longman, 1987. 202 pp. ISBN: 0-582-99865-4.

    Actual newswriting examples, punctuation rules, correct spelling, accepted acronyms, abbreviations, and contractions are discussed. Standardization of script page format, weather reporting, and wire service material are covered. A special section contains a comprehensive usage guide featuring phonetic spelling and a list of words frequently mispronounced or misused.

745. May, Derwent, ed. *Good Talk: An Anthology from BBC Radio.* New York: Taplinger Publishing, 1969. 285 pp.

    Thirteen of the contributions in this book were first broadcast on what used to be the Home Service and is now Radio 4 while 14 were first broadcast on the Third Programme. They are arranged into five categories: People, Problems, Places, Imagination, and Fact.

746. Mayeux, Peter E. *Writing for the Broadcast Media.* Boston: Allyn & Bacon, 1985. 368 pp. ISBN: 0-205-08343-9.

The author states the principal objectives of this book are: (1) to provide a basic study of the script forms, approaches, and techniques used to write effective broadcast script material; (2) to instill an awareness of the role and responsibility of the writer, with emphasis on the audience, content, and impact of the broadcast media; (3) to apply the production and business principles of the broadcasting industry to the design and preparation of effective script material; and (4) to describe and emphasize the process involved in writing for the broadcast media.

747. McGill, Earle. *Radio Directing*. New York: McGraw-Hill, 1940. 370 pp.

Microphones, studios, sound effects, preparation for the broadcast, casting, the board fade, timing and pace, microphone rehearsal, dress rehearsal and air show, and types of productions are the main areas of this book.

748. McLeish, Robert. *The Technique of Radio Production*. 2nd ed. Stoneham, MA: Focal Press, 1988. 250 pp. ISBN: 0-240-51266-9.

All facets of radio broadcasting are covered with particular emphasis on national and local radio. The author describes disc jockey work, interviewing, news-reading, music recording, phone-ins, sequence and drama programming, news, sports commentary, documentaries, commercials, writing, and staff duties. The book was published first in 1978.

749. McWhinnie, Donald. *The Art of Radio*. London: Faber & Faber, 1959. 190 pp.

As he examines "the nature of the medium" of radio, the author divides it into three types of raw materials:

word, sound (music, natural sounds, "musique concrete," and radiophonic effects), and silence. Part two discusses "the participants," and the third part covers "the art as it exists."

750. Miles, Donald W. *Broadcast News Handbook*. Indianapolis: Howard W. Sams, 1975. 385 pp. ISBN: 0-672-21183-1.

Radio is used primarily as the model or "vehicle" for most of the text, and for the discussions, projects, and assignments because the author feels radio is the most practical and economical medium from a teaching standpoint. It is also the most convenient one in which to learn as a beginner in the field, and the country is filled with not just all-news radio stations but with all-news networks and audio services.

751. Miller, Bobby Ray, compiler and ed. *The UPI Stylebook: A Handbook for Writers and Editors*. New York: United Press International, 1977. 196 pp.

The primary purpose of this book is to achieve consistency in spelling, capitalization, punctuation, and usage for newspaper wires. It is intended to be a set of guidelines that reflect current usage so that radio and television broadcasters can do the best job possible with the written material they are provided. The volume is updated regularly.

752. Minkov, Mikail. *Radio Journalism*. Prague: International Organization of Journalists, 1980. 79 pp.

This presents the main features that define radio journalism, describes the creative process of journalistic activities on radio, and gives practical advice for the daily work of the journalist with a microphone.

222 Radio Broadcasting

753. Morgan, Edward P. *Clearing the Air.* Washington: Robert B. Luce, 1963. 267 pp.

    Morgan composed these essays between 1955 and 1962 when he reported the daily news from Washington, mostly by radio, and added some comment on it. They cover areas such as the American scene, international affairs, politics, people, labor and management, censorship, civil rights, holidays and heroes, and the press, radio, and television.

754. Morris, John, ed. *From the Third Programme: A Ten-Years' Anthology.* London: Nonesuch Press, 1956. 339 pp.

    Published to celebrate the completion of ten years of broadcasting by the British Broadcasting Corporation *Third Programme*, this reprints programs in the categories of imagination, argument, experience, and exposition. Among the contributors are V.S. Pritchett, Graham Greene, Elizabeth Bowen, Bertrand Russell, Max Beerbohm, E.M. Forster, Maxim Gorky, Edward Sackville-West, T.S. Eliot, Fred Hoyle, and Thomas Mann.

755. Mosse, Baskett. *Radio News Handbook.* Evanston, IL: Northwestern University Medill School of Journalism, 1947. 64 pp.

    This covers copy preparation, editing, style, the time element, quotations, names, punctuation, wire copy, one-minute summaries, news services, radio sign language, the Illinois Radio Libel Law, sample scripts, etc.

756. Mott, Frank Luther. *The News in America.* Cambridge, MA: Harvard University Press, 1952. 236 pp.

The main subject is the definition and description of news in the United States and the way it is assembled, edited, and disseminated. The author writes about a "typical" newsroom and visualizes a visit to the news department of a 50,000-watt station, WZZZ, which actually is a composite of the operations of WHO, Des Moines, and KGO, San Francisco.

757. Muggeridge, Douglas. *The News War of the Airwaves*. London: British Broadcasting Corporation, 1983. 11 pp.

This booklet contains the text of a speech to the Diplomatic and Commonwealth Writers Association in London on April 14, 1983, given by Muggeridge when he was Managing Director of British Broadcasting Corporation External Broadcasting.

758. Nagler, Frank. *Writing for Radio*. New York: Ronald Press, 1938. 160 pp.

Based on his own experience as Director of Radio for The Players Guild of Manhattan and author of over 300 radio plays, Nagler "tells it like it is." He covers the initial idea, creation of the plot, radio tools, drama, comedy, music, continuity, and "general considerations." He includes specimen scripts and listings of potential markets, advertising agencies, and radio stations.

759. National Association of Broadcasters. *Addresses at the 39th Annual Convention of the National Association of Broadcasters*. Washington: The Association, 1961. 39 pp.

Those speaking at the May 1961 convention were President John F. Kennedy, NAB President LeRoy Collins, FCC Chair Newton N. Minow, Secretary of Health, Education and Welfare Abraham Ribicoff, and

Justin Miller, recipient of NAB 1961 Distinguished Service Award and former President of the NAB.

760. National Association of Broadcasters. *Broadcast Automation: Ready--If You Are*. Washington: The Association, 1978. 44 pp.

Published jointly with the Broadcast Financial Management Association, this presents a comprehensive, industry-wide survey that attempts to answer a number of their members' questions such as: How does automation work? Do we really need it? How much? Can we partially automate? Who are the suppliers? If we buy, will it be obsolete in a few years?

761. National Association of Broadcasters. *Broadcasting in the United States*. Washington: The Association, 1933. 191 pp.

When the National University Extension Association announced in 1933 that one of its debate subjects would be whether the United States should adopt some of the essential features of the British system of radio operation and control, the NAB prepared this booklet. It presents some of the achievements of American broadcasting in order to help debaters in their arguments.

762. National Association of Broadcasters. *Editorializing on the Air*. 2nd ed. Washington: The Association, 1963. 16 pp.

First published in 1959, this report proposes guidelines to assist stations in the practice of editorializing. This edition represents a complete rewriting of the earlier text and has been expanded along with further NAB interpretation of the FCC's editorializing policies.

763. National Association of Broadcasters. *An Operational Guide for Broadcasting the News*. Washington: The Association, 1958. 30 pp.

Prepared by the Association's Freedom of Information Committee, this booklet includes a declaration of principles, the history of broadcast news, organization of a news department, editorials on the air, the right to know, and a code of conduct for the broadcast of public proceedings.

764. National Association of Broadcasters. *Radio Code of Good Practices*. Washington: The Association, 1962. 12 pp.

Promulgated in 1937, this code has been updated and revised periodically ever since. It covers various aspects of program standards (news, public issues, political broadcasts, religious programs, dramatic programs, children's shows, etc.) and advertising standards (time standards, presentation, acceptability of products, contests, premiums, etc.).

765. National Association of Broadcasters. *Radio News: A Primer for the Smaller Operation*. Washington: The Association, 1974. 25 pp.

"Drawn from the positive experiences of the men and women who run and staff the smaller market radio operations, (this) is meant to provide an exchange of practical ideas, all aimed at producing a sound radio news operation." It includes perspective, the wire and how it works, editing, actuality sources, using the telephone, and the tip system.

766. National Association of Broadcasters. *Radio Program Department Handbook*. Washington: The Association, 1975. 28 pp.

The front cover of this booklet calls it "a basic guide for the program director of a smaller operation." It includes information on programming, announcing, copy writing, music, news and program features, public service announcements, traffic, promotion, and publicity.

767. National Association of Broadcasters. *A Source for Public Service Programming.* Washington: The Association, 1973. 22 pp.

Lists of transcriptions, tapes, announcements, and other program material available for local broadcasting from government and civic organizations are in this directory. In addition to listing the name and address of each agency, it identifies the appropriate official to contact in requesting material.

768. National Association of Radio and Television Broadcasters. *Standards of Good Practice for Radio Broadcasters of the United States of America.* Rev. ed. Washington: The Association, 1955. 5 pp.

Originally circulated in 1937, these standards have been revised several times since then. They cover news, public issues, political broadcasts, advancement of education and culture, religion and religious programs, dramatic and children's programs, and general advertising standards.

769. National Broadcasting Company. *Broadcasting in the Public Interest.* New York: The Company, 1939. 80 pp.

Following an account of NBC's history in the pioneering of public service, this booklet itemizes the social responsibilities of the company. Its policies and standards are described, and the last section examines NBC programs.

770. National Broadcasting Company. *Broadcasting to All Homes*. New York: The Company, 1935. 4 vols.

These volumes consist of short, one-page, essays on subjects such as American radio culture, radio as entertainment, and improvement, along with thoughts by a variety of people, from Lord Reith of the British Broadcasting Corporation to the President of Columbia University, Nicholas Murray Butler. Interspersed are charts analyzing quality of NBC programming, sponsored and sustaining program hours, etc.

771. National Broadcasting Company. *The Fourth Chime*. New York: The Company, 1944. 174 pp.

"The Fourth Chime, a note added to the familiar NBC three-chime signal ... rings out from the NBC newsroom only when events of major historical importance occur ... as a confidential 'alert' to effect the immediate gathering of those members of the NBC news staffs, engineers and other operating personnel responsible for broadcasting the news to the people." Thus, the title of this book which tells the story of the NBC newsroom from 1931 through June 7, 1944.

772. National Broadcasting Company. *NBC Handbook of Pronunciation*. 3rd ed. New York: Thomas Y. Crowell, 1964. 418 pp.

Originally compiled by James F. Bender for the National Broadcasting Company in 1943, this became known as "the standard reference book on pronunciation in general American speech." This edition contains more than 20,000 entries, and many outdated ones have been deleted while new words have been introduced. A subsequent edition was edited by Eugene H. Ehrlich and published in 1984. (See item 1639)

228 Radio Broadcasting

773. National Broadcasting Company. *NBC Program Policies and Working Manual.* New York: The Company, 1944. 40 pp.

Policies are spelled out for all productions, news programs, public issues, medical accounts, children's programs, unacceptable business, and commercial standards.

774. National Broadcasting Company. *NBC Radio and Television Broadcast Standards.* New York: The Company, 1951. 46 pp.

This booklet interprets what NBC considers acceptable in the classifications of program content, advertising, and operating procedures. Specific areas mentioned are children's programs, news, religion, sex, dances, impersonations, trade name references, testimonials, premium offers, unrehearsed programs, courtesy announcements, and musical and literary material.

775. *National Morale and Radio.* Columbus: Ohio State University, 1941. 8 leaves (Evaluation of School Broadcasts Bulletin 18, rev.).

Because of the beginning of WW II, an analysis was made to determine the state of morale in a democracy and the part that radio could play in it. This bulletin proposes an agency that would coordinate the use of radio in building and sustaining morale based on scientific experimentation and research.

776. Newsom, Phil. *United Press Radio News Style Book.* New York: United Press Association, 1943. 42 pp.

The author assumes that the reader is already experienced in writing news for newspapers. He points out how this style should be altered in order to make the news stories as clear and effective when they are heard over the radio as they are when seen on the printed page.

777. Niggli, Josephina. *Pointers on Radio Writing.* Boston: The Writer, 1946. 101 pp.

Free-lance writers can succeed in five areas of radio writing that do not require specialization, according to the author. She explains how to write for documentary and education programs, serials (including soap operas, family, cliff hangers, and whodunits), series, dramatic adaptations and originals, and experimental shows.

778. Nisbett, Alec. *The Technique of the Sound Studio for Radio, Television and Film.* 3rd ed. New York: Hastings House, 1972. 559 pp. (Communication Arts Books). ISBN: 0-8038-7096-5.

First published in 1962, this continues the emphasis on general principles rather than rules-of-thumb and insists on the paramount importance of learning to use one's ears properly. Studio and location techniques are described in terms of what each operation does to the sound and why--"and what to listen for." A 4th edition was published in 1979.

779. Nisbett, Alec. *The Use of Microphones.* 2nd ed. London: Focal Press, 1983. 167 pp. (Media Manuals). ISBN: 0-240-51199-9.

Published first in 1974 and reprinted subsequently, this new edition "offers a wealth of tested know-how to professionals, students and amateurs alike." It is about monophonic sound as used for radio, television or film and discusses the many types of microphones available and the skills needed for creatively controlling sound performance transmission or recording.

780. O'Donnell, Lewis B., Philip Benoit, and Carl Hausman. *Modern Radio Production*. 2nd ed. Belmont, CA: Wadsworth Publishing, 1990. 316 pp. (Wadsworth series in Mass Communication). ISBN: 0-534-11622-1.

According to the authors new information was added to this edition until almost the day it rolled off the printing press, especially in the area of technology. Included is expanded coverage of digital recording, satellite feeds and programming services, and an entirely new chapter on digital computer technology in modern radio.

781. O'Donnell, Lewis B., Carl Hausman, and Philip Benoit. *Announcing: Broadcast Communicating Today*. Belmont, CA: Wadsworth Publishing, 1987. 338 pp. ISBN: 0-534-06582-1.

In order to provide both an academic and a practical guide to today's media announcer, this text enumerates the principles of good communication and the specific skills and techniques required. Interviewing, television news announcing, and commercials are among the areas covered.

782. Oringel, Robert S. *Audio Control Handbook for Radio and Television Broadcasting*. 5th ed. New York: Hastings House, 1983. 313 pp. (Communication Arts Books).

The technical and electronic aspects of audio recording for television and radio broadcasting are presented in this non-technical, step-by-step introduction to the field. Focal Press of Boston published a 6th edition in 1989.

783. Orlik, Peter B. *Broadcast Copywriting*. 3rd ed. Boston: Allyn & Bacon, 1986. 618 pp. ISBN: 0-205-08750-7.

The author states that this treats the special requirements and pitfalls of creating the continuity and commercials that are such a central part of the broadcast industry. It is geared toward the basic building blocks of radio and television writing: station IDs, program promos, public service announcements (PSAs), and commercials.

784. Paley, William S. *The Freedom of Radio*. New York: Columbia Broadcasting System, 1944. 18 pp.

    This pamphlet contains the statement of CBS President Paley before the Senate Commerce Committee at a hearing on Senate Bill S. 814, the White-Wheeler Bill, in Washington on November 9, 1943.

785. Paley, William S. *Radio and Its Critics*. New York: Columbia Broadcasting System, 1946. 29 pp.

    The text of an address made by Paley, then Chairman of the Board of CBS, is contained in this booklet. The speech was given at the 24th annual convention of the National Association of Broadcasters in Chicago on October 22, 1946.

786. Paley, William S. *Radio As a Cultural Force*. New York: Columbia Broadcasting System, 1934. 29 pp.

    These notes on the economic and social philosophy of America's radio industry represent the policies and practices of CBS. They were part of a talk CBS President Paley gave to the FCC in its inquiry into proposals to allot fixed percentages of the nation's radio facilities to non-commercial broadcasting.

787. Payne, George Henry. *The Fourth Estate and Radio, and Other Addresses*. Boston: The Microphone Press, 1936. 111 pp.

At the time he wrote this book Payne was a Federal Communications Commissioner and much in demand as a speaker. This is a collection of his talks on safeguarding the public interest, the Federal Communications Act, standards in broadcasting, Otto H. Kahn, Grover Cleveland, Theodore Roosevelt, and the Fourth Estate and radio.

788. Peck, William A. *Anatomy of Local Radio-TV Copy.* 4th ed. Blue Ridge Summit, PA: Tab Books, 1976. 95 pp. ISBN: 0-306-8306-X.

Some of the chapter titles in this book are: Writing Commercials: Creativity and Influence; The Making of Ideas; The Right Words; Motivating the Consumer; Sale Copy and the Sale; The Short Spot; Production Technique; and The Stinger. It is intended to help the reader learn the fundamentals of writing good commercial copy.

789. Pedrick, Gale. *Profitable Scriptwriting for TV and Radio.* London: C. Arthur Pearson, 1961. 204 pp.

A former British Broadcasting Corporation script writer discusses how to go about writing scripts for broadcast. He writes from his own experience of more than 30 years. His topics are fashions in broadcasting, the American influence, the writing of comedy, collaboration, adaptations, and the necessity for and function of an agent.

790. Peet, Creighton. *All About Broadcasting.* New York: Alfred A. Knopf, 1942. 66 pp.

Intended for children, this book describes in basic elementary terms just what radio broadcasting is. It is presented in a narrative format that combines the experiences of a young boy and his father visiting New York and a non-technical presentation of behind-the-scenes radio broadcasting.

791. Phillips, David C., John M. Grogan, and Earl H. Ryan. *Introduction to Radio and Television*. New York: Ronald Press, 1954. 423 pp.

An introductory survey of the subject, this book combines practical information on the production of broadcasts with background material on the development of the industry, its organization, operations, and special problems. It concentrates on current procedures and problems in the industry, such as how stations are organized and equipped, what constitutes successful programming, and production.

792. Poindexter, Ray. *Golden Throats and Silver Tongues: The Radio Announcers*. Conway, AR: River Road Press, 1978. 233 pp.

The author states it is his purpose in this book to portray the significance of the roles played by radio announcers, especially during the early years of radio. He writes about well-known personalities as well as dozens of lesser-known announcers of news, sports, comedy shows, etc.

793. *The Radio Boys*. Chicago: M.A. Donahue; New York: A.L. Burt, 1922- .

Under the basic title *The Radio Boys*, several publishers (and authors) during the 1920s created this series of stories for boys of all ages. Among the titles are *Radio Boys Under the Sea* (J.W. Duffield), *Radio Boys Loyalty, or Bill Brown Listens In* (Wayne Whippe and S.F. Aaron), *The Radio Boys with the Revenue Guards*

(Gerald Breckenridge), and *The Radio Boys with the Iceberg Patrol, or Making Safe the Ocean Lanes* (Allen Chapman).

794. Reck, Franklin M. *Radio from Start to Finish.* New York: Thomas Y. Crowell, 1942. 160 pp.

   Published in association with the Junior Literary Guild, this is a history of radio intended for junior and senior high school students. It is primarily about radio as it was operated prior to WW II, the personnel involved, and the type of work performed.

795. Redfern, Barrie. *Local Radio.* London: Focal Press, 1978. 164 pp. (Media Manuals). ISBN: 0-240-50980-3; 0-8038-4311-9.

   Concentrating on British radio, this book is intended to provide an insight into local radio and the way radio work varies considerably from station to station. Chapters cover studio and recording rooms, sources, manual and automatic controls, cue and talk back, cartridges, transmission, logging, transmitter monitoring, production, editing, and programming.

796. Roberts, Holland D., Helen Fox Rachford, and Elizabeth Goudy. *Airlanes to English.* New York: McGraw-Hill, 1942. 501 pp.

   This is a guide to speaking, listening, reading, and writing, through speech and radio. It contains materials on strange ways of everyday speech and radio, speech down the ages, the ABCs of radio, and producing a script.

797. Robinson, Ernest H. *Broadcasting and a Changing Civilisation*. London: The Bodley Head, 1935. 156 pp. (The Twentieth Century Library).

Among the topics addressed by the author are broadcasting in the home, the appreciation of music, broadcast drama, education and the use of leisure, broadcasting and sport, religion and the British Broadcasting Corporation, propaganda, and international relations.

798. Rogers, Ralph. *Do's and Don'ts of Radio Writing*. Boston: Associated Radio Writers, 1937. 104 pp.

When he couldn't find what he wanted available on the market, the author decided to write "a handy, practical, boiled-to-the-bone working guide containing thoroughly tested 'firing line' helps which could be referred to instantly and applied immediately to the task at hand." This volume is the result.

799. Root, Wells. *Writing the Script: A Practical Guide for Films and Television*. New York: Holt, Rinehart & Winston, 1979. 210 pp. ISBN: 0-03-044226-5.

The discussions in this book came out of extension courses offered by UCLA and taught by Root. They deal primarily with technique, craftsmanship and fundamentals of original stories, conflict, suspense, theme and content, emotion, characterization, and acquisition of an agent.

800. Routt, Edd. *Dimensions of Broadcast Editorializing*. Blue Ridge Summit, PA: Tab Books, 1974. 204 pp. ISBN: 0-8306-3697-8.

In an attempt to encourage broadcasters to write and air more and stronger editorials, the author describes the nature of the medium and contrasts broadcasting with print. He explains the FCC rules and protection of the First Amendment and then discusses how to write and deliver editorials, the editorial practices of a variety of radio stations nationally and in small-to-medium markets.

801. *RTNDA Communicator*. Washington: Radio-Television News Directors Association. ISSN: 0033-7153.

In 1971 this monthly publication superceded the *RTNDA Bulletin* which had begun publication in 1946. It is the "official magazine" of the Association and emphasizes news broadcasting and freedom of information.

802. Rubenstein, Paul Max, and Martin J. Maloney. *Writing for the Media: Film, Television, Video, and Radio*. Rev. ed. Englewood Cliffs, NJ: Prentice-Hall, 1988. 290 pp. ISBN: 0-13-971508-8.

Originally written by Martin Maloney and published under the title *Writing for the Media* in 1980, this revision offers the basics of writing material, such as how to move a story forward, when to begin or end a scene, what body copy is, etc. The most extensive chapters include writing, pitching the story and selling it, coming up with a high concept, and transposing the treatment into a usable script.

803. Ryan, J. Harold. *Radio's Public Service in Time of War*. Washington: National Association of Broadcasters, 1944. 14 pp.

The text of an address presented to the State of New York Department of Health State Conference given by then National Association of Broadcasters President Ryan in July 1944 is published in this pamphlet.

804. Sarnoff, David. *The Message of Radio.* New York: National Broadcasting Company, 1936. 16 pp.

An address on the uses of radio delivered on June 29, 1936, before the 32nd Annual Convention of the Advertising Federation of America.

805. Sarnoff, David. *Radio Communication and Its Import in International Relations.* New York: RCA, 1946. 10 pp.

This pamphlet contains the text of a talk given by General Sarnoff at the Princeton University Bi-Centennial Conference on Engineering and Human Affairs on October 3, 1946.

806. Schechter, A.A. *"Go Ahead, Garrison!" A Story of News Broadcasting.* New York: Dodd, Mead, 1941. 237 pp.

The hero of this novel is Pat Garrison, a recent journalism school graduate, who is a newsman for ABC.

807. Schlosser, Herbert S. *Broadcasters in a Free Society: Common Problems, Common Purpose.* London: British Broadcasting Corporation, 1976. 16 pp. (BBC Lunch-Time Lectures, 10th series, 5). ISBN: 0-563-17087-5.

In celebration of the National Broadcasting Company's 50th year, its President, Herbert S. Schlosser, gave this lecture in the Concert Hall at Broadcasting House, London, on February 12, 1976.

808. Seidle, Ronald J. *Air Time.* Boston: Holbrook Press, 1977. 296 pp. ISBN: 0-205-05602-4.

Divided into studio time, station time, and changing time, the author covers radio and television studios, broadcasting electronics, the history of the medium, station organization, affiliation, and regulation. He tells who's responsible for what, who makes what decisions, and the sort of training and background needed for most positions.

809. Seldes, George. *The Facts Are: A Guide to Falsehood and Propaganda in the Press and Radio.* New York: In Fact, Inc., 1942. 127 pp.

Using copies of newspaper and magazine articles and political cartoons to supplement his text, Seldes asks if the entire press is corrupt and instructs his audience how to read the war news. The last part of the book is a summing up of the people vs. the press and radio, and Seldes offers suggestions concerning what he thinks can be done about the situation.

810. Sergio, Lisa. *Radio--The Conquest of Our Time.* New York: Town Hall, 1939. 31 pp. (A Town Hall pamphlet).

This is the text of an address delivered at Town Hall on January 4, 1939. Sergio began her career as a commentator in 1933 and spoke from personal knowledge as well as a deep interest in the history of broadcasting.

811. Seymour, Katharine, and John T.W. Martin. *How to Write for Radio.* New York: Longmans, Green, 1931. 232 pp.

The authors try to answer questions such as Does radio drama differ fundamentally from play writing or from short-story writing? and How does writing radio advertising differ from writing printed advertising copy? They relate the early history of radio writing, discuss "straight" continuity, dramatic radio writing, and radio adaptations.

812. Seymour, Katharine, and John T.W. Martin. *Practical Radio Writing*. London: Longmans, Green, 1938. 308 pp.

The subtitle of this book is "The Technique of Writing for Broadcasting Simply and Thoroughly Explained"--a concise, apt statement of its contents.

813. Short, K.R.M., ed. *Film & Radio Propaganda in World War II*. Knoxville: University of Tennessee Press, 1983. 341 pp. ISBN: 0-87049-386-8.

Divided into aspects of the Allied experience, propaganda in Fascist Europe, and Japanese propaganda, this contains articles written by various contributors. Erik Barnouw's essay is on Radio Luxembourg in 1944 and 1945, Gordon Daniels presents an overview of Japanese domestic radio between 1937 and 1945, and Namikawa Ryō offers a personal view of Japanese overseas radio broadcasting.

814. Siepmann, Charles A. *Radio in Wartime*. New York: Oxford University Press, 1942. 32 pp. (America in a World at War, 26).

"This pamphlet describes and summarizes the effect of radio on the conduct and impact of modern war. It shows how modern strategy literally depends on use of radio communication and describes, too, the 'fourth front' of propaganda warfare which radio has opened up."

815. Siepmann, Charles A. *The Radio Listener's Bill of Rights: Democracy, Radio and You*. New York: Anti-Defamation League of B'nai B'rith, 1948. 52 pp.

One of the Freedom Pamphlets, this publication was designed to present facts about radio, ideas for action, and "a sketch of radio as it is and as it might be" if listeners played their part and contributed their share of thought and effort. The author states "radio is yours, to make, or to mar by default of ignorance, indifference or inertia."

816. Siepmann, Charles A. *Radio, Television and Society.* New York: Oxford University Press, 1950. 410 pp.

"The first purpose of the book is to bring to the general reader the history of a cultural revolution and to show what has been discovered by research concerning the effects of radio and television upon our tastes, opinions, and values. The second purpose is to deal with broadcasting as a reflection of our time and to throw light upon the problems of free speech, propaganda, public education, our relations with the rest of the world, and upon the concept of democracy itself."

817. Siepmann, Charles A. *Radio's Second Chance.* Boston: Little, Brown, 1946. 282 pp.

Siepmann states that this book is "addressed to the listener, the citizen who must ask the questions and demand the answers ... (it) examines the performance of a great industry on which the health of our democracy depends to a degree that is frightening to the ordinary citizen who stops to think about it."

818. Sieveking, Lance. *The Stuff of Radio.* London: Cassell, 1934. 414 pp.

In addition to chapters on theory and experience, the author chose eight examples from his own plays and provides full text so they could be presented. The appendices cover "the dramatic control-panel," the scoring of radio-works, and "a glance at the future of broadcasting."

819. Siller, Bob, Ted White, and Hal Terkel. *Television and Radio News*. New York: Macmillan, 1960. 227 pp.

Written by two network and one independent radio station professionals, this is based on their own experiences as well as interviews with news executives and questionnaires completed by radio and television stations throughout the country. They draw upon all these data and experiences to present a practical way of handling various problems. The book is divided equally between the two media.

820. Siller, Robert C. *Guide to Professional Radio & TV Newscasting*. Blue Ridge Summit, PA: Tab Books, 1972. 223 pp. ISBN: 0-8306-2535-6.

In a sense this is a how-to book, according to the author who writes that his purpose was to produce a "primer" on newscasting for radio and television. He sets down the basic information needed in order to pursue a career before the microphone or camera.

821. Singletary, Michael W. *Readings in Radio and Television News*. Shippensburg, PA: Michael W. Singletary, 1976. 197 pp.

Compiled, edited and assembled by Singletary, this volume is a selection of reproduced articles divided into several sections titled: Verbal and Visual Aspects of Radio-Television News; Local Radio and Television News; Perception of the Communicator; Values, Professionalism and Research Applications in Radio-TV News; National and International Reporting; and Some Reported Effects of Radio-TV News.

822. Skornia, Harry J., and Jack William Kitson, eds. *Problems and Controversies in Television and Radio*. Palo Alto, CA: Pacific Books, 1968. 503 pp.

Articles emphasizing radio broadcasting were contributed by Carl J. Friedrich, Evelyn Sternberg, Edward P. Morgan, H.V. Kaltenborn, and Albert Namurois. Most of the other essays in the book discuss radio/television together, and a few concentrate only on TV.

823. Skornia, Harry J., Robert H. Lee, and Fred A. Brewer. *Creative Broadcasting: With Twelve Scripts for Broadcast.* New York: Prentice-Hall, 1950. 407 pp.

Part I provides information needed by groups who are beginning to work in radio production and have limited means and facilities. The second part reprints the scripts that are free for broadcast as well as for classroom use and are graded in type and length and accompanied by complete production notes.

824. Slide, Anthony, ed. *Selected Radio and Television Criticism.* Metuchen, NJ: Scarecrow Press, 1987. 213 pp. ISBN: 0-8108-1942-2.

Critical comments on radio programs, television shows, personalities, and celebrities from the late 1920s through the 1950s are reprinted in their entirety. They originally appeared in newspapers and magazines, and some were written by John Crosby, Gilbert Seldes, Herb Golden, Philip Hamburger, Philip Minoff, and Dorothy Thompson.

825. Smeyak, G. Paul. *Broadcast News Writing.* Columbus, OH: Copyright Grid, 1977. 202 pp. ISBN: 0-88244-114-0.

Broadcast news stories are examined in four parts--lead, organization, grammar, and style. Additional chapters cover news judgments, sources, legal judgments, news organization, formats and formulas. A second edition was published in 1983.

826. Smith, Anthony. *Licenses and Liberty: the Future of Public Service Broadcasting*. London: Acton Society Trust, 1985. 19 pp. ISBN: 0-85000-0211.

The third annual John Logie Baird Lecture was presented by Smith, the Director of the British Film Institute, in July 1985.

827. Smythe, Ted C., and George A. Mastroianni, eds. *Issues in Broadcasting: Radio, Television, and Cable*. Palo Alto, CA: Mayfield, 1975. 430 pp. ISBN: 0-87484-330-8.

A variety of articles are presented under categories titled Entertainment, News, Advertising, Government and Broadcasting, Cable Television, Public Broadcasting, International Broadcasting, and Technology and Its Application in Broadcasting. Among the contributors are Wilbur Schramm, Bill Davidson, Douglas O'Connor, Dan Rather, Fred Friendly, Harry J. Skornia, Sig Mickelson, and Herbert I. Schiller.

828. Soley, Lawrence C. *Radio Warfare: OSS and CIA Subversive Propaganda*. Westport, CT: Praeger, 1989. 249 pp. ISBN: 0-275-93051-3.

United States radio propaganda during WW II is examined in detail in this volume as the author analyzes its impact on U.S. postwar strategy. He based much of his writing on recently declassified documents from the National Archives and the British Records Office in order to describe the wartime covert radio operations in detail.

829. Steinberg, Charles S., ed. *Broadcasting: The Critical Challenges*. New York: Hastings House, 1974. 315 pp. (Communication Arts Books). ISBN: 0-8038-0748-1.

This volume is based on the proceedings of the Third Annual Faculty/Industry Seminar of the International Radio and Television Society held at the Tarrytown House Conference Center in 1973. It was devoted to the critical challenges facing broadcasting in the 1970s, what they are and what can be done about them.

830. Stephens, Mitchell. *Broadcast News*. 2nd ed. New York: Holt, Rinehart & Winston, 1986. 360 pp. ISBN: 0-03-071753-1.

The author states that his primary goals in preparing this edition were to strengthen the discussions of television journalism, of radio documentaries, and of reporting in general. He has divided the book into several sections: writing, reporting, producing, television, and the profession itself, and has included updated information in all areas.

831. Stevenson, Wilf, and Nick Smedley, eds. *Responses to the White Paper*. London: British Film Industry, 1989. 85 pp. (The Broadcasting Debate, 3). ISBN: 0-85170-253-8.

The White Paper, "Broadcasting in the '90s: Competition, Choice and Quality," evolved from the 1986 Peacock Report on BBC radio and television. The Stevenson and Smedley publication presents a broad overview of some of the main submissions sent to the government in response to the White Paper and attempts to present a cross-section of the views of the major interested parties.

832. Subcommittee of the Committee on Interstate and Foreign Commerce. U.S. House of Representatives. *Broadcast Editorializing*. Washington: Government Printing Office, 1964. 458 pp.

These hearings were held on a bill to amend the Communications Act of 1934 in order to assure fairness in editorializing by radio and television station licensees in support of or in opposition to candidates for public office by making the equal opportunities provisions of section 315 applicable thereto.

833. Thompson, Dorothy. *Listen, Hans.* Boston: Houghton Mifflin, 1942. 292 pp.

The Thompson broadcasts in this volume were addressed to a personal friend in Germany and were transmitted over the short-wave facilities of CBS as part of its programming to Europe. They were aired every Friday between March and September 1942 and were generated by Thompson's deep conviction that politics was a prime instrument of the war and that was an area with which she was extremely familiar and knowledgeable.

834. Thomson, David Cleghorn. *Radio Is Changing Us.* London: Watts, 1937. 143 pp.

The subtitle states this is a survey of radio development and its problems in our changing world. The book examines the problems affecting broadcasting, the growth of radio, the man and the machinery, and the programs and the public.

835. Tooley, Howard. *The Radio Handbook: Suggestions for the Radio Director and Technician.* Minneapolis: Northwestern Press, 1941. 112 pp.

Among the various ideas is a calendar of historical dates that would suggest special radio shows. A glossary of radio "lingo" and sign language, and instructions on how to create 50 different sound effects provide additional help.

836. Turnbull, Robert B. *Radio and Television Sound Effects*. New York: Rinehart, 1951. 334 pp.

According to the author a few chapters here and there in books on production and writing cover about all that has been written on radio and TV sound effects, and these few are discussed from the producer's or writer's side. In this book the data are presented from the sound technician's viewpoint, and it is intended to explain just what part sound plays in radio and TV drama, how it is affected by writing and production, what some of the problems are in the field, and how they are solved.

837. Tyler, Kingdon S. *Modern Radio*. New York: Harcourt, Brace, 1944. 238 pp.

Because he feels that listeners do not have any idea how modern radio stations, networks, and receivers operate, the author attempts to clear up such radio mysteries. He explains in separate chapters all the aspects of radio from the studio, control room, transmitter, receiving antenna, and finally through the radio set to the loud-speaker.

838. Tyler, Poyntz, ed. *Television and Radio*. New York: H.W. Wilson, 1961. 192 pp. (The Reference Shelf, Vol. 33, No. 6).

In his preface the editor states that this book "simply presents the findings and the views of thoughtful men in the hope that these views, from both within and without the industry, will guide and encourage the reader to arrive at his (her) own conclusions." The articles appeared in *Atlantic Monthly, The Reporter, Harper's, Newsweek, Saturday Review, Holiday, Fortune,* and several other periodicals.

839. Tyler, Tracy F., ed. *Radio As a Cultural Agency.* Washington: National Committee on Education by Radio, 1934. 150 pp.

This volume contains the proceedings of a national conference titled "The Use of Radio As a Cultural Agency in a Democracy" held in Washington in May 1934.

840. U.S. Office of War Information. *When Radio Writes for War.* Washington: Government Printing Office, 1943. 14 pp.

Prepared at the request of the nation's radio writers, this is a digest of practical suggestions on wartime radio scripts.

841. Van Loon, Hendrik Willem. *Air-Storming.* New York: Harcourt, Brace, 1935. 307 pp.

This is a collection of 40 radio talks delivered by the author over the stations of the National Broadcasting Company on Sunday and Thursday evenings in 1935. By and large, he writes, these "little exhortations" are published in the way in which they were originally written and, as expected, broadcast.

842. Wagner, Paul H. *Radio Journalism.* Minneapolis: Burgess Publishing, 1940. 134 leaves.

The author presents to students interested in radio and/or journalism the basic techniques and problems of newscasting, not only as it is practiced in 1940, but as he assumes it will be practiced in the future. Part of this information was presented earlier in his master's thesis at the University of Wisconsin, but additional material has been incorporated.

843. Walters, Roger L. *Broadcast Writing: Principles and Practice.* New York: Random House, 1988. 515 pp. ISBN: 0-394-33089-7.

Organized into four parts and 18 chapters, this paperback textbook emphasizes principles such as aural style, script mechanics, program structure, handling sound and visuals, sponsors, audiences, and persuasion in broadcast messages. Specific program types are described and their special needs are described along with hints about handling material for these formats.

844. Waples, Douglas, ed. *Print, Radio, and Film in a Democracy.* Chicago: University of Chicago Press, 1942. 197 pp.

This volume consists of ten papers on the administration of mass communications in the public interest that were read before the 6th Annual Institute of the University of Chicago Graduate School in 1941. The one essay on radio was written by Paul F. Lazarsfeld and was titled "The Effects of Radio on Public Opinion."

845. Warren, Carl. *Radio News Writing and Editing.* New York: Harper & Brothers, 1947. 439 pp.

Dealing directly with the preparation of news to be broadcast, this has its emphasis on processing rather than the gathering or delivering of news, and on straight news rather than comment. It is intended to be "a teachable, readable, and practical text" in the subject.

846. Weaver, J. Clark. *Broadcast Copywriting As Process: A Practical Approach to Copywriting for Radio and Television.* New York: Longman, 1984. 139 pp.

To help beginning writers gain essential skills, this book is divided into Prewriting, Writing, and Rewriting, with detailed explanations of each stage that cover language, copywriting, and commercials.

847. Weaver, J. Clark. *Broadcast Newswriting As Process*. New York: Longman, 1950. 148 pp. ISBN: 0-582-284538.

This is intended to teach how to write a quality lead, develop a story, devise a logical conclusion, and identify news in relation to human wants, needs and desires. It contains techniques for developing a newswriting style, and preparation for entering the newswriting profession.

848. Weaver, Luther. *The Technique of Radio Writing*. New York: Prentice-Hall, 1948. 593 pp.

Each script in this collection illustrates a specific technical radio writing problem and shows the varying success achieved in its solution. The author has chapters on areas such as theme music and sound effects as well as the usual topics of drama, news, and religious programs.

849. Webster, Bethuel M., Jr. *Our Stake in the Ether*. New York: New York University, 1931. 14 pp.

This is the text of an address given by the Former General Counsel of the Federal Radio Commission under the auspices of the American Academy of Air Law and The New York University School of Law on April 10, 1931.

850. West, Robert. *The Rape of Radio*. New York: Rodin Publishing, 1941. 546 pp.

Chapter titles include: Mikephobia; The Cult of Announcer; Radio Drama Advances; Music, Listen My Children; Major Bowes; Radio Comedians Are Such

Unfunny People; The Church of the Air; Propaganda Rules the Waves; Radio Era of Sports; Censorship; Politics; The Sins of the Sponsor; Public Wants; and Can a Mike Teach?

851. West, Robert. *So-o-o-o You're Going on the Air*. New York: Rodin Publishing, 1934. 215 pp.

Combined with *The Radio Speech Primer*, this book tells what to do when facing the microphone, discusses "comics of the ether," radio music, drama, sponsors, announcers, educational radio, religious broadcasting, fans, women and radio success, and radio's future. The Speech Primer compares faulty radio speech with correct radio speech and includes the "West voice and personality test chart for radio speakers."

852. Whipple, James. *How to Write for Radio*. New York: McGraw-Hill, 1938. 425 pp.

The author states "the sole purpose of this book is to acquaint professional writers, and those who have aspirations to cultivate ability for successful radio writing, with the many basic differences between writing for the radio and writing in other fields of literature ... The material used in this book includes practical examples of all types of radio programs with an analysis of the technique involved in each distinct type."

853. Whitaker-Wilson, Cecil. *Writing for Broadcasting*. London: A. & C. Black, 1935. 150 pp. (Black's Writers' & Artists' Library, 2).

In addition to providing examples of written dramas, the author covers both high and low comedy, burlesque and satire, biographical plays, musical comedy, and historical plays. He touches on characterization, pageants, and the writing and broadcasting of talks.

854. White, Melvin R. *Beginning Radio Production.* Minneapolis: Northwestern Press, 1950. 208 pp.

Written to provide the necessary fundamentals to assist any individual or group of individuals achieve skill in broadcasting, this addresses the production problems of high schools, colleges, universities, little theatres, or church groups. It is intended primarily to develop the basic knowledge and skills essential to the radio worker and not to correct speech, teach reading, or offer training in thinking and expression while on one's feet.

855. White, Melvin R. *Microphone Technique for Radio Actors.* Minneapolis: Northwestern Press, 1950. 54 pp.

This guide describes the correct use of a microphone, including adjustment of its position to suit the volume and pitch of the voice and the avoidance of extraneous noises such as heavy breathing or rattling of the script. It presents a series of exercises to train the actor in conversational style, whispers, shouting, reading, oratory, pauses, etc.

856. White, Melvin R. *Radio Scripts for Practice and Broadcast.* Minneapolis: Northwestern Press, 1950. 208 pp.

Prepared as a workbook to accompany White's *Beginning Radio Production (see item 854)*, this includes material of varying degrees of difficulty. Some require relatively easy characterizations, sound effects and general production activity, while others require more microphone technique and elaborate music and sound.

857. White, Paul W. *News on the Air*. New York: Harcourt, Brace, 1947. 420 pp.

In an author's note White writes that this is actually two books in one: a textbook for beginners attracted to the profession, and a book for those who are full-fledged members of the radio journalism craft. He offers advice on writing and preparing a news program and provides examples of press association copy and scripts.

858. White, Ted, Adrian J. Meppen, and Steve Young. *Broadcast News Writing, Reporting, and Production*. New York: Macmillan, 1984. 314 pp.

New technical developments and techniques have been incorporated into this text with a major emphasis on developing writing and reporting skills. Some basic technical details are provided to introduce the reader to the subject, but they are not intended to train technicians.

859. Williams, Marynelle. *Script-easers: for Radio Commercial Writers*. Richmond, VA: Dietz Printing, 1944. 227 pp.

One- or two-sentence introductions are provided for a variety of commercial subjects: agriculture, automotive, bakery, banks, beverages, books, bowling, Christmas buying, Christmas ads directed to children, circulator heat, men's clothes, dairy, food, footwear, fuel, greetings, headache remedies, insulation, jewelers, laundry, music, newspapers, restaurants, refrigerators, home furnishings, seasonal, soap, sports tie-ins, and women.

860. Willis, Edgar E. *Foundations in Broadcasting: Radio and Television*. New York: Oxford University Press, 1951. 439 pp.

The author had two purposes in mind when he wrote this book: (1) to provide a foundation on which advanced courses in specific phases of radio and television could be based, and (2) to serve as a general introduction to broadcasting for those who will not take other courses in the field.

861. Willis, Edgar E. *Writing Television and Radio Programs.* New York: Holt, Rinehart & Winston, 1967. 372 pp.

In the preface the author states the objective of this book is to provide practical instruction for those seeking a career in broadcasting. The principal program types in American radio and TV writing are discussed, and there is a chapter on writing commercials.

862. Willis, Edgar E., and Camille D'Arienzo. *Writing Scripts for Television, Radio, and Film.* New York: Holt, Rinehart & Winston, 1981. 322 pp. ISBN: 0-03-052706-6.

Published originally in 1967 under the title *Writing Television and Radio Scripts* by Edgar E. Willis, this is meant to provide practical instruction for those seeking careers in broadcasting and film, and to help guide students who are not interested in writing professionally toward attaining fruitful creative experiences.

863. Wimer, Arthur, and Dale Brix. *Workbook for Radio and TV News Editing and Writing.* 5th ed. Dubuque, IA: Wm. C. Brown, 1980. 302 pp.

Based on advice from writers and editors with radio, television and newspaper experience, the authors provide material for use in training students to prepare news for radio and television broadcasting. They include a style manual, a list of common errors to avoid, hints on putting the newscast together, briefs, weather, humor, a

254 Radio Broadcasting

pronunciation dictionary, and numerous rewriting and newscasts exercises.

864. Winfield, Betty Houchin, and Lois B. DeFleur. *The Edward R. Murrow Heritage: Challenge for the Future*. Ames: Iowa State University Press, 1986. 113 pp. ISBN: 0-8138-1191-0.

Murrow set the standards of what to say and how to say it, according to the authors, as they look at these standards in terms of the changing communications industry and its technologies. They discuss the problems he faced covering WW II and interpret the increasingly adversarial press/government relationships. As one recent *Time* reader wrote, "he sounded like God's older brother."

865. Wolverton, Mike. *Reality on Reels: How to Make Documentaries for Video/Radio/Film*. Houston, TX: Gulf Publishing, 1983. 196 pp. ISBN: 0-87201-776-1.

Wolverton states "the documentary is indeed alive and well and living on television with frequent and effective appearances on radio and audio cassette." He advises how to keep the genre healthy and provides basic information on creating, producing, editing, and finally, marketing documentaries.

866. *Write Broadcast Feature Copy*. Washington: Government Printing Office, 1985. 26 pp.

Prepared by the Department of the Army's Office of Public Affairs, this is a manual to train soldiers to identify sources and conduct feature research, identify the five types of features, write radio and television features using the proper format, and ensure features conform to Public Affairs policies and Army regulations.

867. Wulfemeyer, K. Tim. *Beginning Broadcast Newswriting: A Self-Instructional Learning Experience*. 2nd ed. Ames: Iowa State University Press, 1984. 78 pp. ISBN: 0-8138-0210-5.

This workbook is intended to familiarize the student with some of the basic styles, principles, and techniques of broadcast newswriting.

868. Wulfemeyer, K. Tim. *Broadcast Newswriting: A Workbook*. Ames: Iowa State University Press, 1983. 115 pp. ISBN: 0-8138-0226-1.

Writing and reporting guidelines are detailed in sections covering newsroom technology, writing style, story structure, introductions, newscast organization, and script formats. The second half of the book provides writing exercises, style tests, comparative leads, and brief but specific rules on writing for radio and television.

869. Wylie, Max. *Radio and Television Writing*. Rev ed. New York: Rinehart, 1952. 647 pp. (Rinehart Radio and Television series).

Published originally as *Radio Writing* (see next annotation), this is brought up to date in terms of developments over the preceding decade, not only in audience preferences, but in technique as well. This edition is broader in scope than the previous one and, of course, includes material about writing for television as well as radio.

870. Wylie, Max. *Radio Writing*. New York: Farrar & Rinehart, 1939. 550 pp.

The author was Director of Script and Continuity of CBS at the time he wrote this book. In it he describes standard practices of modern broadcasting and illustrates his points with samples of both the problems and properties typical of the industry.

PROGRAMMING

Includes music, comedy, talk shows, call-ins, news, children's programs, farm/rural broadcasting, documentaries, drama, sports, political/public affairs, and religious programming.

* Adair, James R. *M.R. DeHaan: The Man and His Ministry.* Cited above as item 2.

871. Allen, Robert C. *Speaking of Soap Operas.* Chapel Hill: University of North Carolina Press, 1985. 245 pp. ISBN: 0-8078-1643-4.

    The production of this genre is examined in depth along with a detailed analysis of its audience. Allen discusses the economic and institutional functions of such programs and considers their historical development as an advertising vehicle, narrative structure, and "women's fiction." Included are scripts from several soaps from 1931, 1938, 1950, and 1956.

872. Alperowicz, Cynthia. *Radio and Children: An ACT Handbook.* Newtonville, MA: Action for Children's Television, 1984. 24 pp.

    Citing "disenchantment" with children's programming, this author urges increased radio programming geared to young people, offers ideas for the radio industry, advertisers, underwriters, and the community to create a real market, and enumerates the accruing benefits.

873. American Comedy Network. *The Method to the Madness: Radio's Morning Show Madness*. Bridgeport, CT: American Comedy Network, 1985. 61 pp.

Seventy personalities tell what it takes to have a funnier, more creative, and more successful morning show. They completed questionnaires, were interviewed by phone, and provided their own thoughts and comments on the genre of a.m. radio broadcasting.

874. Amin, R.K. *Radio Rural-Forums in Gujarat: An Observation Study*. Gujarat, India: Sardar Vallabhbhai Vidyapeeth, 1966. 63 p.

Studied were the ways and extent the objectives of the Radio Rural Forums had been achieved, an identification of their main defects and failures, and what steps should be taken to improve the working of the forums. They were based on the earlier Radio-Rural Forums in Canada.

875. Armstrong, Ben, ed. *The Directory of Religious Broadcasting*. Morristown, NJ: National Religious Broadcasters, 1989. 344 pp. ISSN: 0731-0331.

Published annually, this provides information about religious radio and TV stations, program producers, and the various agencies and auxiliary services connected with religious broadcasting. It includes a compilation of stations with either a full or partial format of religious programming as well as separate sections for international broadcasting, equipment and technical services, consultants, ad agencies, etc.

876. Armstrong, Ben. *The Electronic Church*. Nashville, TN: Thomas Nelson, 1979. 191 pp. ISBN: 0-8407-5157-5.

Instead of being a comprehensive survey of the hundreds of broadcast ministries on radio and television, this book highlights those ministries that are representative of specific trends.

877. Bachman, John W. *The Church in the World of Radio-Television.* New York: Association Press, 1960. 191 pp.

The author covers not only religious broadcasts but also advertisements, news and entertainment, and the organization and regulation of the American system of broadcasting. He suggests policies and approaches to meet them as the church deals with these forms of media.

878. Bailey, Norman, Romulus Linney, and Dominick Cascio. *Radio Classics.* Minneapolis: Burgess Publishing, 1956. 169 leaves.

Spiral-bound, this is a collection of radio plays of either 15 or 30 minutes in duration and include many original scripts written for this volume. They represent a wide variety of moods and styles; some are based on fairy tales, folk tales, and little-known classics.

879. Baker, John C. *Farm Broadcasting: The First Sixty Years.* Ames: Iowa State University Press, 1981. 342 pp. ISBN: 0-8138-1485-5.

The beginnings of farm broadcasting, USDA weather, market news broadcasting, New England Radio News Service, national networks, and wire news services are profiled. Subsequent chapters are devoted to the extension services of individual states, farm bureaus, broadcasters, and local radio stations featuring farming information.

880. Barnouw, Erik. *Radio Drama in Action: Twenty-five Plays of a Changing World*. New York: Rinehart & Company, 1945. 397 pp. (Rinehart Radio series).

> The complete texts of these plays are reproduced in this volume along with information concerning their original radio broadcasts. Among the authors of the scripts are Orson Welles, Langston Hughes, Arthur Miller, Arch Oboler, Norman Corwin, Stephen Vincent Benét, Norman Rosten, and Pearl S. Buck.

881. Beckett, Samuel. *Cascando and Other Short Dramatic Pieces*. New York: Grove Press, 1968. 88 pp.

> This contains the entire script of the radio play *Cascando* as well as *Words and Music: a Radio Play*, *Eh Joe*, *Play*, *Come and Go*, and *Film*.

882. Beerbohm, Max. *Mainly on the Air*. New ed. New York: Alfred A. Knopf, 1958. 212 pp.

> Eight essays and talks broadcast on the British Broadcasting Corporation have been added to this new edition supplementing the one originally published in 1946. Data about when and where the broadcast took place precedes each essay.

883. Benét, Stephen Vincent. *We Stand United and Other Radio Scripts*. New York: Farrar & Rinehart, 1945. 210 pp.

> The plays in this volume were written during WW II and were intended to help sell Americans on the idea of America. The plays were "written with anger and passion. They are eloquent without being pompous ... (and are important because they) present the author in an entirely new medium, radio."

884. Benson, Dennis C. *Electric Evangelism*. Nashville, TN: Abingdon Press, 1973. 144 pp. ISBN: 0-687-11633-3.

Described on the book jacket as "how to spread the Word through radio and TV," this suggests ways that churches can put together colorful local religious programming. Benson tells how other church groups have created such programming by obtaining free public service time and utilizing the help of professional station personnel.

885. *Best Radio Plays of 1989: The Giles Cooper Award Winners*. London: Methuen London, 1990. 191 pp. (Methuen Modern Plays). ISBN: 0-413-63240-7.

Published first in 1979, this compilation has appeared annually and reprints the full text of the winning plays. Each was broadcast over the British Broadcasting Corporation.

886. Boemer, Marilyn Lawrence. *The Children's Hour: Radio Programs for Children, 1929-1956*. Metuchen, NJ: Scarecrow Press, 1989. 220 pp. ISBN: 0-8108-2270-9.

Boemer writes that the purpose behind this book is to provide the opportunity to find out what the children's radio programs were really like to those who never heard them. She profiles *Jack Armstrong, the All-American Boy*, *Little Orphan Annie*, *The Lone Ranger*, *Uncle Don*, *Captain Midnight*, *Dick Tracy*, and many others, and provides a listing of programs with their networks, years broadcast, and regular characters.

887. Boyd, James, ed. *The Free Company Presents a Collection of Plays About the Meaning of America*. New York: Dodd, Mead, 1941. 312 pp.

The Free Company was the title of a series of radio drama shows about different aspects of Americanism presented over the Columbia Broadcasting System in cooperation with a number of leading American writers. Those contributing to this volume are Maxwell Anderson, Sherwood Anderson, Stephen Vincent Benét, James Boyd, Marc Connelly, Paul Green, Archibald MacLeish, William Saroyan, Robert E. Sherwood, and Orson Welles.

888. British Broadcasting Corporation, *New Radio Drama*, London: The Corporation, 1966. 263 pp.

   The texts of six radio plays are published in this volume. They are *Tonight Is Friday* by Colin Finbow, *A Voice Like Thunder* by Ian Rodger, *A Nice Clean Sheet of Paper* by Rhys Adrian, *Sixteen Lives of the Drunken Dreamer* by Stephen Grenfell, *The Ruffian on the Stair* by Joe Orton, and *The Sconcing Stoup* by Simon Raven.

889. British Broadcasting Corporation. *Tolstoy's War and Peace*. London: The Corporation, 1943. 24 pp.

   In 1943 the BBC broadcast *War and Peace* in a series of six Sunday afternoon and evening programs. This booklet is an introduction to the series and provides a synopsis, identification of the characters, and several short essays regarding the book and this production of it.

890. Brosius, Nancy Bancroft. *Sue 'Em*. New York: Brentano's, 1925. 19 pp.

   The title page credits this as being the first radio play printed in America when it was awarded first prize in the WGBS radio drama contest. It was produced by members of the Provincetown Players at WGBS on December 29, 1925, and had a cast of four.

891. Brunner, Edmund deS. *Radio and the Farmer.* New York: Radio Institute of the Audible Arts, 1935. 65 pp.

    The title article examines the effect on the farmer that radio has as an instrument of both entertainment and education. It precedes an account of "A Symposium on the Relation of Radio to Rural Life" dealing with the same topic.

892. Buckman, Peter. *All for Love: A Study in Soap Opera.* London: Secker & Warburg, 1984. 226 pp. ISBN: 0-436-07506-7.

    The characters peopling every soap opera, the plots and interwoven episodes, the writers, directors and producers, and the actors and actresses are scrutinized in minute detail. The author questions "do we get the soap opera we deserve?" and answers "why we get what we get and why we love it so."

893. Bureau of Agricultural Economics. U.S. Department of Agriculture. *Attitudes of Rural People Toward Radio Service.* Washington: USDA, 1946. 113 pp.

    A nation-wide survey of farm and small-town people was conducted by the Bureau to examine several major areas: how important is radio to rural people and in what ways, what are their attitudes toward their present service, what are their program preferences, and what proportion of the rural population does not have radios in working order. This report gives the results of that survey.

894. Cantor, Muriel G., and Suzanne Pingree. *The Soap Opera.* Beverly Hills: Sage, 1983. 167 pp. (Sage CommText series, 12). ISBN: 0-8039-2004-0.

The first three chapters are concerned with an introduction to the subject, the background of the genre, and soaps on the radio. The balance discusses TV soaps, an analysis of *The Guiding Light*, (first on radio and then television for over 40 years), soap opera content, and audiences.

895. Carmer, Carl. *Taps Is Not Enough*. New York: Henry Holt, 1945. 12 pp.

This is a radio script copyrighted by CBS and has a small cast of only a narrator, a woman, a soldier, and a "realist."

896. Chase, Gilbert, ed. *Music in Radio Broadcasting*. New York: McGraw-Hill, 1946. 152 pp. (NBC-Columbia University Broadcasting series).

Based on the course, Music for Radio, given by Columbia University Extension in cooperation with NBC, this is the first book devoted exclusively to music in radio broadcasting. It is a general orientation course that covers all aspects of music as it is used in broadcasting without attempting to teach the applied techniques of any one of them.

897. Chester, Edward W. *Radio, Television and American Politics*. New York: Sheed & Ward, 1969. 342 pp. ISBN: 0-8362-0180-9.

The preface states this book represents the first comprehensive attempt to answer questions such as: Precisely what qualities made Franklin Roosevelt the great radio speaker that he was? What use has been made of radio and TV in state and local elections? What has been the nature of the radical right's invasion of the radio following WW II? and In what ways are political radio and political television similar and in what ways are they different?

898. *The Church in the Sky*. New York: Federal Council of the Churches of Christ in America, 1938. 38 pp.

The texts of several short addresses presented at an anniversary celebration of National Religious Radio are reprinted in this volume. Among the participants were representatives of NBC, various church federations, and the Federal Council of the Churches of Christ in America.

899. Codrescu, Andrew. *A Craving for Swan*. Columbus: Ohio State University Press, 1986. 314 pp. ISBN: 0-8142-0415-5.

The essays in this book were broadcast on National Public Radio's *All Things Considered* between 1983 and 1985. Some of them appeared in a slightly different form on the Op-Ed page of the *Baltimore Sun* during that same period.

900. Columbia Broadcasting System. *Serious Music on the Columbia Broadcasting System*. New York: CBS, 1938. 67 leaves

This is a survey of series, soloists and special performances from 1927 through 1938 broadcast over CBS. It sketches the highlights in the musical activity of the network and divides the programs into two basic categories, sustaining and commercial.

901. Columbia Broadcasting System. *The Sound of Your Life: A Record of Radio's First Generation*. New York: CBS, 1950. 133 pp.

An imaginary family of radio listeners was created who listened to broadcasts over a 20-year period. In this manner CBS was able to offer a summary of news events of the times and illustrate them with photographs.

902. Columbia Broadcasting System. *We Now Take You To....* New York: CBS, 1937. 128 pp.

Among the places CBS takes the reader are South America, Great Britain, Spain, Italy, and China--in a series of 311 broadcasts from 27 foreign countries during 1936. This publication was issued as a Foreign Affairs Supplement to *Talks*, a digest of addresses of diversified interest broadcast over the Columbia Network and published quarterly throughout the year.

903. Corwin, Norman. *More by Corwin.* New York: Henry Holt, 1945. 412 pp.

This anthology incorporates 16 radio dramas that were broadcast between 1941 and 1943. Along with the names of the cast there is a commentary by Corwin about the writing of the play or the actual performance. Similar volumes of radio plays written by Corwin published by Holt around the same time were titled *Thirteen by Corwin*, *Untitled and Other Radio Dramas*, and *This Is War!*

904. Corwin, Norman. *On a Note of Triumph.* New York: Simon & Schuster, 1945. 71 pp.

Late in 1944 the Columbia Broadcasting System asked Corwin to write an hour's program hailing the hoped-for victory in Europe during WW II. This is the script of the program that was broadcast immediately after V-E Day, May 8, 1945.

905. Corwin, Norman. *They Fly Through the Air with the Greatest of Ease.* Weston, VT: Vrest Orton, 1939. 56 pp.

> First broadcast on February 19, 1939, this was the 11th in a series of programs entitled *Norman Corwin's Words Without Music.* Production notes and cast lists are included.

906. Coulter, Douglas, ed. *Columbia Workshop Plays.* New York: McGraw-Hill, 1939. 378 pp.

> The scripts of 14 radio plays are presented in this collection. They include some written by Irving Reis, Norman Corwin, and Archibald MacLeish, along with adaptations of stories by Stephen Vincent Benét, DuBose Heyward, and William March.

907. Dikshit, Kiranmani A., et al. *Rural Radio: Programme Formats.* Paris: Unesco, 1979. 94 pp. (Monographs on Communication Technology and Utilization). ISBN: 92-3-101616-4.

> The focus is on the various methods of reaching the rural audience with news and information on farm techniques, organization, general rural development, and other relevant topics. The farm forum is perhaps the best-known type of rural broadcasting, but it seldom is used in many areas except for the developing countries.

908. Dimond, Sidney A., and Donald M. Andersson. *Radio and Television Workshop Manual: A Practical Guide to Creative Radio and Television.* New York: Prentice-Hall, 1952. 301 pp.

> The preface states that this manual provides suitable material of sufficient depth of thought which, at the same time, employs a minimum of production problems so that

it can be used by the smallest radio or television setup with simplified cast, music and technical equipment. A number of scripts are reproduced.

909. Dinwiddie, Melville. *Religion by Radio: Its Place in British Broadcasting.* London: George Allen & Unwin, 1968. 136 pp.

Religion by radio began at a time when the skepticism created by the First World War still exerted a strong influence, according to the author's introduction. He enlarges on this statement by telling what is possible in religious broadcasting and, more specifically, the British Broadcasting Corporation's approach to the subject.

910. Drakakis, John, ed. *British Radio Drama.* Cambridge, Eng.: Cambridge University Press, 1981. 288 pp. ISBN: 0-521-22183-8.

A volume of criticism, this has full appraisals of the radio writing of Louis MacNeice, Dylan Thomas, and Henry Reed, along with detailed studies of particular aspects of the work of Dorothy L. Sayers, Susan Hill, Giles Cooper, and Samuel Beckett. A final essay assesses the current trends in radio drama in the light of the developing technology of the medium itself and of the rival claims of television.

911. Duff, Willis P., Jr. *The Talk Radio Handbook.* (No publisher or place of publication shown), 1969. 61 pp.

In his preface Duff writes "This book is for broadcasters who are doing, who have done, or who may ever do telephone-talk programming." It evolved from a series of memos to the broadcast personalities or other station personnel involved in the first 24-hour talk radio station,

KLAC in Los Angeles. It is a how-to book along the lines of a problem-solving manual.

912. Durfey, Thomas C., and James A. Ferrier. *Religious Broadcast Management Handbook.* Grand Rapids, MI: Academie Books/Zondervan, 1986. 294 pp. ISBN: 0-310-39741-3.

The authors state Christian broadcasters need to know everything secular professionals in the same field need to know--and more. The sections cover development, ownership options, engineering, programming, management, sales, and promotions.

913. Dykema, Peter W. *Men and Radio Music.* New York: Radio Institute of the Audible Arts, 1935. 7 pp.

Sections in this brochure are titled Restoring Man's Birthright; Choose Your Music, Gentlemen!; You Control the Dial; Bathing in Music; Recognizing Old Friends; Good Form in Sport and Music; What Makes Rhythm?; Digging for More Gold; Counting Up to Ten; and a bibliography of "music books for various tastes."

914. Dykema, Peter W. *Music As Presented by the Radio.* New York: Radio Institute of the Audible Arts, 1935. 6 pp.

The first in a series of brochures, this looks at how radio is revolutionizing listening to music and the various ways music can enrich one's life.

915. Dykema, Peter W. *Radio Music for Boys and Girls.* New York: Radio Institute of the Audible Arts, 1935. 8 pp.

The author, a professor of music education at Columbia University Teachers College, discusses why youths crave music and how important music is both in school and at home. He shows how radio enriches music and describes various broadcasts by youths including grade school children singing and choral music by older children in junior and senior high schools.

916. Dykema, Peter W. *Women and Radio Music*. New York: Radio Institute of the Audible Arts, 1935. 8 pp.

    The fourth in a series of brochures by Dykema on the general subject of music as presented by radio, this is a companion volume to *Men and Radio Music* (see item 913). It tells how women can develop personality with music, and how a woman's taste influences others. There is a very short bibliography of "books that lead to greater satisfactions."

917. Eberly, Philip K. *Music in the Air: America's Changing Tastes in Popular Music, 1920-1980*. New York: Hastings House, 1982. 406 pp. ISBN: 0-8038-4743-2.

    The author attributes the ultimate testing ground of what makes music "popular" to radio. It "will decree what tunes and artists will succeed and how long they will last. The wide range of music available up and down the dials of our radio music boxes is proof there is no single American popular music. *There are dozens and dozens!*"

918. Edmondson, Madeleine, and David Rounds. *From Mary Noble to Mary Hartman*. New York: Stein & Day, 1976. 256 pp. ISBN: 0-8128-2094-X.

    A revised, updated, and expanded edition of Edmondson's, *The Soaps* (see next annotation), this begins with a radio quiz, continues with the early history of the genre, or what the authors call "birth of a notion", and ends with the reasons why radio soap opera died. In between are chapters on "radio soapland," "soaperstars," the "soap du jour," and "the once and future soap."

919. Edmondson, Madeleine, and David Rounds. *The Soaps: Daytime Serials of Radio and TV*. New York: Stein & Day, 1973. 256 pp. ISBN: 0-8128-1639-0.

Originally broadcast with a 15-minute format, daytime serials attracted millions of fans (usually housewives) and became a staple of daytime radio broadcasting. They later achieved great or greater popularity on television and eventually drove the radio soaps off the air. This volume recalls the genre and furnishes information on the writers, the performers, and, of course, the actual long-running stories.

920. Eisenberg, Azriel L. *Children and Radio Programs*. New York: Columbia University Press, 1936. 237 pp.

Based on a study of more than 3,000 children in the New York metropolitan area, this examines the radio-listening activities of children, the programs they listen to, and their reactions to such programs. Other results discuss the attitudes of parents to their children's listening, the role of the radio in the home, and the reliability and validity of the responses made by the children.

921. Felton, Felix. *The Radio-Play: Its Technique and Possibilities*. London: Sylvan Press, 1949. 151 pp.

Among the aspects of drama production covered are the stage and the studio, adaptation, sound effects, dramatization of short stories, narration, documentaries, the use of music, and script interpretation. Several pages of photographs illustrate these various points.

922. Furlonger, Brian, compiler. *Vietnam: A Reporter's War.* Sydney: Australian Broadcasting Commission, 1975. 87 pp. ISBN: 0-642-97473-X.

Produced just after the South Vietnamese government surrendered, ABC Radio created a special public affairs program surveying the longest and best reported war of the 20th century. The program lasted two hours and told the story of the Vietnam War in the words of the people who made the news and those who saw it happen. This is the written version of that Australian program.

923. Gielgud, Val. *British Radio Drama, 1922-1956.* London: George G. Harrap, 1957. 207 pp.

This is a survey conducted by the Head of BBC Drama (Sound). The preface states that it "*is* survey, and *not* history ... The aim has been to present the general picture--not omitting imperfections, failures, and shortcomings."

924. Gielgud, Val. *How to Write Broadcast Plays.* London: Hurst & Blackett, 1932. 190 pp.

In addition to describing the basic knowledge necessary to succeed in the field, Gielgud includes three examples of his own writings: *Friday Morning, Red Tabs,* and *Exiles.* All three were broadcast by the British Broadcasting Corporation.

925. Gielgud, Val. *Radio Theatre.* London: MacDonald, 1946. 199 pp.

Complete texts of seven plays that were specially written for broadcasting comprise this anthology. Production notes are provided giving the date of production and the cast.

926. Gielgud, Val. *The Right Way to Radio Playwriting*. Kingswood, Eng.: Right Way Books, 1948. 133 pp.

Gielgud discusses the art of writing in general, basic elements, subjects, length, use of music, sound effects, and adaptation. He offers "a glimpse of the machine" as he writes about the play library, play readers, the preliminary read-through, and the final stage of production.

927. Gordon, Dorothy. *All Children Listen*. New York: George W. Stewart, 1942. 128 pp. (Radio House series).

Active from the beginning of radio and a performer on children's radio programs, Dorothy Gordon criticizes the shows that are being produced for children and discusses the movement of women (and mothers in particular) to modify such programming. She compares American broadcasting with that in Great Britain, Scandinavia, Europe, Russia, Japan, and Nazi Germany.

928. Gordon, George N., and Irving A. Falk. *On-the-Spot Reporting: Radio Records History*. New York: Julian Messner, 1967. 191 pp.

In the early 1930s publishers decided that press associations would hurt newspapers if they made their news wires available to radio personnel. Radio was deprived of its principal sources of news and had to plunge into an expansion of its own limited news-covering facilities. This book recalls the results of that expansion.

929. Grandin, Thomas. *The Political Use of Radio*. Geneva: Geneva Research Centre, 1939. 116 pp.

This book comprises Volume X, Number 3, of *Geneva Studies*. The first three chapters examine broadcasting for national and European consumption as well as intercontinental broadcasting. The final two chapters cover the effect of political transmissions upon the public, and efforts to control the political uses of radio. This was reprinted in 1971 as part of the History of Broadcasting: Radio to Television series published by Arno Press/New York Times.

930. Griswold, Clayton T., and Charles H. Schmitz. *Broadcasting Religion*. Rev. ed. New York: National Council of the Churches of Christ, 1954. 103 pp.

The front cover of this paperback states that it is a manual for local use. It covers writing, programming, and production, plus church policy and church council policy as resources.

931. Gruenberg, Sidonie Matsner. *Radio and Children*. New York: Radio Institute of the Audible Arts, 1935. 22 pp.

Written before the advent of television, this study indicates that children begin to take an interest in radio programs between the age of 4 and 5 years, and that this interest becomes general at about age 6. The author shows how children become more exacting as they get older, their tastes change, and they need guidance. She then identifies characteristics peculiar to radio.

932. Guimary, Donald L. *Citizens' Groups and Broadcasting*. New York: Praeger, 1975. 170 pp. (Praeger Special Studies in U.S. Economic, Social and Political Issues).

Commercial broadcasting has been a public concern since its acceptance as a mass communications medium in the 1920s. This recalls the earliest citizen's groups concerned with radio broadcasting at that time and the effect they and subsequent groups had on broadcasting policy, licensing, advertising, programming, and employment policies of radio and television stations.

933. Hackett, Walter. *Radio Plays for Young People*. Boston: Plays, Inc., 1950. 277 pp.

Hackett has gathered 15 stories adapted for royalty-free performance. All are easy to produce and are based on well-known British and American classics.

934. Hackett, Walter. *Radio Plays from History and Literature*. Boston: Baker's Plays, 1952. 100 pp.

All the six plays in this booklet have been produced over various major and/or regional networks as commercial or sustaining shows. Each one is either 15 or 30 minutes long.

935. Hall, Claude, and Barbara Hall. *This Business of Radio Programming*. New York: Billboard Books, 1977. 360 pp. ISBN: 0-8230-7760-8.

The title page states that this is a comprehensive look at modern programming techniques used throughout the radio world. The introduction is written by Jack G. Thayer, President, NBC Radio.

936. Havig, Alan. *Fred Allen's Radio Comedy*. Philadelphia: Temple University Press, 1990. 187 pp. (American Civilization). ISBN: 0-87722-713-6.

The author "explores the roots of Allen's comedy, the themes it exploited, the problems and challenges that faced the radio comedy writer, and Allen's unique success with the one-dimensional medium of radio." He traces Allen's long career from 1912 into the 1950s and describes his "verbal slapstick" style.

937. Henry, Robert D., and James M. Lynch, Jr. *History Makers*. Evanston, IL: Row, Peterson, 1941. 92 pp.

Eight radio plays are incorporated in this book, and they are designed to teach the fundamentals of broadcasting along with an appreciation of American history. All are adaptable for classroom use.

938. Hewitt, John. *Air Words: Writing for Broadcast News*. Mountain View, CA: Mayfield, 1988. 226 pp. ISBN: 0-87484-844-X.

Designed to provide skills needed for the broadcast medium, this workbook contains a collection of definitions, rules, warnings, short cuts, and exercises to sharpen style. They offer "a load of hints, suggestions, and rules, but they are not absolute."

939. Higgins, C.S., and P.D. Moss. *Sounds Real: Radio in Everyday Life*. St. Lucia: University of Queensland Press, 1982. 237 pp. ISBN: 0-7022-1900-2.

Chapters cover interaction analyses of talk-back radio and are titled: Some Cultural Meanings; Private Meanings, Public Channels; Commercial Radio and Culture; Radio: a Dramatizing Medium; Realities and Pseudo-realities: Radio News and Current Affairs; and Media Culture--General Culture.

940. Hill, George H., and Lenwood Davis. *Religious Broadcasting, 1920-1983: A Selectively Annotated Bibliography*. New York: Garland, 1984. 243 pp. ISBN: 0-8240-9015-2.

In addition to religious radio and television data, this includes biographies, dissertations, theses, and material on religious public relations, journalism, and communications within the United States.

941. Holloway, Donald F. *Adult Radio: Annual Project Report*. Morehead, KY: Morehead State University, 1970. 43 pp.

Prepared by the Institute of Public Broadcasting, this implemented a project for cultural, recreational, and area development in Eastern Kentucky and describes the programming by station WMKY-FM especially designed for elderly and/or retired people in the area.

942. Howard, Herbert H., and Michael S. Kievman. *Radio and TV Programming*. Ames: Iowa State University Press, 1986. 372 pp. (Grid series in Advertising and Journalism). ISBN: 0-8138-0347-0.

Basically intended as a textbook, this is actually a how-to book to help enhance the reader's skills. It introduces broadcast programming, puts it into a historical perspective, tells how to manage a program department, and goes into detail about programming on both commercial and public broadcast stations.

943. Huber, Louis J. *Short Radio Plays*. Minneapolis: Northwestern Press, 1938. 96 pp.

A collection of nine short plays intended for radio broadcasting. The parts are simple, there is no difficult dialect, and the sound effects are easy to create. Each play is about 13 minutes in length.

944. Irvin, Lee. *Radio Workshop: A Collection of Radio Scripts for Radio Broadcasting*. Minneapolis: Northwestern Press, 1946. 101 pp.

The sketches in this collection were intended primarily for radio presentation but can be used in various ways by schools. They are fairly short, and all have small casts.

945. Jones, Carless, ed. *Short Plays for State and Radio.* Albuquerque: University of New Mexico Press, 1939. 191 pp.

The intent of this book is to provide script material that can be adapted for radio use. Included are well-known plays and original dramas such as *The Necklace* by Guy de Maupassant, *The Importance of Being Ernest* by Oscar Wilde, and *Bardell vs. Pickwick* by Charles Dickens.

946. *Journeys Behind the News: Radio Scripts.* Denver, University of Denver, 1937. 2 vols.

Formerly available annually, these volumes contain the typescripts of a weekly radio program presented by the Social Science Foundation of the University of Denver in cooperation with The Rocky Mountain Radio Council. The programs were carried by a number of stations in Colorado, New Mexico, Oregon, Wyoming, Illinois, Kansas, Indiana, Minnesota, and Wisconsin.

947. Kaplan, Milton Allen. *Radio and Poetry.* New York: Columbia University Press, 1949. 333 pp.

This was originally the Ph.D. dissertation Kaplan wrote for Columbia University. After briefly recounting radio's beginnings, he concentrates on the different aspects of the radio verse play--dramatic, poetic and documentary techniques--and the adaptation of poetry and poetry reading on the air.

948. Kaufman, Schima. *Everybody's Music.* New York: Thomas Y. Crowell, 1938. 320 pp.

Published with the cooperation of the Columbia Broadcasting System, this contains commentary from the CBS series of Sunday afternoon programs called

Everybody's Music. The broadcasts consisted of orchestral masterpieces and these commentaries.

949. Keirstead, Phillip O. *All-News Radio*. Blue Ridge Summit, PA: Tab Books, 1980. 222 pp. ISBN: 0-8306-9779-0.

This book is devoted to one format, one medium: all-news radio. It describes radio stations that broadcast news and news-related material from 18 to 24 hours a day, along with those that mix their programming with lengthy, play-by-play sports schedules, or those with significant time blocks given over to telephone call-in programs.

950. Keirstead, Phillip O. *Modern Public Affairs Programming*. Blue Ridge Summit, PA: Tab Books, 1979. 251 pp. ISBN: 0-8306-8977-X.

The author's aim, he states, is to encourage more station managers to sort out public affairs functions and assign someone the task of giving that area of programming direction and organization. He uses several radio stations as practical examples of good planning: WGMS, WCBS, WRFM, WRKL, KVOX, KKUA, and WBLX.

951. Keith, Michael C. *Radio Programming: Consultancy and Formatics*. Boston: Focal Press, 1987. 195 pp. ISBN: 0-240-51792-X.

The role of the programming consultant is closely examined in this book that looks at all aspects of modern radio programming. The practices and methods employed by consultants are described in one chapter while the rest of the book is devoted to the unique programming considerations of different formats such as adult contemporary, easy listening, news and talk, classical, country music, and public broadcasting.

952. Keller, Evelyn L. *The Script Shop Presents Eleven Radio Plays.* Boston: Christopher Publishing House, 1944. 256 pp.

> The plays are: Battle Hymn; *If You Want Anything, Just Yell*; *Carnival Kid*; Reflection; *The Happy Ending*; *International Incident*; *A Little Closer to God*; *And Thorns Have Roses*; The Bartering Bride; *Fantasy in F*; and *Voices in the Wilderness.*

953. Kinscella, Hazel Gertrude. *Music on the Air.* New York: Viking Press, 1934. 438 pp.

> In an introduction written by Walter Damrosch, the statement is made that "it is important that their (the greater number of listeners who have never heard real music before) musical intelligence should be sharpened and their power of appreciation increased." Kinscella does just that as she selects essays on folk music, opera, choral music, classical and popular music, etc.

954. Klages, Karl W. *Sportscasting.* Logan, UT: Sportscasters, 1963. 154 pp.

> The preface states that "this book is prepared for the professional broadcaster. Its purpose is to provide a philosophy of approach to a sportscaster's functions--to inform and to entertain."

955. Kozlenko, William, ed. *American Scenes.* New York: John Day, 1941. 269 pp.

> "The underlying purpose of this volume, apart from trying to collate an interesting group of plays, is to picture dramatically the humor, tragedy, character, and idiom of certain regions of our country." Notes are provided about the authors of the radio plays, but no production information is given.

956. Kozlenko, William, compiler. *One Hundred Non-Royalty One-Act Plays*. New York: Greenberg, 1940. 802 pp.

Any strictly amateur group may produce on the stage or as a non-commercial radio broadcast, without permission or royalty payment, any of the plays published in this compilation. Most are original plays, but there are a number of radio adaptations of well-known stories.

957. Kozlenko, William, compiler. *One Hundred Non-Royalty Radio Plays*. New York: Greenberg, 1941. 683 pp.

A companion volume to the compiler's book of one-act plays (see previous annotation), this reprints scripts that are especially good for radio broadcasts. There are plays to satisfy all tastes and needs, and most have been previously aired by various radio stations and/or the major networks.

958. Krulevitch, Walter, and Rome C. Krulevitch. *Radio Drama Production: A Handbook*. New York: Rinehart, 1946. 330 pp. (Rinehart Radio series).

This handbook is a compilation of the most successful of the authors' materials in combining active participation in radio writing, production, and teaching. It offers suggestions for procedure and provides a background of production theory.

959. LaGuardia, Robert. *From Ma Perkins to Mary Hartman: The Illustrated History of Soap Operas*. New York: Ballantine Books, 1977. 421 pp.

Heavily illustrated, this begins with the Golden Age of radio soaps from 1930 to 1960, continues with the first television soaps, and concludes with details of the current TV serials. Radio shows featured include *Vic and Sade*,

The Romance of Helen Trent, *Myrt and Marge*, *Big Sister*, *Young Widder Brown*, *Life Can Be Beautiful*, and the daytime mystery, *Perry Mason*.

960. LaGuardia, Robert. *Soap World*. New York: Arbor, 1983, 408 pp.

    After a general history of the genre, the major current soap operas and several past favorites are discussed. Complete plot summaries and background information with cast lists and credits are provided. Appendices show cast and credits for some radio soaps and canceled television soaps which lasted less than ten years.

961. Lampell, Millard. *The Long Way Home*. New York: Julian Messner, 1946. 174 pp.

    These scripts were first produced over an official Army Air Force program, *First in the Air*, on CBS and were later repeated over Mutual as part of another series, *Wings for Tomorrow*. Individual ones were rebroadcast both by NBC and CBS.

962. LaPrade, Ernest. *Broadcasting Music*. New York: Rinehart, 1947. 236 pp. (Rinehart Radio series).

    Because the author felt that the broadcasting of music "has hitherto received scant attention in print," he has written this book "to depict for the student--and for the music-loving listener ... the entire process of broadcasting music, from the planning of programs to their production in the studio. The requisite organization, equipment, and techniques are described; underlying principles are analyzed; and the historical and technical background is sketched in."

963. Lass, A.H., Earle L. McGill, and Donald Axelrod, eds. *Plays from Radio*. Cambridge, MA: Houghton Mifflin, 1948. 342 pp.

Included in this anthology are plays written by Lucille Fletcher, Norman Corwin, Charles Tazewell, Frederick and Pauline Gilsdorf, Joseph Ruscoll, Ted Key, James and Elizabeth Hart, Milton Geiger, Ruth Barth, James Boyd, Arthur Miller, Bernard Schoenfeld, Charles Jackson, John Mason Brown, and Howard M. Teichmann.

964. Latham, Jean Lee. *Nine Radio Plays*. Chicago: Dramatic Publishing, 1940. 132 pp.

The plays in this anthology are primarily for particular holidays: Columbus Day, Halloween, Thanksgiving, Christmas, St. Valentine's Day, Washington's Birthday, St. Patrick's Day, and Mother's Day.

965. Lawton, Sherman P. *Radio Drama*. Boston: Expression Company, 1938. 404 pp.

Growing out of the author's own experience in the classroom, this book is directed toward enabling students to learn by doing. The material is arranged in a step-by-step basis so that the student is led from the simpler forms of radio dramatic writing to the more difficult.

966. Lea, Gordon. *Radio Drama and How to Write It*. London: George Allen & Unwin, 1926. 91 pp.

The foreword states that this author has the distinction of being the first to publish a work in volume form upon the subject of radio drama. Mr. Lea writes about the limitations of the stage-play, the technique for writing radio plays, sound effects, and radio actors.

967. Lee, Alfred McClung, and Elizabeth Bryant Lee, eds. *The Fine Art of Propaganda: A Study of Father Coughlin's Speeches*. New York: Harcourt, Brace, 1939. 140 pp.

The foreword states that the radio talks of the Rev. Charles E. Coughlin of Detroit were chosen for analysis "because they represent a fairly typical borrowing of foreign anti-democratic propaganda methods by an American propagandist." Father Coughlin had a wide following for his regular weekly radio broadcasts during the 1930s.

968. LeRoy, David J., and Christopher H. Sterling, compilers. *Mass News: Practices, Controversies, and Alternatives*. Englewood Cliffs, NJ: Prentice-Hall, 1973. 334 pp. ISBN: 0-13-559898-2.

This compilation includes articles contributed by Ben H. Bagdikian, Irving Fang, Edwin Emery, Philip H. Ault, Warren Agee, Burton Paulu, Verne E. Edwards, Jr., Eric J. Light, Frank Stanton, Edith Efron, George A. Bailey, Lawrence W. Lichty, Neil Hickey, M.L. Stein, John Tebbel, and the compilers.

969. Leverton, Garrett H., ed. *On the Air: Fifteen Plays for Broadcast and for Classroom Use*. New York: Samuel French, 1947. 259 pp.

The plays in this anthology are generally short and require only small casts. Several were adapted for radio from short stories by prominent authors.

970. Levin, Murray B. *Talk Radio and the American Dream*. Lexington, MA: D.C. Heath/Lexington Books, 1987. 170 pp. ISBN: 0-669-13216-0.

This is the first book that "documents and analyzes a period of American history through tape recordings of hundreds of hours of talk radio." The author views talk radio as "a particularly sensitive barometer of alienation because the hosts promote controversy and urge their constituencies to reveal the petty and grand humiliations dealt by the state, big business and authority." Such programs have become a gold mine of Americana beginning with the 1960s.

971. Lewis, Dorothy. *Broadcasting to the Youth of America.* Washington: National Association of Broadcasters, 1943. 78 pp.

This is a report on present-day activities in the field of children's radio programs prepared by the Vice-Chairman of the Radio Council on Children's Programs. It was jointly sponsored by the Radio Council on Children's Programs and the NAB.

972. Lewis, Dorothy, and Dorothy L. McFadden. *Program Patterns for Young Radio Listeners in the Field of Children's Radio Entertainment.* Washington: National Association of Broadcasters, 1945. 80 pp.

Among the program patterns recounted in this book are comics, forums, hobbies, holidays, local history, music, nature, newscasts, quizzes, spelling bees, religion, safety, science, stories, talent, vocational, war service, and youth organizations. Special programming for pre-school, kindergarten age, and teenagers are mentioned as well as some foreign station and national network programs.

973. Lewis, Peter, ed. *Radio Drama.* London: Longman, 1981. 278 pp. ISBN: 0-582-49052-9.

The main theme of this book is radio drama as presented through the BBC Radio Drama Department. Individual subject areas include the producer and radio drama, the nature of radio drama, the writer and the medium, popular radio drama, adaptations of stage plays, classic fiction, sociological perspectives on radio drama, and radio drama in North America and Australia.

974. Liss, Joseph, ed. *Radio's Best Plays*. New York: Greenberg, 1947. 383 pp.

The plays in this anthology are divided into three classifications: Cycle From Fear to Fear, Plays With a Purpose, and Plays about People. Twenty are reprinted here.

975. Loizeaux, Marie D., compiler. *Library on the Air*. New York: H.W. Wilson, 1940. 364 pp.

Rather than use original material or scripts from a single library, the compiler has selected representative scripts from libraries doing successful broadcasting throughout the country. Approximately one-fifth of those submitted are included in this anthology.

976. MacDonald, J. Fred. *Don't Touch That Dial! Radio Programming in American Life, 1920-1960*. Chicago: Nelson-Hall, 1979. 412 pp. ISBN: 0-88229-528-4.

The first part of this work traces the history of radio and its programs between 1920 and 1960 as it explains the rise of the medium and its collapse after the advent of national television. The second looks closely at distinct types of programs or social themes during this time period.

977. MacFarland, David T. *Contemporary Radio Programming Strategies*. Hillsdale, NJ: Lawrence Erlbaum Associates, 1990. 211 pp. (Communication Textbook series). ISBN: 0-8058-0664-4.

Radio's Arena, Attributes, and Audiences constitute part I of this book while part II covers Formats, Soundscapes, and Voices. Music programming is the subject of the last portion with chapters on the appeals of radio music, music moods research, and the components of a mood-evoking music progression.

978. MacFarland, David T. *The Development of the Top 40 Radio Format*. New York: Arno Press, 1979. 626 pp. (Dissertations in Broadcasting). ISBN: 0-405-11765-5.

Originally presented as the author's Ph.D. dissertation at the University of Wisconsin in 1972, this analyzes the evolution of the general and specialized radio formats incorporating the 40 or so most popular records as an essential ingredient. The main focus of the author's research is on the station owners, managers, and program directors who were influential in determining the content and style of Top 40 radio.

979. Mackey, David R. *Drama on the Air*. New York: Prentice-Hall, 1951. 468 pp.

The preface states that radio actors, directors, and playwrights have a lot in common, and this book attempts to explore their common lot. The primary emphasis is on the problems of radio acting and production, but as a whole the book attempts to correlate the activities of the various parts rather than to separate them still farther.

980. MacLeish, Archibald. *Air Raid: A Verse Play for Radio*. New York: Harcourt, Brace, 1938. 36 pp.

The Columbia Broadcasting System broadcast this play on October 27, 1938. It is interesting to note in the cast list that several of the actors played more than one role-- a not uncommon thing in radio drama.

981. MacLeish, Archibald. *The American Story: Ten Broadcasts.* New York: Duell, Sloan & Pearce, 1944. 231 pp.

The radio scripts in this book were broadcast over the National Broadcasting Corporation in February, March, and April 1944. They were written for the network's *University of the Air* program, and their theme is the "American experience--the experience common to the Americans of the early settlements and voyages, of whatever race."

982. MacLeish, Archibald. *The Fall of the City: A Verse Play for Radio.* New York: Farrar & Rinehart, 1937. 33 pp.

The first performance of this play was in April 1937 over the Columbia Broadcasting System network and lasted a half-hour. Orson Welles was the voice of the announcer, Dwight Weist the Second Messenger, and Burgess Meredith the Orator.

983. MacNeice, Louis. *Persons from Porlock, and Other Plays for Radio.* London: British Broadcasting Corporation, 1969. 144 pp. ISBN: 0-563-08452-9.

Four plays are included in this volume: *Enter Caesar, East of the Sun and West of the Moon, They Met on Good Friday,* and *Persons from Porlock.* Information is included about when each was broadcast on BBC, along with a list of the cast members.

984. Matelski, Marilyn J. *The Soap Opera Evolution: America's Enduring Romance with Daytime Drama.* Jefferson, NC: McFarland, 1988. 212 pp. ISBN: 0-89950-324-1.

What account for the popularity of "the soaps" and the loyalty of viewers to particular favorites? This book studies the subject from a sociological point of view and tells which people watch which soap and why. Synopses (and genealogical tables) of 13 radio and television programs are provided.

985. Mathur, J.C., and Paul Neurath. *An Indian Experiment in Farm Radio Forums.* Paris: Unesco, 1959. 132 pp. (Press, Film and Radio in the World Today).

Farm Radio Forum, started in Canada in 1941, was a radio discussion program aimed at rural audiences. It was later expanded and produced as a pilot project to be broadcast in Southeast Asia at the request of the Indian government; this volume tells the story of that project.

986. Mayorga, Margaret. *The Best One-Act Plays of 1940.* New York: Dodd, Mead, 1941. 399 pp.

Part of an annual series, this edition has scripts written by Tennessee Williams, William Saroyan, Robert Finch, and Betty Smith, among others. Bibliographies contain lists of 50 selected plays of the year and new collections of one-act plays in print.

987. McDonagh, Richard. Robert H. Connery, ed. *The Land of the Free: Six Radio Plays.* Washington: Catholic University of America Press, 1941. 120 pp.

As part of its citizenship program, the Commission on American Citizenship presented, in cooperation with the National Council of Catholic Men and the National

Broadcasting Company, a series of six radio plays over *The Catholic Hour*. This volume contains the complete scripts of these plays along with full instruction for adapting them to school use.

988. McKinney, Eleanor, ed. *The Exacting Ear: The Story of Listener-Sponsored Radio, and an Anthology of Programs from KPFA, KPFK, and WBAI*. New York: Pantheon Books, 1966. 339 pp.

    Pacifica Foundation is the owner of the three radio stations named in the title. This book is an anthology of some of the Foundation's diverse radio broadcasts and reflects only fragments of the range of uncommon radio programming that became world-famous.

989. Mickel, Joseph. *Radio and Television Drama: A Collection of Tested Plays for All Groups*. New York: Exposition Press, 1953. 126 pp.

    Some of the plays in this anthology have been broadcast over WLSU, WJMR, KMLB, KNOE, WTPS, and other stations. All were part of the workshop productions of the Lin-Rey School of Broadcasting in New Orleans.

990. Migala, Joseph. *Polish Radio Broadcasting in the United States*. Boulder, CO: East European Monographs, 1987. (Distributed by Columbia University Press, New York.) 309 pp. (East European Monographs, 216). ISBN: 0-88033-112-7.

    The position of Polish radio programs in the American broadcast system is explained in part one while part two describes Polish radio programs in large Polish-American communities. The role of radio in the service of American ethnic groups is discussed and the response to a public opinion survey about Polish radio in the United States is analyzed.

991. Milton, Ralph. *Radio Programming: A Basic Training Manual.* London: Geoffrey Bles, 1968. 384 pp. ISBN: 0-7138-0216-2.

All the basic details of radio programming are included in this manual that was designed primarily for students in Asia, Africa, the Middle East, and Latin America. It was begun in 1963 as part of a Southeast Asia Radio Workshop held in the Philippines and has grown to cover short talks, interviews, translating, audience studies, panel discussions, live programs, music, news, and drama.

992. Morris, James M. *Radio Workshop Plays.* Rev. ed. New York: H.W. Wilson, 1943. 559 pp.

The first edition of this anthology was published in 1940, and this volume includes a few plays from that as well as many new dramatizations. They were written especially for radio or adapted from short stories and stage forms, and were presented at KOAC, the public-owned station of the state of Oregon.

993. Mourne, William. *NBC Matinee Theatre Presents "Miracle at Carville."* New York: National Broadcasting Company, 1950. 1 vol.

This script is for the production that was adapted by Mourne from an autobiography by Betty Martin and Evelyn Wells.

994. National Association of Broadcasters. Freedom of Information Committee. *Broadcasting Public Proceedings: Coverage Guide-Posts.* Washington: The Association, 1972. 20 pp.

Many of the points included are elementary, but they cover the people's right to know, access to the news, and responsibilities of the broadcaster. Technical suggestions for operation of equipment are made.

995. Nicol, John, Albert A. Shea, and G.J.P. Simmins. *Canada's Farm Radio Forum.* Paris: Unesco, 1954. 235 pp. (Press, Film and Radio in the World Today series).

The National Farm Radio Forum is a discussion-group project for the rural people of Canada sponsored by the Canadian Broadcasting Corporation, the Canadian Association for Adult Education, and the Canadian Federation of Agriculture. A Farm Forum is a group of neighbors who meet weekly from November to March to listen to a special radio broadcast and to study and discuss the topic of that broadcast.

996. Oboler, Arch. *Fourteen Radio Plays.* New York: Random House, 1940. 257 pp.

Before the scripts of the actual plays are presented there is an essay "The Art of Radio Writing" written by Oboler. Irving Stone has contributed an introduction, "On Reading a Radio Play."

997. Oboler, Arch. *Ivory Tower, and Other Radio Plays.* Chicago: William Targ, 1940. 79 pp.

The "other radio plays" are *Alter Ego* and *The Ugliest Man in the World.* All three are for the reading public only, and no performance of them of any sort can be given without permission from the National Broadcasting Company.

998. Oboler, Arch. *Oboler Omnibus: Radio Plays and Personalities.* New York: Duell, Sloan & Pearce, 1945. 309 pp.

In addition to creating these radio plays, Oboler adds a brief commentary about each script to tell an anecdote or two about the actors and actresses who performed in the plays or an account describing the inspiration behind each one. Oboler wrote a number of other anthologies of radio plays including *Fourteen Radio Plays* (see item 996), *This Freedom*, *Plays for Americans*, and *Free World Theatre: Nineteen New Radio Plays*.

999. O'Brien, Mae. *Children's Reactions to Radio Adaptations of Juvenile Books*. New York: King's Crown Press, 1950. 143 pp.

Before the growth of television, it was true that children listened extensively to radio programs--a fact which generated this study. It had two purposes: to find ways in which children's reactions to broadcasts could be made more directly available to producers of public service and commercial juvenile broadcasts, and to discover ways in which certain types of radio materials could be better utilized in classrooms.

1000. Olfson, Lewy. *Radio Plays of Famous Stories: A Collection of Royalty-free Radio Dramatizations of Great Stories*. Boston: Plays, Inc., 1956. 250 pp.

Among the novels dramatized in this manner are *Wuthering Heights*, *Jane Eyre*, *Silas Marner*, *Cyrano de Bergerac*, *Captains Courageous*, *David Copperfield and Uriah Heep*, *The Pickwick Papers*, *A Connecticut Yankee in King Arthur's Court*, and a Christmas story, *Which of the Nine?*

1001. Paquin, Lawrence, ed. *Radio Manual*. Washington: Federal Security Agency, U.S. Office of Education, 1941. 15 pp.

Suggestions are presented to schools and non-professional groups for the preliminary arrangements, general organization, and production of radio programs. They are intended for persons who have had no experience whatsoever in radio production.

1002. Parikhal, John, and David Oakes. *Programming Radio to Win in the New America*. Washington: National Association of Broadcasters, 1989. 191 pp. ISBN: 0-89324-062-1.

The introduction states that this is actually a report on the future of the broadcasting industry. The authors "take a 'macro' or overall look at how those in charge see the future of radio ... how the changes in the American lifestyle will affect every radio station in the country and how ... (broadcasters) can move in step with these important trends."

1003. Parker, Everett C., David W. Barry, and Dallas W. Smythe. *The Television-Radio Audience and Religion*. New York: Harper & Brothers, 1955. 464 pp. (Studies in the Mass Media of Communication).

This volume evolved from a study report supervised by Yale University as part of its Communications Research Project. It concentrates on metropolitan New Haven, its people, its religious practices, the religious broadcasters' views and actions, and the radio-TV audience in that city.

1004. Parker, Everett C., Elinor Inman, and Ross Snyder. *Religious Radio: What to Do and How*. New York: Harper & Brothers, 1948. 271 pp.

Intended as a primer for religious broadcasting, this points out the importance of radio in the communication of religious ideas and then goes on to discuss religious radio programming for the total community and the service goals of such broadcasting. Subsequent chapters describe how to write and produce programs for the widest audiences.

1005. Passman, Arnold. *The Deejays*. New York: Macmillan, 1971. 320 pp.

In his introduction Passman states "The uniting of radio with phonograph that constitutes the average radio program yields a very special pattern quite superior in power to the combination of radio and telegraph press that yields our news and weather programs. The disc jockey ... is the servant and sorcerer of this media mix which makes up at least 80 percent of all broadcast time in the U.S." Passman relates the history of the format, its ups and downs and the personalities involved--all in a scholarly manner.

1006. Pear, T.H. *Voice and Personality As Applied to Radio Broadcasting*. New York: John Wiley & Sons, 1931. 247 pp.

After specifying why voices are important and identifying voice characteristics, the author writes about radio drama from the listener's standpoint. She defines the "radio personality" and tells what effect it has on radio drama.

1007. Poling, Daniel A. *Radio Talks to Young People, with the Questions and Answers*. New York: George H. Doran, 1926. 268 pp.

The addresses in this book are the ones given by Dr. Poling at the Young People's Conferences that were begun in December 1925 and broadcast throughout the New York City area. They were part of the earliest religious programs on radio and attracted extremely large listening audiences.

1008. *Radio Broadcasting News.* East Pittsburgh, PA: Westinghouse Electric & Manufacturing Company.

First published in 1927, this was a weekly periodical that was meant "to increase interest and enjoyment in radio broadcasting." It listed programs for the week in the districts of Pittsburgh, New York and the East, Chicago and the Midwest, and the South, as well as a special section on religious broadcasting.

1009. *Radio Broadcasting Serves Rural Development.* Paris: Unesco, 1965. 51 pp. (Reports and Papers on Mass Communication, 48).

Two articles are included in this publication: "Radio Rural Forums Spread Throughout India," by B.P. Bhatt and P.V. Krishnamoorthy, and "Training for Rural Broadcasting in Africa," by Ram Marathey and Michael Bourgeois.

1010. *Radio Listener's Book of Operas.* Boston: Lothrop, Lee & Shepard, 1910. 2 vols.

Many well-known operas contain music which appeals to the public and which has ever-increasing popularity and are broadcast in their entirety. This book is intended to help the radio listener become familiar with the plots and stories of these standard operas.

1011. *Radio Programs for Children.* New York: Radio Institute of the Audible Arts, 1936. 17 pp.

Published for the 1935-36 winter season, this is a revision of an earlier listing selected by the Child Association of America for the Radio Institute of the Audible Arts. Nineteen programs are mentioned along with news commentators Boake Carter, Gabriel Heatter, Edwin C.

Hill, H.V. Kaltenborn, and Lowell Thomas, and sports commentators Ted Husing, Stan Lomax, Eddie Dooley, Lou Little, and Fritz Crisler.

1012. *Radio Programs in the Public Interest.* New York: American Civil Liberties Union, 1946. 5 pp.

This booklet provides answers to the radio industry's objections to the Federal Communications Commission's new standards of judging the public service of radio.

1013. Reid, Seerley. *Tales From Far and Near.* Columbus: Ohio State University, 1941. 44 leaves. (Evaluation of School Broadcasts Bulletin, 38).

The Columbia Broadcasting System produced a series of programs for children that were aired in 1940 and 1941 titled *Tales from Far and Near.* This report provides a critical appraisal of 25 of these broadcasts.

* Reymer & Gersin Associates. *Radio W.A.R.S.: An In-Depth Look at Full Service Fans.* Cited above as item 521.

1014. Riley, Donald W. *Handbook of Radio Drama Techniques.* Ann Arbor, MI: Edwards Brothers, 1939. 77 pp.

The introduction states that the material in this handbook was collected and arranged to instruct the beginner who wants to enter any one or all the various phases of radio drama activities. It is also intended to provide a highly condensed manual of specific techniques for the teacher.

1015. Robertson, Milton. *Meet the Russians: 6 Radio Plays.* New York: National Council of American-Soviet Friendship, 1943. 100 pp.

The first script in the series "Meet the Russians" was offered through a New York station to the American radio audience in the early 1940s and was very well received by its listeners. The Ohio State Radio Institute examined the programs and this volume contains a small part of the 70 scripts that were aired up to the publication date of this book.

1016. Rodger, Ian. *Radio Drama*. London: Macmillan, 1982. 166 pp. ISBN: 0-333-29428-9.

Chapters discuss national responses to radio, the conflict between theatre and radio, the revolution in diction, the National Theatre, the drama schools, and technical advances.

1017. Routt, Edd, James B. McGrath, and Fredric A. Weiss. *The Radio Format Conundrum*. New York: Hastings House, 1978. 314 pp. (Communication Arts Books). ISBN: 0-8038-6355-1.

Calling this book "a tool box of radio information," the authors present an accounting of radio's past, its then-state-of-the-art status, and some predictions for the medium's future. Chapters consider formats, music (classicial, contemporary, and country), black ethnic programming, information programs, religious broadcasting, the classical format, and educational facilities.

1018. Rouverol, Jean. *Writing for the Soaps*. Cincinnati: Writer's Digest Books, 1984. 220 pp. ISBN: 0-89879-146-4.

Daytime drama is a genre of its own with special rules to be followed. Rouverol explains them along with providing a good summary of how episodes are planned, written, cast, and produced.

1019. Rowland, J. Howard, I. Keith Tyler, and Norman Woelfel. *Criteria for Children's Radio Programs.* Washington: Federal Radio Education Committee, 1942. 24 pp.

The authors attempt to answer a variety of questions in this volume: Who is interested in children's radio programs? What makes the problem so complicated? What basic purposes should children's programs serve? By what criteria should children's radio programs be judged? and How were these criteria developed?

1020. Scholastic Radio Guild. *Radio Plays.* Pittsburgh: Scholastic Publications, 1935. 1 vol.

Originally published separately by Scholastic Publications and bound together by the University of Illinois library, this volume contains the scripts of 16 radio plays suitable for classroom, auditorium, or club programs.

1021. Seligman, Marjorie, and Sonya Fogle. *More Solo Readings for Radio and Class Work.* New York: Dramatists Play Service, 1944. 50 pp.

Most of the material in this volume consists of paragraphs taken from a variety of serious, semi-serious, or comic short stories, plays, or books.

1022. Seligman, Marjorie, and Sonya Fogle. *Solo Readings for Radio and Class Work.* New York: Dramatists Play Service, 1941. 55 pp.

Intended primarily for use in the radio field, a good number of the selections are considerably longer than actual audition requirements. They have been included because the authors felt such characterizations would recommend themselves to all students of the drama, regardless of the area of participation.

1023. Shane, Ed. *Programming Dynamics: Radio's Management Guide*. Overland Park, KS: Globecom Publishing, 1984. 118 pp.

"Three basic tenets recur in this book: (1) radio is a business, albeit a creative business; (2) radio is the fastest, most responsive information and entertainment medium; and (3) if you know your audience, you know your business." The author has several chapters on these ideas titled: Program Philosophy, Program Practice, Arbitron, Advertising, Research, and The Future Is Now.

1024. Sheats, Paul H. *Forums on the Air*. Washington: Federal Radio Education Committee, 1939. 63 pp.

Sheats reports on plans and procedures developed in the broadcasting of public affairs discussion programs over local radio stations. This pamphlet was published with the cooperation of the U.S. Office of Education Federal Security Agency.

* Sklar, Rick. *Rocking America: An Insider's Story. How the All-Hit Radio Stations Took Over*. Cited above as item 238.

1025. Smith, Curt. *Voices of the Game: The First Full-Scale Overview of Baseball Broadcasting, 1921 to the Present*. South Bend, IN: Diamond Communications, 1987. 594 pp. ISBN: 0-912083-21-2.

Written by someone who obviously loves the game, this "weaves into its main theme the social, political, and cultural events of the times, the drama of baseball's pennant races, and the actual play-by-play of the pastime's greatest moments." Smith discusses Mel Allen, Red Barber, Vin Scully, Joe Garagiola, Bob Prince, Jack Brickhouse, and one of his favorites, Harry

Caray, and describes their antics both in and out of the booth.

1026. Smith, V. Jackson. *Programming for Radio and Television*. Rev. ed. Washington: University Press of America, 1983. 170 pp. ISBN: 0-8191-2888-0.

Designed to be used as a study guide by which an instructor could structure a college course in programming, this presents an overview of early radio programming, networks, the Golden Age of radio, and radio programming today. Other sections discuss the audience, the actual program, and the duties and responsibilities of the program director. The first edition was published in 1980.

1027. Stedman, Raymond William. *The Serials: Suspense and Drama by Installment*. Norman: University of Oklahoma Press, 1971. 514 pp. ISBN: 0-8061-0927-0.

The author declares that serial drama was born in 1912 and grew out of continued stories in magazines and newspapers and then on to film, radio, and television. He writes about many old favorite radio shows (*The Shadow*, *The Lone Ranger*, *I Love a Mystery*, *Mr. Keen, Tracer of Lost Persons*, etc.) as he recalls the excitement such programs held for their listeners and how they acquired and maintained a loyal following.

1028. Stoppard, Tom. *Four Plays for Radio*. London: Faber & Faber, 1984. 150 pp. ISBN: 0-571-13428-9.

The plays printed in their entirety are *Artist Descending a Staircase*, *If You're Glad, I'll Be Frank*, *Albert's Bridge*, and *Where Are They Now?*

1029. Stupp, Irene M. *How and Where to Sell Radio Scripts.* New York: Thesis Publishing, 1942. 30 pp.

Along with a complete list of stations, this book provides advice to new writers on breaking into radio. Stupp reveals how stations obtain and/or commission scripts, what the contents should include, and ways of getting radio producers to read a submitted script.

1030. Taylor, Sherril W., ed. *Radio Programming in Action: Realities and Opportunities.* New York: Hastings House, 1967. 183 pp.

Edited by the National Association of Broadcasters Vice-President for Radio, this volume has articles on news and public service, modern music, country music, "beautiful" music, FM radio, and "the sports bonanza." The articles were written by officers, general managers, and/or program directors of national radio stations.

1031. Thorne, Sylvia, and Marion Norris Gleason. *The Pied Piper Broadcasts: Radio Programs for Children.* New York: H.W. Wilson, 1943. 380 pp.

Adaptations for radio of seven famous stories, these were first broadcast over station WHAM in Rochester, New York, as part of a series intended to provide a juvenile audience with entertainment on their own level of experience.

1032. Tooley, Howard. *Radio Guild Plays.* Minneapolis: Northwestern Press, 1941. 125 pp.

Tooley has compiled a collection of radio scripts suitable for special holidays and historical occasions. They are intended primarily for the use of radio groups, high school students, and club radio guilds.

1033. *The Use of Radio in Farm Advisory Work and Farmer Education*. Paris: Organisation for European Economic Co-Operation, 1956. 67 pp.

This booklet presents the report on the workshop sponsored by the European Productivity Agency of the Organisation for European Economic Co-Operation by arrangement with the U.S. Foreign Operations Administration which was held in Italy in May 1954.

1034. Van Doren, Carl, and Carl Carmer. *American Scriptures*. New York: Boni & Gaer, 1946. 302 pp.

The vignettes in this volume were selected from the series of the same name originally broadcast for the radio audience during the intermissions of the Philharmonic Symphony Sunday concerts in 1943 and 1944. They were intended to lift American spirits by recalling the wise and heroic things said and done in the American past.

1035. Verwey, Norma Ellen. *Radio Call-ins and Covert Politics: A Verbal Unit and Role Analysis Approach*. Aldershot, Eng.: Avebury, 1990. 246 pp. ISBN: 0-566-05349-7.

The author compares the approach and content of Canadian commercial call-in shows with those aired on the British public network. There were a number of Canadian programs that were similar as well as dissimilar in either content or listener's reactions, and she details these features. *Election Call* was the main British program Verwey analyzed, and she studied that show for five years although she does mention a few other BBC call-ins at the end of the book.

1036. Walker, E. Jerry. *Religious Broadcasting*. Washington: National Association of Broadcasters, 1945. 19 pp.

This is "a manual of techniques ... a guide to those who prepare and present religious programs." It includes information on basic planning (value of a committee, station contact), program planning (format, personnel, materials, building an audience), administration (church, station, and listener relations), program presentation, and rights and obligations.

1037. Warner, W. Lloyd, and William E. Henry. *The Radio Day Time Serial: A Symbolic Analysis*. Provincetown, MA: Journal Press, 1948. 99 pp.

Published first in the February 1948 issue of *Genetic Psychology Monographs Quarterly*, this is a scholarly treatise of a program titled *Big Sister* and the reactions of a typical listener group. As the authors analyze this program, they also examine the social and psychological functions of the daytime serial as a genre.

1038. Watson, Katherine Williams. *Once Upon a Time: Children's Stories Retold for Broadcasting*. New York: H.W. Wilson, 1942. 263 pp.

In response to a demand for better children's programs in 1935, the Denver Public Library began a story-telling series titled *Once Upon a Time* that was broadcast weekly over station KOA. This is a collection of some of the stories that were used.

1039. Watson, Katherine Williams. *Radio Plays for Children*. New York: H.W. Wilson, 1947. 281 pp.

The plays in this anthology are categorized as Children of Many Lands, Book Week, Fairy Tales, Holidays, Animals, Humor, Mystery, and Western. All are easy to produce and run from five to thirty minutes.

1040. Weinberg, Steve, ed. *The IRE Book: Summaries of Many Top Investigations from 1983.* Columbia, MO: Investigative Reporters & Editors, 1984. 98 pp.

Synopses of the winning stories in IRE's annual contest for the best investigative reporting in the U.S. are included, along with other entries representing categories covering newspapers, magazines, television, and radio.

1041. Weiser, Norman. *The Writer's Radio Theater: Outstanding Plays of the Year.* New York: Harper & Bros., 1941. 213 pp.

The first of several annual compilations, this reproduces ten scripts that were chosen from the several thousand that were broadcast during 1940. The foreword states that "Each of the dramas selected for inclusion was forced to meet the most rigid requirements thus far established for the writing of broadcast material."

1042. Welch, Constance, and Walter Prichard Eaton. *Yale Radio Plays: The Listeners' Theatre.* Boston: Expression Company, 1940. 390 pp.

The plays in this volume were selected from those produced on a weekly sustaining program broadcast by WICC, New Haven, a station of the Yankee network. They were written and acted by students of the Yale University Department of Drama.

1043. Wertheim, Arthur Frank. *Radio Comedy.* New York: Oxford University Press, 1979. 439 pp. ISBN: 0-19-502481-8.

The evolution of radio comedy from the fledgling years of the 1920s through the impact of television in the early 1950s is recounted. The relationship of radio comedy to

American values and society during the Great Depression and WW II is stressed.

1044. West, W.J., ed. *Orwell: The War Broadcasts*. London: Gerald Duckworth/British Broadcasting Corporation, 1985. 304 pp. ISBN: 0-7156-1916-0.

In addition to being the author of *1984* and *Animal Farm*, Orwell wrote for the BBC and went on the air himself. This book contains 16 of his more than 75 wartime scripts as well as a selection of his letters from the same period.

1045. West, W.J., ed. *Orwell: The War Commentaries*. London: Gerald Duckworth/British Broadcasting Corporation, 1985. 248 pp. ISBN: 0-7156-2073-8.

Recently discovered in the BBC archives, these are the lost texts of George Orwell's radio commentaries on WW II. They were transmitted weekly from December 1941 to February 1943, and the text is given in full along with background details furnished by the editor.

1046. Westinghouse Broadcasting Company. *The Controversial Car*. New York: The Company, 1966. 44 pp.

This pamphlet is made up of excerpts from the series of seven radio programs produced by Group W, Westinghouse Broadcasting Company, in association with Wayne State University, and broadcast in June 1965 on stations WBZ, WINS, KYW, KDKA, WOWO, and WIND.

1047. White, James R. *Let's Broadcast*. New York: Harper & Brothers, 1939. 266 pp.

Twelve one-act plays constitute this collection written expressly for young people. The method of presentation is rather unusual in that each play is a make-believe radio broadcast so there is little or no memorizing, stage business, costuming, or play properties required.

1048. White, James R. *Three Way Plays*. New York: Harper & Brothers, 1944. 165 pp.

White has compiled several non-royalty one-act plays and comedy sketches that are ideal for radio broadcasting because the size of the casts may be reduced or increased by doubling up on parts or by adding technicians or actors for the mob scenes or extra musicians.

1049. White, Melvin R. *Children's Programs for Radio Broadcast*. Minneapolis: Northwestern Press, 1948. 126 pp.

The author collected scripts that have been tested in actual broadcast for a "children's hour" type of program. They have been proven to be both easy to produce and of interest to younger children.

1050. Wishengrad, Morton. *The Eternal Light*. New York: Crown Publishers, 1947. 412 pp.

Twenty-six radio plays from the series that interpreted Judaism are reprinted here. Each has an introduction and production notes listing the cast and pertinent information about the play.

1051. Wolfe, Kenneth M. *The Churches and the British Broadcasting Corporation, 1922-1956: The Politics of Broadcast Religion*. London: SCM Press, 1984. 627 pp. ISBN: 0-334-01932-X.

The first phase in relations between the religious and broadcasting institutions in the United Kingdom is examined in this volume that considers the principal aspects and evolution of BBC policy in respect to religious broadcasting. At least one additional volume is expected to follow.

1052. Wright, Gene. *Horrorshows: The A-to-Z Horror in Film, TV, Radio, and Theater.* New York: Facts on File Publications, 1986. 296 pp. ISBN: 0-8160-1014-5.

Black-and-white photographs illustrate this catalog of the best and worst of the genre. Categories include Crazies and Freaks; Mad Scientists; Monsters; Cataclysmic Disasters; Ghouls; Ghosts; Demons; Witches; Vampires; Mummies; Werewolves; and Zombies.

1053. Writer's Guild of America. *The Prize Plays of Television and Radio, 1956.* New York: Random House, 1957. 309 pp.

Part of a series published annually, this book reprints texts of the best of serious dramas, comedies, and children's shows that were broadcast on radio and television during the year. Those radio shows in this volume are *Bring on the Angels, The Penny,* an episode from *The Edgar Bergen Show,* and the radio documentary, *Decision for Freedom.*

1054. Zimmermann, Ed. *Love in the Afternoon.* Indianapolis: Bobbs-Merrill, 1971. 186 pp.

The author is an actor who appeared in the radio serial *The Guiding Light.* This is a novel about the events and happenings of the people who are in the cast of a soap opera.

INTERNATIONAL BROADCASTING

Includes Africa, Asia, Australia, Canada, Europe, Great Britain, India, Latin and South America, Malaysia, Mexico, Scandinavia, the Third World, Radio Free Europe, and Radio Liberty.

1055. Adhikarya, Ronny, et al. *Broadcasting in Peninsular Malaysia*. London: Routledge & Kegan Paul, 1977. 102 pp. (Case Studies on Broadcasting Systems). ISBN: 0-7100-8530-3.

In addition to the Government-controlled Radio/TV Malaysia, Rediffusion, the media structures covered here include the Royal Australian Air Force Radio, telecommunications, magazines, books, and newspapers. This volume tells how broadcasting is structured, what purposes it is meant to fulfill in educational developmental and other fields, and how it may evolve in the future.

1056. *An African Experiment in Radio Forums for Rural Development: Ghana, 1964/1965*. Geneva: Unesco, 1968. (Reports and Papers on Mass Communication, 51). 71 pp.

An experiment in radio forums for rural development was carried out in Ghana from December 1964 to April 1965 and adapted the technique of farm radio forums as applied earlier in Canada and India to the social context of rural life in an African country. This paper describes and assesses the Ghana project and continues the Unesco series of publications on the subject.

1057. Aldington, Toby Low. *The Use of Radio Frequencies for Sound and Television Broadcasting in the United Kingdom.* London: British Broadcasting Corporation, 1974. 11 pp.

This paper, prepared by the BBC for its General Advisory Council, sets out the way in which the various allocated broadcasting frequencies are used by the Corporation for its sound and television services. It draws attention to some of the difficulties encountered and proposes possible courses of action.

1058. Alexeyeva, Ludmilla. *U.S. Broadcasting to the Soviet Union.* New York: Helsinki Watch, 1986. 136 pp. ISBN: 0-938579-87-8.

The U.S. Helsinki Watch Committee commissioned this report on the work of the Russian-language broadcasting services of Radio Liberty and the Voice of America. It was written by a former Soviet historian and one of the founders of the Moscow Helsinki Watch Committee.

1059. Allard, T.J. *The C.A.B. Story, 1926-1976: Private Broadcasting in Canada.* Ottawa: Canadian Association of Broadcasters, 1976. 68 pp.

Individual sections are devoted to the Infant Years; the Advent of Authority; the Years of Shadow (1931-34); the Rebirth; First Interlude; the Reconstruction Years; the Third Structural Change; 1944-46; 1946-48; 1948-58; and 1958-73. Appendices provide data and photographs of officers and officials of the CAB and its Board of Directors.

1060. Allard, T.J. *Straight Up: Private Broadcasting in Canada, 1918-1958.* Ottawa: Canadian Communications Foundation, 1979. 280 pp. ISBN: 0-9690948-0-9.

Written by a knowledgeable insider this book "... bluntly challenges nearly every generally accepted concept about Canadian broadcasting" It traces the development of broadcasting and outlines public and behind-the-scenes events involved in shaping the structure of Canada's broadcasting.

* Amin, R.K. *Radio Rural Forums in Gujarat: An Observation Study*. Cited above as item 874.

1061. Australian Broadcasting Corporation. *ABC Achievements and the Implementation of Dix, 1983-85*. Sydney: The Corporation, 1985. 40 pp. ISBN: 0-642-53032-7.

The ABC Committee of Review (known as the Dix Committee after its Chairman, Alex Dix) reported to the Australian Parliament in May 1981 following a major inquiry into the corporation. Over 270 specific recommendations were made. This report gives, in summary form, the progress that has been made in implementing these recommendations.

1062. Australian Broadcasting Corporation. *ABC Powers and Functions*. Sydney: The Corporation, 1984. 8 pp. ISBN: 0-642-97583-3.

Funding, the legal basis, staffing and management, divisions, and studio descriptions are included in this booklet. Stereo FM radio, Radio Australia, and state symphony orchestras are also described.

1063. Australian Broadcasting Corporation. *Corporate Plan, 1985-1988*. Sydney: The Corporation, 1985. 40 pp. ISBN: 0-642-5302-4-6.

The plan offers a strategic view of the corporation's activities for three years, anticipates likely changes in broadcasting, and sets priorities so that ABC can respond to such changes. A financial statement and expansion plans for electronic data- processing are included.

1064. Australian Broadcasting Corporation. *History and Development of the ABC*. Sydney: The Corporation, 1984. 16 pp. ISBN: 0-642-97607-4.

The national broadcasting service actually began operations in July 1932 and expanded considerably during the post-WW II years. This booklet describes the progress in both words and figures. Included is a listing of the various stations added since 1956.

1065. Australian Broadcasting Corporation. *The Role of a National Broadcaster in Contemporary Australia*. Sydney: The Corporation, 1985. 20 pp. ISBN: 0-642-53016-5.

The Board's Chairman, Kenneth Myer, refers to this as a philosophical statement that reveals a changing but still crucial role for a national broadcasting organization. It examines roles and principles, community values, standards, and the Australian national culture as it relates to public service broadcasting.

1066. Australian Department of Communications. *Sound and Television Broadcasting Stations*. 5th ed. Canberra: Australian Government Publishing Service, 1984. 146 pp. ISSN: 0812-2016.

Published regularly since 1979, this periodical provides the call sign, location, frequency, power, aerial type and height, geographic co-ordinates, and opening date for each of the national, commercial, and public broadcasting stations.

1067. Australian Department of Transport and Communications. *Review of National Broadcasting Policy.* Canberra: Government Publishing Service, 1988. 1 vol. ISBN: 0-644-07862-6.

This is a selection of six discussion papers of the Australian Broadcasting Corporation. The first two are about the role of Australia's national broadcasters and the funding of ABC; the other four discuss Parliamentary broadcasting, the ABC orchestra, the infrastructure of national broadcasting, and the TV broadcasting environment.

1068. Awasthy, G.C. *Broadcasting in India.* Bombay: Allied Publishers, 1965. 268 pp.

The author was a member of the All India Radio programming staff for over 15 years and wrote this book because he says he was unable to find a single book on the subject and felt one was long overdue. It tells of Indian broadcasting's struggle for survival, the programming and programming policies, administration, and growth.

1069. Bakke, Marit, and Karen Siune. *Radio and TV News in Denmark and Norway.* Aarhus, Denmark: University of Aarhus, 1974. 9 leaves.

Using samples of three consecutive weeks of news programs selected over a long period of time, this pamphlet presents some results from a content analysis comparing newscasts transmitted in two mass media in the two countries.

1070. Ball, W. Macmahon, ed. *Press, Radio and World Affairs: Australia's Outlook.* Melbourne: Melbourne University Press, 1938. 146 pp.

A report issued under the auspices of the Victorian Branch of the Institute of Pacific Relations, this is a collection of essays on Australia's relations with other countries regarding media. Chapters discuss the Australian press and world affairs, Japan, the USSR, the League of Nations in the Abyssinian War, imperial ideas, and radio broadcasting and world affairs.

1071. Baron, Mike. *Independent Radio: The Story of Independent Radio in the United Kingdom*. Lavenham, Eng.: Terence Dalton, 1975. 192 pp. ISBN: 0-900963-65-4.

Until October 8, 1973, the British Broadcasting Corporation had a 50-year monopoly on radio broadcasting. On that date London Broadcasting launched commercial radio in Britain. This book discusses the early days of British broadcasting and the growth of BBC, but concentrates on the "upstart independent radio broadcasting."

1072. Baruah, U.L. *This Is All India Radio: A Handbook of Radio Broadcasting in India*. New Delhi: Ministry of Information and Broadcasting, Publications Division, 1983. 367 pp.

Written by AIR's former Director-General, this presents an informed analysis of the organizational structure of Indian broadcasting and the growth and development it has undergone. There is an account of the programming provided and various development activities in progress at the time of publication.

1073. Beachcroft, T.O. *British Broadcasting*. London: Longmans Green, 1946. 39 pp. (British Life & Thought, 25).

In this essay Mr. Beachcroft explains the constitution and scope of the British Broadcasting Corporation and the particular place it occupies in British democratic life.

1074. Bennett, Jeremy. *British Broadcasting and the Danish Resistance Movement, 1940-1945*. Cambridge, Eng.: Cambridge University Press, 1966. 266 pp.

Bennett presents a study of the wartime broadcasts of the BBC Danish Service. He begins with its first broadcast in Danish on April 9, 1940, the day of the German invasion of Denmark, continues with chapters on the Danish Crisis of October 1942, the election of March 1943, black propaganda, and concludes with a story of radio and the resistance movement.

1075. Beveridge, Sir William, et al. *Changes in Family Life*. London: Allen & Unwin, 1932. 160 pp.

The seven wireless talks reprinted in this volume were presented in 1932 as part of a British Broadcasting Corporation plan to secure the interest and help of listeners in collecting information of scientific interest. They became part of the BBC series, *The Changing World*.

1076. Bird, Roger, ed. *Documents of Canadian Broadcasting*. Ottawa: Carleton University Press, 1988. 756 pp. ISBN: 0-88629-073-2.

Categorized into the pre-broadcasting era, the radio age, television, and the CRTC years, this includes reports of the Deputy Minister of Public Works, the Wireless Telegraphy Act of 1905, the Radiotelegraph Act of 1913, reports of the Royal Commission on Radio Broadcasting, BBC Radio (TV) broadcasting regulations, a 1966 White paper on broadcasting, the CBC Journalistic Policy, CRTC broadcasting regulations, etc.

1077. Blackburn, Adrian. *The Shoestring Pirates: Radio Hauraki.* Auckland, N.Z.: Hodder & Stoughton, 1974. 194 pp. ISBN: 0-340-195711.

The New Zealand Broadcasting Corporation exercised a monopoly over radio and television broadcasting until a small group determined to break this monopoly. This book is the story of that attempt and its aftermath.

1078. Blatnỳ, Milan K. *Heralds of False Freedom: Who Is Who in Radio Free Europe and in Radio Liberty.* Bratislava: Journalistic Study Institute in the Obzor Publishing House, 1977. 35 pp.

Printed by Pravda, this is a listing of names and brief backgrounds of people who were employed by Radio Free Europe and Radio Liberty. Included are agents of the CIA and other American intelligence services, employees of the Czechoslovak, Hungarian, and Policy sections of RFE, and agents of Western special services involved in espionage operations.

1079. Boyd, Douglas A. *Broadcasting in the Arab World: A Survey of Radio and Television in the Middle East.* Philadelphia: Temple University Press, 1982. 306 pp. (International and Comparative Broadcasting series). ISBN: 0-87722-237-1.

The developments, trends and constraints of Arab World broadcasting are discussed in Boyd's introduction. In the balance of the book he goes into great detail about the various national systems of Egypt, the Sudan, Lebanon, Syria, Jordan, North and South Yemen, the Arabian Gulf States, North Africa, and international radio broadcasting in Arabic.

1080. Brack, Hans. *The Evolution of the EBU Through Its Statutes from 1950 to 1976.* Geneva: European Broadcasting Union, 1976. 179 pp. (EBU Legal and Administrative Monographs, 11).

This describes the founding of the European Broadcasting Union, the development of its objects, the status of its members, the position of the General Assembly, the Administrative Council, its president, the EBU permanent services, its committees, finances, appointments, and achievements.

1081. Brack, Hans. *German Radio and Television: Organization and Economic Basis.* Geneva: European Broadcasting Union, 1968. 68 pp. (EBU Legal and Administrative Monographs, 6).

In a historical outline, this looks first at the organization and economic basis of radio in Germany prior to WW II, in the Federal Republic of Germany in 1968, and then in the German Democratic Republic. The second part examines international broadcasting organizations in general and as part of the European Broadcasting Union.

* Briggs, Asa. *The History of Broadcasting in the United Kingdom.* Cited above as item 42.

1082. British Broadcasting Corporation. *The BBC and the Arts.* London: The Corporation, 1968. 28 pp. ISBN: 0-563-07415-9.

Based on a recent study made by the BBC for its General Advisory Council, this examines BBC programming and relations with music and musicians, opera and ballet, performers and composers, concerts and festivals, drama, the theatre, and competitions. Special attention is given to broadcasting to Scotland,

Wales, and the Regions, and to the general overall role of broadcasting itself.

1083. British Broadcasting Corporation. *BBC Local Radio: Some Questions Answered.* London: The Corporation, 1967. 11 pp. ISBN: 0-563-07405-1.

In 1967 the BBC began an experiment in local broadcasting with eight communities in Leicester, Sheffield, Merseyside, Nottingham, Brighton, Stoke-on-Trent, Leeds, and Durham. The Government expected to consider in 1969 whether the experiment had been a success, and this booklet answers questions evoked by this trial, such as Why local radio? What do listeners hear? Serious or pop? and How many miles?

1084. British Broadcasting Corporation. *BBC Services Available to Other Broadcasters.* London: The Corporation, 1971. 7 pp.

Among the services described are rebroadcasting of BBC programs, recorded programs, transcription service, BBC topical tapes, special programs, English language lessons, and educational recordings. Also described are TV programs, broadcast facilities in London for other broadcasters, and staff training courses.

1085. British Broadcasting Corporation. *The BBC's Medical Programmes & Their Effects on Lay Audiences.* London: The Corporation, 1976. 63 pp. ISBN: 0-563-17262-2.

While this study prepared for the BBC General Advisory Council concentrates mainly on television, there are several sections about Network Radio, the Science Unit of the BBC. Coverage of medical matters on the BBC's regional and local radio services are described along with some examples of medical programs broadcast on both network TV and radio.

1086. British Broadcasting Corporation. *Broadcasting in the Seventies: The BBC's Plan for Network and Nonmetropolitan Broadcasting.* London: The Corporation, 1969. 13 pp. ISBN: 0-563-08562-2.

The proposals in this paper deal mainly with the future of radio so that BBC radio can play a full part in the broadcasting pattern of the 1970s. They cover network radio (Radios One, Two, Three, and Four), news, education, local radio, broadcasting for the Regions, frequencies, and music programming.

1087. British Broadcasting Corporation. *Talking Points.* London: The Corporation, 1968. 1 vol.

This is the first volume of an irregularly published series of BBC comments on questions that viewers and listeners asked. The articles are reprinted from *Radio Times*.

1088. British Broadcasting Corporation. *This Is Local Radio: The BBC Experiment at Work.* London: The Corporation, 1969. 30 pp. ISBN: 0-563-08485-5.

A follow-up to *BBC Local Radio: Some Questions Answered* (see item 1083), this is the promised 1969 evaluation of the BBC experiment in local radio broadcasting in eight communities. This booklet gives some idea of what the eight local stations are doing so that people not living in those areas could get some understanding of the programming output of the stations and the results achieved.

1089. British Broadcasting Corporation. *The Western Tradition.* London: Vox Mundi Books, 1951. 110 pp.

This contains a series of talks presented on the BBC about a variety of topics all relating to western civilization. Among the subjects are Science and Present Day Problems, Nature and Origin of Scientific Method, the Roman Catholic View of Church and State, Science and the Future, Totalitarianism, Nationalism and the Western Tradition, and Skepticism and Tolerance.

1090. British Broadcasting Corporation. *What Do You Think So Far?* London: The Corporation, 1977. 64 pp. ISBN: 0-563-17480-3.

Based mainly on the *BBC Annual Report and Accounts* for 1976-77, this is a "shorter, cheaper version" to inform the public how BBC spends the public's money and how it tries to keep in touch with that public.

1091. BBC World Service. *London Calling.* London: British Broadcasting Corporation. ISSN: 0024-600X

This monthly publication "is the programme journal of the BBC World Service." It is available throughout the world and offers a guide to the current recommended transmission and frequency times for various areas as well as articles about programs and listings for the programs.

1092. *Broadcasting.* London: Her Majesty's Stationery Office, 1966. 11 pp.

A pamphlet presented to Parliament by the Postmaster General, this summarizes the various major aspects of British broadcasting policy. Detailed are the finances of the British Broadcasting Corporation, sound radio, hours of broadcasting, and the common responsibilities of the broadcasting authorities.

* *Broadcasting in Britain.* Cited above as item 45.

1093. *Broadcasting Laws: Documents on Politics and Society in the Federal Republic of Germany.* Bonn-Bad Godesberg, Ger.: Inter Nationes, 1979. 70 pp.

Articles describe broadcasting corporations, their legal forms, organs, functions, financial bases, and the cooperation between the corporations. The second part of this book reprints excerpts from the Basic Law of the Federal Republic of Germany along with a selection of the broadcasting norms laid down by law.

1094. Browne, Donald R. *International Radio Broadcasting: The Limits of the Limitless Medium.* New York: Praeger, 1982. 369 pp. (Praeger Special Studies). ISBN: 0-03-059619-X.

The author has drawn on his nearly 25 years of exploration of international broadcasting and on articles, books and reports dating back to the 1920s to provide historical treatment of the subject. His central thesis is that international radio broadcasting functions within some rather severe limitations, principally political, cultural, technical, and economic, and he explains these restrictions within the text.

* Buehler, E.C., compiler. *American vs. British System of Radio Control.* Cited above as item 326.

1095. Bumpus, Bernard, and Barbara Skelt. *Seventy Years of International Broadcasting.* Paris: Unesco, 1985. 117 pp. (Communication and Society, 14).

"This study traces the history of international broadcasting from its earliest days to the present. It also takes a look at the impact of these broadcasts, and how this can be measured. It considers the reason why there are so many international broadcasters, many of whom persist in spite of the difficulties and rising costs ... looks at some of the problems which broadcasters face today, and considers the future of the medium."

1096. Burke, Richard C. *Comparative Broadcasting Systems*. Chicago: Science Research Associates, 1984. 43 pp. (Masscomm Modules in Mass Communication). ISBN: 0-574-22603-6.

An overview of broadcasting in the United Kingdom, Canada, Western Europe, Soviet Union, Japan, the Developing World, and the U.S. is presented along with background on services offered, programming, regulation, financing, and future plans.

* Burns, Tom. *The BBC: Public Institution and Private World*. Cited above as item 50.

1097. Canada. Committee on Broadcasting. *Report*. Ottawa: Queen's Printer, 1965. 416 pp.

The Canadian Broadcasting System is the subject of this report that was commissioned for the Secretary of State and Registrar General of Canada in 1964. It examines programming, facilities, coverage, relations with Parliament and the government, control, mandate, commercial activities, private broadcasting, and radio's financing.

1098. Canadian Association of Broadcasters. *A Broadcasting Strategy for the Future*. Ottawa: The Association, 1982. 19 pp.

This pamphlet contains the text of policy and legislative recommendations proposed by Canada's private broadcasters. They cover general broadcast policy, copyright and program exclusivity, Canadian content and production, satellite services, radio services, ownership, incentives for TV, and the role of the CBC.

1099. Canadian Broadcasting Corporation. *Canadian Radio Year Book.* 1st ed. Toronto: The Corporation, 1946. 147 pp.

This annual publication provides data on provincial radio, actors, administrative personnel, musicians, networks, programs, unions, writers, etc. It subsequently was retitled *The Canadian Radio and Television Annual* and combined directory information with yearbook facts.

1100. Canadian Broadcasting Corporation. *What the Canadian Public Thinks of the CBC.* Ottawa: The Corporation, 1963. 1 vol. (A CBC Research Report to Management).

The subtitle states this is "An empirical study of public attitudes to the Canadian Broadcasting Corporation and to certain other aspects of broadcasting in Canada." It examines public support for certain CBC aims, the extent of public knowledge about aspects of CBC commercial activities and financing, and the identifying characteristics of those who prefer CBC-owned to non-CBC stations.

1101. Canadian Radio-Television and Telecommunications Commission. *FM Radio in Canada: A Policy to Ensure a Varied and Comprehensive Radio Service.* Ottawa: The Commission, 1975. 27 pp.

This document sets out, in English and in French, the Commission's objectives and requirements for the development of FM radio in Canada. It provides background material, discusses the development of Canadian radio broadcasting in general, lists some concerns about radio, and summarizes the measures adopted by the Commission in connection with FM radio.

1102. Canadian Radio-Television and Telecommunications Commission. Public Hearing Division. *Radio and Television Stations in Canada by Province, by Program*

Source, by Call Signs. Ottawa: The Commission, 1980. 156 pp.

Just as the title indicates, this contains lists of Canadian radio and television stations arranged in several ways.

1103. Canadian Radio-Television Commission. *CRTC Ownership: Radio and Television Stations*. Ottawa: The Commission, 1970. 1 vol.

In a loose-leaf format so that amendments can be easily inserted, this consists of lists showing the ownership of broadcasting stations licensed by the Canadian Radio-Television Commission. In addition to name and address of each individual or organization, it includes names of directors, executive officers, and shareholders.

1104. Canadian Radio-Television Commission. *Directory: Multilingual Broadcasting in Canada*. Ottawa: Information Canada, 1974. 117 pp.

The aim of this booklet is to promote more interaction among the broadcasters and stations listed in it, to help the multilingual community expand, and improve its broadcasting activities. It lists producers (by language and alphabetically) and stations (by medium--AM and FM radio and television).

1105. Canadian Radio-Television Commission. *Radio Frequencies Are Public Property*. Ottawa: The Commission, 1974. 143 pp.

This is a public announcement and decision of the Commission on the applications for renewal of the CBC's radio and television licenses. It contains the report of a public hearing held in March 1974.

1106. Canadian Royal Commission on Broadcasting. *Report*. Ottawa: The Commission, 1957. 518 pp.

This report submitted by the Commissioners to the Governor General covers Canada's special problems in broadcasting, programming, regulation, private broadcasters, public relations, research in broadcasting, the CBC, radio's future, finances, and broadcasting in the French language.

1107. Cathcart, Rex. *The Most Contrary Region: The BBC in Northern Ireland, 1924-1984*. Belfast: Blackstaff Press, 1984. 306 pp. ISBN: 0-85640-323-7.

From its beginnings as a "chamber of horrors" single studio, the BBC has grown to become "one of the most important institutions in Northern Ireland." Cathcart describes its fluctuations and discusses the various programming disputes that have arisen as its influence has expanded over the past 60 years.

1108. Cave, Martin. *Broadcasting Regulation and the New Technologies*. Canberra: Australian National University. Centre for Economic Policy Research, 1984. 32 pp. (Discussion Paper, 105).

Following the Spence-Owen model of broadcasting regulation, this paper states that both pay-broadcasting and competition within the industry become more attractive as frequencies restrictions are relaxed, It compares regulatory policies of Great Britain, the U.S., and Australia.

1109. Chang, Won Ho. *Mass Media in China: The History and the Future*. Ames: Iowa State University Press, 1989. 308 pp. ISBN: 0-8138-0272-5.

The change of leadership in China with the advent of Deng Xiaoping ushered in a new era of development in all aspects of society in China, including the mass media and journalism, prior to the June 1989 student protest in Tiananmen Square in Beijing. This book presents the early history, an overview and analysis of the development of the press and broadcasting before the student protest.

1110. Chatterji, P.C. *Broadcasting in India*. New Delhi; Newbury Park, CA: Sage Publications India, 1987. 210 pp. (Case Studies on Broadcasting Systems). ISBN: 0-8039-9529-6.

Indian broadcasting today is described against a demographic, economic and linguistic background. Management and financial procedures, programming, and the structure and organization of radio and television are examined as are the reports of the First Committee that inquired into the state of Indian broadcasting and the two Working Groups set up by the Janata and Congress-I governments.

* Childs, Harwood L., and John B. Whitton, eds. *Propaganda by Short Wave*. Cited above as item 642.

1111. Coase, R.H. *British Broadcasting: A Study in Monopoly*. Cambridge, MA: Harvard University Press, 1950. 206 pp.

Published for the London School of Economics and Political Science of the University of London, this tells how broadcasting in Great Britain came to be organized on a monopolistic basis, the effect such a monopoly has on the development of and policy toward competitive services, and the views which have been held on this monopoly. The author states it is not his aim to come to a conclusion as to whether or not it is desirable that broadcasting should be organized as it is, but it is published to "be of assistance in any reasoned discussion of this question."

1112. Codding, George A., Jr. *World Administrative Radio Conference for the Planning of HF Bands Allocated to the Broadcasting Service: A Pre-Conference Briefing Paper.* London: International Institute of Communications, 1983. 40 pp.

This report discusses the problems associated with the high frequency portion of the radio spectrum and its importance, particularly for domestic use in developing countries, and for international broadcasting in general. It reviews past developments and identifies the principal tasks of the 1984 conference.

1113. *Commercial Radio in Africa.* Bonn, West Ger.: German Africa Society, 1970. 207 pp.

The Deutsche Afrika-Gesellschaft e.V. (German Africa Society) found it advisable to compile a reference book devoted to the possibilities of radio and television advertising in Africa. The purpose of this book is to provide all who are interested in the structure of the new market with reliable and detailed information regarding industry, commerce, and publicity.

1114. Committee on Foreign Affairs. U.S. House of Representatives. *The Board for International Broadcasting, Radio Free Europe and Radio Liberty.* Washington: Government Printing Office, 1974. 108 pp.

These hearings are similar to a number of annual ones held to authorize appropriations for a specific fiscal year to support the operations of RFE, Radio Liberty, and the Board for International Broadcasting.

328 Radio Broadcasting

1115. Committee on Foreign Affairs. U.S. House of Representatives. *Radio Broadcasting to Cuba (Radio Marti)*. Washington: Government Printing Office, 1982. 210 pp.

   This publication contains a transcript of the hearings before the Committee in March 1982.

1116. Committee on Foreign Relations. U.S. Senate. *Funding of Radio Free Europe and Radio Liberty*. Washington: Government Printing Office, 1972. 83 pp.

   The purpose of these hearings was to further amend the U.S. Information and Educational Exchange Act of 1948 to continue funding of Radio Free Europe and Radio Liberty for another year. Similar hearings have been held annually.

1117. Committee on Foreign Relations. U.S. Senate. *Radio Broadcasting to Cuba*. Washington: Government Printing Office, 1983. 548 pp.

   Administration witnesses testified at this hearing held on July 1, 1982, on S. 1853, a bill to authorize support of radio broadcasting to Cuba.

1118. Committee on Foreign Relations. U.S. Senate. *Radio Free Europe and Radio Liberty Authorization*. Washington: Government Printing Office, 1974. 62 pp.

   This hearing was on S. 3190 to authorize appropriations for fiscal year 1975 for carrying out the Board for International Broadcasting Act of 1973.

1119. Committee on International Relations. U.S. House of Representatives. *Board for International Broadcasting Authorization for Fiscal Year 1976 (Radio Free*

Europe/Radio Liberty). Washington: Government Printing Office, 1975. 50 pp.

The June 12, 1975, hearing was for the purpose of funding for the Board for International Broadcasting to support Radio Free Europe and Radio Liberty.

1120. Commonwealth Broadcasting Association. *Handbook.* London: The Association, 1976. 122 pp.

The Commonwealth Broadcasting Association was founded in London in February 1945 as the Commonwealth Broadcasting Conference and is an association of 45 national broadcasting organizations in 42 Commonwealth countries pledged to work for the professional improvement of broadcasting in member organizations through collective study and mutual assistance. This handbook records the origins of the Association, gives examples of the kind of practical cooperation that goes on, and summarizes the proceedings of the organization's general conferences.

1121. Contreras, Eduardo, et al. *Cross-Cultural Broadcasting.* Geneva: Unesco, 1976. 49 pp. (Reports and Papers on Mass Communication, 77). ISBN: 02-3-101353-X.

Cross-cultural broadcasting was defined rather broadly, according to the introduction, to mean any radio or television broadcasting situation where one cultural group produces the programming and another cultural group receives it. The main purpose of the study was to discover the effects of such a situation in four areas: cultural, linguistic, psychological, and/or political.

1122. Crisell, Andrew. *Understanding Radio.* London: Methuen, 1986. 236 pp. (Studies in Communication series). ISBN: 0-416-38330-0.

330 Radio Broadcasting

A short history of institutional radio in Britain and a survey of current developments are provided in this in-depth study. Crisell discusses educational radio, phone-ins, outside broadcasts, and the ways in which the listener can best use the medium.

* Crocker, Patti. *Radio Days: A Personal View of Australia's Radio Heyday.* Cited above as item 73.

1123. *Cultural Radio Broadcasts: Some Experiences.* Paris: Unesco, 1956. 59 pp. (Reports and Papers on Mass Communication, 23).

Part one consists of the texts of speeches made during an International Meeting of Cultural Radio Programme Directors or Producers held at Unesco headquarters in 1956. Part two is a report by Mr. Nicolae David on the cultural role of broadcasting in various countries.

1124. Curran, Charles. *A Seamless Robe: Broadcasting--Philosophy and Practice.* London: Collins, 1979. 358 pp. ISBN: 0-00-211-864-5.

Curran was Director-General of the British Broadcasting Corporation and was "determined not to write a book of 'secrets'" about the BBC. Instead he has "set down some of my thoughts about the philosophy and practice of broadcasting as I had known it." He includes much information about Radios One, Two, Three, and Four as well as Radio Telefis Eireann.

1125. *Developing Information Media in Africa: Press, Radio, Film, Television.* Paris: Unesco, 1962. 57 pp. (Reports and Papers on Mass Communication, 37).

This publication reproduces the report of a meeting of experts on development of information media in Africa that was held at Unesco headquarters in 1962. The section on radio broadcasting discussed the current situation, means of transmission, telecommunication, planning of broadcasting services, means of reception, group listening, programming, news programs, educational role of radio, and program cooperation.

1126. Dizard, Wilson P. *Space WARC and the Role of International Satellite Networks*. Washington: Georgetown University Center for Strategic & International Studies, 1984. 40 pp.

A major attempt to redefine international rules for satellite development was the agenda of an International Telecommunications Union World Administrative Radio Conference in August 1985 and was to be continued at a second session in 1988. This preliminary report provides background, summarizes the prevailing attitudes of the countries involved, and describes the recommended U.S. strategy.

1127. Duggal, K.S. *What Ails Indian Broadcasting*. New Delhi: Marwah Publications, 1980. 183 pp.

The author, a long-time broadcaster in India, states that All India Radio had never known any interference from the provincial government "until freedom came in 1947." He blames Indian broadcasting troubles and the misuse of mass media on the government as he writes about radio drama, mishandling, the need for proper feedback, and language policy.

1128. Durham, F. Gayle. *Amateur Radio Operation in the Soviet Union*. Cambridge, MA: Massachusetts Institute of Technology, 1965. 71 pp.

Published by MIT's Center for International Studies, this is part of its Research Program on Problems of

Communication and International Security. It examines the administration of Soviet amateur radio activity, the amateur radio operator, types of amateur communications being encouraged, activities of Soviet operators, and the radio equipment used.

* Durham, F. Gayle. *News Broadcasting on Soviet Radio and Television.* Cited above as item 667.

1129. Durham, F. Gayle. *Radio and Television in the Soviet Union.* Cambridge, MA: Massachusetts Institute of Technology, 1965. 127 pp.

   Processed for the Defense Documentation Center, Defense Supply Agency, this unclassified document deals with the broadcasting network within the Soviet Union. The author delves into radio broadcasting, broadcasting situations, and radio and television in rural localities. She also studies the Soviet audience with her focus on its size, nature, audience feedback, and listening behavior.

1130. Eckersley, Peter. *The Power Behind the Microphone.* London: Jonathan Cape, 1941. 255 pp.

   The author states that any book about British broadcasting is inevitably concerned with the British Broadcasting Corporation. He criticizes the BBC in this volume but does not consider it a personal attack upon individuals. Rather, his disagreement is with the BBC policy itself, and this is the focus of his book.

1131. Eguchi, H., and H. Ichinohe, eds. *International Studies of Broadcasting, with Special Reference to the Japanese Studies.* Tokyo: NHK Radio & TV Culture Research Institute, 1971. 301 pp.

The essays look at the historical, legal and economic aspects of the broadcasting industry in Japan, its programming and production, political process, and public opinion. Other articles examine radio and television broadcasting research trends in the United States, Germany, the United Kingdom, Canada, and the Scandinavian countries.

1132. Emery, Walter B. *National and International Systems of Broadcasting: Their History, Operation and Control*. East Lansing: Michigan State University Press, 1969. 752 pp.

The foreword states "this book represents the first attempt by an author to analyze in some depth the important broadcasting systems in all parts of the world, and to explain their origin, development, and present operation. A global study with emphasis on the managerial and regulatory aspects of radio and television, both national and international, it also covers the quantitative dimensions of the media and describes in detail their programming patterns."

1133. Etzioni-Halevy, Eva. *National Broadcasting Under Siege: A Comparative Study of Australia, Britain, Israel, and West Germany*. London: Macmillan, 1987. 228 pp. ISBN: 0-333-42775-0.

The author writes that this is a comparative study of the pressures which political establishments exert on national public broadcasting corporations in four Western-style democracies, the broadcasters' reactions to them, and the resulting tensions and conflicts. She points out the differences and similarities among the corporations in their relations with their governments.

1134. Faenza, Roberto. *The Radio Phenomenon in Italy*. Strasbourg: Council for Cultural Co-Operation, 1977. 29 pp.

Published through the Council of Europe as part of its Education & Culture publications, this discusses the use of radio as a force in society, its power and the consequences of that power in the Italian context. It looks at "thirty years of monopoly," the various political aspects of that monopoly, pirate radio, and proposals for the future.

1135. Federal Radio Corporation of Nigeria. *Radio-TV Times*. Lagos, Nigeria: FRC.

A monthly program journal of the Federal Radio Corporation of Nigeria, this serial began publication in 1968 and includes letters, articles, and program schedules.

1136. Fejes, Fred. *Imperialism, Media, and the Good Neighbor: New Deal Foreign Policy and United States Shortwave Broadcasting to Latin America*. Norwood, NJ: Ablex, 1987. 190 pp. (Communication & Information Science series). ISBN: 0-89391-321-9.

The author applied a "revisionist history" approach as he examined the complex dynamics between economic interests and public policy and their inter-relationships. He describes the early development of North American shortwave broadcasting, how it was affected by an "activist" Good Neighbor Policy, and how it expanded during WW II.

1137. Ferrell, Oliver P. *Confidential Frequency List*. 6th ed. Park Ridge, NJ: Gilfer Associates, 1984. 304 pp. ISBN: 0-914-542-13-3.

Published posthumously, this book represents the then-latest available information on the most interesting communications stations operating on the shortwave bands. It represents stations actually in operation and being heard internationally by active monitors and the text explains Piccolo Signals, RTTY, Russian language transmissions, aeronautical mobile bands, and Z-codes.

1138. *Final Acts of the World Administrative Radio Conference for the Mobile Services (MOB-83)*. Geneva: International Telecommunications Union, 1983. 200 pp. ISBN: 92-61-01731-2.

This contains the partial revision of the radio regulations, their appendices, the final protocol, and the resolutions, along with the names of the signatories.

1139. Fischer, Desmond. *Broadcasting in Ireland*. London: Routledge & Kegan Paul, 1978. 120 pp. (Case Studies on Broadcasting Systems). ISBN: 0-7100-8885-X.

Regular broadcasting began in Ireland in 1926, and its development was bound up with the process of building the political, economic, and social framework of the Irish Free State. This chronicles the progress and problems of Ireland's broadcasting service as it competes with other British broadcasting systems.

1140. Fowler, Gene, and Bill Crawford. *Border Radio*. Austin: Texas Monthly Press, 1987. 282 pp. ISBN: 0-87719-066-6.

The colorful story of the powerful radio stations just across the Mexican border that commanded a nationwide audience in the U.S. from the 1930s through the 1960s is told in this volume. They broadcast with more than 500,000 watts and could be heard on AM all over the country and were primarily owned by American broadcasting "wildcatters." The foreword was written by radio personality Wolfman Jack.

1141. Frederick, Howard H. *Cuban-American Radio Wars: Ideology in International Telecommunications*. Norwood, NJ: Ablex, 1986. 200 pp. (Communication and Information Science series). ISBN: 0-89391-264-4.

The latest volume in this series examines radio broadcasting as a primary vehicle of ideological confrontation among nations, specifically Cuba and the U.S. It concentrates on the meaning and importance of this confrontation as it reflects on telecommunications and democracy in general.

* Golding, Peter, and Philip Elliott. *Making the News*. Cited above as item 694.

1142. Gorham, Maurice. *Forty Years of Irish Broadcasting*. Dublin: Talbot Press, 1967. 356 pp.

Published for Radio Telefis Eireann, this recounts the story of Irish radio broadcasting as compiled from newspaper files, daily reports, office records, and personal memories of the people who were involved. It is confined to radio broadcasting; television is mentioned only insofar as it had an impact on radio.

1143. Graves, Harold N., Jr. *War on the Short Wave*. New York: Foreign Policy Association, 1941. 64 pp. (Headline Books, 30).

The titles of the various sections are: Round the World on the Air Waves; The Story of International Broadcasting; Weapons in the Radio Armory; The Tragedy of *Paris-Mondial*; The Soviet Engima; The BBC Takes Up the Cudgels; and What Is the Radio Weapon Worth?

1144. Guback, Thomas H., and Steven P. Hill. *The Innovation of Broadcasting in the Soviet Union and the Role of V.I. Lenin*. Urbana: University of Illinois Institute of Communications Research, 1972. 56 leaves.

This presents an overview of the history of Soviet broadcasting from its beginnings to the mid-1920s. It includes the technological precursors and the political, economic and administrative character of the emerging Soviet nation as well.

1145. Haak, Kees van der, with Joanna Spicer. *Broadcasting in the Netherlands*. London: Routledge & Kegan Paul, 1977. 92 pp. (Case Studies on Broadcasting Systems). ISBN: 0-7100-8780-2.

In describing Dutch broadcasting, this concentrates on providing the factual basis of the country's radio and television systems. It analyzes the relationship between government and broadcasters and how advertising is regulated.

1146. Hale, Julian. *Radio Power: Propaganda and International Broadcasting*. Philadelphia: Temple University Press, 1975. 196 pp. (International and Comparative Broadcasting series). ISBN: 0-87722-0492.

Hale calls radio the only unstoppable medium of mass communication and the only one that reaches across the entire globe instantaneously to convey a message from any country to another. For this reason he feels that radio is the most powerful weapon of international propaganda and cites examples in the British Broadcasting Corporation, Nazi Germany, Communist countries, the Third World, and the Middle East as well as existing clandestine radio stations.

1147. Hallman, E.S., with H. Hindley. *Broadcasting in Canada.* London: Routledge & Kegan Paul, 1977. 90 pp. (Case Studies on Broadcasting Systems). ISBN: 0-7100-8528-1.

The Canadian Broadcasting System is a single system of broadcasting regulated by an independent public authority, and both public and private initiative have roles to play in bringing radio and television service to the community. This book describes the state of Canada's broadcasting system, its history, the laws and regulations governing it, and its various broadcasting organizations such as Radio-Quebec, CBC, Alberta Educational Communications Corporation (ACCESS), and Global Communications Ltd.

1148. Harding, Richard. *Outside Interference: The Politics of Australian Broadcasting.* Melbourne: Sun Books, 1979. 219 pp. ISBN: 0-72510315-9.

The author provides "fresh insights into many of the issues that made Australian headlines: the Bland affair, the staff commissioner, the continuing crisis and cries of 'bias' in current affairs programs, 2JJ and access radio, FM, the department of the media, the sports coverage tangle, etc."

1149. Harris, Paul. *Broadcasting from the High Seas: The History of Offshore Radio in Europe, 1958-1976.* Edinburgh: Paul Harris Publishing, 1977. 361 pp. ISBN: 0-904505-07-3.

Pirate radio ships have threatened government-controlled broadcasting monopolies throughout the European continent, and their popularity has grown in Denmark, Sweden, Britain, Holland, and Belgium. This book describes events around the Radio City fort in London's Thames Estuary which resulted in the shooting of its owner and proved to be the catalyst in the British Government's legislation against offshore broadcasters.

1150. Harris, Paul. *When Pirates Ruled the Waves.* 3rd ed. Aberdeen, Scot.: Impulse Publications, 1969. 213 pp.

The main difficulty the author faced in writing this book, he states, was in singling out the facts from the mass of rumors and fiction that have surrounded the often romanticized activities of the offshore radio stations. He tries to set the story straight as he describes the background, problems, legalities, and solutions to the offshore pirating of British radio programming.

1151. Harrison, Kate. *Press and Television Interests in Australian Commercial Radio.* Sydney: Federation of Australian Radio Broadcasters, 1982. 21 pp.

The extent of radio ownership by newspaper interests and by companies holding interests in commercial television licenses is presented in this study commissioned by the Federation. It updates previous studies and includes FM commercial radio stations.

1152. Head, Sydney W., ed. *Broadcasting in Africa: A Continental Survey of Radio and Television.* Philadelphia: Temple University Press, 1974. 453 pp. (International and Comparative Broadcasting series). ISBN: 0-87722-027-1.

Head states in his introduction that "radio is the only medium in Africa able to scale the triple barrier of illiteracy, distance, and lack of transportation." He therefore solicited a series of essays that describe the individual broadcasting systems, an appraisal of cross-system functions on a continental scale, and a critique leading to an inventory of subjects suggested for further study.

1153. Head, Sydney W. *World Broadcasting Systems: A Comparative Analysis*. Belmont, CA: Wadsworth Publishing, 1985. 457 pp. (Wadsworth series in Mass Communication). ISBN: 0-534-04734-3.

The author examines the origins of broadcasting, its politics, ownership, access concepts, laws and regulation, economics, facilities, programs and programming, and international aspects.

1154. Hein, Kurt John. *Radio Bahá'í, Ecuador: A Bahá'í Development Project*. Oxford, Eng.: George Ronald, 1988. 215 pp. ISBN: 0-85398-273-2.

Conceived as a way for Bahá'ís to keep in touch with one another, Radio Bahá'í soon emerged as the primary link among all the country people of the Otavalo region of Ecuador. It has become the main transmitter of local heritage, music, and information in its broadcast area.

1155. Hind, John, and Stephen Mosco. *Rebel Radio: The Full Story of British Pirate Radio*. London: Pluto Press, 1985. 163 pp. ISBN: 0-7453-0055-3.

Beginning with a history of pirate radio, the authors examine various aspects of pirating: black music, political programming, and community stations. One chapter is devoted to "oddities, eccentricities, and gestural swipes" while another looks at radio abroad in America, France, and Australia.

1156. Hoggart, Richard, and Janet Morgan, eds. *The Future of Broadcasting: Essays on Authority, Style, and Choice*. London: Macmillan, 1982. 155 pp. ISBN: 0-333-28848-3.

The essays in this volume are papers that were presented at a May 1980 conference whose theme was "The Foundations of Broadcasting Policy." The authors examine Britain's broadcasting systems in terms of authority, style, and choice. Contributors are Shirley Williams, Asa Briggs, Jeremy Isaacs, Dennis Lawrence, Randolph Quirk, Karl Deutsch, Mary Douglas, Karen Wollaeger, and the editors.

1157. Holt, Robert T. *Radio Free Europe*. Minneapolis: University of Minnesota Press, 1958. 249 pp.

In 1949 a private organization, the Free Europe Committee, was created, and Radio Free Europe was its oldest and most important division. This book recalls the origins of RFE, its basic purposes and policies, organization, personnel, setting, policy formulation, programming, effectiveness, its various successes, and few failures.

1158. Howell, W.J., Jr. *World Broadcasting in the Age of the Satellite: Comparative Systems, Policies, and Issues in Mass Telecommunication*. Norwood, NJ: Ablex, 1986. 329 pp. (Communication and Information Science series). ISBN: 0-89391-390-1.

The three divisions in this book examine frames of reference in world broadcasting, four worlds of national broadcasting, and a preview and review of the whole topic of world broadcasting. Within that framework the author compares and contrasts the field as it is practiced throughout the world and anticipates the way it will go in the future.

1159. Howkins, John, Neville Hunnings, and Joanna Spicer. *Satellite Broadcasting in Western Europe*. London: International Institute of Communications, 1982. 84 pp.

Beginning with the April 1982 plans and proposals for satellite use in broadcasting in Western Europe, this paper summarizes satellite characteristics, broadcasting development, and legal aspects.

1160. Hughes, Patrick. *British Broadcasting: Programmes and Power.* Bromley, Eng.: Chartwell-Bratt, 1981. 223 pp. ISBN: 0-862380-23-5.

According to the introduction, the essays in this book survey different approaches to the study of broadcasting in Britain with particular emphasis on the implications of each approach for an understanding of the power relations which constitute current broadcasting practice. They share a common concern without attempting to be a systematic whole.

1161. Huth, Arno. *Radio Today.* New York: Arno Press/New York Times, 1971. 155 pp. (History of Broadcasting: Radio to Television). ISBN: 0-405-03585-3.

This is a reprint of *Radio Today: The Present State of Broadcasting* that was published by the Geneva (Switzerland) Research Centre in July 1942. The author defines the structure of broadcasting and details its organization, financing, transmission, programs, and reception. He also summarizes radio broadcasting in Europe, America, Africa, Asia, and Oceania.

1162. Independent Broadcasting Authority. *Independent Broadcasting: 30 Years and Beyond.* London: The Authority, 1985. 31 pp.

Transcripts from three major speeches on the development and future of Independent Broadcasting are reprinted in this booklet. Titles are "Thirty Years of Independent Television," "Thirty Years of Independent

Broadcasting," and "The Pursuit of Excellence in the New Age of Broadcasting."

1163. Independent Broadcasting Authority. *Television & Radio 1987: The IBA's Yearbook of Independent Broadcasting.* London: The Authority, 1988. 224 pp. ISBN: 0-900485-52-3.

Published annually, this offers an overview of the IBA along with sections on independent radio, technical services, advertising, audience research, staff and training, reference, and various aspects of television.

1164. India Ministry of Information and Broadcasting. *Radio and Television.* New Delhi: The Ministry, 1966. 249 pp.

A report of the Committee on Broadcasting and Information Media, this discusses the history and development of broadcasting in India, including the several development plans, radio in wartime, and radio rural forums. Other chapters cover technical coverage, problems of programming, audience research, language, and types of programs.

1165. Inglis, K.S. *This Is the ABC: The Australian Broadcasting Commission, 1932-1983.* Melbourne: Melbourne University Press, 1983. 521 pp. ISBN: 0-522-84258-5.

Based on the Commission's own archives, this recounts the formation and growth of the radio network serving Australia which was modeled on the British Broadcasting Corporation but soon acquired an independent identity.

1166. International Broadcasting Union, Geneva. *Broadcasting Abroad.* Chicago: University of Chicago Press, 1934. 103 pp.

344 Radio Broadcasting

This is basically a comparison of American and foreign, particularly European, broadcasting stations made as a result of direct observation. Included is a supplemental memorandum on radio broadcasting in the Far East and the South Pacific written by the American Council, Institute of Pacific Relations.

1167. International Communication Agency. Office of Research and Evaluation. *Communist International Radio Broadcasting, 1977.* Washington: Government Printing Office, 1978. 27 pp. (Research Report R-30-78).

This report compares 1977 developments in Communist international radio broadcasting with those during 1976. The main source for the report is the Foreign Broadcast Information Service (FBIS).

1168. International Communication Agency. Office of Research and Evaluation. *International Radio Listener Discussion Panels: Final Report and Recommendations.* Washington: Government Printing Office, 1978. 14 pp. (Research Report R-27-78).

Summarized in this report are the findings of a series of listener panel-discussions that took place in Malaysia, Colombia, Kuwait, Nigeria, and the Ivory Coast. They present opinions on Voice of America, other international broadcasters, and the content and style of such programming.

1169. International Institute of Intellectual Co-operation. *Broadcasting and Peace: Studies and Projects in the Matter of International Agreements.* Paris: League of Nations, 1933. 231 pp. (Intellectual Co-operation series).

Besides questions of technical organization, the use of radio broadcasting raises a series of international problems of a moral and jurisdictional nature. This volume examines technical aspects as well as other possible controversies and the pending agreements that could ease their consequences.

1170. Ito, Masami, et al. *Broadcasting in Japan*. London: Routledge & Kegan Paul, 1978. 125 pp. (Case Studies on Broadcasting Systems). ISBN: 0-7100-0043-X.

Ito and his associates describe comprehensively the growth of broadcasting in Japan from the dawn of radio and television to satellite communication and to the multiplex broadcasting of the future. They examine the Broadcast Law and the interaction of the public service Nippon Hoso Kyokai (NHK) system and the 51 radio and 91 television broadcasting organizations.

1171. Jamieson, Don. *The Troubled Air*. Fredericton, Can.: Brunswick Press, 1966. 236 pp.

The title page describes this as "a frank, thorough and sometimes disturbing look at the present state of Canadian broadcasting by a noted broadcaster." Jamieson writes about the nature of radio, encouraging Canadian talent, the public and private sectors, controlling broadcasting, and the new complexities of the medium.

1172. Kaftanov, S.V., ed. *Radio and Television in the USSR*. Washington: U.S. Joint Publications Research Service, 1961. 243 pp.

Available in photocopy form from the Library of Congress, this is a translation of the book *Radio i televidensiye v SSSR* that was published by the State Committee on Radio Broadcasting and Television of the Council of Ministers USSR, Moscow, in 1960. In a condensed form, it cites basic data that characterize Soviet radio and television and is designed to give an overall understanding about the programs in the USSR, some of the more important broadcasts of the central and local services, radio and television newspapers and magazines, the extent of the service, etc.

1173. Katz, Elihu, and George Wedell. *Broadcasting in the Third World: Promise and Performance*. Cambridge, MA: Harvard University Press, 1977. 305 pp. ISBN: 0-674-08341-5.

The preface states that the majority of people in the world live within reach of a domestic radio signal, however poor the quality of the signal in many areas, however remote the language of the medium from the vernacular of the listeners. This study concentrates on the ways in which broadcasting institutions have been transplanted and have taken root in the developing countries. It is based on an extensive review of statistical and documentary data concerning broadcasting in 91 developing countries.

1174. Khalid, Muhammad. *Mass Communication in Developing Countries: Development of Radio Broadcasting in Pakistan*. West Berlin: Freien University, 1986. 234 pp.

Written in English, this is the author's Ph.D. dissertation, and he states it is the first comprehensive study of its kind on the subject. It traces the history of radio broadcasting in Pakistan and assesses the role of varying social, political, and economic pressures that helped shape its development.

1175. Kuhn, Raymond, ed. *Broadcasting and Politics in Western Europe*. London: Frank Cass, 1985. 174 pp. ISBN: 0-7146-3274-0.

Essays on the influence of broadcasting on the political scene and vice versa were contributed by Desmond Bell, Kees Brants, Kenneth Dyson, Dimitrios Katsoudas, Esteban López-Escobar, Angel Faus-Belau, Donald Sassoon, Jean Seaton, Arthur Williams, and Raymond Kuhn.

1176. Kuhn, Raymond, ed. *The Politics of Broadcasting*. London: Croom Helm, 1985. 305 pp. ISBN: 0-7099-1542-X.

Concentrating on Australia, Canada, France, Great Britain, Italy, Japan, the United States, and West Germany, this treats political debate over broadcasting and identifies the principal participants. It investigates such aspects as government monopolies, private broadcasting, and public service responsibilities. The book was also published by St. Martin's Press in 1985.

1177. Lent, John A., ed. *Broadcasting in Asia and the Pacific: A Continental Survey of Radio and Television.*. Philadelphia: Temple University Press, 1978. 429 pp. (International and Comparative Broadcasting series). ISBN: 0-87722-068-9.

A systematic, descriptive treatment of all broadcasting services of the area is provided in this volume. It recounts the problems, challenges, and prospects of Asian broadcasting, details the national systems, explains the cross-system functions of the various specialized program services, and international and regional cooperation.

1178. Lichty, Lawrence W. *World and International Broadcasting: A Bibliography*. Washington: Association for Professional Broadcasting Education, 1970. 1 vol.

This bibliography is intended to provide information on domestic broadcasting throughout the world with the exception of the United States. It also covers international broadcasts and propaganda. Lichty cites his sources in his introductory section and arranges the material first by regions and then alphabetically.

1179. Lisann, Maury. *Broadcasting to the Soviet Union: International Politics and Radio.* New York: Praeger, 1975. 199 pp. (Praeger Special Studies in International Politics and Government). ISBN: 0-275-05590-6.

The preface states that "radio broadcasting may account for more communication between the Communist and non-Communist parts of the world than all forms of private and laboriously negotiated intergovernmental exchanges combined; it is also probably the form of contact about which least is known." The author tries to rectify this shortcoming through this study.

1180. Liu, Alan P.L. *Radio Broadcasting in Communist China.* Cambridge, MA: Massachusetts Institute of Technology, 1964. 71 pp.

Processed for the Defense Documentation Center, Defense Supply Agency, of the Department of Commerce, this unclassified document is a result of a four-month study on the subject. The data have been integrated into the text and are accompanied by a map survey providing regional statistics.

1181. Lord Simon of Wythenshawe. *The B.B.C. from Within.* London: Victor Gollancz, 1953. 360 pp.

A former British Broadcasting Corporation chairman discusses its constitution, program production, commercial broadcasting, and the problems of monopoly as he sees them. He apologizes for not having a chapter on BBC engineering because it is so highly technical that it is impossible to include in a book intended for the general public.

* Lucas, Peter. *The Constant Voice*. Cited above as item 176.

1182. Luther, Sara Fletcher. *The United States and the Direct Broadcast Satellite: The Politics of International Broadcasting in Space*. New York: Oxford University Press, 1988. 230 pp. ISBN: 0-19-505138-6.

The social, political, and economic factors underlying the evolving international controversy affecting DBS are identified. The rise of international regulation through the International Telecommunications Union, the role of American radio interests, and the effect of mass communication research and scholarship are discussed.

1183. Luthra, H.R. *Indian Broadcasting*. New Delhi: Ministry of Information and Broadcasting, 1986. 531 pp.

The author has tried to create a readable history of broadcasting in India and to catch something of the flavor of its various stages of growth. He discusses the early planning of the 1920s, its shaky development, and finally the status it has achieved in the mid-1980s.

1184. MacCabe, Colin, and Olivia Stewart, eds. *The BBC and Public Service Broadcasting*. Manchester, Eng.: Manchester University Press, 1986. 116 pp. (Images of Culture series). ISBN: 0-7190-1964-8.

Contributed articles were written by Anthony Smith, Janet Morgan, William Maley, Krishan Kumar, Charles Jonscher, Brenda Maddox, David Elstein, Margaret Matheson, Jeremy Isaacs, John Caughie, and Colin MacCabe.

1185. Mackay, Ian K. *Broadcasting in New Zealand.* Wellington, N.Z.: A.H. & A.W. Reed, 1953. 159 pp.

The first in Mackay's series on radio broadcasting, this describes his own experiences with New Zealand broadcasting from what he calls "a detached viewpoint." He relates the story of the 25-watt radio club licensed under the call letters of 2ZR that eventually became 1XN in the New Zealand Broadcasting Service network as well as the growth of the entire field from 1921 until his 1953 date of publication.

1186. Mackay, Ian K. *Broadcasting in Nigeria.* Ibadan, Nigeria: University Press, 1964. 158 pp.

Nigeria entered the broadcasting era in 1932 when the British Broadcasting Corporation launched the world's first regularly scheduled shortwave service. Nigeria operated its own Nigerian Broadcasting Service from 1951 to 1957 when the Nigerian Corporation was formed to replace NBS.

1187. Mackay, Ian K. *Broadcasting in Papua New Guinea.* Melbourne, Aust.: Melbourne University Press, 1976. 190 pp.

In 1934 Major Charles Marr, Australian minister in charge of territories and a distinguished WW I wireless operator, chaired a meeting that "discussed the need for making wireless broadcasting available to residents of the Pacific Territories." This heralded the beginning of island broadcasting, and the author chronicles the progress that occurred under the jurisdiction of the Australian Broadcasting Commission and the National Broadcasting Commission up to 1976.

1188. Magne, Lawrence, and Tony Jones, eds. *Passport to World Band Radio*. New York: International Broadcasting Services, 1990. 383 pp. ISBN: 0-914941-20-8. ISSN: 0897-0157.

Schedules for every station on the air, articles on how to get started and what can be heard, and a buyer's guide to portable radios and tabletop receivers are included. The book is called "the closest thing to *TV Guide* for world band radios" and data are provided for news and entertainment shows from 161 countries along with glossaries, a summary of broadcasting activity, and a directory of advertisers.

1189. Mansell, Gerard. *Let Truth Be Told: 50 Years of BBC External Broadcasting*. London: Weidenfeld & Nicholson, 1982. 300 pp. ISBN: 0-297-78158-8.

Saturday, December 19, 1932, was a red-letter day for the British Broadcasting Corporation when it started the Empire Service and thus began its initial venture into international broadcasting. The first transmission lasted two hours and was beamed at Australia and New Zealand. The growth and progress of this phase of the BBC is told in this volume.

1190. Martelanc, Tomo, et al. *External Radio Broadcasting and International Understanding: Broadcasting to Yugoslavia*. Geneva: Unesco, 1977. 51 pp. (Reports and Papers on Mass Communication, 81). ISBN: 92-3-101523-0.

The three chapters constituting this volume are concerned with external radio broadcasting and propaganda, the complementary or supplementary role of external broadcasting to Yugoslavia, and the specific content and value orientations of external radio broadcasting to that country.

1191. Masani, Mehra. *Broadcasting and the People*. 2nd ed. New Delhi: National Book Trust, 1985. 178 pp.

All India Radio (AIR) and television Doordarshan have expanded rapidly since the first edition of this book was published in 1975. The author relates the changes that have occurred and their effects, and discusses the launching of the Indian National Satellite (INSAT 1A).

* Mathur, J.C., and Paul Neurath. *An Indian Experiment in Farm Radio Forums*. Cited above as item 985.

1192. McCavitt, William E. *Broadcasting Around the World*. Blue Ridge Summit, PA: Tab Books, 1981. 336 pp. ISBN: 0-8306-9913-9.

Each chapter was written by an individual either directly involved in broadcasting or else connected with the official national broadcasting system. Eighteen different countries are represented.

* McFadyen, Stuart, Colin Hoskins, and David Gillen. *Canadian Broadcasting: Market Structure and Economic Performance*. Cited above as item 444.

* McNair, W.A. *Radio Advertising in Australia*. Cited above as item 446.

1193. McNeil, Bill, and Morris Wolfe. *Signing On: The Birth of Radio in Canada*. Toronto: Doubleday Canada, 1982. 303 pp. ISBN: 0-385-17742-9.

Public radio officially arrived in Canada in 1932, and this book is a celebration of the half-century of Canadian public broadcasting. It "contains interviews with 125 broadcasters, producers, technicians, entrepreneurs, and ordinary listeners ... Three chapters are devoted to private broadcasting, three to public, and a final one on the coming of television in 1952, when this book ends."

1194. McPhail, Thomas L. *Electronic Colonialism: The Future of International Broadcasting and Communications*. 2nd ed. Newbury Park, CA: Sage, 1987. 311 pp. (Sage Library of Social Research, 126). ISBN: 0-8039-2730-4.

Chapters discuss the New World Information Order, the role of Unesco, the International Telecommunications Union, the World Administration Radio Conference (WARC), the MacBride International Commission, the Maitland Commission, and related international issues.

* European Broadcasting Union. *Medium and Long-Range Economic Planning in Broadcasting Organizations*. Cited above as item 371.

1195. Meo, L.D. *Japan's Radio War on Australia, 1941-1945*. Carlton, Aust.: Melbourne University Press; London: Cambridge University Press, 1968. 300 pp. ISBN: 0-522-83891-1.

Mrs. Meo presents a "careful survey of a sustained Japanese effort to communicate with Australians from 1941 to 1945. Her book is mainly based on Japanese wartime propaganda broadcasts to Australia."

1196. Mickelson, Sig. *America's Other Voice: The Story of Radio Free Europe and Radio Liberty*. Westport, CT: Praeger, 1983. 269 pp. ISBN: 0-03-063224-2.

"Mickelson, following a long career as President of CBS News and later as President of RFE/RL, tells the story of RFE/RL in broad perspective, lacing it with fascinating details, and employing detachment and restraint. It is the story, as he says, ' of intrigue, mystery, clandestine planning, sophisticated intelligence concepts, and heavy-handed Communist attempts to demoralize or disrupt the flow of broadcasts.' It is also the story of broadcast operations that can have enormous long-term impact if handled with wisdom and restraint."

1197. Mullick, K.S. *Tangled Tapes: The Inside Story of Indian Broadcasting.* New Delhi: Sterling Publishers, 1974. 159 pp.

The author states that "two types of tape are used in All India Radio--the brown tape which records programs for broadcast, and the red tape of bureaucracy; one a vehicle for creative enterprise, the other a symbol of rigid formalism." They "are always getting into a tangle" which became the central theme of his book, and he suggests a way to resolve this tangle.

1198. Muscio, Winston T. *Australian Radio: The Technical Story, 1923-1983.* Kenthurst, Aust.: Kangaroo Press, 1984. 243 pp. ISBN: 0-949924-82-2.

Sixty years of technical developments ranging from early broadcast receivers and transmitters to the latest communication systems are presented in this concise history of the industry in Australia. It is supplemented by numerous drawings and a few photographs.

1199. Namurois, Albert. *Structure and Organization of Broadcasting in the Framework of Radiocommunications.* Geneva: European Broadcasting Union, 1972. 211 pp. (EBU Monograph, 8).

The author explains the sources of telecommunications law, the organization of the International Telecommunications Union, and the principles governing international telecommunications. He goes into radio and television service, its mission, some structural problems, and problems of organization.

* Nicol, John, Albert A. Shea, and G.J.P. Simmins. *Canada's Farm Radio Forum*. Cited above as item 995.

1200. Nippon Hoso Kyokai. *50 Years of Japanese Broadcasting*. Tokyo: NHK, 1977. 429 pp.

March 22, 1975, marked the 50th anniversary of the start of broadcasting in Japan, and the first half of that period consisted of radio broadcasting only. This volume recounts the story of NHK's early history, wartime broadcasting, the years of occupation, and radio's new age. It goes on to discuss the birth and rapid growth of the television industry.

1201. Nippon Hoso Kyokai. *The History of Broadcasting in Japan*. Tokyo: NHK, 1967. 436 pp.

Japan's radio broadcasting began in March 1925 and has gone through numerous changes in political and social life and conditions. This is the story of its development and includes the history of Japanese television which was inaugurated in February 1953.

1202. Nordic Council of Ministers. *Nordic Radio and Television via Satellite*. Stockholm, Sweden: Secretariat for Nordic Cultural Cooperation, 1980. 210 pp.

Translated into English from the Norwegian/Swedish edition, this is the main report, NU A 1979:4E. It looks at the possibility of a Nordic broadcasting satellite project whereby all existing nationwide radio and television channels in the Nordic countries would be distributed to all of them.

1203. Noriega, Luis Antonio de, and Frances Leach. *Broadcasting in Mexico*. London: Routledge & Kegan Paul, 1979. 89 pp. ISBN: 0-7100-04168.

Published in association with the International Institute of Communications, this study traces the birth and growth of Mexico's broadcasting services against the background of her geographical, cultural, demographic, economic, and political structures. One section is devoted to commercial and non-commercial radio while others cover the advent and development of broadcasting in Mexico, broadcasting structures and regulatory frames, and the advent of television.

1204. Ontario Ministry of Transportation and Communications. Communications Division. *Radio Broadcasting in Canada: A Policy Paper*. Toronto: The Ministry, 1983. 25 leaves.

This paper consolidates many of Ontario's stated views on radio regulation and presents them in the context of a timely, overall policy framework. Its key issue is how radio can maintain its local character and commercial viability in the face of new technological developments and increasing competition.

1205. Paulu, Burton. *British Broadcasting in Transition*. Minneapolis: University of Minnesota Press, 1961. 250 pp.

A sequel to the author's *British Broadcasting (see next annotation)*, this is a report on the effects of competition on the broadcasting services of a country that introduced commercial television after some 30 years of service from a non-commercial monopoly. While its main focus is on television, there is a history of the British Broadcasting Corporation, data on the impact of television on radio, press and the cinema, as well as information about radio and TV audiences.

1206. Paulu, Burton. *British Broadcasting: Radio and Television in the United Kingdom*. Minneapolis: University of Minnesota Press, 1956. 457 pp.

Intended for readers in both the United Kingdom and the United States, this is "a sympathetic and yet critical description of (the British) system of broadcasting by an American." Paulu was able to interview key members of the British Broadcasting Corporation staff, watched programs in rehearsal and production, and had access to the library and much unpublished data as he compiled this history.

1207. Paulu, Burton. *Radio and Television Broadcasting in Eastern Europe*. Minneapolis: University of Minnesota Press, 1974. 592 pp. ISBN: 0-8166-0721-4.

Paulu's purpose is to describe and appraise the theory and practice of radio and television in the socialist countries of Eastern Europe which he defines as including Albania, Bulgaria, Czechoslovakia, East Germany, Hungary, Poland, Romania, the Soviet Union, and Yugoslavia. This is a companion volume to the one he wrote concerning broadcasting on the European continent (see next annotation).

1208. Paulu, Burton. *Radio and Television Broadcasting on the European Continent*. Minneapolis: University of Minnesota Press, 1967. 290 pp.

The facilities, structure and organization, and finances of continental broadcasting are described. Radio developed during the early 1920s and was well established by the middle 1930s. Paulu recalls its beginnings and growth, then discusses its interaction with television following WW II.

1209. Paulu, Burton. *Television and Radio in the United Kingdom.* Minneapolis: University of Minnesota Press, 1981. 476 pp. ISBN: 0-8166-0941-1.

The historical development and operations of the British Broadcasting Corporation are recounted in this overview of British radio and television. Paulu discusses technical facilities, finances, personnel, programming, audience research, and external broadcasting, particularly before and during WW II.

1210. Peers, Frank W. *The Politics of Canadian Broadcasting 1920-1951.* Toronto: University of Toronto Press, 1969. 466 pp. ISBN: 0-8020-5214-2.

This volume traces the development of broadcasting policy in Canada up to the inception of television in 1952. It looks at the Aird Commission, nationalization, the Canadian Radio-Broadcasting Commission, and private broadcasting between 1939 and 1945.

1211. Pilgert, Henry P., with the assistance of Helga Dobbert. *Press, Radio and Film in West Germany, 1945-1953.* Bad Godesberg-Mehlem, Ger.: Office of the U.S. High Commissioner for Germany, 1953. 123 pp.

The emphases are on German developments in the press, radio, and film, and on U.S. policies and programs with respect to these mass communications media. Chapters examine radio in the British and French zones, finance, allocation of frequencies, and the High Commissioner's relations with German broadcasting companies.

1212. Pirsein, Robert William. *The Voice of America: An History of the International Broadcasting Activities of the United States Government, 1940-1962.* New York: Arno Press,

1979. 589 pp. (Dissertations in Broadcasting series). ISBN: 0-405-11754-X.

Originally prepared as the author's Ph.D. thesis at Northwestern University in 1970, this reiterates the story of the International Broadcasting Service of the United States or, as it is better known, Voice of America. The period described goes from 1942 to its 20th anniversary celebration on February 26, 1962.

1213. Ploman, Edward W. *Broadcasting in Sweden*. London: Routledge & Kegan Paul, 1976. 65 pp. (Case Studies on Broadcasting Systems). ISBN: 0-7100-8529-X.

The first volume in the series, this provides an authoritative and overall view of the evolution, present structure, and future possibilities of Sweden's broadcasting system. The author reveals the relationship between national characteristics and broadcasting policies and structures.

1214. Potts, John. *Radio in Australia*. Kensington, NSW: New South Wales University Press, 1989. 189 pp. ISBN: 0-86840-331-8.

In addition to describing the history of Australian radio broadcasting, this highlights the differences between radio and other media. According to the cover, the author explores the nature of listening and of sound itself.

1215. *Radio and Television in the Service of Education and Development in Asia*. Geneva: Unesco, 1967. 58 pp. (Reports and Papers on Mass Communication, 49).

This is the principal working paper distributed in advance of "a meeting convened at Bangkok to provide for those responsible for broadcasting, education, and development

360 Radio Broadcasting

in Asia, an opportunity to take a 'new look' at the contribution which radio and television can make to the important tasks facing them in their countries ... (It) presents and analyzes conditions and experiences throughout the world with respect to the application of broadcasting to education and national development, and raises issues for examination by the meeting."

1216. *Radio Broadcasting: A.S.I.C. Class 9114.* Melbourne, Aust.: Ibis Research Services, 1978. 75 pp.

An overview of the field, this is a statistical summary of the radio broadcasting industry in Australia from 1924 to 1979, along with projections into the 1980s. It begins with a history of the original four radio stations and continues to discuss the more than 240 extant in 1978.

* *Radio Broadcasting Serves Rural Development.* Cited above as item 1009.

1217. Radio Free Europe. Audience and Public Opinion Research Department. *The Image of RFE in Poland.* Munich: RFE, 1967. 10 leaves.

Radio Free Europe published a series of comparative studies on the reception of its programming in several countries (Poland, Hungary, Bulgaria, Czechoslovakia, etc.) It was a way to determine the effectiveness of RFE radio broadcasts to those living in western and eastern Europe, as well as European refugees and visitors to the area. This title is one of that series, and the other publications are similar in format and length.

1218. *Radio Study: A Research Report to Establish the Need for and Type of Training for Radio.* North Sydney, Aust.: Reark Research, 1979. 112 pp.

Prepared for the Australian Film and Television School, this report is in three parts. The first examines the organization and structure of Australian radio, the second looks at types of radio training found in that country, and the third discusses training and attitudes toward training within the radio industry itself.

1219. Reith, John C.W. *Broadcast Over Britain.* London: Hodder & Stoughton, 1924. 231 pp.

Written while the author was Managing Director of the British Broadcasting Company, this is "an exposition of the ideals which animate the policy of the British Broadcasting Company." The four parts are titled In the Beginning, What Say They?, The Radio Way, and The Unending Pursuit.

1220. Rosen, Philip T., ed. *International Handbook of Broadcasting Systems.* Westport, CT: Greenwood Press, 1988. 336 pp. ISBN: 0-313-24348-4.

Arranged by country, each section covers specific aspects of broadcasting systems, including the history of radio and television, government regulation, economic structure, programming, broadcast reform, alternative structures, new technologies, and a forecast for the future. The book enables the user to determine what the broadcasting structure is in a given nation, how it came to be, and the direction it is going.

1221. Sanders, Ron. *Broadcasting in Guyana.* London: Routledge & Kegan Paul, 1978. 76 pp. (Case Studies on Broadcasting Systems). ISBN: 0-7100-0025-1.

In the 1960s Guyana had two radio channels, both operated by Rediffusion Limited in Britain, and in 1968 the Government of Guyana started its own radio station on one of those channels. At the time of publication of this book there was no television, and these two still were the only radio stations. The author discusses their evolution along with that of other media in the country.

1222. Sherman, Charles, and Donald Browne, eds. *Issues in International Broadcasting*. Washington: Broadcast Education Association, 1976. 171 pp. (Broadcast Education Association Monograph, 2).

Contributors to this volume are Thomas H. Guback, Sig Mickelson, Fred S. Siebert, Richard R. Colino, Art Kane, Chris Jeans, Sydney W. Head, Thomas F. Gordon, Andrew T. Faller, Paul Prince, Richard C. Burke, Leonard Marks, W. Peter Janicki, Douglas A. Boyd, Kenneth Adam, Don R. Le Duc, Donald R. Browne, Charles E. Sherman, Bruce A. Linton, James M. Kushner, and Benno Signitzer.

1223. Shore, Peter. *International Radio Stations Guide*. Rev. ed. London: Bernard Babani, 1988. 312 pp. ISBN: 0-85934-200-X.

Data are provided on worldwide short wave radio stations, European, Middle East, and North African long and medium wave stations as well as Canadian and American medium wave stations. Other sections deal with International Telecommunications Union country codes, United Kingdom FM radio stations, time differences from GMT, and wave length/frequency conversion.

1224. Skolnick, Roger. *A Bibliography of Selected Books and Significant Articles in Foreign and International Broadcasting*. East Lansing: Michigan State University, 1963-1966. 3 vols.

Material is arranged into the following categories: History and Background of International Broadcasting; Control by Government Corporation; Control by Government Alone; Mixed System of Control; External or International Broadcasting Between Countries; Distribution Systems; Current Problems; and References in International and Foreign Broadcasting. Brief bibliographical information on books and articles is included.

1225. Skues, Keith. *Radio Onederland: The Story of Radio One*. Lavenham, Eng.: Landmark Press, 1968. 223 pp.

The author attempts to paint as accurate a picture as possible of Radio One and the people who work for it and make it work. He provides "a few facts & figures," discusses the plans for a land-based pop station, tells of Radio One's early days, and then details the roles of disc jockeys, producers, news readers, technical assistants, the controller, and the chief assistant.

1226. Smith, Anthony, compiler and ed. *British Broadcasting*. Newton Abbot, Eng.: David & Charles, 1974. 271 pp. (David & Charles Sources for Contemporary Issues series). ISBN: 0-7153-6326-3.

"The medium of radio was identified from its birth in Britain as an instrument of a kind of cultural democracy" according to Smith as he describes the foundations of the British Broadcasting Corporation as "diversity through monopoly." Later sections cover the birth of television, the end of the monopoly, the consequences of competition, standards, plans for reform, and codes of practice.

1227. *Socio-economic Aspects of National Communication Systems.* Paris: Unesco, 1979. 3 vols. (Communication and Society 10, 11, 12).

This series of studies examines the role of radiobroadcasting in the process of socio-economic and cultural change in Austria, Czechoslovakia, and Venezuela. They deal with cultural implications of broadcasting structures, ownership and financing, and advertising as well as offering a short description of the historic and legal evolution of their national broadcasting systems. Benno Signitzer and Kurt Leger prepared the report on Australia, Alice Bunzlová and Leopole Slovák the one on Czechoslovakia, and INICO (Institute of Communication Research, Central University of Caracas) the one on Venezuela.

1228. Soley, Lawrence C., and John S. Nichols. *Clandestine Radio Broadcasting: A Study of Revolutionary and Counterrevolutionary Electronic Communication.* Westport, CT: Praeger, 1987. 384 pp. ISBN: 0-275-92259-6.

The authors state they "have attempted to report as accurately as possible the past and present of clandestine radio broadcasting and, in interpreting the subject matter, to make our guesswork as educated as possible" as they tried to build a documentary foundation for future research. They have included as appendices lists of clandestine radio stations from 1948 through 1985 and information about the Voice of Palestine and related broadcasts of 1973.

1229. Sound Broadcasting Society. *Unsound Broadcasting: The Case Against the BBC's New Policy.* London: Faber & Faber, 1958. 47 pp.

On April 8, 1957, the British Broadcasting Corporation announced far-reaching changes in its Sound Broadcasting Services which aroused a storm of controversy. This pamphlet has comments by T.S. Eliot, Sir Laurence Olivier, Ralph Vaughan Williams, Michael Tippett, and several others criticizing the new policy.

1230. *Sparks Into the USSR: The Story of Radio Liberation*. New York: American Committee for Liberation. Press and Publications Division, 1957. 47 pp.

This pamphlet summarizes how Russians who are exiled from the USSR and reside in Munich are able to broadcast to their German countrymen.

1231. Sterling, Christopher H. *Foreign and International Communications Systems: A Survey Bibliography*. Washington: George Washington University Center for Telecommunications Studies, 1983. 20 pp. (Basic Bibliography, 3). (GW Occasional Papers).

This is an annotated listing of selected current books and documents on foreign communications systems and international communication. In 1989 there was a new edition published by the Center for Advanced Study in Telecommunications at the Ohio State University.

1232. Sterling, Christopher H., ed. *International Telecommunications and Information Policy*. Washington: Communications Press, 1984. 496 pp. (NTIA Report).

Papers from a symposium held at George Washington University in May 1983, and a report of the National Telecommunications Administration published in 1983 and titled "Long-range Goals in International Telecommunications and Information," form the basis for this volume.

1233. Subcommittee on Telecommunications, Consumer Protection, and Finance. Committee on Energy and Commerce. U.S. House of Representatives. *Radio Broadcasting to Cuba.* Washington: Government Printing Office, 1982. 239 pp.

The main concern of the Subcommittee at this hearing was to understand the impact that Radio Marti could have on American broadcasting practices and institutions. The hearing was held on May 10, 1982.

* Swaziland Government. *Survey of Radio Listenership, 1977.* Cited above as item 565.

1234. Thomas, Ruth. *Broadcasting and Democracy in France.* London: Bradford University Press, 1976. 211 pp. ISBN: 0-258-97006-5.

This study explores some aspects of the relationship between broadcasting as an institution and the exercise of democracy in France. It presents a summary of the establishment of the official "Paris-PTT" station in 1927, describes the formation in 1940 of Radiodiffusion nationale, and the formation of Office de radiodiffusion-télévision française (ORTF) in 1964.

1235. Tomlinson, John D. *The International Control of Radiocommunications.* Ann Arbor, MI: J.W. Edwards, 1945. 314 pp.

Originally presented as a dissertation at the University of Geneva, Switzerland, in 1938, this discusses the rise of international radio legislation, the expansion of radio and the extension of international control, international regulations concerning traffic and operation of services, international interference, allocation of frequencies, and regional and bilateral agreements.

1236. Tyson, James L. *U.S. International Broadcasting and National Security*. New York: Ramapo Press, 1983. 153 pp. ISBN: 0-915071-00-2.

The author outlines briefly the history of American international broadcasting in its relation to foreign policy. He proposes several areas for strengthening such efforts in the future. His focus is primarily on broadcasting to the Soviet Union and the Warsaw Pact countries.

1237. Unesco. *Press, Radio, Film*. New York: Arno Press, 1972. 3 vols. (International Propaganda and Communications series). ISBN: 0-405-04740-1 (set).

Published originally in 1947, 1948, and 1950, these volumes contain the Report of the Unesco Commission on Technical Needs in Press, Radio and Film Following the Survey in Twelve War-Devastated Countries. A fourth volume covers television.

1238. U.S. Foreign Broadcast Information Service. *Broadcasting Stations of the World*. Washington: Government Printing Office, 1971. 4 vols.

The first three parts of this set are concerned with radio broadcasting while the fourth is devoted to television. Included are data on amplitude modulation broadcasting stations according to country and city, AM broadcasting stations according to frequency, and FM stations.

1239. U.S. Information Agency. Office of Research. *Communist International Radio Broadcasting--1976*. Washington: Government Printing Office, 1977. 28 pp.

"This report outlines developments in the volume of Communist international radio broadcasting during 1976 as compared to 1975. The main source for the report is the Foreign Broadcast Information Service (FBIS)."

1240. U.S. Information Agency. Office of Research. *Listening Habits of Soviet Citizens to the Voice of America.* Washington: Government Printing Office, 1978. 17 pp.

The listening habits of a sample of 1100 former or current Soviet citizens to Voice of America are described in this study. Variables examined include attitude toward VOA programs, frequency of listening, length of listening sessions, time listening begins, language service monitored, reason for listening, and other stations monitored by Soviet listeners.

1241. U.S. Information Agency. Office of Research. *VOA Russian Listeners' Panel.* Washington: Government Printing Office, 1978. 8 pp.

The abstract states that this unclassified report is an analysis of information gathered from a panel on Soviet reactions to Voice of America broadcasts. It is designed to aid VOA in its programming decisions.

1242. U.S. Information Agency. Office of Research and Intelligence. *Geographic Distribution of Radio Sets and Characteristics of Radio Owners in Countries of the World.* Washington: Government Printing Office, 1954. 96 pp.

Supplementing an earlier report on the total number of radio sets in each country by the type of sets, here the focus is on the ownership of such sets. It is intended to answer the questions of *who* owns the radios and *where* within the country these sets are to be found.

1243. Venmore-Rowland, John. *Radio Caroline: The Story of the First British Off-Shore Radio Station*. Lavenham, Eng.: Landmark Press, 1967. 184 pp.

Intended primarily to tell the story of Radio Caroline, the author does not attempt to make a case for or against off-shore radio, and states that he prefers that term to "pirate radio." He presents the events in chronological order within the first few chapters and then details information about the ships, supply, commercial aspects, and the disc jockeys involved.

1244. Vittet-Philippe, Patrick, and Philip Crookes. *Local Radio and Regional Development in Europe*. Manchester, Eng.: European Institute for the Media, 1987. 161 pp. (Media Monograph, 7). ISBN: 0-948195-07-X. ISSN: 0267-4467.

Following an overview of local radio and communications systems in Europe, the authors present some comparative aspects in Denmark, Ireland, the Netherlands, Norway, Portugal, Sweden, and Switzerland. Additional essays discuss local radio in France, Germany, Italy, and the U.K.

1245. *Voice of America at the Crossroads: A Panel Discussion on the Appropriate Role of the VOA*. Washington: Media Institute, 1982. 70 pp. ISBN: 0-937790-13-3.

This is a transcript of a panel discussion sponsored by the Media Institute on June 24, 1982. Among the speakers were Philip Nicolaides, Bernard Kamenske, M. William Haratunian, and Jozsef Takacs.

1246. Von Utfall, Johan, compiler and ed. *Broadcasting in Sweden: Material Resources*. Stockholm: Sveriges Radio, 1970. 1 vol.

The history of Swedish sound broadcasting, its enabling legislation, status, financing, accounting, and the Radio Council are all described. There are charts and maps showing administration, broadcast schedules, transmitter locations, Eurovision international circuits, etc.

1247. *WARC-85: International Perspectives*. Washington: Annenberg School of Communications Washington Program, 1985. 99 pp. (International Telecommunications Policy series). ISBN: 0-93441-01-0.

The papers and comments assembled in this book were presented in Washington in November 1984 at a conference that aimed at anticipating the problems and opportunities that would be discussed at the planned August 1985 World Administrative Radio Conference of the International Telecommunications Union.

1248. Ward, John E., Ithiel de Sola Pool, and Richard J. Solomon. *A Study of Future Directions for the Voice of America in the Changing World of International Broadcasting*. Cambridge, MA: MIT Laboratory for Information and Decision Systems, 1983. 118 leaves.

This document presents the final report on a study of the present international broadcast operations of the VOA and makes recommendations for actions felt necessary for it to maintain its present stature among world broadcasters in future.

1249. Wavell, Stewart. *The Art of Radio: A C.B.C. Training Manual*. Colombo, Ceylon: Ceylon Broadcasting Corp., 1969. 175 pp.

The existing broadcasting system had been in operation for over 30 years at the time this manual was published and was treated primarily as an entertainment medium.

Its focus has been altered as its potential as a catalyst for social change is being emphasized, and thus this manual was created to train staff, administrators, and anyone else involved in broadcasting.

1250. Wedell, George. *Making Broadcasting Useful: The African Experience*. Manchester, Eng.: Manchester University Press; European Institute for the Media, 1986. 306 pp. ISBN: 0-7190-1865-X.

The development of radio and television in Africa in the 1980s is described in this collection of articles. The contributors are all individuals who have been involved in broadcasting in African countries and who have experienced difficulties in creating their own modern broadcasting system.

1251. Weir, E. Austin. *The Struggle for National Broadcasting in Canada*. Toronto: McClelland & Stewart, 1965. 477 pp.

The author wrote a number of prefaces and explanations to papers about the early days of Canadian radio which he deposited in the Public Archives of Canada. This book originated from this material and his notes that cover early radio and the CNR, pioneer programming, the national network, early transAtlantic broadcasts, and eventually, television.

1252. Wettig, Gerhard. *Broadcasting and Détente: Eastern Policies and Their Implication for East-West Relations*. London: C. Hurst, 1977. 110 pp. ISBN: 0-903983-91-5.

The Eastern Bloc Campaign against the flow of information from West Germany and discussions in the United Nations and the CSCE on freedom or constraint on the air are the two main topics of this book. There are chapters on Radio Free Europe and Radio Liberty as well as an appendix providing information on the five international radio stations in West Germany.

1253. Williams, Arthur. *Broadcasting and Democracy in West Germany*. London: Bradford University Press/Crosby Lockwood Staples, 1976. 198 pp. ISBN: 0-258-96996-2.

Part one summarizes the Allies and West German broadcasting and compares the early system with the then-present West German Broadcasting System. The second part examines a question of balance within the system, its control, politics in public broadcasting, and the internal problem of freedom of broadcasting.

1254. Williams, J. Grenfell. *Radio in Fundamental Education in Undeveloped Areas*. Paris: Unesco, 1950. 152 pp. (Press, Film and Radio in the World Today series).

Concentrating primarily on the rural areas of India, China, Indonesia, Malaya, Africa, and South America, this discusses "the role of radio" with emphasis on the program rather than its technical side. It describes some of the experiments in radio for these areas and explains the aims and techniques used in the various studies.

1255. Windschuttle, Keith. *The Media: A New Analysis of the Press, Television, Radio, and Advertising in Australia*. Victoria: Penguin Books, 1985. 436 pp. ISBN: 0-14-00-6848-1.

Are the media trivial and mindless or are they expressing our cultural needs asks the author as he examines the political economy and the culture as they affect the media and vice versa. Some of his topics include sexuality, popular music, talk shows, unions, strikes and the news, the New Right, self-regulation of advertising, and media ownership.

1256. Wood, Richard E. *Shortwave Voices of the World.* Park Ridge, NJ: Gilfer Associates, 1969. 96 pp.

The text explains the "how, what, and why" of this unique hobby activity. The author tells about "the broad panorama of international shortwave broadcasting, how it is organized, why some countries use it more than others, what broadcasters are trying to accomplish, etc."

1257. *World Radio and Television.* Paris: Unesco Publications Center, 1965. 159 pp.

Published to meet the widespread demand for information on radio and television throughout the world, this describes existing facilities in nearly 200 countries. Part one relates the pattern of radio and television while part two details radio and television country by country from Aden to Zanzibar.

1258. Yoder, Andrew R. *Pirate Radio Stations: Tuning in to Underground Broadcasts.* Blue Ridge Summit, PA: Tab Books, 1990. 182 pp. ISBN: 0-8306-3268-9.

The author provides a complete history of pirate radio since its emergence in the 1920s along with station biographies and interviews with some of the personnel involved. Numerous diagrams illustrate the operation of pirate radio systems.

1259. Yugoslav Institute of Journalism. *Press, Radio, Television, Film in Yugoslavia.* Beograd: The Institute, 1961. 131 pp.

Roughly less than one-third of this book is actually devoted to radio broadcasting, but it does offer an overview of the medium that is not readily available elsewhere. It describes the development of radio stations, how they were founded and are funded, their programming, along with lists of stations, duration of programs, times, and wave lengths.

PUBLIC BROADCASTING

Includes national public radio, community broadcasting, educational radio, and the use of radio in education.

1260. Aarnes, Hale, and Kenneth Christiansen, eds. *Problems in College Radio*. Columbia, MO: Stephens College, 1948. 158 pp.

This book comprises the proceedings of the 1946 Conference on College Radio held at Stephens College. It includes papers on radio curriculum, subject matter fields in radio, programming trends, radio management in the college and university, radio careers for women, and a look at radio from both the industry itself and the university administrator.

1261. *American Public Radio Qualitative Profile*. Washington: Corporation for Public Broadcasting, 1987. 1 vol.

Taken from *National Demographics & Lifestyles* of March 1987, this provides a qualitative analysis of a sampling of public radio listeners. The report also includes discussion of the study methodology and of the application of research for public radio stations.

1262. Atkinson, Carroll. *American Universities and Colleges That Have Held Broadcast License*. Boston: Meador Publishing, 1941. 127 pp. (Nelson Memorial Library series).

The table of contents lists discussions about standard broadcast licenses, the elimination of weaker stations, commercial operations, cooperative broadcasting, public relations broadcasting, adult education, and instruction by radio.

1263. Atkinson, Carroll. *Broadcasting to the Classroom by Universities and Colleges*. Boston: Meador Publishing, 1942. 128 pp. (Nelson Memorial Library series).

At the time this book was published, 38 American universities and colleges broadcast programs intended for classroom use. Atkinson summarizes the historical development of these programs according to chronological order from the first attempt to reach the classroom via radio (Nebraska Wesleyan University in 1921).

1264. Atkinson, Carroll. *Development of Radio Education Policies in American Public School Systems*. Edinboro, PA: Edinboro Educational Press, 1939. 279 pp.

Intended for educators who are seeking ideas for the creation or improvement of radio education policies, this "records the most important historical facts" and describes present policies of 126 (10.3%) of the American public school systems representing population centers of 8,000 or more. Atkinson provides a summary for each of these cities based on data furnished by them.

1265. Atkinson, Carroll. *Education by Radio in American Schools*. Nashville, TN: George Peabody College for Teachers, 1938. 126 pp.

The author's Ph.D. dissertation, its purpose was to determine the status of the relationship between the American school and radio as Atkinson looks at how extensive the use of radio has been in the schools, the success of such practices, and future implications of radio as an educational tool.

1266. Atkinson, Carroll. *Public School Broadcasting to the Classroom*. Boston: Meador Publishing, 1942. 144 pp. (Nelson Memorial Library series).

Atkinson compiles all available data concerning attempts made by public school systems to create a radio program service for classroom listening. At the time of publication of this book there were 29 American public school systems that provided this type of educational service, and each is described in detail.

1267. Atkinson, Carroll. *Radio Extension Courses Broadcast for Credit*. Boston: Meador Publishing, 1941. 128 pp. (Nelson Memorial Library series).

As the title indicates, this is a listing of schools and universities offering extension courses in broadcasting. It lists three institutions that offer certificates but not academic credit, three universities with extension courses, and 13 institutions that give academic credit for broadcast extension courses.

1268. Atkinson, Carroll. *Radio in State and Territorial Educational Departments*. Boston: Meador Publishing, 1942. 136 pp. (Nelson Memorial Library series).

The author feels that since radio has become a recognized educational force in all levels of instruction, there should be a definite policy as to its use within the classroom and as a medium for public relations work. He details the status of such policies in each individual state although not all the states are represented.

1269. Atkinson, Carroll. *Radio Network Contributions to Education.* Boston: Meador Publishing, 1942. 128 pp. (Nelson Memorial Library series).

This examines the contributions of the major networks in a variety of areas: forum-panels, information-quizzes, dramas, music, children, educator-produced subject matter, and several miscellaneous types.

1270. Atkinson, Carroll. *Radio Programs Intended for Classroom Use.* Boston: Meador Publishing, 1942. 128 pp. (Nelson Memorial Library series).

A frank appraisal of radio programs intended for classroom use, this recommends certain programs and tells briefly their histories as they have been developed by the major networks, local stations, universities, colleges, etc. The author includes times of presentation as closely as he can determine them with regard to changing of program schedules.

1271. Bailey, K.V. *The Listening Schools: Educational Broadcasting by Sound and Television.* London: British Broadcasting Corporation, 1957. 184 pp.

The author provides a guide to the history, organization and output of educational broadcasting in the United Kingdom and makes some overall assessment of the part such broadcasts play in the schools. Several appendices include composition of school broadcasting councils, a guide to school broadcasts, and a select bibliography of works published since 1945 on school broadcasting in the UK.

1272. Bartlett, Kenneth L. *How to Use Radio.* Washington: National Association of Broadcasters, 1938. 42 pp.

Public Broadcasting 379

Professor Bartlett presents an outline of practical suggestions for the teacher and the radio chairperson in schools. Contents include contributions to radio made by educational groups and civic organizations, what radio can do for education, and the problem of adapting educational material to the air.

This book has been cataloged through OCLC and other shared cataloging under the name of the author as Kenneth Gill Bartlett; however, the copy examined clearly shows his middle initial as L.

1273. Berry, Lola. *Radio Development in a Small City School System*. Boston: Meador Publishing, 1943. 126 pp. (Nelson Memorial Library series).

Lewiston, Idaho, is the city that Berry uses as an example of what can be done with radio "to build poise within individual students, to create life interests, and to make the high school more definitely a part of the community life."

1274. Beville, Hugh Malcolm, Jr., and Cuthbert Daniel. *Classification of Educational Radio Research*. Washington: Federal Radio Education Committee, 1941. 13 leaves.

Reproduced from typewritten copy, this offers readers very brief summaries of what is known in certain areas in the field of audience research. The scheme of classification proposed by the authors is expected to be valuable to civic and educational groups and to broadcasters.

1275. Bird, Win W. *The Educational Aims and Practices of the National and Columbia Broadcasting Systems*. Seattle:

University of Washington, 1939. 82 pp. (University of Washington Extension series, 10).

Because only NBC and CBS had sufficiently long experience with educational broadcasting and because they are the only ones to employ educational directors, they were chosen as the subjects of Bird's study of educational broadcasting and the broadcasts that are available to the country. He selected programs that had been on the air for at least one academic year and analyzed their content.

1276. Blakely, Robert J. *To Serve the Public Interest: Educational Broadcasting in the United States.* Syracuse, NY: Syracuse University Press, 1979. 274 pp. ISBN: 0-8156-2198-1.

In his preface McGeorge Bundy writes that Mr. Blakely's central theme is that noncommercial broadcasting owes its very life and most of its present strength to the individual citizens who have cared enough to fight for it. Blakely states that this book's purpose is to tell the story of the achievement of educational broadcasting--how it began, its struggle for survival, and what its future prospects are.

1277. Bloch, Louis M., Jr. *The Gas Pipe Networks: A History of College Radio, 1936-1946.* Cleveland, OH: Bloch, 1980. 126 pp. ISBN: 0-914276-02-6.

At the time of publication there were slightly over 1,000 colleges with campus radio stations operated by students. The author was involved with the development of college radio from its very beginning at Brown University in 1936, and he tells the story of his involvement in college radio, "affectionately called 'The Gas Pipe Networks'"

1278. Boutwell, William Dow. *FM for Education.* Washington: Government Printing Office, 1944. 54 pp.

Prepared for distribution by the Federal Security Agency of the U.S. Office of Education, this offers suggestions for planning, licensing and utilizing educational FM radio stations owned and operated by school systems, colleges, and universities.

1279. Brant, Billy G. *The College Radio Handbook.* Blue Ridge Summit, PA: Tab Books, 1981. 224 pp. ISBN: 0-8306-9763-2.

The preface states that the purpose of this book is twofold: first to survey the history and development of college radio in the United States, and second, to provide practical suggestions concerning programming, promotional work, public support, management, and operations.

1280. Broadcast Institute of North America. *College Carrier Current: A Survey of 208 Campus-Limited Radio Stations.* New York: The Institute, 1972. 29 pp.

The findings indicate that most campus-limited stations are run as undergraduate student activities, few are used for training, and most carry commercial advertising but rely upon institutional or student-generated funds for their main support. Their programming consists mainly of recorded music (generally progressive rock or top 40), and little or no opportunity is available for student self-expression. News or public affairs programming is offered, and most stations appear to be relatively free from outside or institutional controls.

1281. *Broadcasting to Schools.* Paris: Unesco, 1949. 211 pp.

The contents of this volume are reports on the organization of school broadcasting services in various countries. Those featured are Australia, Belgium, Brazil, Canada, Chile, Great Britain, India, Mexico, Poland, Sweden, Switzerland, Union of South Africa, and the United States.

1282. Broderick, Gertrude G. *Educational AM and FM Radio and Educational Television Stations by State and City.* Washington: U.S. Office of Education, 1965. 26 pp.

This is an updated version of Broderick's *List of Educational AM and FM Radio and Television Stations* (see next annotation) published in 1955 and has the same format.

1283. Broderick, Gertrude G. *List of Educational AM and FM Radio and Television Stations by State and City.* Washington: U.S. Office of Education, 1955. 11 pp.

The first list prepared by Broderick, this is arranged alphabetically by state and then by city and provides call letters, licensee, and the general manager's and/or program director's names.

1284. Burke, Richard C. *The Use of Radio in Adult Literacy Education.* Tehran, Iran: Hulton Educational Publications, 1976. 116 pp. (Literacy in Development). ISBN: 0-7175-0760-2.

"The purpose of this monograph is to provide literacy field workers with some practical advice about using radio broadcasting as an important and integral part of their work."

1285. Busby, H.S., et al. *How to Use Radio in the Classroom.* Washington: National Association of Broadcasters, 1941. 21 pp.

The materials for this introductory handbook were gathered during a six-week radio education seminar held in connection with the Progressive Education Association's Eastern Workshop in 1938. The preface states that it offers suggestions to teachers who are interested in using radio in their classroom and is intended to be introductory and provocative, rather than comprehensive and conclusive.

1286. Caldwell, S. Carlton, and Harold Niven. *Broadcast Programs in American Colleges and Universities.* Washington: National Association of Broadcasters, 1981. 45 pp. (Broadcast Education Association, 15th report).

A listing of the colleges and universities offering degrees or coursework in broadcasting as well as two-year colleges offering broadcasting programs, this is arranged alphabetically by state. It summarizes graduation requirements, facilities, financial aid, and faculty. A 1986 edition updated these data to 1986-87, and a new one is being planned as a directory in 1990.

1287. Callahan, Jennie Waugh. *Radio Workshop for Children.* New York: McGraw-Hill, 1948. 398 pp.

This book was written to aid instructors of college courses in radio and to serve as a text for those who are preparing to use radio broadcasting as a teaching tool. Photographs of workshop groups taken during rehearsals and broadcasts help illustrate the types of activities involved.

1288. Carle, Wayne M., ed. *Education on the Air: Yearbook of the 1959 Institute for Education by Radio-Television.* Columbus: Ohio State University, 1959. 264 pp.

The essays in this volume cover a wide range of topics: broadcasting's social responsibility, current problems and issues, progress in educational aspects of broadcasting, communications research, and areas of special interest. First published in 1930, the Yearbook has been continued on an annual basis. (See alto item 1346.)

1289. Cater, Douglass, and Michael J. Nyhan, eds. *The Future of Public Broadcasting.* New York: Praeger, 1976. 372 pp. ISBN: 0-275-56990-X.

A number of experts in the area of communications were asked to examine the many serious policy questions facing public broadcasting, to explore possible solutions, and to propose future directions. This book is the compilation of their thoughts, questions, answers, and suggestions.

1290. Charters, W.W., ed. *Research Problems in Radio Education.* Rev. ed. New York: National Advisory Council on Radio in Education, 1934. 41 pp. (Information series, 4).

The purpose of this publication is to call the attention of investigators to certain specific problems in the field of research in education by radio. It classifies and lists the problems so that an individual investigator can define the problem more sharply as well as assimilate personal research with other research studies being undertaken.

1291. Clausse, Roger. *Education by Radio: School Broadcasting.* Paris: Unesco, 1949. 72 pp. (Press, Film and Radio in the World Today).

Following an introduction concerning education and the radio, the author describes management, administration, educational considerations, radio and the school, and school broadcasting at different educational levels. This series of studies concentrates on specific problems of mass communications.

1292. Cleveland Public Schools. *Report of Radio Activities, 1938-1939: Station WBOE*. Cleveland, OH: Cleveland Board of Education, 1939. 163 pp.

The Cleveland public schools have experimented in the use of radio for broadcasting lessons to regular classes since 1925. Through a cooperative arrangement with the General Education Board the Cleveland Board of Education developed its own station, WBOE, which was in operation nearly all the 1938-39 school year. This report tells the story of that year.

* Clifford, Theresa R., ed. *Sourcetap: A Directory of Program Resources for Radio*. Cited above as item 645.

1293. Cooper, Isabella M. *Bibliography on Educational Broadcasting*. New York: Arno Press/New York Times, 1971. 576 pp. (History of Broadcasting: Radio to Television). ISBN: 0-405-03587-X.

"The chief aim of the compiler was to produce a bibliography of practical utility which should give access to reference and research material in the historical, technical, and educational fields of broadcasting and the particular application of this art in methods of use for instruction." The book was originally published in 1942 by the University of Chicago Press.

* Corporation for Public Broadcasting. *Audience 88: A Comprehensive Analysis of Public Radio Listeners.* Cited above as item 354.

1294. Corporation for Public Broadcasting. *Public Radio Handbook.* Washington: The Corporation, 1979. 1 vol. ISBN: 0-89776-013-1.

    The main divisions of this loose-leaf volume are Planning and Pre-broadcast Activities, Station Management and Organization, Legal Considerations, Program Theory and Planning, Program Management and Scheduling, Technical Considerations, Development, Communication Research, Special Services, and a Directory of Organizations and Services.

1295. Corporation for Public Broadcasting. *Public Radio/Telephone Survey.* Washington: The Corporation, 1978. 34 pp.

    This report is one of four describing a nationwide study of (1) awareness of and listening to public radio, as well as reactions to on-air fund raising and to programming on public radio and (2) reactions to on-air fund raising by public television stations. This survey was repeated in later years.

1296. Corporation for Public Broadcasting. *Public Television and Public Radio Awareness Viewing and Listening On-Air Fund Raising.* Washington: The Corporation, 1982. 92 pp.

    The public radio portion of this survey is a repetition of studies completed in 1978 and 1979 (see previous annotation). It is intended to provide a measure of changes in public reaction over the years.

1297. Corporation for Public Broadcasting. *A Report to the People: 20 Years of Your National Commitment to Public*

Public Broadcasting 387

Broadcasting, 1967-1987. Washington: The Corporation, 1987. 96 pp.

Actually the Corporation's 1986 *Annual Report*, this publication is different from the usual format in that it provides a 20-year history of the organization, discusses programming in depth, presents audience profiles, and suggests plans for the future. The usual financial statements and grant allocations are listed in a separate section.

1298. Council on Radio Journalism. *Council on Radio Journalism*. Washington: The Council, 1945. 12 pp.

This pamphlet provides a history of the organization, its constitution, and a list of its standards for education for radio journalism. There is a checklist for a program of education in radio journalism published for the convenience of colleges and universities who offer courses in the field.

1299. Curtis, Alberta. *Listeners Appraise a College Station*. Washington: Federal Radio Education Committee, U.S. Office of Education, 1940. 70 pp.

Station WOI of Iowa State College in Ames is the subject of this study and evaluation. Particular areas of concentration include WOI's book programs, music shop, homemaking programs, vocational guidance, and market news service.

1300. Darrow, Ben H. *Radio: The Assistant Teacher*. Columbus, OH: R.G. Adams, 1932. 271 pp.

The author describes the origin and growth of educational broadcasting and puts an emphasis on participation by individual states. He continues with the purposes of educational broadcasting, necessary preparation, ways of presentation, and actual classroom usage.

1301. Darrow, Ben H. *Radio Trailblazing.* Columbus, OH: College Books, 1940. 137 pp.

The founder of "The Little Red Schoolhouse of Radio"--WLS, Chicago--relates a brief history of the Ohio School of the Air and its implications for educational broadcasting.

1302. Denison, Merrill. *The Educational Program.* New York: Radio Institute of the Audible Arts, 1935. 13 pp.

In this brochure the author presents a discussion of facts and techniques in educational broadcasting. He recommends what educators should do to adapt their programs to radio's requirements.

1303. Department of Elementary School Principals. Michigan Education Association. *Implications of the Radio in Education.* Lansing, MI: The Association, 1940. 128 pp.

The 12th Yearbook of the Association, this examines the influence of radio on children and includes a survey of the radio listening of approximately 1,000 elementary school children in Michigan. Other chapters project ways to develop discriminate listening, utilize radio for instruction, and acquire radio equipment.

1304. Department of Elementary School Principals. National Education Association. *Radio and the Classroom.* Washington: The Association, 1940. 97 pp.

This monograph is a practical discussion by educators experienced in both the fields of education and radio. It is intended for other educators who want to experiment with radio as a tool of learning in the classroom.

1305. Dunham, Franklin. *FM for Education.* 2nd ed. Washington: Government Printing Office, 1948. 30 pp.

Prepared for the Federal Security Agency of the U.S. Office of Education, the first edition of this title appeared in 1944 and urged educators and school board members to take advantage of the 20 FM channels reserved by the FCC for education. This edition presents evidence of the rapid growth in use of this tool as some 100 school systems and colleges were on their way to ownership and operation of FM stations by April 1948.

1306. *Editorial Integrity in Public Broadcasting: Proceedings of the Wingspread Conference, November 28-30, 1984.* Columbia, SC: Southern Educational Communications Association, 1985. 85 pp.

The Conference studied the questions of legality, accountability, and creditability as well as a review of issues, policy implications, and code development.

1307. Federal Radio Education Committee. *Suggested Standards for College Courses in Radio Broadcasting.* Washington: Government Printing Office, 1945. 12 pp.

Published with the cooperation of the U.S. Office of Education, this set of standards is designed as a guide to those institutions already offering, or planning to develop, undergraduate courses in the program, business, and/or listener aspects of modern broadcasting.

1308. Frost, S.E., Jr. *Education's Own Stations: The History of Broadcast Licenses Issued to Educational Institutions.* Chicago: University of Chicago Press, 1937. 480 pp.

During the period 1921 through 1936, a total of 202 broadcast licenses were granted by the federal government to educational institutions and held in the names of those institutions while a few others were granted to a high school faculty member, and still others were special or temporary permits. This volume describes the various licensees and their subsequent histories. It has been reprinted as part of the 1971 History of Broadcasting: Radio to Television series published by Arno Press/New York Times.

1309. Garland-Compton, Ltd. *Community Radio: Missing Link?* London: Garland-Compton, 1965. 30 pp.

"This booklet discusses the establishment of a local radio service (in Great Britain), and the implications of local radio being financed by the sale of air-time."

1310. Gibson, George H. *Public Broadcasting: The Role of the Federal Government, 1912-1976.* New York: Praeger, 1977. 236 pp. (Praeger Special Studies in U.S. Economic, Social, and Political Issues).

Title chapters are The Secretary of Commerce and the Federal Radio Commission; The Federal Communications Commission and the Office of Education--AM Radio; The Federal Communications Commission--FM Radio; The Federal Communications Commission--Television; The Congress and the Department of Health, Education and Welfare--Funds; The Congress and the President--Public Broadcasting; and The Congress and the President--Long-Range Financing.

1311. Gibson, Pauline. *Handbook for Amateur Broadcasters.* Pittsburgh, PA: Scholastic Radio Guild, 1937. 58 pp.

The first Radio Workshop of the Educational Radio Project of the Office of Education undertook the preparation of this booklet as one of its first important projects. It is intended to improve the technique of educational broadcasting through a study of the methods used successfully by important educational and commercial broadcasters throughout the country.

1312. Giovannoni, David. *The Personal Importance of Public Radio*. Washington: Corporation for Public Broadcasting, 1988. 20 pp.

The topics of this selection of material from *Current* magazine's "Radio Intelligence" columns deal with "the importance of being important." They cover the demographics, program content, and the search for personal importance.

1313. Giovannoni, David, and George Bailey. *Appeal and Public Radio's Music*. Washington: Corporation for Public Broadcasting, 1988. 27 pp.

This compilation is adapted from articles originally published in *Current*'s "Radio Intelligence" column, funded by CPB's Office of Policy Development and Planning. The intent is to examine existing research and devise new strategies which can be applied immediately by public broadcasters.

1314. Grinspan, Mel G., ed. *News and Views from National Public Radio*. Memphis, TN: Rhodes College, 1987. 36 pp.

In 1987 the M.L. Seidman Memorial Town Hall lectures were presented by Bob Edwards, host of NPR's *Morning Edition*, Cokie Roberts, reporter for *Morning Edition* and *All Things Considered*, and *Weekend Edition* host Scott

392 Radio Broadcasting

Simon. The texts of all three lectures comprise this volume.

1315. Harrison, Margaret. *Radio in Rural Schools: An Investigation.* New York: Columbia University Teachers College, 1930. 103 leaves.

This is a preliminary report of a study made by the author in 1929-1930. Its whole purpose was to lay the groundwork for further experimentation and research.

1316. Harrison, Margaret. *Radio in the Classroom: Objectives, Principles and Practices.* New York: Prentice-Hall, 1938. 260 pp.

The primary purpose of this book is to offer suggestions to those concerned with the classroom use of radio. It is designed to help supervisors, principals, and teachers make use of programs broadcast throughout the country, but it purposely omits the use of state and local "schools of the air."

1317. Haussman, John F., Jr. *Radio in Education.* Harrisburg: Pennsylvania Department of Public Instruction, 1939. 47 pp.

The 12th in a series of books and pamphlets compiled and published by the Federal Writers' Project in Pennsylvania, this bulletin was conceived and published as a means of introducing Pennsylvania's teachers to the development of radio in schools, of relating interesting experiments, and of speculating upon the future possibilities of radio and television as educational media. It explains the problems of educational broadcasts and provides a program analysis and program construction. Plans are suggested for program improvement.

1318. Herzberg, Max J., ed. *Radio and English Teaching: Experiences, Problems, and Procedures.* New York: Appleton-Century, 1941. 246 pp.

A series of essays were written on the background of radio, history, and problems of educational broadcasts. The last part provides a bibliography of publications and sources of useful material on radio as a tool in education.

1319. *The Hidden Medium: A Status Report on Educational Radio in the United States.* New York: Herman W. Land Associates, 1967. 1 vol.

Prepared for National Educational Radio, this report is based on a survey conducted during the winter of 1966-67 by means of a 25-page questionnaire containing 112 questions mailed to 320 educational radio stations. Forty-two percent of those surveyed responded, and an additional 50 telephone and field interviews were conducted by station managers to provide the results published here.

1320. Hill, Frank Ernest. *Listen and Learn: Fifteen Years of Adult Education on the Air.* New York: American Association for Adult Education, 1937. 248 pp.

The author states that this book is the product of an effort to collect and relate to one another the important facts about adult education, past and present. He writes about the problems faced in the beginning and some of the victories and successes. He states that he looks forward to the development of a stronger program for the field.

1321. Hill, Frank Ernest. *Tune in for Education: Eleven Years of Education by Radio.* New York: National Committee on Education by Radio, 1942. 109 pp.

This summarizes the events in which the Committee has participated. The Committee is composed of the representatives of nine national educational associations and has devoted its activities to the promotion of radio as an educational medium.

1322. Internationales Zentralinstitut für das Jugend- und Bildungsfernsehen, ed. *School Radio in Europe.* München: K.G. Saur, 1979. 198 pp. (Communication Research and Broadcasting, 1). ISBN: 3-598-20200-8.

This is a compilation of contributions from the European School Radio Conference held in Munich in 1977. Subjects include reports from European school radio departments, an overview of school radio, issues in perception and attention in relation to the reception of radio broadcasts, foreign language teaching and school radio, and music education.

1323. Irvin, Lee. *The School Radio Club.* Minneapolis: Northwestern Press, 1941. 137 pp.

Suggestions for conducting radio activities are offered along with 11 radio scripts from the series "Looking Ahead."

1324. Isber, Caroline, and Muriel Cantor. *Report of the Task Force on Women in Public Broadcasting.* Washington: Corporation for Public Broadcasting, 1975. 141 pp.

The three objectives of this study were (1) to examine the extent to which women are employed at all levels in broadcasting and are integrated into its policy-making and operations, (2) to examine the visibility and image of women in all radio and television programming and the coverage of issues pertinent to women, and (3) to make recommendations for improvement to the CPB Board of Directors.

1325. Jamison, Dean T., and Emile G. McAnany. *Radio for Education and Development*. Beverly Hills: Sage, 1978. 224 pp. (People and Communication series). ISBN: 0-8039-0865-2.

In 1975 the Education Department of the World Bank initiated a study of the role of radio in education and development communication. This volume presents an overview of the subject based on case studies and other sources.

1326. Jansky, C.M., Jr., R.C. Higgy, and Morse Salisbury. *The Problem of the Institutionally Owned Station*. Chicago: University of Chicago Press, 1934. 31 pp.

Three essays discuss the problems facing radio stations owned by educational institutions. They concentrate on various aspects of educational broadcasting stations and their administration.

1327. Jones, J. Morris. *Americans All--Immigrants All: A Handbook for Listeners*. Washington: U.S. Office of Education, 1939. 120 pp.

Prepared in association with the Federal Radio Education Committee, this booklet is intended to be used in connection with a series of radio programs originally broadcast from coast to coast under the auspices of the Office of Education and later made available to schools and listener groups. The programs "demonstrated that the making of the United States goes on--today as always--by endless cooperative effort" and relate the history of this country.

1328. Josephson, Larry, ed. *Telling the Story: The National Public Radio Guide to Radio Journalism*. Dubuque, IA: Kendall Hunt, 1983. 228 pp. ISBN: 0-8403-2861-3.

Produced by NPR's Education Services and Station Services Departments, this book is about "the art and craft, theory and practice, ethics and pragmatics, legal underpinnings, and marketing of news and information radio." It emphasizes personal qualities, role models, professional skills, practice, and luck.

1329. Kansas State Department of Education. *The Radio Classroom*. Topeka: The Department, 1945. 142 pp.

Accompanied by a 130 page teacher's manual, this presents a series of radio programs, sponsored by the State Department of Education and Emporia State Teachers College and broadcast over the Kansas State Network. They were designed for classroom instruction in the rural schools.

1330. Katz, Joan H., and Denise E. Wood. *Public Radio Stations' Educational Services, 1982-83*. Washington: Corporation for Public Broadcasting, 1984. 1 vol. ISBN: 0-89776-091-3.

Part of a comprehensive research project supported by CPB and the National Center for Education Statistics, this report presents the highlights of the survey which monitored certain educational services provided by public radio stations to elementary, secondary, and post-secondary educational institutions in the United States.

1331. Koon, Cline M. *The Art of Teaching by Radio*. Washington: Government Printing Office, 1933, 91 pp.

Published by the U.S. Department of the Interior as its 1933 *Bulletin No. 4*, this analyzes some of the forms which broadcasting has taken and gives some attention to the preparation and delivery of these forms. It contains a lengthy bibliography of journal articles for additional reference.

1332. Koon, Cline M. *School Use of Radio*. Laramie: University of Wyoming, 1936. 64 leaves.

Mimeographed by the University and not actually intended for wide circulation, this is the preliminary draft of a text for teachers and school administrators and was conceived for experimental use in teacher-training courses at Wyoming, the University of Illinois, Ohio State University, and Columbia University's Teachers College during the summer session of 1936.

1333. Koon,Cline M., compiler. *Some Public Service Broadcasting*. Chicago: University of Chicago Press, 1934. 35 pp.

The National Advisory Council on Radio in Education and the Federal Office of Education conducted a survey about programs and broadcast activities of national voluntary organizations that have public service objectives. This volume is a report of that survey.

1334. Kumar, Narenda. *Educational Radio in India*. New Delhi: Arya Book Depot, 1967. 116 pp.

This volume combines the author's earlier publications, *School Broadcasting in India* and *Adult Education Through Radio*, in one volume. It was based on research done in 1954-55.

1335. Laine, Elizabeth. *Motion Pictures and Radio: Modern Techniques for Education*. New York: McGraw-Hill, 1938. 165 pp.

Published for the Regents' Inquiry into the Character and Cost of Public Education in the State of New York, this examines the role and background of motion pictures and then devotes the second half of the book to radio. Areas studied include radio as a medium for mass impression, adaptation of radio to education, educational projects in radio broadcasting, and the role of the state in an educational radio program.

1336. Lambert, Richard S. *School Broadcasting in Canada*. Toronto: University of Toronto Press, 1963. 223 pp.

Lambert describes the origin, growth, and achievements of school broadcasting in Canada. He emphasizes the cooperation achieved between both the Canadian government and the provincial governments.

1337. Leach, Eugene E. *Tuning Out Education: The Cooperation Doctrine in Radio, 1922-38*. Washington: Current, 1983. 19 pp.

This is a reprint, with footnotes added, of the series "Snookered 50 Years Ago," that appeared in the newspaper *Current* in January, February, and March 1983.

1338. Lee, S. Young, and Ronald J. Pedone. *Summary Statistics of CPB-Qualified Public Radio Stations, Fiscal Year 1972*. Washington: Government Printing Office, 1973. 91 pp.

This publication--one in a continuing series of statistical reports on public broadcasting--is based on data provided annually by public radio and television licensees to the Corporation for Public Broadcasting. It summarizes fundamental statistics in finance, employment, and broadcast and production activities of 121 educational public radio stations.

1339. Levenson, William B. *Teaching Through Radio.* New York: Farrar & Rinehart, 1945. 474 pp. (Farrar & Rinehart Radio series).

Written by the director of radio activities in the Cleveland, Ohio, schools, this book is an outgrowth of the writer's experience in classroom use of radio and in directing the operation of the Cleveland Board of Education's station WBOE. It presents the techniques and basic information needed by teachers and school administrators in a variety of situations, including broadcasting activities within the school, public relations broadcasting, commercial programs for children, and the school radio station.

1340. Levenson, William B., and Edward Stasheff. *Teaching Through Radio and Television.* Rev. ed. New York: Greenwood Press, 1969. 560 pp.

When this book underwent revision, it also acquired a co-author and a title change from *Teaching Through Radio* (see previous annotation) in order to encompass the new medium. Its goal, as was the earlier edition, is "the improvement of school broadcasting and the encouragement of more effective use of educational programs."

1341. Lifset, Reid. *Public Radio and State Governments.* Washington: National Public Radio, 1981. 132 pp.

Description and Analysis is the title of Volume 1 in this series that describes how each state and United States territory is involved in public broadcasting with an emphasis on public radio. There are 229 full-service public radio stations qualified to receive funds from the Corporation for Public Broadcasting, and state governments provide a significant percentage of the total income for these stations, along with individual contributions.

1342. Lingel, Robert. *Educational Broadcasting: A Bibliography*. Chicago: University of Chicago Press, 1932. 162 pp.

In the fall of 1930 the National Advisory Council on Radio in Education came into existence and one of its first tasks was the compilation of a bibliography on the subject. This book is the result and covers a variety of subject areas from adult education and advertising to writing and zoology, along with specific categories for a number of countries and American states.

1343. Lowdermilk, R.R. *The School Radio-Sound System*. Washington: Federal Radio Education Committee, 1941. 58 pp.

This pamphlet was written primarily in terms of the educational uses to which radio sound equipment may be put, and it treats technical matters in relation to such uses.

1344. Lowdermilk, R.R. *Teaching with Radio*. Columbus: Ohio State University. Bureau of Educational Research, 1938. 48 pp. (Radio Bulletin, 16).

This is intended to help educators prepare classes for radio, instruct them in how to listen, and carry on discussions after the broadcast.

1345. Lumley, Frederick H. *Broadcasting Foreign-Language Lessons*. Columbus: Ohio State University. Bureau of Education Research, 1934. 90 pp. (Research Monographs, 19).

Written from a background of nearly ten years of broadcasting foreign-language lessons, the author summarizes what has been both good and bad in the field. Tables show the number of stations broadcasting in the area, the number of actual lessons aired, the number of teachers involved, and a list of textbooks used to supplement the courses.

1346. MacLatchy, Josephine, ed. *Education on the Air: First Yearbook of the Institute for Education by Radio.* Columbus: Ohio State University, 1930. 400 pp.

This is the first printed Proceedings of the ten-day Institute of Radio Education sponsored by the Payne Fund, the State Department of Education of Ohio, and the Ohio State University that was held in June 1930. This book has evolved into an annual publication that discusses administration, international activity, radio in educational institutions, schools of the air, college stations, and educational techniques in broadcasting. It was edited for the first 18 years by MacLatchy, and by O. Joe Olson until 1952, and since then by a series of editors. (See also item 1288.)

1347. Maddison, John. *Radio and Television in Literacy.* Geneva: Unesco, 1971. 82 pp. (Reports and Papers on Mass Communication, 62).

The present report is based on experience in 38 member states of Unesco and on documentation already published. It is a survey of the use of the broadcasting media in combating illiteracy among adults.

1348. Marsh, C.S., ed. *Educational Broadcasting 1937.* Chicago: University of Chicago Press, 1937. 386 pp.

One of a series, this contains the Proceedings of the Second National Conference on Education Broadcasting that was held in Chicago in the winter of 1937. The main intent of these conferences is to provide a national forum where interests concerned with education by radio can come together to exchange ideas and experiences and to examine and appraise the situation in American broadcasting as a background for present and future public service.

1349. McClendon, Natalie. *Go Public! The Traveler's Guide to Non-Commercial Radio*. Lincoln, NB: Wakerobin Communications, 1987. 219 pp. ISBN: 0-9617989-0-4.

The book is a boon to anyone who travels by car and wants to find out the frequency of the local AM/FM public broadcasting station. It is organized geographically by regions of the United States and is composed of maps for each area along with a listing of stations, arranged in alphabetical order by call letter. In addition, it provides the format of the stations and in many cases offers a log showing type of program by time period.

* McNeil, Bill, and Morris Wolfe. *Signing On: The Birth of Radio in Canada*. Cited above as item 1193.

1350. Mendel, Robin, Natan Katzman, and Solomon Katzman. *Public Radio Programming Content by Category, Fiscal Year 1982*. Washington: Corporation for Public Broadcasting, 1982. 54 pp. ISBN: 0-89776-094-8.

The figures presented in this report are based on data covering the 1982 fiscal year and represent each one of 228 public radio stations sampled for seven days, on a different day of the week, in each of seven seasons. Similar reports have been published previously.

1351. Merrill, I.R. *Benchmark Television Radio Study, Part I: Lansing*. East Lansing: Michigan State University, 1956. 74 leaves (WKAR-TV Research Report 561M).

Although the bulk of this report deals with television, there are sections covering educational broadcast audiences for radio and educational radio programs in general.

1352. Methold, Kenneth. *Broadcasting with Children: Broadcasting Techniques As an Aid to Teaching.* London: University of London Press, 1959. 128 pp.

   A very personal account, this describes the author's own experiences with broadcasting techniques in modern secondary schools.

1353. Milam, Lorenzo Wilson. *The Original Sex and Broadcasting: A Handbook on Starting a Radio Station for the Community.* 3rd ed. San Diego: MHO and MHO Works, 1988. 348 pp. ISBN: 0-917320-01-8.

   Published first in June 1971 because the author got "sick and tired of writing up single-space five page letters for all those people wanting to set up alternative, community radio stations," this edition "is now about ten times longer, with about one-third of the bombast of the first edition." It still provides help for those interested in the subject and may make their endeavors to go on the air a bit easier.

1354. Milam, Lorenzo Wilson. *The Radio Papers: From KRAB to KCHU.* San Diego: MHO and MHO Works, 1986. 166 pp. ISBN: 0-917320-18-2.

   Subtitled "Essays on the Art and Practice of Radio Transmission," this is a collection of articles written between 1962 and 1977 for the program guides of five non-commercial community radio stations: KRAB (Seattle), KBOO (Portland), KDNA (St. Louis), KTAO (Los Gatos), and KCHU (Dallas).

1355. Miles, J. Robert. *Sixty School Broadcasts*. Columbus: Ohio State University, 1941. 14 leaves (Evaluation of School Broadcasts Bulletin, 31).

This report presents an appraisal of the "best" in classroom radio programs during 1939-40. All 60 broadcasts were entered in the Fourth American Exhibition of Recordings of Educational Radio Programs held in conjunction with the 11th Institute for Education by Radio in 1940.

1356. Millikan, Robert A. *Radio's Past and Future*. Chicago: University of Chicago Press, 1931. 15 pp.

This is the text of an address given by Dr. Millikan over NBC and CBS on May 22, 1931. It was to be published as part of *Radio and Education*, a book containing the complete proceedings of the first annual assembly of the National Advisory Council on Radio in Education.

1357. Moemeka, Andrew A. *Local Radio: Community Education for Development*. Zaria, Nigeria: Ahmadu Bello University Press, 1981. 118 pp. ISBN: 978-125-018-6.

The author analyzes the problems of the media that direct their comments and broadcasting to the urban population rather than those in rural areas. He presents what he calls "a manifesto for action" to make a strong case for a radical innovation of taking education to the countryside, particularly through radio and television broadcasting.

1358. Mohanty, Jagannath. *Educational Broadcasting: Radio and Television in Education*. New Delhi: Sterling, 1984. 168 pp.

This examines the history of educational broadcasting in India beginning with children's programs on All India Radio. School broadcasting began in 1932 and television was introduced in 1960. Dr. Mohanty describes the evolution of both media.

1359. Muller, Helen M., compiler. *Education by Radio*. New York: H.W. Wilson, 1932. 175 pp. (The Reference Shelf, Vol. 8, No.1).

Following a brief resolution stating legislation should be enacted reserving to educational agencies at least 15 percent of all radio channels available for American broadcasting, there are several points presenting both affirmative and negative viewpoints. Eighteen additional articles are included as part of general, affirmative and negative discussions of the issues.

1360. National Advisory Council on Radio in Education. *Present and Impending Applications to Education of Radio and Allied Arts*. Chicago: University of Chicago Press, 1934. 83 pp.

This report of the Committee on Engineering Developments grew out of a bulletin setting down interpretations of the technicalities of radio and the allied arts in education. This is a complete revision of the earlier work and its subsequent supplements.

1361. National Association of Educational Broadcasters. *Live Radio Networking for Educational Stations*. Urbana, IL: The Association, 1960. 97 pp.

The NAEB Professional Development Committee planned and partially underwrote a seminar devoted to discussion of present networking endeavors and a consideration of future steps. It was held at the University of Wisconsin in July 1960, and this publication contains some of the talks, discussions, and conclusions of the seminar.

1362. National Association of Educational Broadcasters. *National Educational Radio: Blueprint for the Future.* Washington: The Association, 1964. 37 pp.

This is the report of an NAEB seminar held in January 1964 at the University of Chicago Center for Continuing Education. The main talks were presented by William G. Harley and Robert E. Underwood, Jr., of NAEB, E.G. Burrows from WUOM, University of Michigan, and Jack D. Summerfield from Riverside Radio WRVR in New York City.

1363. National Association of Educational Broadcasters. *Radio's Role in Instruction.* Washington: The Association, 1972. 42 pp.

Prepared by its National Educational Radio Division, this is a report containing the recommendations of the Instructional Radio Task Force. It presents findings, offers guidelines for developing effective audio instruction, asks some basic questions, examines the future outlook, and has several supplementary papers on the subject.

1364. National Broadcasting Company. *How Schools Can Use Radio: A Handbook for Schools on the Practical Use of Radio in Education.* New York: The Company, 1942. 28 pp.

This pamphlet offers simple suggestions for teachers in the use of radio in classrooms. Included are a section on basic facts, hints on fitting radio into the curriculum, and data on organizing radio workshops in schools.

1365. National Committee on Education by Radio. *Educational Radio Stations: A Pictorial Review.* New York: The Committee, 1936. 41 pp.

Featured are radio stations located at Purdue, St. Lawrence, Cornell, St. Louis, Wisconsin, Illinois, Minnesota, Oklahoma, Ohio State, Florida, Iowa State, North Dakota, Kansas, South Dakota State School of Mines, Rensselaer Polytechnic Institute, Grove City College, World Wide Broadcasting Foundation, South Dakota State, Oregon State, Kansas State, and the State College of Washington.

1366. New York Academy of Medicine. *Radio in Health Education.* New York: Columbia University Press, 1945. 120 pp.

Two studies comprise the main parts of this volume--one called Radio Broadcasting: A Critical Study of Health Education, and the other The Radio in Health Education, which were part of the New York Academy of Medicine Health Education Conference. Along with these are several articles written by people involved in the joint areas of radio and education.

1367. Noel, Francis W., George W. Ormsby, and Harry J. Skelly. *Using Radio in the Classroom.* Sacramento: California State Department of Education, 1953. 31 pp.

The February 1953 issue of the *Bulletin of the California State Department of Education* is designed to serve as a guide to educators to point out the most effective ways to use radio as an instructional tool. Practical suggestions are provided, and it can be used to foster discussions among school administrators, supervisors, and teachers.

1368. O'Steen, Alton, and J. Robert Miles. *Ideas That Came True.* Columbus: Ohio State University, 1941. 11 leaves. (Evaluation of School Broadcasts Bulletin, 32).

Two series of programs were presented by NBC on Thursday afternoons in 1939 and 1940 and were intended primarily for grade school children. One was titled "Transportation and Communication" and the other "The Greatest Idea of Them All--Democracy!"; both are appraised in this report.

1369. Parker, Lester Ward. *School Broadcasting in Great Britain.* Chicago: University of Chicago Press, 1937. 160 pp.

Mr. Parker calls attention to the wide and fundamental differences between British and American methods of education and points out that British and American radio are organized under basically different conditions. He then describes just how British educational broadcasting is handled and the success it has achieved.

1370. Partridge, Simon. *Not the BBC/IBA: The Case for Community Radio.* London: Comedia, 1982. 74 pp. (Comedia/Minority Press Group series, 8). ISBN: 0-906890-18-7.

On July 14, 1981, Partridge, the Home Secretary, gave the first official recognition to community radio when he stated in Parliament that "he proposed to give further consideration to this matter" after receiving requests for such a service. In this volume he outlines the possibilities of the new service and describes how these may be tested in actual practice.

1371. Perry, Armstrong. *Radio in Education: The Ohio School of the Air and Other Experiments.* 2nd ed. New York: The Payne Fund, 1929. 166 pp.

The Ohio School of the Air was organized by the Ohio State Department of Education in the fall of 1928 as a cooperative venture with Ohio educators, the Payne Fund, and radio stations WKW and WEAO. This describes the undertaking, what it did, how it went about it, and what the results were.

1372. Power, Leonard. *College Radio Workshops.* Washington: Federal Radio Education Committee, 1940. 51 pp.

This report is intended to enable station managers to discover and utilize the valuable radio resources that may be found in some nearby college, to enable the college to find a practical means for providing its students with broadcasting experience, and to enable civic leaders to learn how they can best use talents of students in production of their own programs.

1373. Power, Leonard. *Local Cooperative Broadcasting: A Summary and Appraisal.* Washington: Federal Radio Education Committee, 1940. 28 pp.

Published with the cooperation of the U.S. Office of Education, Federal Security Agency, the materials in this report summarize correspondence with more than 500 radio stations and interviews with more than 100 station managers. They provide constructive solutions to problems and examples of local, state, and regional cooperation.

1374. Power, Leonard. *Public Service Broadcasting: Station WMBD, Peoria, Ill.* Washington: Federal Radio Education Committee, 1940. 38 pp.

This study, part of a general one to examine cooperative efforts between broadcasters and educators, reports how one station has successfully cooperated with local non-

410 Radio Broadcasting

profit service groups that broadcast. It looks at station policies and how WMBD encourages public service promotion.

1375. Power, Leonard. *Schools of the Air and Radio in the High School Curriculum.* Washington: Federal Radio Education Committee, 1940. 61 leaves. (American Cooperative Broadcasting, Supplementary series, Bulletin 4).

Issued by the U.S. Office of Education, Federal Security Agency, this contains a survey of cooperation between education authorities and radio stations. It includes a case study of one state department of education and two case studies of city school systems.

1376. Power, Leonard. *Small Station Cooperation.* Washington: Federal Radio Education Committee, 1940. 31 leaves. (American Cooperative Broadcasting, Supplementary series, Bulletin 1).

This presents the results of a survey of successful cooperative efforts between small radio stations and educational, religious, and other non-profit civic groups.

1377. *Public Radio Stations with Early Experience Under the 1985 FCC Rules on NCE-FM/TV6 Interference.* Washington: Corporation for Public Broadcasting, 1987. 1 vol.

This pamphlet contains lists of stations that applied to or amended applications to the Federal Communications Commission for upgrade, for modification, new facilities, impact on active construction, etc. Each entry shows call letters, city, state, frequency, call letters of nearest TV6, and call letters of second TV6.

1378. Radio Corporation of America. Department of Information. *Radio-Electronics in Education.* New York: The Corporation, 1943. 48 pp.

David Sarnoff, RCA President, writes in his foreword that this booklet presents briefly the various types of aid which radio, both as a science and as a system of communication, renders to the cause of education.

1379. Radio Four Seminar. *Radio & Community Development, 3rd-4th December 1983.* Jongwe, Zimbabwe, ZBC Radio Four, 1984. 64 pp.

The papers presented by delegates from Government Ministries and voluntary organizations concern both formal and non-formal educational programming. They also describe the role of the radio media in promoting governmental development projects in various fields.

1380. Reed, Albert A. *Radio Education Pioneering in the Mid-West.* Boston: Meador Publishing, 1943. 128 pp. (Nelson Memorial Library series).

The question is asked, in this book, why the Mid-West was such an especially fertile soil for pioneering in the educational possibilities of radio and several factors are given as the answer: the great distances over which settlements extend; the rapid development of most forms of education; and the boundless enthusiasm of the people to communicate with each other. These reasons are expanded along with a history of the genre as it originated and grew.

1381. Reed, Thomas H. *Civic Education by Radio.* New York: Radio Institute of the Audible Arts, 1935. 9 pp.

The pamphlet describes how radio has revolutionized politics, itemizes problems to be solved, and suggests ways that organized groups can effect better programs. The last few pages are about listening groups and civic education broadcasts for schools.

1382. Reid, Seerley. *Network School Broadcasts: Some Conclusions and Recommendations*. Columbus: Ohio State University, 1941. 14 leaves. (Evaluation of School Broadcasts Bulletin, 35).

After examining and reviewing a number of radio programs broadcast to schools primarily by CBS in 1940-41, the author's findings indicate that the American School of the Air programs have significance and over-all value as educational materials for American schools.

1383. Reid, Seerley. *New Horizons*. Columbus: Ohio State University, 1941. 48 leaves. (Evaluation of School Broadcasts Bulletin, 37).

Reid makes a critical appraisal of 26 school broadcasts produced by CBS during the 1940-41 school year. He examines their educational value, the clarity and comprehensibility of the broadcasts, and their audience appeal.

1384. Reid, Seerley. *Radio and the Teaching of English*. Columbus: Ohio State University, 1941. 56 leaves. (Evaluation of School Broadcasts Bulletin, 22).

This study is a report of an evaluation of some of the important aspects of a 10th grade English class in Rochester, New York, that was centered around the radio.

1385. Reid, Seerley. *Radio in the Schools of Ohio.* Washington: Federal Radio Education Committee, 1942. 34 pp.

Published with the cooperation of the U.S. Office of Education Federal Security Agency, this pamphlet reiterates the results of a survey studying the extent that schools possess radio and sound equipment of varied kinds, the use of broadcasting by schools and teachers, and the content and techniques of radio in curricular and extra-curricular activities.

1386. Reid, Seerley, and Norman Woelfel. *How to Judge a School Broadcast.* Columbus: Ohio State University, 1941. 24 pp. (Evaluation of School Broadcasts Pamphlet series, 2).

This manual is recommended for use in introducing radio programs into a school system or building and/or as a basis for selecting recordings for a school library. It can also be used as a guide to script writers of school broadcasts in indicating criteria to be observed in preparing scripts.

1387. *A Resource for the Active Community.* Ottawa: Canadian Radio-Television Commission, 1974. 125 pp.

The foreword states this is a collection of articles gathered from people who have themselves been involved in community broadcasting for the past several years. It is not to be considered as an expression of CRTC policy or even as a guideline on how community expression might best be achieved.

1388. Robbins, Irving. *This Living World.* Columbus: Ohio State University, 1941. 13 leaves. (Evaluation of School Broadcasts Bulletin, 33).

This report is an evaluation of the Friday series of "The School of the Air of the Americas" that was broadcast by Columbia Broadcasting System during 1940 and 1941.

1389. Roeder, Mary, and Mary Urmston. *The Radio Enters the Classroom*. New York: Columbia University Teachers College, 1932. 17 pp.

Developed in grades 3, 6, and 7 of the Scarsdale, New York, public schools, this is intended as a means of sharing lesson units with other teachers. Its focus is on the technique of broadcasting and the presentation of a program by the children.

1390. Scupham, John. *School Broadcasting and the Newsom Report*. London: British Broadcasting Corporation, 1965. 16 pp.

Published for the School Broadcasting Council for the United Kingdom, the text of this pamphlet was prepared as a talk which Mr. Scupham gave to the Council. It refers to the Report of the Central Advisory Council for Education (England) on the education of pupils aged 13 to 16 of average and less than average ability, and treats the communications revolution (primarily broadcasting) as a new educational tool.

1391. Spain, Peter L., Dean T. Jamison, and Emile G. McAnany. *Radio for Education and Development: Case Studies*. Washington: World Bank, 1977. 2 vols. (World Bank Staff Working Paper, 266).

In this document are papers describing radio's use for in-school education, for formal education out-of-school, for non-formal education, and for interactive development communications. Most of the papers are case studies from the World Bank project, but several of them are more general papers to assist in planning the use of radio. See also item 1325 titled *Radio for Education and Development*.

1392. Sterner, Alice P. *A Course of Study in Radio and Television Appreciation*. Maplewood, NJ: Educational and Recreational Guides, 1950. 34 pp.

Intended for high school classes, this emphasizes verbal values that are especially necessary to a study of communication. Free listening, music, popular programs, sports broadcasts, comedy, drama, discussion, speeches, and literary programs are among the topics covered. An earlier edition was published in 1941 under the title *A Course of Study in Radio Appreciation*.

1393. Sterner, Alice P. *Radio, Motion Picture, and Reading Interests: A Study of High School Pupils*. New York: Columbia University Teachers College, 1947. 102 pp. (Contributions to Education, 932).

To gather data for this study the author had students complete checklists of radio programs heard along with maintaining a diary record of radio listening for seven consecutive days. The findings are presented in text and tables showing radio's relationship among adolescents, the types of programs preferred, and activities followed while listening to the radio.

1394. Stewart, Irvin, ed. *Local Broadcasts to Schools*. Chicago: University of Chicago Press, 1939. 239 pp.

Intended primarily for those cities in the United States (approximately 490) in which broadcast stations are located, this book is concerned solely with broadcasts to schools and how such broadcasting can be improved. A series of articles tell of the experiences of Detroit, Cleveland, Rochester (New York), Portland (Oregon),

Akron (Ohio), and Alameda, (California), in creating and maintaining school broadcasting.

1395. Strack, Irene Lydia, ed. *Public Broadcasting Directory, 1987-1988*. Washington: Corporation for Public Broadcasting, 1987. 134 pp. ISBN: 0-89776-104-9.

Data presented cover national and regional organizations and networks, organizations by state, related organizations and agencies, public radio stations, and public television stations. The latter two provide geographical listing, personnel index, and indexes by call letters and by licensee type.

1396. Subcommittee on Communications and Power. Committee on Interstate and Foreign Commerce. U.S. House of Representatives. *Educational Television and Radio Amendments of 1969*. Washington: Government Printing Office, 1969. 315 pp.

These hearings were on bills to amend the Communications Act of 1934 by extending the provisions relating to grants for construction of educational television or radio broadcasting facilities and the provisions relating to support of the Corporation for Public Broadcasting.

1397. Subcommittee on Communications and Power. Committee on Interstate and Foreign Commerce. U.S. House of Representatives. *Financing for Public Broadcasting--1972*. Washington: Government Printing Office, 1972. 254 pp.

These hearings were held in February 1972 on H.R. 11807, H.R. 7443, and H.R. 12808, all bills to provide for improved financing for the Corporation for Public Broadcasting.

1398. Subcommittee on Telecommunications and Finance. Committee on Energy and Commerce. U.S. House of Representatives. *Public Broadcasting.* Washington: Government Printing Office, 1988. 623 pp.

Hearings were held in November 1987 and March 1988 on H.R. 4118, a bill primarily to amend and extend the authorization of appropriations for public broadcasting. This is a transcript of these hearings.

1399. *The Teacher and the Radio Program.* Chicago: School Broadcast Conference, 1941. 26 leaves.

The role of the teacher is defined in this publication that is basically a handbook for the in-service teacher who uses radio in the classroom and was prepared by a committee of elementary school teachers. The second part of this mimeographed pamphlet explains school organization for the effective use of radio programs.

1400. Temporary Commission on Alternative Financing for Public Telecommunications. *Alternative Financing Option for Public Broadcasting.* Washington: The Commission, 1982. 2 vols.

Printed also by the Government Printing Office for the use of the Subcommittee on Telecommunications, Consumer Protection and Finance of the Committee on Energy and Commerce, U.S. House of Representatives, this report consists of two volumes. The first contains an analysis of the current state of public broadcasting, a discussion of existing and reasonably available funding options, and the conclusions and recommendations of the Commission to ensure the survival of public broadcasting services. The second volume contains staff papers which review in detail the enterprises considered as potential options for funding public broadcasting.

1401. Thomas, Thomas J., and Theresa R. Clifford. *The Public Radio Legal Handbook: A Guide to FCC Rules and Regulations*. 3rd ed. Washington: National Federation of Community Broadcasters, 1986. 1 vol.

This is one of a series of information manuals for non-commercial radio stations published by the NFCB. It provides a station operations checklist, regular filings and reports, fund raising and underwriting programming regulations, the Fairness Doctrine, political broadcasts, logs, files and station records, operating rules, technical regulations, and methods of dealing with the Federal Communications Commission. It is in a loose-leaf format for easy reference.

1402. Tyler, I. Keith. *How to Judge a Radio Program*. Chicago: Scholastic, 1936. 2 pp.

The January 11, 1936, issue of *Scholastic, The American High School Weekly*, was devoted to radio and had features on its many phases. Dr. Tyler wrote the lead editorial for this issue on the quality of broadcasting, and this pamphlet contains that article.

1403. Tyler, I. Keith. *Radio in the Elementary School*. Sacramento, CA: California State Department of Education, 1936. 6 pp.

Reprinted from the *California Journal of Elementary Education*, this pamphlet discusses the widespread influence of the radio, how it is used in elementary school instruction and the central control system utilized to present such programs.

1404. Tyler, I. Keith. *Radio in the High School*. Columbus, OH: Educational Research Bulletin, 1935. 4 pp.

This is a reprint that was intended for private circulation and was part of the *Educational Research Bulletin* published on November 13, 1935. It describes the state of radio broadcasting in Ohio high schools.

1405. Tyler, I. Keith, and R.R. Lowdermilk. *Aids to School Use of Radio*. Columbus: Ohio State University, 1936. 10 pp. (Radio Bulletin, 12).

"The two articles included in this publication are reprinted from *The Ohio Radio Announcer*. Since the usefulness of these articles is by no means confined to Ohio readers, it seemed desirable to make them available to a wider public than that represented by the mailing list of the *Announcer*."

1406. Tyler, I. Keith, and R.R. Lowdermilk. *Radio As an Aid in Teaching*. Columbus: Ohio State University, 1937. 18 pp. (Radio Bulletin, 13).

The five articles in this booklet are reprinted from *The Ohio Radio Announcer*. They are "Using Radio News," "Radio in the Social Studies," "Music and Radio," "Radio and English," and "Radio and Science."

1407. Tyler, Tracy Ferris. *An Appraisal of Radio Broadcasting in the Land-Grant Colleges and State Universities*. Washington: National Committee on Education by Radio, 1933. 150 pp.

Prepared under the direction of the Joint Radio Survey Committee, this examines financial aspects, existing facilities, and administrative aspects of college radio programs. The opinions of college and university administrators concerning broadcasting are expressed.

1408. Tyler, Tracy Ferris. *Some Interpretations and Conclusions of the Land-Grant Radio Survey.* Washington: National Committee on Education by Radio, 1933. 25 pp.

Seventy-one land-grant colleges and separate state universities were studied in this survey. Some of the points stressed were the extent to which the institutions use radio, the nature of their programming, the type and costs of equipment owned and used, the amount of money spent annually on broadcasting, personnel, and the extent to which such broadcasting has been effective.

1409. Tyson, Levering. *Education Tunes in: A Study of Radio Broadcasting in Adult Education.* New York: American Association for Adult Education, 1930. 119 pp.

This study examines government control of broadcasting, the attitudes of educators and broadcasters, educational broadcasting in Europe and the United States, its financing, and some of the problems for further research and experimentation.

1410. Tyson, Levering, and William J. Donovan. *Retrospect and Forecast in Radio Education.* Chicago: University of Chicago Press, 1936. 27 pp.

The two articles in this booklet are based upon addresses delivered by the authors before the section on "Radio in Adult Education" at the 10th Anniversary Celebration of the American Association for Adult Education in New York City on May 21, 1936.

1411. Tyson, Levering, and Judith Waller. *The Future of Radio and Educational Broadcasting.* Chicago: University of Chicago Press, 1934. 31 pp.

A preprint of a paper for the 5th Annual Institute on Education by Radio, this speculates on what the trends for the immediate and more remote future seem to be for the field of educational broadcasting and what has been accomplished previously. The first article projects future accomplishments while the second examines recent past history.

1412. Underwood, Robert, compiler. *Survey on Degrees and Courses Offered in Radio and Television in Colleges and Universities in the United States*. Urbana, IL: National Association of Educational Broadcasters, 1955. 13 leaves.

This provides a list of the degrees given and courses offered for 22 colleges and universities who replied to the NAEB February 1955 *Newsletter* request for such data.

1413. U.S. Department of the Interior. *Report of the Advisory Committee on Education by Radio*. Washington: The Committee, 1930. 246 pp.

Appointed by the Secretary of the Interior, this is the report of the Committee whose purpose was to examine the possibilities of radio as an educational tool that would appeal to educators, broadcasters, manufacturers, and the public at large.

1414. U.S. Department of the Interior. Office of Education. *Radio Manual*. Washington: The Department, 1937. 18 leaves.

First published in 1937 and updated in later editions, this offers suggestions to schools and non-professional groups for the production of educational radio programs.

1415. Westley, Bruce H., and Philip P. Anast. *An Audience for Educational Radio*. Madison: University of Wisconsin

Television Laboratory, 1960. 53 leaves. (Research Bulletin 13).

Focusing on "the audience for educational radio in one city where it has been available longer than anywhere else in the world," this describes the listening tastes of the residents of Madison, Wisconsin. They answered the survey if they listened to WHA-radio and told how many hours per day they listened and the kinds of programs they particularly liked on that station.

1416. Willey, Roy DeVerl, and Helen Ann Young. *Radio in Elementary Education*. Boston: D.C. Heath, 1948. 450 pp.

After introducing radio as a dynamic educational force, the authors discuss techniques of teaching by radio, including specialized areas such as language and creative arts. They include one part on the administration of radio education and another on radio's past and future.

* Williams, J. Grenfell. *Radio in Fundamental Education in Undeveloped Areas*. Cited above as item 1254.

1417. Willis, Frederic A. *Widening Horizons*. Chicago: University of Chicago Press, 1934. 13 pp.

"The attitude of the forward-looking broadcaster concerning the part he (or she) might play in education is set forth in these pages." This actually is the text of a speech delivered by the author, a CBS executive, at an annual convention of the National Association of Broadcasters.

1418. Wisconsin Research Project in School Broadcasting. *Radio in the Classroom*. Madison: University of Wisconsin Press, 1942. 203 pp.

A project report, this contains experimental studies in the production and classroom use of lessons broadcast by radio.

1419. Witherspoon, John, and Roselle Kovitz. *The History of Public Broadcasting*. Washington: Current, 1987. 85 pp.

Reprinted from *Current*, this is described in the introduction as "a guide to how public broadcasting came to be structured as it is, and how its principal issues--from long-range financing to program decision-making--have developed over time." It is an edited version of *A Tribal Memory of Public Broadcasting: Missions, Mandates, Assumptions, Structure* which was commissioned by the Corporation for Public Broadcasting.

1420. Woelfel, Norman, ed. *How to Use Radio in the Classroom*. Rev. ed. Washington: National Association of Broadcasters, 1941. 23 pp.

The outline of contents answers the following questions: Does radio have a place in education? What's on the air? How can we fit radio into the curriculum? What about equipment for classroom listening? How shall we select school broadcasts? How (do we) prepare to use school broadcasts? Is out-of-school listening important? What part can the teacher play in the planning of educational broadcasts? How may teachers learn more about radio in education?

1421. Woelfel, Norman, and Irving Robbins. *School-Wide Use of Radio*. Washington: Federal Radio Education Committee, 1942. 56 pp.

Part of the Evaluation of School Broadcasts research project at the Ohio State University, the authors describe how one Ohio junior high school used network radio programs to learn the historical and contemporary background of the American war effort immediately prior to this country's entry into WW II. This was also published as Ohio State University Evaluation of School Broadcasts Bulletin 30, in 1941.

1422. Woelfel, Norman, and I. Keith Tyler, eds. *Radio and the School: A Guidebook for Teachers and Administrators.* Yonkers-on-Hudson, NY: World Book Company, 1945. 358 pp. (Radio in Education series).

A part of the Evaluation of School Broadcasts Project, this is "an attempt to clarify the position of radio in education and to point out the specific things which need to be done. It embodies the findings and judgments" of the project staff after five years' intensive investigation.

REGULATION AND LEGAL ASPECTS

Includes station ownership, radio control, licensing, Federal Communications Commission rulings, allocation of frequencies, copyright, censorship, right to access, the Fairness Doctrine, and the First Amendment.

1423. *Access to the Air.* New York: Columbia University, 1969. 46 pp.

Conducted by Columbia's Journalism School, the Office of Communication of the United Church of Christ, and the American Jewish Committee, this describes a conference on the public responsibility of broadcast licensees and the ethical and legal considerations of equal time, editorializing, personal attacks, balanced programming, and the Fairness Doctrine.

1424. Albert, James A. *The Broadcaster's Legal Guide for Conducting Contests and Promotions.* Chicago: Bonus Books, 1985. 237 pp. ISBN: 0-933893-08-6.

Among the chapters are The Popularity of Station Contests, The Quiz Show Scandals of the 1950s, The Contest Laws Now on the Books, and Petitions to Amend the FCC's Contest Rules and Regulations. Other areas covered are contests which resulted in stations losing their licenses, were fined, were censured, and cases where licenses were renewed or ownership transferred.

1425. Aly, Bower, and Gerald D. Shively, eds. *A Debate Handbook on Radio Control and Operation*. Columbia, MO: Staples Publishing, 1922. 220 pp.

Prepared for the High School Debating League "in each of the thirty-two states," this is a bibliography and collection of selected articles for and against the resolution: That the United States should adopt the essential features of the British system of radio control and operation. It is the Official Debate Handbook for 1933-1934 of the National University Extension Association.

1426. Aly, Bower, and Gerald D. Shively, eds. *A Debate Handbook Supplement on Radio Control and Operation*. Columbia, MO: Staples Publishing, 1933. 224 pp.

Consisting entirely of reprints, this has 54 articles on the control of international and general aspects of broadcasting, American broadcasting, and British broadcasting. Another similar book was also published in 1933 by the University of Iowa, and it contained 20 articles on the same subjects.

1427. Ashley, Paul P., in collaboration with Camden M. Hall. *Say It Safely: Legal Limits in Publishing, Radio, and Television*. 5th ed. Seattle: University of Washington Press, 1976. 238 pp.

Since the first edition was published in 1956, there have been numerous important legal decisions affecting the media. This edition places special emphasis on the problems of the political broadcast, on-the-spot radio and TV reports, and cases involving contempt of court, literary property, and the right of privacy.

1428. Ashmore, Harry S. *Fear in the Air.* New York: W.W. Norton, 1973. 180 pp. ISBN: 0-393-08368-3.

Subtitled "Broadcasting and the First Amendment: the Anatomy of a Constitutional Crisis," this points out the dimensions of the controversy over First Amendment protection and who plays what role within it. Chapters discuss the right of access, the public network, the political atmosphere, and an alternative to regulation.

1429. *Attitudes of Rural People Toward Radio Service: A Nation-wide Survey of Farm and Small-town People.* Washington: U.S. Department of Agriculture, Bureau of Agricultural Economics, 1946. 133 pp.

This report was prepared as part of the general preparation for the Clear Channel Hearing, Docket No. 6741 which was ordered by the Federal Communications Commission on February 20, 1945. Its purpose is generally to determine what changes, if any, should be made in the policies regarding allocation of so-called clear channels in the standard radio broadcast band.

1430. Babe, Robert E., and Conrad Winn. *Broadcasting Policy and Copyright Law: An Analysis of a Cable Rediffusion Right.* Ottawa: Canadian Department of Communications, 198-. 247 pp.

Cable copyright liability is examined from the perspective of Canada's broadcasting policy. The authors consider the two areas as individual interactive and complementary streams of policy instead of grouping them together as has been done in the past.

1431. Barnett, Steven. *Pricing the Radio Spectrum.* London: Broadcasting Research Unit, 1987. 13 pp. (A Broadcasting Research Unit Working Paper).

This discusses the assignment of radio or electromagnetic spectrum space by international agreements and the allocation of frequencies. The author poses the nature of the problem and offers possible solutions, including spectrum fees.

1432. Bensman, Marvin R. *Broadcast Regulation: Selected Cases and Decisions.* 2nd ed. Lanham, NY: University Press of America, 1985. 192 pp. ISBN: 0-8191-4900-4.

Citations are provided primarily in the fields of copyright, contracts, tax labor law, antitrust, tort law, and libel as they affect the electronic media. Specific cases include the WOR music copyright decision, the Federal Radio Commission's power over intrastate radio, WAAT "code message" broadcasts, and radio station rights to broadcast away games.

1433. Berry, Tyler. *Communications by Wire and Radio.* Chicago: Callaghan, 1937. 462 pp.

The title page describes this as "A treatise on the law of wire and wireless communications in interstate and foreign commerce based on the Federal Communications Act of June 19, 1934, as amended, with a discussion of the rules of practice and procedure before the Federal Communications Commission and the courts, and suggested forms."

1434. Bittner, John R. *Broadcast Law and Regulation.* Englewood Cliffs, NJ: Prentice-Hall, 1982. 441 pp. ISBN: 0-13-083492-7.

Several areas are emphasized in this volume: the regulatory framework, programming and policy, broadcast and cable operations, self-regulation and legislation, the legal system, and legal research. Of particular interest to radio broadcasters are the chapters on history and development, the FCC, regulation of entertainment and political programs, the Fairness Doctrine, regulation of commercial programming, and self-regulation.

1435. *Blacklisting: Two Key Documents.* New York: Arno Press/New York Times, 1971. 507 pp. (History of Broadcasting: Radio to Television series). ISBN: 0-405-03579-9.

The two documents are *Report on Blacklisting* by John Cogley, published in 1956 by the Fund for the Republic, and *The Judges and the Judged* by Merle Miller, published in 1952 by Doubleday. Both deal with investigations of the radio and television industry in the 1950s.

1436. Brindze, Ruth. *Not to Be Broadcast: The Truth About Radio.* New York: Vanguard Press, 1937. 310 pp.

In her discussion of censorship in the early days of radio Brindze asks who owns the air as she questions the bigness of NBC, CBS, and Mutual Broadcasting System. She cites political interference and has a chapter criticizing the FCC's "star chamber proceedings." Other chapters are titled "His Master's Voice" and "The Medicine Men's Show."

1437. *Broadcasting and Government Regulation in a Free Society.* Santa Barbara, CA: Center for the Study of Democratic Institutions, 1959. 39 pp.

At a series of day-long meetings held at the Center, persons with many points of view were given an opportunity to speak fully and frankly on the subject of government regulation of broadcasting. This booklet contains stenographic transcripts of these discussions.

* Broadcasting Laws: Documents on Politics and Society in the Federal Republic of Germany. Cited above as item 1093.

* Buehler, E.C., compiler. *American vs. British Systems of Radio Control*. Cited above as item 326.

1438. Burke, J. Frank. *Keep Radio for the People*. Pasadena, CA: Login Printing, 1943. 20 pp.

    Written by an attorney and president of Pacific Coast Broadcasting Company and independent station KPAS, this pamphlet is addressed to the members of Congress and particularly the Interstate Commerce Committee. It concerns "the White-Wheeler Bill, a proposed amendment to the Communications Act, which would take the control of radio from representatives of the people and turn it over to the licensee."

* Cave, Martin. *Broadcasting Regulation and the New Technologies*. Cited above as item 1108.

1439. Cole, Barry, and Mal Oettinger. *Reluctant Regulators: The FCC and the Broadcast Audience*. Reading, MA: Addison-Wesley, 1978. 303 pp. ISBN: 0-201-01039-9.

    The introduction states that "some of the more dramatic stories in this book involve confrontations between FCC regulators and groups and individuals who have no direct financial interest in broadcasting but who have learned 'how to talk back.'"

1440. Columbia Broadcasting System. *What the New Radio Rules Mean*. New York: CBS, 1941. 33 pp.

    This is an analysis of new radio rules adopted by the FCC and is directed to "people who like good radio programs, radio stations that carry network programs, government officials and others who seek a nation-wide radio audience, religious, educational, cultural and social groups who use radio, businessmen who advertise on the radio, (and) all who believe in free radio, as against a government-dominated radio."

* Committee on Interstate and Foreign Commerce. U.S. House of Representatives. *Regulation of Radio and Television Cigarette Advertisements*. Cited above as item 348.

1441. Committee on Merchant Marine, Radio and Fisheries. U.S. House of Representatives. *Radio Broadcasting*. Washington: Government Printing Office, 1934. 226 pp.

These hearings held in March 1934 were on a bill to amend the Radio Act of 1927. Witnesses included counsel for and members of the Watch Tower Bible and Tract Society, representatives from the National Association of Broadcasters, CBS, NBC, National Council of Catholic Men, Federal Council of Churches of Christ in America, and the chairman of the Federal Radio Commission.

1442. Committee on Rules. U.S. House of Representatives. *Providing for Radio and Television Coverage of House Proceedings*. Washington: Government Printing Office, 1977. 3 pp.

This is a very brief report created to accompany House Resolution 866. It offers background, purposes, a summary of major provisions, and committee actions.

1443. Committee on the Merchant Marine and Fisheries. U.S. House of Representatives. *Federal Radio Commission*. Washington: Government Printing Office, 1929. 1080 pp.

This volume consists of the hearings held before the Committee of the 70th Congress, 2nd Session, on H.R. 15430, which was a bill continuing the powers and authority of the Federal Radio Commission under the Radio Act of 1927. The hearings were held in January and February 1929.

1444. *Communications and the Law*. Westport, CT: Meckler Corp. ISSN: 0162-9093.

Published quarterly, this journal is a review of expanding technologies, censorship, public opinion as influenced by the government and aggressive use of the media by business. It is devoted to the communication issues that have daily impact upon legislative, legal, and judicial affairs.

1445. Cooper, Louis F., and Robert E. Emeritz. *Pike & Fischer's Desk Guide to the Fairness Doctrine*. Bethesda, MD: Pike & Fischer, 1985. 183 pp.

The authors provide a summary of the evolution of the Fairness Doctrine and describe how it is being practiced at the time of the book's publication. There is a practical guide for complaints, sanctions, and negotiated resolution as well as an article relating the Doctrine to new technologies.

1446. Davis, Stephen. *The Law of Radio Communication*. New York: McGraw-Hill, 1927. 206 pp.

Awarded the Linthicum Foundation Prize by the Faculty of Law of Northwestern University in June 1927, this book explains the existing legal conditions, the right to engage in radio communication, and federal and state jurisdiction. Chapters also discuss the Radio Act of 1927, conflicting rights in reception and transmission, broadcasting of copyright matter, and control of broadcast programs.

1447. Davis, W. Jefferson. *Radio Law.* Los Angeles: Parker, Stone & Baird, 1929. 364 pp.

Topics covered are the trend of radio, European progress in radio control, the Radio Act of 1927, text of the Act and Amendments of 1928 and 1929, state and municipal regulations, copyright and radio, libel and slander, and the Washington Conference of 1927 describing a new world code for radio. Also included are the Washington Radiotelegraph Convention, results of the North American Radio Conference and the 1929 Conference at Prague, and the procedure before the Federal Radio Commission.

1448. *Decisions of the National Labor Relations Board Affecting Radio Broadcasting Stations.* Washington: National Association of Broadcasters, 1943. 83 pp.

Radio broadcasting cases, along with those affecting other industries, are bound together in a series of volumes. "The NAB has collected the texts of all 'representation' cases affecting radio into Part One of this volume. Part Two contains a list of all radio broadcasting decisions involving alleged unfair labor practices."

1449. Dill, Clarence C. *Radio Law: Practice and Procedure.* Washington: National Law Book Company, 1938. 353 pp.

This is "a book designed to inform the legal practitioner of the theory of radio together with enough history of the development of radio law to make it possible to handle radio cases before the Commission in an intelligent manner." The author was a member of the bar of the

State of Washington and the District of Columbia, a member of the House of Representatives, and a Washington State Senator and draws on this experience for the text.

* Donahue, Hugh Carter. *The Battle to Control Broadcast News: Who Owns the First Amendment?* Cited above as item 661.

1450. Edelman, Jacob Murray. *The Licensing of Radio Services in the United States: A Study in Administrative Formulation of Policy.* Urbana: University of Illinois Press, 1950. 229 pp.

Originally prepared as the author's 1948 University of Illinois Ph.D. dissertation, this study was undertaken to "offer a basis for determining to what degree the licensing authority in the field has found it possible or thought it wise to reduce its discretion to rule."

1451. Emery, Walter B. *Broadcasting and Government: Responsibilities and Regulation.* Rev. ed. East Lansing: Michigan State University Press, 1971. 569 pp. ISBN: 0-87013-159-1.

What has been and what should be the function of government in the regulation of broadcasting are the questions the author attempts to answer in this book. He examines the basis and scope of governmental controls, the character, classification and utilization of radio frequencies, and the problems of getting on the air as well as looking to the future of broadcasting.

1452. *Entertainment Law Reporter.* Santa Monica, CA: Entertainment Law Reporter Publishing. ISSN: 0170-3831.

This monthly publication provides information about motion pictures, television, radio, music, theatre, publishing, and sports. A separately printed index is published annually and is included in the subscription price.

1453. Erickson, Don V. *Armstrong's Fight for FM Broadcasting: One Man vs. Big Business and Bureaucracy*. University, AL: University of Alabama Press, 1973. 226 pp. ISBN: 0-8173-4818-2.

Edwin Howard Armstrong was recognized as the inventor of present-day FM, and he and his widow maintained a legal struggle that the Supreme Court refused to hear. Motorola, Inc. settled the last of 20 FM patent infringement court cases in 1968, and Mrs. Armstrong was paid the last of some ten million dollars. This volume tells the story of both the invention and the ensuing legal actions.

1454. Ernst, Morris L. *The First Freedom*. New York: Macmillan, 1946. 316 pp.

The main sections explore the philosophy of freedom, look at the "trends, practices and controls of press, radio and movies" and the author's suggestions for "reversing the monopoly trend and upsetting the present cartelization of press, radio and movies."

1455. Fischer, Henry G., et al. *Pike & Fischer Radio Regulation*. Washington: Pike & Fischer, 1948-to date.

The first series of this title consisted of 25 volumes of reports, a digest, and cases. A second series was begun in 1963, and was kept up-to-date by annual supplements. The third series has been published since 1989 and is divided into Decisions, Desk Book, and Digest. All are loose-leaf and include indices.

1456. Fly, James Lawrence. *Chain Broadcasting Regulations and Free Speech*. Washington: Federal Communications Commission, 1942. 1 vol.

The first half of this volume contains remarks made by FCC Chairman Fly before the House Interstate and Foreign Commerce Committee on June 30, 1942. The balance of the book consists of a list and description of exhibits that Fly refers to in his address.

1457. Frost, S.E., Jr. *Is American Radio Democratic?* Chicago: University of Chicago Press, 1937. 232 pp.

A reprint of the author's Ph.D. dissertation at Columbia University, this is "a study of the American system of radio regulation, control, and operation as related to the democratic way of life with emphasis upon its educational aspects." He examines the nature of radio, federal regulation, the station owner, the advertiser, the educator, and the public and also considers radio on the college campus.

1458. Ginsburg, Douglas H. *Regulation of Broadcasting: Law and Policy Towards Radio, Television and Cable Communications*. St. Paul, MN: West Publishing, 1979. 741 pp. (American Casebook series). ISBN: 0-8299-2017-X.

As the title and series indicate, this is a book about the laws governing the electronic mass media and the policy-making process by which those laws are formed, publicized, and administered. Numerous applicable cases are described. One practice receiving extensive coverage is payola and the regulation it required.

1459. Grundfest, Joseph A. *Citizen Participation in Broadcast Licensing Before the FCC.* Santa Monica, CA: Rand, 1976. 195 pp.

Treating an area of increasing concern, this report has several components: (1) it describes some of the avenues open to citizens who want to influence FCC policies, (2) it describes the history of past citizen participation, (3) it traces the evolution of an FCC policy statement regarding citizen agreements and analyzes it, and (4) it makes recommendations for future FCC policy.

* Herring, James M., and Gerald C. Gross. *Telecommunications: Economics and Regulation.* Cited above as item 388.

1460. Hogan, John V.L. *Radio Facts and Principles: Limiting the Total Number of Broadcasting Stations Which May Operate Simultaneously in the United States.* Washington: Government Printing Office, 1928. 21 pp.

This is the testimony of Hogan, a consulting radio engineer in New York City, before the Federal Radio Commission in Washington on July 23, 1928.

1461. *Inter-American Radio Agreement.* Washington: Government Printing Office, 1949. 1 vol.

Printed in four languages, this agreement was passed at the Fourth Inter-American Radio Conference held in Washington, D.C., in 1949. It replaces the earlier agreement of 1940.

1462. Jennings, Ralph M., and Pamela Richard. *How to Protect Your Rights in Television and Radio.* New York: United Church of Christ, 1974. 167 pp.

438 Radio Broadcasting

This book is intended to be a handbook to help citizens participate in the setting of policies for broadcasting so that radio and television will become more responsible in serving the needs, tastes, and desires of the citizenry. It was written as part of a program to combat discrimination against minorities by broadcasters.

1463. Kahn, Frank J., ed. *Documents of American Broadcasting*. 4th ed. Englewood Cliffs, NJ: Prentice-Hall, 1984. 501 pp. ISBN: 0-13-217133-3.

This is "a collection of primary source materials in the field of public policy formulation in broadcasting and related media." It contains "laws, commission materials, court decisions, and other documents spanning electronic media development from their prehistory to the 1980s in chronological fashion."

1464. Kassner, Minna F., with the collaboration of Lucien Zacharoff. *Radio Is Censored: A Study of Cases Prepared to Show the Need of Federal Legislation for Freedom of the Air*. New York: American Civil Liberties Union, 1936. 56 pp.

The ways radio is censored are described in chapters titled The Voice of Monopoly, Editorial Selection Pressure Groups, How the Censor Works, Political Censorship, Discrimination of Labor News, Race Taboos, Call It a Social Disease, Gags and Funnymen, and Selected Cases of Radio Censorship.

1465. Kerwin, Jerome G. *The Control of Radio*. Chicago: University of Chicago Press, 1934. 26 pp. (Public Policy Pamphlets, 10).

The author examines the issue of freedom of speech for radio broadcasting and questions how much of that freedom the current system of radio control provides. He compares the English and Canadian systems with the American one to provide answers to that and other related questions.

1466. Kittross, John M. *Administration of American Telecommunications Policy, Vol. 1*. New York: Arno Press, 1980. 1 vol. (Historical Studies in Telecommunications). ISBN: 0-405-13197-7.

This volume is a reprint of three titles published earlier: *The Licensing of Radio Services in the United States, 1927-1947: A Study in Administrative Formulation of Policy*, by Murray Edelman; *Staff Report on the Federal Communications Commission*, by William W. Golub, and *Licensing of Major Broadcast Facilities by the Federal Communications Commission*, by William K. Jones.

1467. Kittross, John M., ed. *Documents in American Telecommunications Policy*. New York: Arno Press, 1977. 2 vols. (Historical Studies in Telecommunications). ISBN: 0-405-07756-4.

Among the material included is a program promulgated by the President's Communications Policy Board in 1951, a Joint Technical Advisory Committee, IRE-RTMA, report on radio spectrum conservation written in 1952, and a reprint from the *University of Illinois Bulletin*, volume 54, 1957, titled "The Structure and Policy of Electronic Communication."

1468. Krasnow, Erwin G., and Lawrence D. Longley. *The Politics of Broadcast Regulation*. New York: St. Martin's Press, 1973. 148 pp.

Dealing primarily with the Federal Communications Commission, this discusses broadcasting and the regulatory process, five determiners of regulatory policy, and an analytic view of broadcast regulation. Case studies involve FM broadcasting, license renewal challenges, and litigation on commercial advertisements on radio. A third edition was published in 1982.

1469. Labunski, Richard E. *The First Amendment Under Siege: The Politics of Broadcast Regulation.* Westport, CT: Greenwood Press, 1981. 184 pp. (Contributions in Political Science, 62). ISBN: 0-313-22756-X. ISSN: 0147-1066.

This study examines the major issues raised by federal regulation of electronic communication and the environment in which that regulation takes place. Chapters examine the case law in broadcasting and discuss the evolution of broadcasters' First Amendment rights.

1470. Labunski, Richard E. *Libel and the First Amendment: Legal History and Practice in Print and Broadcasting.* New Brunswick, NJ: Transaction Books, 1987. 251 pp. ISBN: 0-88738-082-4.

The historical and contemporary issues relating to libel suits against media organizations are explored in this volume. Labunski emphasizes the consequences of the development of libel law for the First Amendment and outlines the special problems that broadcasters have with libel suits and their potential for inhibiting television news coverage.

1471. Lawrence, John Shelton, and Bernard Timberg. *Fair Use and Free Inquiry: Copyright Law and the New Media.* 2nd ed. Norwood, NJ: Ablex, 1989. 408 pp. (Communication and Information Science series). ISBN: 0-89391-484-3.

The main structural change in this new edition is that there is no longer a section about international perspectives in fair use. Sixteen essays have been retained from the earlier edition of which nine have been revised. There are seven new sections documenting significant trends in legal and social issues associated with fair use as well as full texts of three landmark fair use cases.

1472. Le Duc, Don R. *Beyond Broadcasting: Patterns in Policy and Law*. New York: Longman, 1987. 216 pp. ISBN: 0-582-29039-2.

Federal deregulation policies and their effect on future electronic mass media in the United States are detailed. Licensing and competition, content, controls, the extent of deregulation, and patterns in media law are topics covered in various chapters.

1473. Le Duc, Don R., ed. *Issues in Broadcast Regulation*. Washington: Broadcast Education Association, 1974. 151 pp. (BEA Monograph 1)

This volume contains a collection of presentations that were given at BEA (APBE) Broadcast Regulation seminars in 1969 and 1972. Two of them deal with the broadcast license cases of stations WMAL and WHDH.

1474. LeRoy, Howard S. *Air Law: Outline and Guide to Law of Radio and Aeronautics*. Washington: Howard LeRoy, 1935. 120 pp.

Evolving from a course of lectures on air law in a Washington law school, the purpose of this outline is to offer a concise and comprehensive survey of available legal materials showing the rapid world growth in the field.

* Levin, Harvey J. *Broadcast Regulation and Joint Ownership of Media.* Cited above as item 431.

1475. Levin, Harvey J. *The Invisible Resource: Use and Regulation of the Radio Spectrum.* Baltimore: Johns Hopkins Press, 1971. 432 pp. ISBN: 0-8018-1316-6.

Published for Resources for the Future, the author attempts to describe and analyze the economic characteristics of the radio spectrum--that portion of electromagnetic waves used to transmit information through the air. He identifies the participants in this industry and the roles they play, analyzes the economic efficiency with which the radio spectrum is utilized, and suggests some alternatives for its management.

1476. McMahon, Robert Sears. *Federal Regulation of the Radio and Television Broadcast Industry in the United States: with Special Reference to the Establishment and Operation of Workable Administrative Standards.* New York: Arno Press, 1979. 358 pp. (Dissertations in Broadcasting).

This is a reprint of the author's Ph.D. dissertation at the Ohio State University in 1959. It examines the regulation of broadcasting prior to 1934, the events leading up to the abolition of the Federal Radio Commission and the establishment of the Federal Communications Commission. It also presents an analysis of the Federal Communications Act.

1477. Minor, Dale. *The Information War.* New York: Hawthorn Books, 1970. 212 pp.

With the major emphasis on radio, Minor details the conflict between the media and the government. He claims that while "many aspects of our society have experienced virtual revolutions, the press has evolved improvements on techniques and practices which were already aging in 1930 and (it) is still woefully behind in dealing with the problems raised by its own changing technology and degree of impact."

1478. Moser, Julius G. *Radio and the Law*. Los Angeles: Parker, 1947. 386 pp.

Among the topics covered are program control, transmission to foreign stations, professional advertising, defamation, right of privacy, unfair competition, trademarks and trade names, common law literary and artistic property rights, copyright, contracts, employee relations, international broadcasting stations, and FM.

1479. Murray, John. *The Media Law Dictionary*. Washington: University Press of America, 1979. 139 pp. ISBN: 0-8191-0616-X.

The author brings together words and phrases commonly appearing in media law. Many are standard law terms while others have acquired "artful meanings within mass media decisions and are not readily available to non-lawyers." Following the definition section of the book is a listing of pertinent cases and terms.

1480. National Association of Broadcasters. *Broadcasting and the Bill of Rights*. Washington: The Association, 1947. 322 pp.

Included in this volume are statements presented by several representatives of the broadcasting industry during hearings on the White Bill (S. 1333) to amend the Communications Act of 1934. The hearings were held by a subcommittee of the Senate Committee on Interstate and Foreign Commerce in June 1947.

1481. National Association of Broadcasters. *Is Your Hat in the Ring?* Washington: The Association, 1944. 14 pp.

This offers guidance in writing, timing, and presenting a radio talk. It reproduces FCC rules and regulations on the topic of broadcasts by candidates for public office.

1482. National Association of Broadcasters. *Legal Guide to Broadcast Law and Regulation.* 3rd ed. Washington: The Association, 1988. 448 pp. ISBN: 0-89324-051-6.

This publication "is designed to give the broadcaster a more comprehensive analysis and understanding of the many rules, regulations, and laws that affect broadcasters in their day-to-day operations." Included are new chapters and sections on libel and invasion of privacy, new developments in commercial speech, minimum wage rules, satellite earth station regulations, copyright and trademark issues, and antitrust law as it relates to broadcasters.

1483. National Association of Broadcasters. *Political Broadcast Catechism.* 12th ed. Washington: The Association, 1988. 96 pp. ISBN: 0-89324-014-1.

Prepared for NAB members, this provides broadcasters with the latest rules, regulations, and interpretations governing political broadcasting. It "places great importance on broadcasters' responsible execution of their obligations in this area." The first edition was published in 1960.

1484. National Association of Broadcasters. Legal Department. *NAB Radio-Television Program Log Recommendations.* Rev. ed. Washington: The Association, 1976. 36 pp.

Replacing the 1969 edition, this incorporates the Federal Communications Commission's new rules regarding the following: automatic logging; sponsorship identification; correction of logs; sister-station promotional announcements; broadcasts of taped, filmed or recorded material; station identification announcements; and other matters closely related to program logging requirements.

1485. Nelson, Harold L., Dwight L. Teeter, Jr., and Don R. Le Duc. *Law of Mass Communications: Freedom and Control of Print and Broadcast Media.* 6th ed. Westbury, NY: Foundation Press, 1989. 803 pp. ISBN: 0-88277-715-7.

Originally published 20 years ago, this new edition has undergone a revision that updates advertising and broadcasting regulations, rulings on defamation, obscenity, copyright, and disclosure information. It covers more recent developments such as electronic news gathering, satellite networks and videotext.

1486. Newspaper-Radio Committee. *Freedom of the Press: What It Is, How It Was Obtained, How It Can Be Retained.* New York: The Committee, 1942. 105 pp.

This booklet presents selections from the testimony of a few of the witnesses who appeared before the Federal Communications Commission in the newspaper-radio hearings held in 1941 on the subject of what policy should be followed regarding applications for FM stations by personnel affiliated with the publication of one or more newspapers. This testimony, however, deals more with the issue of free speech than with procedural or other limited issues.

1487. Olsson, Harry R., Jr. *Business and Legal Problems of Television and Radio.* 2nd ed. New York: Practicing Law

Institute, 1971. 208 pp. (Trademark and Literary Property Course Handbook series, 19).

A variety of subjects are covered in this volume that was prepared for distribution at a seminar presented in cooperation with the National Association of Broadcasters. Among the topics are acquisition of material, network affiliation, music, acceptability of broadcast material, controls over commercials, news operations, and regulation by the Federal Communications Commission.

1488. Paley, William S. *Why We Need a New Radio Law.* New York: Columbia Broadcasting System, 1941. 84 pp.

In May 1941 the Federal Communications Commission ordered drastic changes in radio broadcasting and announced that stations which did not comply would forfeit their licenses. This had a dramatic effect on broadcasters and this pamphlet is a printed copy of Paley's statement delivered before the U.S. Senate Committee on Interstate Commerce the following month.

1489. Pember, Don R. *Mass Media Law.* 4th ed. Dubuque, IA: Wm. C. Brown, 1987. 668 pp. ISBN: 0-697-04368-1.

With libel laws getting more publicity through national media, the author of this textbook has expanded sections on freedom of the press, libel, and invasion of privacy. Other chapters discuss gathering information, protection of sources, free trial, copyright, obscenity, and the regulation of advertising and broadcasting.

1490. Pennybacker, John H., and Waldo W. Braden, eds. *Broadcasting and the Public Interest.* New York: Random House, 1969. 175 pp. (Issues and Spokesmen series).

The articles in this anthology examine aspects of the Federal Communications Commission, programming, the Fairness Doctrine, and implications of the communications revolution.

1491. Perry, Larry, and Barry Selvidge. *Perry's Broadcast Regulation Political Primer*. Knoxville, TN: Perry Publications, 1984. 89 pp.

The goal of the authors is to furnish the public the tools it needs to reach an informed decision on any political broadcast problem. Topics discussed include political advertising, reasonable access, equal time, censorship, debates, and the Fairness Doctrine.

1492. Pons, Eugène. *General Considerations on License Fees for Radio and Television Sets*. Geneva: European Broadcasting Union, 1964. 42 pp. (Legal monograph 1).

This addresses the question of whether radio and television license fees are a world-wide phenomenon and the basis behind such fees. Separate chapters cover the application of the tax or license fee; its assessment; special cases of increases or reduction or even exemptions; organization of the licensing service; census of users; collection of fees; the cost of the service; and the appropriation of the revenue.

1493. Powe, Lucas A., Jr. *American Broadcasting and the First Amendment*. Berkeley: University of California Press, 1987. 295 pp. ISBN: 0-520-05918-2.

Why are radio and television treated differently from the print medium? The author pursues this topic, describes why regulatory licensing was enacted to best serve "the public interest" and wonders if the system should be changed and, if so, how.

1494. Practicing Law Institute. *Legal and Business Problems of Television and Radio 1976.* New York: The Institute, 1976. 574 pp. (Patents, Copyrights, Trademarks and Literary Property Course Handbook series, 72).

These lectures and discussions are on the subjects of the broadcasting station and its relationship with the network, acquisition of programs for broadcasting, antitrust and broadcasting, station licenses and renewals, current advertising problems, the investigative powers and procedures of the FCC, restraint on broadcast content, broadcasting and the copyright law, the Canadian border war, and tort liability for broadcast matter.

1495. Presidential Study Commission on International Radio Broadcasting. *The Right to Know.* Washington: Government Printing Office, 1973. 91 pp.

Prepared for the President of the United States, this report is based on the "assumption that one indispensable ingredient in a comprehensive program for peace is genuine human understanding among all the peoples of the world." How and when appropriate information can be dispensed is the focus of this booklet as the Commission reports on its findings and offers suggestions for improving world broadcasting.

1496. *Radio Regulations.* London: His Majesty's Stationery Office, 1948. 307 pp.

This volume contains the appendices to the *Radio Regulations* and *Additional Radio Regulations* presented at the International Telecommunication Convention held in Atlantic City, New Jersey, in 1947. They were originally published by the Bureau of the International Telecommunication Union, Berne, and signed by the delegates to the conference.

1497. *Radio Regulations*. Geneva: International Telecommunication Union, 1959. 641 pp.

This volume includes additional radio regulations, additional protocols, resolutions, and recommendations to supplement those passed by the International Radio Conference in Atlantic City, New Jersey, in 1947 (see previous annotation). These were passed in Geneva in 1959.

1498. Ray, Verne M., ed. *Interpreting FCC Broadcast Rules and Regulations*. Thurmont, MD, and Blue Ridge Summit, PA: Tab Books, 1966-1972. 3 vols.

The material in this set was originally published as a series of articles in *BM/E Magazine* to clarify some of the controversial questions which had plagued station operators for many years. They cover a wide range of subjects including in-depth views on Section 315, community leadership, public surveys, lotteries, multiple ownership, and CATV rules, among others.

1499. Ray, William B. *FCC: The Ups and Downs of Radio-TV Regulation*. Ames: Iowa State University Press, 1990. 193 pp. ISBN: 0-8138-0227-X.

The author attempts to provide some insight into the endless problems that the FCC has faced in the constantly changing field of electronic communications and how it has fared in trying to deal with them. He concentrates on the FCC vs. obscene/indecent language, the Fairness Doctrine, "radio medicine men," radio preachers, and its ongoing battles with Congress and, more recently, the Reagan Commission which he terms "a national disgrace."

1500. Rhyne, Charles S. *Municipal Regulations, Taxation and Use of Radio and Television*. Washington: National Institute of Municipal Law Officers, 1955. 84 pp. (Report 143).

This study looks at radio and television transmitters, antennas, interception, the use of police radio messages by others, examination and licensing of repair personnel, regulation of program content, local taxation of commercial broadcasting, municipal use of radio and television, and interference to radio and television reception.

1501. Rorty, James. *Order on the Air!* New York: John Day, 1934. 32 pp.

In this pamphlet the author "analyzes radio's sins of commission and omission, and describes the several kinds of conflicting censorship by which radio is shackled and minority pressure groups are kept off the air. He calls for order--or at least orderly conflict--on the air and joins with the American Civil Liberties Union in urging as a basis for legislation, an investigation and recommendations by a non-political commission appointed by the President."

1502. Rowan, Ford. *Broadcast Fairness: Doctrine, Practice, Prospects*. New York: Longman, 1984. 214 pp. (Longman series in Public Communication).

The question "Does enforcement of the Fairness Doctrine result in equal access to the airwaves?" is discussed with contrasting points of view being presented.

1503. Sarnoff, David. *Communications and the Law*. Washington: Radio Corporation of America, 1962. 16 pp.

This pamphlet contains the text of an address prepared by David Sarnoff for presentation at the Law and Layman Conference, Section of Judicial Administration of the American Bar Association in San Francisco, on August 7, 1962.

* Sarnoff, David. *Principles and Practices of National Radio Broadcasting.* Cited above as item 535.

* Schmeckebier, Laurence F. *The Federal Radio Commission: Its History, Activities and Organization.* Cited above as item 230.

1504. Segal, Paul M., and Paul D.P. Spearman. *State and Municipal Regulation of Radio Communication.* Washington: Government Printing Office, 1929. 16 pp.

"In response to numerous requests for guidance and information, the members of the Legal Division of the Commission feel an obligation to transmit the fruit of their experience to less experienced persons engaged in the formulation of regulatory measures." The two authors are from the Legal Division of the Federal Radio Commission and have experience to discuss the engineering aspects of the subject, which form an indispensable basis for all forms of regulation, according to the foreword.

1505. Shapiro, Andrew O. *Media Access: Your Rights to Express Your Views on Radio and Television.* Boston: Little, Brown, 1976. 297 pp. ISBN: 0-316-78287-4.

The focus of this book is upon one key aspect of broadcasting law: those rules which require a broadcaster to provide air time to concerned citizens for self-expression. It is primarily a how-to book and is intended to translate for lay readers the often technical legal rules and make it easier for those who wish to express opinions and views on the air.

1506. Simmons, Steven J. *The Fairness Doctrine and the Media*. Berkeley: University of California Press, 1978. 285 pp. ISBN: 0-520-03585-2.

The author provides a narrative history of the complicated development of the Fairness Doctrine and reminds the reader that the quality of regulation is related to standards observed by those doing the regulating. He points out important areas for reform and recommends expanded airwave access in order to minimize the need for regulation.

1507. Smead, Elmer E. *Freedom of Speech by Radio and Television*. Washington: Public Affairs Press, 1959. 182 pp.

This book describes the long history behind the problems involving freedom of speech and censorship, their origins and development, and the difficulties involved in their solution. It demonstrates the unavoidable complexity of the interrelations of Congress, the Federal Communications Commission, courts, and broadcasters which are encountered in the attempt to solve each problem.

1508. Socolow, A. Walter. *The Law of Radio Broadcasting*. New York: Baker, Voorhis, 1939. 2 vols.

Among the topics presented are federal jurisdiction to regulate radio broadcasting, international regulation of telecommunication, jurisdiction to tax radio broadcasting, broadcast stations and their studios, program operations, contracts, labor relations, simultaneous transmission of programs, employees' injuries, taxes, defamatory broadcasts, copyright, censorship, and advertising.

1509. Special Committee on Radio and Television of the Association of the Bar of the City of New York. *Radio, Television and the Administration of Justice.* New York: Columbia University Press, 1965. 321 pp.

Part one of this book examines the effects of radio and television on the administration of justice and includes a sampling of specific, generally documented, occurrences on the media that may be relevant to the problem being studied. The second part looks at actual documents and includes a selective bibliography on the topic.

1510. *Studies in the Control of Radio.* New York: Arno Press/New York Times, 1971. 1 vol. (History of Broadcasting: Radio to Television). ISBN: 0-405-03581-0.

This reprint edition contains six studies from the Broadcasting Research Project at the Littnauer Center of Harvard University that were published between 1940 and 1948. Each appeared as a separate publication, and the authors were Carl Joachim Friedrich, Jeanette Sayre Smith, and Evelyn Sternberg. They are titled (1) *The Development of the Control of Advertising on the Air*; (2) *Controlling Broadcasting in Wartime: A Tentative Public Policy*; (3) *An Analysis of the Radiobroadcasting Activities of Federal Agencies*; (4) *Radiobroadcasting and Higher Education*; (5) *Congress and the Control of Radio-Broadcasting*; and (6) *Small Station Management and the Control of Radiobroadcasting.*

1511. Subcommittee of the Committee on Interstate and Foreign Commerce. U.S. House of Representatives. *Communications Act, 1934.* Washington: Government Printing Office, 1938. 123 pp.

This presents the text of the House hearings on H.R. 1038 to amend Section 313 of the Communications Act of 1934. They were held in May and June 1938 and included statements and reports from the Budget Bureau, the FCC, the State Department, and others.

1512. Subcommittee of the Committee on Interstate and Foreign Commerce. U.S. House of Representatives. *Responsibilities of Broadcasting Licensees and Station Personnel.* Washington: Government Printing Office, 1960. 2 vols.

The hearings in these volumes were conducted on payola and other deceptive practices in the broadcasting field. They were particularly concerned with secret payments made to obtain plugs for a product on radio and television programs.

1513. Subcommittee of the Select Committee on Small Business. U.S. Senate. *Daytime Radio Broadcasting--1957.* Washington: Government Printing Office, 1957. 428 pp.

The hearings involved problems arising out of the petition filed by the Daytime Broadcasters Association, Inc., with the Federal Communications Commission for extended hours of operation.

1514. Subcommittee on Activities of Regulatory Agencies. Select Committee on Small Business. U.S. House of Representatives. *The Allocation of Radio Frequency Spectrum and Its Impact on Small Business (1969).* Washington: Government Printing Office, 1969. 399 pp.

This is the original report on H.R. 66, which is a resolution creating a select committee to conduct studies and investigations of the problems of small business. The report iself consists of 399 pages as indicated above as well as an attached appendix of 333 pages of related text and tables.

1515. Subcommittee on Telecommunications and Finance. Committee on Energy and Commerce. U.S. House of Representatives. *Broadcasters and the Fairness Doctrine*. Washington: Government Printing Office, 1989. 191 pp.

Testimony in this hearing was presented by John H. Buchanan, Jr., Chairman of People for the American Way; Thomas Goodgame, President, Television Station Group, Westinghouse Broadcasting Company; Philip Jones, Executive Vice-President, Meredith Corp., on behalf of the National Association of Broadcasters; David Lichtenstein, general counsel for Accuracy in Media; and John Spain, News Director of WBRZ-TV, on behalf of the Radio and Television News Directors Association.

1516. Summers, Harrison B., ed. *Radio Censorship*. New York: Arno Press/New York Times, 1971. 297 pp. (History of Broadcasting: Radio to Television). ISBN: 0-405-03582-9.

Originally part of The Reference Shelf series published by H.W. Wilson in 1939, this volume is a reprint of a collection of discussions and articles that appeared in various publications. Topics include radio as a social factor; radio programs under fire; editorial selection; program policies of broadcasters; government censorship of programs; the broadcaster as censor; examples of "editorial selection;" and the policy of equal opportunity.

1517. Summers, Robert E., compiler. *Wartime Censorship of Press and Radio*. New York: H.W. Wilson, 1942. 197 pp. (The Reference Shelf, Vol. 15, No. 8).

This volume is planned to tell the story of the development of censorship in WW II with reference to its operation, origin, problems, and purpose. Materials relating to every phase of censorship of news are brought together to present a well-rounded picture of the situation as it existed at the time. The majority of the writings about radio appeared in either *Variety* or *Broadcasting*.

1518. Swearer, Harvey F., and Joseph J. Carr. *Commercial FCC License Handbook*. 3rd ed. Blue Ridge Summit, PA: Tab Books, 1982. 383 pp. ISBN: 0-8306-0053-1.

The authors present a complete guide to preparing for the General Radiotelephone Operator exam. It covers basic law and solid-state electronics and has sections on basic radiotelephone, the radar endorsement, and FCC rules.

* Thomas, Thomas J., and Theresa R. Clifford. *The Public Radio Legal Handbook: A Guide to FCC Rules and Regulations*. Cited above as item 1401.

1519. U.S. Department of Commerce. Bureau of Navigation. Radio Service. *Radio Communication Laws of the United States and the International Radiotelegraphic Convention*. Washington: Government Printing Office, 1914. 100 pp.

This edition, as of July 27, 1914, publishes the regulations governing radio operators and the use of radio apparatus on ships and on land. Later editions update these regulations.

1520. U.S. Federal Communications Commission. *An ABC of the FCC*. Washington: Government Printing Office, 1947. 15 pp.

Updated in later editions, this pamphlet basically answers questions such as What is the Federal Communications Commission? What does it do? How does it regulate? and How did it come into being? It spells out licensing procedures, assignment of call letters and frequencies, and censorship.

1521. U.S. Federal Communications Commission. *The Communications Act of 1934, as Amended, and Other Selected Provisions of Law*. Washington: Government Printing Office, 1985. 300 pp.

This contains the complete text of the Communications Act of 1934 which is "an act to provide for the regulation of interstate and foreign communication by wire or radio, and for other purposes, enacted by the Senate and House of Representatives of the United States of America in Congress assembled." This edition includes the texts of the Communications Satellite Act of 1962, as amended, some selected provisions from the United States Code, enacted through January 1983, Public Law 98-214, FCC Authorization Act of 1983, and Public Law 98-549, Cable Communications Policy Act of 1984.

1522. U.S. Federal Communications Commission. *Public Service Responsibility of Broadcast Licensees*. Washington: The Commission, 1946. 59 pp.

This report, known as "The Blue Book," explains the FCC's concern with and its jurisdiction over program service. It defines various aspects of "public interest" and discusses the carrying of local live programs, public issues programming, and advertising excesses.

1523. U.S. Federal Communications Commission. *Report on Chain Broadcasting*. Washington: Government Printing Office, 1941. 139 pp.

"The FCC on March 18, 1938, by Order No. 37, authorized an investigation 'to determine what special regulations applicable to radio stations engaged in chain or other broadcasting are required in the public interest, convenience, or necessity.'" This is the report of a committee of three Commissioners who held hearings on this subject.

1524. U.S. Federal Communications Commission. *Report on Social and Economic Data Pursuant to the Informal Hearing on Broadcasting, Docket 4063, Beginning Oct. 5, 1936.* Washington: Government Printing Office, 1937. 197 pp.

Prepared by the Engineering Department of the FCC, this was presented before the informal hearing on the subject of allocation improvements in the standard broadcast band 550-1600 kc. It brings together "the most complete information available with respect to the broad subject of allocation, not only in its engineering, but also in its corollary social and economic phases."

1525. U.S. Federal Communications Commission. *Responsibility for Broadcast Matter.* Washington: The Commission, 1960. 254 pp.

Prepared by the staff of the Office of Network Study, this is an interim report that covers the relevant portions of the record made to date in the program inquiry. It includes the conclusions and suggestions of the Office of Network Study.

1526. U.S. Federal Communications Commission. *A Short History of Radio Regulation.* Washington: The Commission, 1942. 28 leaves.

Actually an FCC interoffice information memo, this summarizes the preliminary regulation, the Radio Acts of 1910 and 1912, and the creation of the Federal Radio Commission. There is a chronology of both the Federal

Radio Commission and the succeeding Federal Communications Commission.

1527. U.S. Federal Communications Commission. *Supplement No. 1 to Study Guide and Reference Material for Commercial Radio Operator Examinations.* Washington: The Commission, 1948. 5 pp.

Strictly an addendum, this provides additional material for Element Four--Advanced Radiotelephone Operator Examinations.

1528. U.S. Federal Radio Commission. *Rules and Regulations.* Washington: Government Printing Office, 1931. 156 pp.

The forerunner of the Federal Communications Commission, the Federal Radio Commission issued these rules effective February 1, 1932. They govern the administration of the Radio Act of 1927, as amended.

1529. U.S. Federal Radio Commission. *Rules and Regulations.* Rev. ed. Washington: Government Printing Office, 1934. 186 pp.

A revised version of the previous title, this spells out the general rules and regulations for radio broadcasters. It covers practices and procedures, applications, broadcast services, classes of stations, allocation of facilitites, and technical operation. A final section describes "services other than broadcast" and includes areas such as fixed public service, aviation, coastal, ship, mobile press, and experimental services.

1530. U.S. House of Representatives. *Fairness in Broadcasting Act of 1987.* Washington: Government Printing Office, 1987. 102 pp.

This report contains the amendment to the Communications Act of 1934 and a summary of the various issues involved. There is a section-by-section analysis and discussion and the findings reached. Additional and dissenting views are also presented.

1531. Warner, Harry P. *Radio and Television Law: A Standard Reference Book on the Legal and Regulatory Structure of the Radio Industry*. Albany, NY: Matthew Bender, 1948. 1 vol.

Warner details the administrative practice, procedures, and processes of the Federal Communications Commission, administrative control of program standards, network regulations, licensing, FM, and television. A 1952 cumulative supplement was issued to cover cases and materials reported up to and including October 1, 1952, as well as the Revised Rules adopted June 2, 1949, as amended.

1532. Warner, Harry P. *Radio and Television Rights: A Standard Reference Book on the Law of Copyright, Trade-marks and Unfair Competition and the Broadcasting Industry*. Albany, NY: Matthew Bender, 1953. 1254 pp.

A companion volume to Warner's *Radio and Television Law* (see item 1538), this is concerned with the subject matter and remedies available for protecting radio and television programs. It examines the content, service marks and ideas in radio and television programs, and individual rights in connection with such programs.

1533. Whitley, Jack W., and Gregg P. Skall. *The Broadcaster's Survival Guide: A Handbook of FCC Rules and Regulations for Radio and TV Stations*. New York: Scripps Howard Books, 1988. 127 pp. ISBN: 0-88687-337-1.

Summarized are some of the basic legal principles affecting today's broadcasting industry. Specific cases or rules are not cited, but rather an explanation of the basic conduct expected of broadcasters by the Federal Communications Commission tells what is prohibited and what is required.

1534. Zollmann, Carl. *Law of the Air*. Milwaukee: Bruce Publishing, 1927. 286 pp.

This is an expansion of three articles by the author that appeared in 1919 in issues of *The American Law Review*. They are primarily about the interaction of aeronautics and radio and a discussion of the Air Commerce Act of 1926, the Radio Act of 1927, and the Uniform State Law of Aeronautics adopted by a number of states and territories.

1535. Zuckman, Harvey L., et al. *Mass Communications Law in a Nutshell*. 3rd ed. St. Paul, MN: West Publishing, 1988. 538 pp. (Nutshell series). ISBN: 0-314-62943-2.

This paperback offers concise information about the legal aspects affecting mass communication. It covers the First Amendment, defamation, privacy, restraint, the free press, the rights of newspeople, and regulation of commercial speech. Other sections deal with the electronic mass media, FCC control, and various new technologies.

AMATEUR/HAM RADIO

Includes history of amateur radio, licensing requirements and station operations.

1536. *The Amateur Radio Handbook*. 2nd ed. London: Incorporated Radio Society of Great Britain, 1941. 328 pp.

Because there was so much demand for the first edition of this volume when it was published in 1939, it was necessary to prepare a reprint and then a complete second edition. This has two new chapters, one dealing with workshop practice and the other with crystal band pass filters, but most of the volume remains virtually unchanged from the first edition.

1537. *The ARRL Handbook for the Radio Amateur*. 67th ed. Newington, CT: American Radio Relay League, 1990. 1 vol. (Radio Amateur's Library Publication 6). ISBN: 0-87259-167-0.

First published in 1926, the *Handbook* provides up-to-date information and construction projects for beginners and advanced radio hobbyists alike. It has "something for everyone ... from simple low-power transmitters and easy-to-build receivers to sophisticated amplifiers and satellite antennas."

1538. Bennett, Hank, Harry L. Helms, and David T. Hardy. *The Complete Shortwave Listener's Handbook*. 3rd ed. Blue Ridge Summit, PA: Tab Books, 1986. 294 pp. ISBN: 0-8306-2655-7.

464 Radio Broadcasting

Completely revised, updated, and expanded, this edition of the classic book for worldwide shortwave listeners includes the latest on equipment, stations, procedures, and operating practices. It covers all the basics and includes all-new material on low frequencies, selectivity and image rejection, station identification, clubs, etc.

1539. Carr, Joseph J. *The Tab Handbook of Radio Communications*. Blue Ridge Summit, PA: Tab Books, 1984. 1048 pp. ISBN: 0-8306-1636-5.

Information is provided on every aspect of radio communications with chapters on electrical fundamentals, circuits, receivers, antennas, radioteletype, and TV to form a basis for study for amateur and/or commercial radio operators' licenses.

1540. Clarricoats, John. *World at Their Fingertips*. London: Radio Society of Great Britain, 1967. 307 pp.

The title page explains that this is both the story of amateur radio in the U.K. and a history of the Radio Society of Great Britain. Clarricoats was secretary of the Society from 1930 to 1963 and is well-qualified to author this history.

1541. Collins, A. Frederick. *The Radio Amateur's Hand Book*. 3rd ed. New York: Thomas Y. Crowell, 1924. 413 pp.

The subtitle states that this is "a complete, authentic and informative work on wireless telegraphy and telephony." This edition was revised throughout and new illustrations have been added as well as "up-to-date material on new low voltage detecting and amplifying vacuum tubes and power amplifiers, transformer-coupled radio frequency amplifiers, improved Armstrong super-regenerative circuits, transmitting antenna systems, (and) the new radio receiving circuits." Subsequent editions have since been published.

1542. DeSoto, Clinton B. *Calling CQ: Adventures of Short-Wave Radio Operators*. New York: Doubleday, Doran, 1941. 291 pp.

Written by an ardent short-wave fan, this tells the story of ham operators who have maintained communications during fires, floods, disasters, and other sorts of emergencies. Their various escapades and experiences related here are true and generally exciting.

1543. DeSoto, Clinton B. *Two Hundred Meters and Down: The Story of Amateur Radio*. West Hartford, CT: American Radio Relay League, 1936. 184 pp.

Intended primarily for radio hams, but of interest to anyone concerned with radio, this is the history of amateur radio from its beginning through the development and recognition of the wartime services it rendered. The last section covers international high-frequency communication, the International Amateur Radio Union, and uses of amateur radio in expeditions and emergencies throughout the world.

1544. Dexter, Gerry L. *Shortwave Radio Listening with the Experts*. Indianapolis: Howard W. Sams, 1986. 518 pp. ISBN: 0-672-22519-0.

This provides help in identifying foreign and local broadcasts, recognizing frequencies for exclusive stations, differentiating between various languages, obtaining QSL reports or cards to confirm the stations heard, and offering tips on record-keeping.

* Durham, F. Gayle. *Amateur Radio Operation in the Soviet Union.* Cited above as item 1128.

1545. Gibson, Stephen W. *How to Enjoy Your Amateur Radio License: An Operator's Manual.* Englewood Cliffs, NJ: Prentice-Hall, 1988. 164 pp. ISBN: 0-13-023748-5.

Nearly 425,000 ham radio operators share this hobby in the United States, and this book is aimed specifically at those who have recently acquired a license or hope to do so soon. It shows what can be done with such a license and the privileges that come with it.

1546. Hood, W. Edmund. *How to Be a Ham.* 3rd ed. Blue Ridge Summit, PA: Tab Books, 1986. 302 pp. ISBN: 0-8306-0653-X.

This latest edition of a classic source book for amateur radio enthusiasts has been completely revised and updated to include the recent innovations in operating practices and equipment availability. It also contains changes in FCC rules, regulations, and licensing requirements.

1547. Kasser, Joe. *Software for Amateur Radio.* Blue Ridge Summit, PA: Tab Books, 1984. 284 pp. ISBN: 0-8306-0360-3.

Computerization has reached amateur radio as it has ever so many other areas. Computer-aided design and circuit analysis, logging, simulations, modeling, antenna positioning, and pointing are only a few of the ways computer programs can serve the ham radio operator. These and others are described here.

1548. Laster, Clay. *The Beginner's Handbook of Amateur Radio.* 2nd ed. Blue Ridge Summit, PA: Tab Books, 1988. 418 pp. ISBN: 0-8306-2965-3.

Included is information on the introduction and history of ham radio, principles of electricity and magnetism, radio communication theory, electronic circuits, fundamentals of radio transmitters and receivers, system descriptions of transmission lines and antennas, an illustrated presentation of the International Morse Code, and latest information on the new Novice License privileges.

1549. Lescarboura, Austin C. *Radio for Everybody.* New York: Scientific American Publishing Company; Munn & Company, 1922. 334 pp.

The title page describes this as a popular guide to practical radio-phone reception and transmission and to the dot-and-dash reception and transmission of the radio telegraph (amateur radio). It is intended for the layperson who wants to use radio for pleasure and profit without going into the special theories and intricacies of the art.

1550. Lodge, Oliver. *Talks About Radio.* New York: George H. Doran, 1925. 267 pp.

The subtitle reads: "With Some Pioneering History and Some Hints and Calculations for Radio Amateurs." The author calls this book "a message of greeting to the great army of wireless amateurs and experimenters, from one who--always enthusiastic about ether waves--did some pioneering work and who now admires the remarkable progress that has been made by others."

1551. Luciani, Vince. *Amateur Radio, Super Hobby!* New York: McGraw-Hill, 1984. 275 pp. (McGraw-Hill/VTX series).

Ham radio has long been a popular hobby for the young and old alike. What it is, who is participating, and how to join in are explained in an easy-going style. There is a short practice test (with answers), a glossary of terms, and sample conversations.

* McMahon, Morgan E. *A Flick of the Switch: 1930-1950.* Cited above as item 189.

1552. Orr, William I. *Radio Handbook.* 22nd ed. Indianapolis: Howard W. Sams, 1981. 1200 pp. ISBN: 0-672-21874-7.

    Revised every few years, this presents recent technological breakthroughs of interest to the radio amateur. Its first edition appeared in 1935 as a slim paperback titled *The Radio Handbook for Amateurs and Experimenters* and was informally known as the "West Coast Handbook." The 23rd edition was published in 1986.

1553. Palmer, Eric. *Riding the Air Waves with Eric Palmer.* New York: Horace Liveright, 1930. 329 pp.

    Described as "the story of the most fascinating hobby and its relation to science and public service--as told by a typical devotee," this is a first-person account of amateur radio. Palmer had been fascinated by radio from the age of ten, made his first crystal set soon after, and then entered the world of ham operators. In this book he tells what happened after that.

1554. Radio Amateurs of North America. *Radio Amateur Callbook.* 68th ed. Lake Bluff, IL: Radio Amateurs Callbook, 1989. 1591 pp.

    Similar to the telephone book in format and published regularly since 1920, this lists by call number the names and addresses of licensed ham radio operators in North America and includes those in Hawaii and U.S.

possessions. A similar book lists international operators exclusive of North America and Hawaii.

1555. Subcommittee on Communications and Power. Committee on Interstate and Foreign Commerce. U.S. House of Representatives. *Alien Amateur Radio Operators*. Washington: Government Printing Office, 1971. 15 pp.

Hearings were held on one Senate and three House bills to amend the Communications Act of 1934 which provided that certain aliens admitted to the United States for permanent residence shall be eligible to operate amateur radio stations in this country and to hold licenses for their stations. This describes these hearings.

* Wood, Richard E. *Shortwave Voices of the World*. Cited above as item 1256.

WOMEN AND MINORITIES

Includes ownership and/or management of radio stations, career opportunities, and station programming.

1556. Anwar, Muhammad. *Ethnic Minority Broadcasting: A Research Report*. London: Commission for Racial Equality, 1983. 80 pp. ISBN: 0-907920-39-X.

This report deals with ethnic minorities access to the various channels of communication, in particular the broadcasting media, radio, and television. It describes reactions to programming and attitudes toward the media and also makes recommendations for future advances.

1557. Baehr, Helen, and Michele Ryan. *Shut Up and Listen! Women and Local Radio: A View from the Inside*. London: Comedia, 1984. 64 pp. ISBN: 0-906890-54-3.

Telling it like it is (or was), two women describe life inside CBC, Cardiff's independent local radio station. They offer guidelines for women seeking careers in radio.

* Bartlett, Kenneth G., and Douglass W. Miller. *Occupations in Radio*. Cited below as item 1577.

1558. *Black Radio Exclusive*. Hollywood, CA: Black Radio Exclusive. ISSN 0745-5992.

Published weekly except for one week in June, Thanksgiving, Christmas, and New Year's, this periodical presents black radio news and programming information. Special sections offer news about publishers, music reports, music reviews, jazz notes, and film reviews. Also included are charts and research data about albums, singles, new releases, programmer's polls, and special columns.

* Broadcast Advertising Bureau. *Radio's Feminine Touch*. Cited above as item 313.

* Brown, Stanley J., and Jay L. Birnbaum. *A Broadcaster's EEO Handbook*. Cited below as item 1623.

1559. Canadian Radio-Television and Telecommunications Commission. *Images of Women*. Quebec: Canadian Government Publishing Centre, 1983. 189 pp. ISBN: 0-660-90921-9.

Published in 1982 and reprinted in 1983, this is the report of the Task Force on Sex-Role Stereotyping in the Broadcast Media. The CRTC was requested to "take steps to see that guidelines and standards to encourage the elimination of sex-role stereotyping from the media it regulates are formulated." This report provides examples of such sterotyping and is the first step taken by the Commission to fulfill its charge.

* Dykema, Peter W. *Women and Radio Music*. Cited above as item 916.

1560. Eiselein, E.B. *Minority Broadcasting*. Tucson, AZ: Society of Professional Anthropologists, 1978. 31 pp.

Intended as a general introductory survey of the major areas in minority broadcasting, this discusses target audience programming, ownership, advertising, research, stereotypes, employment, the Fairness Doctrine, ascertainment, and license challenges of radio stations, networks, public radio, and, to a lesser degree, television and cable.

* Ellis, Elmo I. *Opportunities in Broadcasting.* Cited below as item 1584.

1561. Garnett, Bernard E. *How Soulful Is "Soul" Radio?* Nashville, TN: Race Relations Information Center, 1970. 42 pp.

This special report looks at black-owned broadcasting facilities and their programming. Chapters focus on television's threat to radio, the failure of the National Negro Network, and listeners' preferences in programming. An 18-page appendix illustrates the promotions, news broadcasts, and public affairs performances of six black-oriented broadcasting chains.

1562. Grame, Theodore C. *Ethnic Broadcasting in the United States.* Washington: Government Printing Office, 1980. (American Folklife Center, 4). 171 pp.

The first part of this volume describes the state of ethnic broadcasting and provides a bibliographic survey, historical background, cultural and intellectual settings, economic situations, religious and ethnic broadcasting, program contents, and audiences. The rest of the book is devoted to the actual broadcasts which are arranged by geographic areas.

1563. Gutiérrez, Félix F., and Jorge Reina Schement. *Spanish-Language Radio in the Southwestern United States.* Austin: University of Texas at Austin. Center for Mexican American Studies, 1979. 130 pp. ISBN: 0-292-77550-4.

Beginning with a statement about the "surprising growth of Spanish-language radio," this continues to discuss the medium in the United States and particularly in the Southwest. The authors make a comparison of news and public affairs programming between a Spanish and an

English-language station and provide a case study of one Spanish-language station.

1564. Hill, George H. *Black Media in America: A Resource Guide*. Boston: G.K. Hall, 1984. 333 pp. (A Publication in Black Studies). ISBN: 0-8161-8610-3.

Black media in this book refers to black-owned media outlets and non-black-owned media that are oriented toward the black community and the black consumer. Data on blacks working at non-black-owned media are included. This bibliography covers books, monographs, dissertations, theses, journal references, and articles in newspapers and magazines.

1565. Hosley, David H., and Gayle K. Yamada. *Hard News: Women in Broadcast Journalism*. Westport, CT: Greenwood Press, 1987. 196 pp. (Contributions in Women's Studies, 85). ISBN: 0-313-25477-X.

In an overview of how the evolution of women in news has contributed to and reflected changes in our society, this book identifies the newswomen pioneers who had the greatest impact on radio and television. It examines issues such as equal pay, equal opportunity, sexual harassment, and, in particular, the changing roles of women in broadcast news and the effects on the individual as careers and family life are juggled.

* Isber, Caroline, and Muriel Cantor. *Report of the Task Force on Women in Public Broadcasting*. Cited above as item 1324.

1566. Kaland, William J. *The Great Ones*. New York: Washington Square Press, 1970. 176 pp.

This paperback contains the dramatized stories of ten remarkable black Americans. It is based on a 1967 radio series produced by Group W, Westinghouse Broadcasting Company.

1567. Kerr, Frances Willard. *Women in Radio: Illustrated By Biographical Sketches*. Washington: Government Printing Office, 1947. 30 pp. (Department of Labor Bulletin, 322)

Among the professional positions and the women holding them that are profiled in this bulletin are those of commentator, radio actress, producer, director, station program manager, UN radio officer, sports commentator, musician, retail advertiser, network executive, network librarian, employment manager, public relations representative, and continuity acceptance editor.

1568. Knight, Ruth Adams. *Stand by for the Ladies: The Distaff Side of Radio*. New York: Coward-McCann, 1939. 179 pp.

The experiences of women already established in broadcasting and a survey of the various available opportunities are summarized in an effort to "map out a path for the novice who wants to enter and master such a complex profession."

1569. Lewels, Francisco J., Jr. *The Uses of the Media by the Chicano Movement: A Study in Minority Access*. New York: Praeger, 1974. 185 pp. (Praeger Special Studies in U.S. Economic, Social and Political Issues).

In an effort to gain better access to broadcasting and other media, various minority groups have organized and begun challenging the media. They have formed advisory councils to ascertain community needs, examine employment, programming, scholarships, training, and public service announcements. This book tells the story of the movement and its successes and failures.

* MacDonald, J. Fred, ed. *Richard Durham's Destination Freedom: Scripts from Radio's Black Legacy, 1948-50.* Cited above as item 179.

1570. McBride, Mary Margaret. *Tune in for Elizabeth: Career Story of a Radio Interviewer.* New York: Dodd, Mead, 1946. 191 pp. (Dodd, Mead Career books).

This novel tells the story of Elizabeth from Glendale, Illinois, who acquires a job with XBC in Radio City and gains fame in radio as a pioneering interviewer.

1571. Newman, Mark. *Entrepreneurs of Profit and Pride: from Black-Appeal to Radio Soul.* Westport, CT: Praeger, 1988. 186 pp. (Media and Society series). ISBN: 0-275-92888-8.

According to Newman black radio programming began "when the concept of 'black appeal' first occurred to certain entrepreneurs, a concept that played a pivotal role in the rise of cultural pride and 'soul.'" He uses case studies of three representative black radio stations to reveal the evolution of programming practices "dictated not only by pride but by profits gained through successful marketing strategies."

* Office of the Superintendent of Public Instruction. State of Illinois. *A Survey of Jobs in Radio for Girls.* Cited below as item 1597.

* *Radio Today: The Black Listener.* Cited above as item 512.

* *Radio Today: The Hispanic Listener.* Cited above as item 513.

1572. Sioussat, Helen. *Mikes Don't Bite*. New York: L.B. Fischer, 1943. 303 pp.

Written by one of the few top women executives in radio broadcasting at the time, this is both a guide to speaking over the radio and an account of her own personal history. She writes about the medium's requirements for speakers, singers, technicians, and executives, and passes on practical advice on how to make the grade in the profession.

* Subcommittee on Communications. Committee on Commerce, Science, and Transportation. U.S. Senate. *Minority Ownership of Broadcast Stations*. Cited above as item 561.

* Subcommittee on Telecommunications and Finance. Committee on Energy and Commerce. U.S. House of Representatives. *Radio Broadcasting Issues*. Cited above as item 562.

1573. Surlin, Stuart H. *Ascertainment of Community Needs by Black-Oriented Radio Stations*. Athens, GA: University of Georgia, 1972. 54 leaves.

Supported by a 1971 National Association of Broadcasters grant, the author presents the findings and conclusions based upon data collected from the then-current license renewal applications submitted by a sample of radio stations that are primarily black-oriented in their programming.

1574. Taves, Isabella. *Successful Women and How They Attained Success*. New York: E.P. Dutton, 1943. 320 pp.

This book profiles three women who achieved great success in radio broadcasting. Mary Margaret McBride was a radio columnist who had a wide following for her interview shows, Anne Hummert attained success as a radio executive, and Jane Crusinberry gained fame as a script writer, especially for her soap opera scripts.

1575. *Women in the Media.* Paris: Unesco, 1980. 119 pp. ISBN: 02-3-101687-3.

The first part of this volume is an inquiry on participation of women in radio, television, and film in Australia, Canada, the United Kingdom, and the United States. The second part focuses on women in cinema.

CAREERS IN BROADCASTING

Includes vocational guidance and job descriptions.

1576. Arnold, Frank A. *Do You Want to Get into Radio?* New York: Frederick A. Stokes, 1940. 140 pp.

This is the story of radio broadcasting written for young people who are considering radio as a possible career. Arnold discusses the entire field of broadcasting and covers educational requirements, training, areas of specialization, and future prospects.

* Baehr, Helen, and Michele Ryan. *Shut Up and Listen! Women and Local Radio: A View from the Inside.* Cited above as item 1557.

1577. Bartlett, Kenneth G., and Douglass W. Miller. *Occupations in Radio.* Chicago: Science Research Associates, 1940. 48 pp. (Occupational Monographs series).

This discusses the rise of radio and explains how radio stations and networks are organized. It provides data on employment with service organizations, qualifications and training necessary for radio and/or technical jobs, and has a short section on the opportunities for women in radio.

1578. Blume, Dan. *Making It in Radio: Your Future in the Modern Medium.* Hartford, CT: Continental Media, 1983. 175 pp. ISBN: 0-9123-4900-X.

Written in simple, understandable terms, this paperback recalls the development of commercial radio, station management, staffing, performing, sales, audiences, and programming.

1579. Bouck, Zeh. *Making a Living in Radio*. New York: McGraw-Hill, 1935. 222 pp.

Chapters discuss career opportunities as radio operator, engineer, on-the-air broadcaster, writer, radio executive, or repair person. Bouck even includes such related jobs as factory work in a radio manufacturing company and selling radios.

1580. *Careers in Radio*. Chicago: Institute for Research, 1950. 24 pp.

Reiterates the history of the field, job opportunities and education required. It provides data on four categories of the industry: (1) apparatus manufacture, sales and service; (2) broadcasting; (3) communications; and (4) industrial radio or radio-electronics.

1581. Carlisle, Norman V., and Conrad C. Rice. *Your Career in Radio*. New York: E.P. Dutton, 1941. 189 pp.

Illustrated by a number of photographs, this is intended to be a guide to anyone wanting to pursue a career in radio broadcasting.

1582. Council on Radio Journalism. *Report on Radio News Internships*. Washington: National Association of Broadcasters, 1946. 16 pp.

The subtitle of this pamphlet is "Documented Results of First Planned Cooperation Between Broadcasters and Teachers of Journalism." It describes internships at WGAR Cleveland, WFAA Dallas, WTIC Hartford, KMBC Kansas City, KFI Los Angeles, WOW Omaha,

KOIN Portland (Oregon), WSYR Syracuse, and KVOO Tulsa.

1583. DeHaven, Robert, and Harold S. Kahm. *How to Break into Radio.* New York: Harper & Brothers, 1941. 162 p.

This book provides straight-from-the-shoulder advice on how to go about applying for a radio job and what to do after one is obtained. The authors answer questions such as What are the various types of radio jobs? What experience is needed? Where can such experience be acquired? How have others broken into radio? and What area of radio is open to a beginner?

1584. Ellis, Elmo I. *Opportunities in Broadcasting.* Skokie, IL: VGM Career Horizons, 1981. 149 pp.

The evolution of broadcasting is described in the beginning of this career guide. Later chapters discuss working conditions, preparing for a broadcasting career, radio and television jobs, women and minorities in broadcasting, and various broadcast-related jobs.

1585. Evans, Elwyn. *Radio: A Guide to Broadcasting Techniques.* London: Barrie & Jenkins, 1977. 174 pp. ISBN: 0-214-20378-6.

The author wrote this book primarily for those who want to enter the broadcasting field as contributors, programming staffs, and mass communications students. He offers some rules of thumb on script writing, interviewing, disc jockeying, phone-in programs, features and documentaries, plays, music, and outside broadcasts.

1586. Firth, Ivan, and Gladys Shaw Erskine. *Gateway to Radio.* New York: The Macaulay Company, 1934. 319 pp.

An early guide to beginning a radio career, this is divided into chapters covering writing for the air, commercial credits, radio drama, music, the radio market, recorded programs, spot broadcasting, studio production, announcing, acting, children's programming, the engineer, and the sales department. There is information on British production methods as well as a chapter on press relations and another on the future of the medium.

1587. Gorham, Maurice. *Training for Radio*. Paris: Unesco, 1949. 105 pp. (Press, Film and Radio in the World Today).

The author explains the value of training and relates what is being done in the area. He writes about the optimum method and what can be done in the future.

* Hayes, John S., and Horace J. Gardner. *Both Sides of the Microphone: Training for the Radio*. Cited above as item 698.

1588. Hornung, J.L. *Radio As a Career*. New York: Funk & Wagnalls, 1940. 212 pp. (Kitson Careers series).

The whole focus of this book is radio engineering. The author explains the various career opportunities available in the field and includes material on self-study preparation, home study or correspondence schools, and college training in engineering.

1589. Jackson, Gregory. *Getting into Broadcast Journalism: A Guide to Careers in Radio and TV*. New York: Hawthorn Books, 1974. 156 pp.

Written by a veteran news correspondent, this is intended for young people who think they might want to get into radio and television news. He describes the field, tells how to prepare for it, and suggests where to start looking for a job.

1590. Jennings, George. *The Program Side of Radio.* Boston: Bellman Publishing, 1941. 15 pp. (Vocational and Professional Monographs, 44).

Topics covered here include training, applying for a job, promotion and salary increases, and specific areas such as announcing, acting, music, producing, etc.

* *The Job of the Radio Announcer.* Cited above as item 717.

1591. Keats, John. *Careerscope 6: Careers in Radio.* 3rd ed. London: Hamilton House, 1983. 32 pp. ISBN: 0-906888-52-2.

Part of a series on career advisement, this covers the growth of local (British radio), British Broadcasting Corporation external stations, Radio Luxembourg, stations overseas, and the BBC itself. Other information is provided about sales agencies, training, writing, musicians, free lance work, and engineering.

* Knight, Ruth Adams. *Stand by for the Ladies: The Distaff Side of Radio.* Cited above as item 1568.

1592. Larson, Raymond D., ed. *Employment Outlook in Radio and Television Broadcasting Occupations.* Washington: Government Printing Office, 1949. 69 pp.

Published for the U.S. Department of Labor and the Bureau of Labor Statistics in cooperation with the Veterans Administration, this is one of a series for use in vocational counseling of veterans, young people in schools, and others interested in choosing a field of work. It describes broadcast occupations and their anticipated earnings along with a state and/or geographical area outlook.

1593. Lent, Henry B. *"This Is Your Announcer:"* Ted Lane Breaks into Radio. New York: Macmillan, 1945. 199 pp.

Not intended to be a handbook on how to begin a radio career, this "is merely the story of what happened once to a returned AAF flier by the name of Ted Lane--and of what might easily happen again, to any beginner." The author did talk with announcers, producers, engineers, and radio station executives to gather facts so that he could tell the story accurately.

1594. Lerner, Mark. *Careers with a Radio Station*. Minneapolis: Lerner Publications, 1983. 36 pp. ISBN: 0-8225-0312-3.

This describes 15 careers, including announcer, sports director, sales manager, music director, researcher, traffic manager, promotions director, account executive, and chief engineer.

1595. National Advisory Council on Radio in Education. *Listener's Handbook*. Chicago: University of Chicago Press, 1932. 32 pp.

This was prepared to accompany a series of broadcasts on vocational guidance which had dramatizations and addresses by well-known men. These programs were broadcast on Sunday evenings during February, March, and April 1932.

1596. National Association of Broadcasters. *Careers in Radio*. Washington: The Association, 1986. 23 pp.

Helpful hints are provided for obtaining jobs in various aspects of radio broadcasting: programming, engineering, sales, and general administration. There is information also about the education required and the best ways to go about job hunting. An earlier version, published in 1974, contained 16 pages of similar material.

1597. Office of the Superintendent of Public Instruction. State of Illinois. *A Survey of Jobs in Radio for Girls*. Springfield: State of Illinois, 1942. 42 leaves.

This dated report "is recommended as an authoritative, accurate road map to their goals (for) girls who have a real interest in entering radio--who are not afraid of hard, concentrated work." It then addresses positions as switchboard operators, mail clerks, stenographers, secretaries, sales people, program managers, musicians, receptionists, traffic clerks, and continuity writers, along with salaries and qualifications.

1598. *Passbooks for Career Opportunities: Radio Station Manager*. New York: National Learning Corp., 1984. 1 vol. (The Passbook series). ISBN: 0-8373-2935-3.

The entire field is reviewed and sample questions and answers are provided in order to prepare the student for an examination in radio broadcast management.

1599. Pearlman, Donn. *Breaking into Broadcasting: Getting a Good Job in Radio or TV--Out Front or Behind the Scenes*. Chicago: Bonus Books, 1986. 156 pp. ISBN: 0-933893-16-7.

Advice on finding, keeping, and progressing in that first job in television or radio is offered in great detail by an experienced Chicago television newsman. He covers opportunities in news, writing, producing, sports, engineering, sales, and disc jockeying. He includes charts comparing median weekly salaries in radio and TV news by market.

1600. Ranson, Jo, and Richard Pack. *Opportunities in Radio*. New York: Vocational Guidance Manuals, 1946. 104 pp.

Individual chapters are devoted to announcing, acting, radio writing, production, publicity, special events and news, sales, sales promotion, research, and engineering.

1601. Rider, John R. *Your Future in Broadcasting*. Rev. ed. New York: Richards Rosen Press, 1978. 125 pp. ISBN: 0-8239-0233-1.

The various jobs available in radio and television broadcasting are described along with the requirements for a career in either field. An appendix lists broadcast organizations, educational broadcasting organizations, and government agencies dealing with broadcasting.

1602. Sarnoff, David. *Opportunities in Radio and Electronics for Returning Service Men*. New York: RCA, 1945. 28 pp.

General Sarnoff and RCA prepared this booklet to assist returning WW II veterans begin careers in the areas in which they had been trained and gained practical experience during their military service. He summarizes some of the related fields where jobs would be available, such as radio relay, short-wave, radio and television broadcasting, FM, and some industrial applications of electronics.

1603. Stone, Vernon A. *Careers in Radio and Television News*. 6th ed. Washington: Radio-Television News Directors Association, 1989. 20 pp.

The author states that the purpose of this careers booklet is to inform those who are undecided about a career but it is not necessarily meant to recruit. It is intended to help students decide whether broadcast and/or cable news is the right future.

1604. Tighe, C.R. *Crashing Radio*. New York: Radio Art, 1935. 103 pp.

Tighe provides practical help to would-be radio performers as well as those who have already started their careers. He offers some idea of how to proceed in getting that first job or upgrading to a better one.

1605. Vahl, Rod. *Exploring Careers in Broadcast Journalism*. New York: Rosen Publishing Group, 1983. 122 pp.

After some background advice, the author provides interviews with a wide range of broadcast journalists from nationally known Jane Pauley to Steve Olson, a television news reporter in Rock Island, Illinois.

REFERENCE SOURCES

Includes handbooks, guidebooks, dictionaries, glossaries, directories, encyclopedias, and bibliographies.

1606. Abbot, Waldo. *Handbook of Broadcasting: The Fundamentals of AM, FM, FAX, and TV.* 3rd ed. New York: McGraw-Hill, 1950. 494 pp.

As the subtitle indicates, this is intended to offer a background in all the fundamentals of broadcasting. This edition is an extensive revision of the 1941 text and is updated to include material on specific forms of broadcasting such as amplitude modulation, wired and wireless systems, frequency modulation, transit radio, low power, closed-circuit and color television, facsimile, and audio-fax. A 4th edition was published in 1957.

1607. Advertising Research Foundation. Radio-Television Ratings Review Committee. *Radio-TV Bibliography.* New York: The Foundation, 1954. 17 leaves.

Certain rules were observed in deciding whether or not a title should be included: the material had to be directly concerned with audience-size measurements, and it had to bear directly on methods, objectives, standards, comparisons of results, or validations. Almost every entry is for a periodical article although a few textbooks are listed.

1608. Alicoate, Jack, ed. *The 1938 Radio Annual.* New York: Radio Daily, 1938. 960 pp.

The first in a 26-year run, this was an annual compiled by the staff of *Radio Daily*. It has articles about the medium and includes statistical and informative data. The three main sections are titled Stations and Networks, Backstage, and The Business Side.

1609. American Council for Nationalities Service. *Radio Stations in the U.S. Broadcasting Foreign Language Programs*. New York: The Council, 1966. 113 leaves

At the time of publication there were 1073 radio stations in the United States broadcasting foreign language programs and more than 2000 different languages broadcast. This lists these stations by state and provides call letters, addresses, names of general managers, and numbers of hours for each language broadcast.

1610. Andrews, Cyrus, compiler. *Radio and Television Who's Who*. 2nd ed. London: Vox Mundi, 1950. 262 pp.

This furnishes biographical information about British actors, actresses, directors, and journalists who worked in radio and/or television. A later edition consisting of 516 pages was published in 1954 by George Young.

1611. *The B & T Yearbook*. 29th ed. Chippendale, Aust.: Thomson Publications, 1986. 833 pp. ISSN: 0810-6694.

This is an annual directory providing data on advertising agencies; advertisers; legislation, regulation and standards; government bodies (e.g., Australian Broadcasting Tribunal, Department of Communications, Trade Practices Commission); codes; networks; services to radio stations; industry associations; the consumer press; exhibitions and conventions; and photographic services.

1612. *Bacon's Radio/TV Directory.* 2nd ed. Chicago: Bacon, 1988. 700 pp. ISSN: 0891-0103.

This lists call letters, channel numbers, phone numbers, mailing addresses, network affiliations, studio addresses, staff, and programs for more than 10,000 commercial and non-commercial broadcast stations in the United States. Also included are major market maps, network information, and data about cable satellite systems.

1613. Baden, Anne L., chief compiler. *Radio and Radio Broadcasting: A Selected List of References.* Washington: Library of Congress, 1941. 109 pp.

Published fairly regularly by the Library of Congress under the direction of the Chief Bibliographer and compiled by different librarians, this lists the bibliographies, books, pamphlets, and periodical writings on the subject of radio broadcasting held by the Library of Congress.

1614. Baker, John. *A Radio Handbook for Extension Workers.* Washington: U.S. Dept. of Agriculture, 1939. 15 leaves.

The purpose of this booklet is to teach extension workers in agriculture, home economics, and 4-H work how to make the best use of radio. It first answers the question "Why use radio?" and then discusses a variety of aspects of radio broadcasting such as what to broadcast, how long, how to write for radio, publicity, and preparing the county extension program.

1615. Bond, C.A., and W.H. Zipf. *Radio Handbook for Extension Workers.* Washington: Government Printing Office, 1946. 21 pp. (U.S. Department of Agriculture Miscellaneous Publication 592).

This is a guide describing radio's role and how it can be expanded to reach farm people who may not attend meetings or get information elsewhere. It discusses formats, scripts, on-the-farm recordings, getting cooperation from stations, what and when to broadcast, and how often. This was first published by the USDA Office of Information and Extension Service in 1939 and was originally written by John Baker. (See previous annotation.)

1616. British Broadcasting Corporation. *BBC Handbook 1980*. London: The Corporation, 1980. 283 pp. ISBN: 0-563-17811-6.

Published annually, this includes the BBC *Annual Report and Accounts* for the year preceding. Articles cover programs, external broadcasting, engineering, personnel, publications and enterprises, and a pictorial review of BBC programs.

1617. British Broadcasting Corporation. *Books About Broadcasting*. London: The Corporation, 1948. 16 pp.

This volume attempts to collate the non-technical material that has been published about broadcasting in England during the previous 25 years. Magazine articles are excluded.

1618. British Broadcasting Corporation. *British Broadcasting: A Bibliography*. London: The Corporation, 1954. 35 pp.

This bibliography replaces *Books About Broadcasting* that was issued in September 1948 (see previous annotation). It covers books published in England on sound and television broadcasting but excludes those on engineering subjects. Later editions appeared in 1958 and 1972.

1619. *Broadcasting/Cable Yearbook.* Washington: Broadcasting Publications, 1990. 1 vol. ISSN: 0732-7196.

Published since 1931 this reference book has had several title changes. It incorporates information about radio, pay cable, and television stations arranged geographically by state and city. There are specific sections on "The ABCs of the Fifth Estate," FCC rules, group ownership, cross-ownership, cable systems, advertising agencies, brokers, technical consultants, satellites, an ADI market atlas, and a buyer's guide.

1620. Broderick, Gertrude G. *Radio and Television Bibliography.* Washington: Government Printing Office, 1952. 48 pp.

Prepared for the Federal Security Agency of the Office of Education, this itemizes materials on careers, production, writing, educational uses, engineering and servicing, FM, receiving and recording equipment, records and transcriptions, scripts, books, and plays.

1621. Broderick, Gertrude G., and Ruth M. Rowland. *Radio Bibliography.* Washington: Government Printing Office, 1945. 16 pp.

This is the original edition of item 1624 above. It was prepared for the Educational Radio Script and Transcription Exchange of the Office of Education and classifies books into categories such as careers, broadcasting techniques and script writing, education, radio sources, technical aspects, television, educational recordings and equipment, FM, periodicals, and sources of general information on education by radio. All entries are annotated.

1622. Brown, Donald E. *Reference Shelf for Radio-Television Newsmen*. Iowa City: Radio-Television News Directors Association, 1962. 15 pp.

"An annotated list of useful books and booklets for broadcast newsmen," this pamphlet organizes the material largely into the following categories: editorials, legal problems, news broadcasting texts, news reporting, news film photography, still photography, style books, word usage, surveys, and criticisms.

1623. Brown, Stanley J., and Jay L. Birnbaum. *A Broadcaster's EEO Handbook*. 2nd ed. Washington: National Association of Broadcasters, 1989. 165 pp. ISBN: 0-89324-0745.

This offers an overview of equal employment opportunity (EEO) procedures and describes the interaction between EEO and the Federal Communications Commission. Particular categories of illegal discrimination are defined, and guidelines are offered to help in hiring and/or terminating employees.

1624. Canadian Radio-Television and Telecommunications Commission. *Bibliography of CRTC Studies*. Ottawa: The Commission, 1982. 75 pp. ISBN: 0-6625-2054-8.

An indexed bibliography of the numerous special reports, studies, and working papers produced by the Commission since 1968 listed in both English and French.

1625. Cheydleur, Raymond D., compiler. *A Compilation of Radio Theses in American Colleges and Universities, 1918-1950*. Huntingdon, WV: Marshall College, 1950. 73 pp.

Based on a study of data submitted by 83 academic institutions, this compilation of radio theses attests to the

Reference Sources 495

steady interest and growth in both the technical and nontechnical aspects of radio since 1918.

* Clearinghouse on Development Communication. *A Sourcebook on Radio's Role in Development*. Cited above as item 340

* Clifford, Theresa R., ed. *Sourcetap: A Directory of Program Resources for Radio*. Cited above as item 645.

1626. Columbia Broadcasting System. *Radio Alphabet: A Glossary of Radio Terms*. New York: Hastings House, 1946. 85 pp.

   In addition to defining terms from AAAA (American Association of Advertising Agencies or Associated Actors and Artistes of America) to Zilch (the standard name used to describe anyone who walks into the studio and whose name is not known), this includes illustrations of radio sign language that describes how to stretch out a program, raise or lower the volume, cut, etc.

1627. Columbia Broadcasting System. *Radio and Television Bibliography*. 6th ed. New York: CBS, 1942. 96 pp.

   Prepared to help students and others interested in radio and television find the principal books, pamphlets, and articles in the field, this also includes names and addresses of radio and advertising trade periodicals containing "radio sections" and the main publishers and other organizations issuing material on broadcasting. The entries are arranged by advertising and audience studies, drama, education, engineering, music, news and special events, techniques and careers, and television. A later edition appeared in 1946.

1628. Commonwealth Broadcasting Association. *Who's Who: Annual List of Members*. London: The Association, 1990. 34 pp. ISSN: 0144-6150.

Member organizations are listed in this regularly published directory that provides addresses, telephone numbers, and telex information along with the names of executives and key personnel.

1629. Congress of Industrial Organizations. Political Action Committee. *Radio Handbook*. New York: The Congress, 1944. 47 pp.

This handbook was compiled for labor leaders and for all those interested in labor education. It tells what the people's rights are to radio time, how labor may obtain time on the air, and how that time can be used to great advantage for political action.

1630. Connors, Tracy Daniel. *Longman Dictionary of Mass Media & Communication*. New York: Longman, 1982. 255 pp. ISBN: 0-582-28336-1.

While this reference book contains definitions of terms other than those applicable to radio broadcasting, it also includes both well-known and unfamiliar radio jargon. Examples are night side, hot mike, rocker, spot sales, and some acronyms (AFRTS, BPA, HAAT, PSAs, RTTY, etc.).

* Cooper, Isabella M. *Bibliography of Educational Broadcasting*. Cited above as item 1293.

1631. *Current Mass Communication Research I*. Paris: Unesco, 1957. 60 pp. (Reports and Papers on Mass Communication, 21).

Two areas are covered in this publication: a register of mass communication research projects in progress and in planning, and a bibliography of books and articles on mass communication published after January 1, 1955. The entries, including data on radio, are arranged geographically by country of origin.

1632. Diamant, Lincoln. *The Broadcast Communications Dictionary.* Rev. ed. New York: Hastings House, 1978. 201 pp. (Communication Arts Books. ISBN: 0-8038-0788-0.

Swelling "the original word stock (of the first edition) by almost 100%," this defines terms from AA (Advertising Association) to Zworykin (U.S. television pioneer). In between are hundreds of terms, jargon, acronyms, and techologese, each *very* briefly defined. A third edition was published in 1989 by Greenwood Press.

1633. Dick, Ernest J. *Guide to CBC Sources at the Public Archives.* Ottawa: Public Archives Canada, 1987. 125 pp. ISBN: 0-662-54911-2.

Written in both English and French, this is a catalog of Canadian Broadcasting Commission holdings for each of its various divisions. Included are reports, photographs, files, microfilms, sound recordings, videotapes, minutes, and miscellaneous papers. There are indices by name, book title, program title, and subject.

1634. Drinkwater, Jane. *Get It on Radio and Television: The London Media Project.* London: Pluto Press, 1984. 261 pp. ISBN: 0-86104-785-0.

Described as "a practical guide to getting air time," this tells how-to and is a directory of London's local broadcast media. Although it deals mainly with London, there is information on programs and contacts throughout the United Kingdom.

1635. Drury, Francis K.W. *The Broadcaster and the Librarian*. New York: National Advisory Council on Radio in Education, 1931. 28 pp. (Information series, 3).

The contents describe how the radio station and the library can interact to help each other. The book explains what the public library offers to broadcasting studios, educational programs available, and ways to stimulate reading through broadcasting.

1636. Duncan, James H., Jr. *American Radio*. Kalamazoo, MI: James H. Duncan. ISSN: 0738-8675.

Completed in February 1986, this particular edition offers data about formats, leading stations, various changes since fall 1984, and the best and worst markets for various formats. An alphabetical listing of cities provides individual market reports in this semi-annual publication.

1637. Dunlap, Orrin E., Jr. *Dunlap's Radio & Television Almanac*. New York: Harper & Brothers, 1951. 211 pp.

This describes "men, events, inventions, and dates that made history in electronics from the dawn of electricity to radar and television." It is arranged chronologically from 640 B.C. to 1950.

1638. Editors of Broadcasting Magazine. *Across the Dial: Where the Action Is on AM and FM Radio in North America*. 5th ed. Washington: Broadcasting Publications, 1986. 177 pp.

Combined with *Around the Channels*, this publication provides a convenient and current list of radio and television stations in North America. Stations and their formats are arranged alphabetically by state and city, and the book is sized conveniently for storage in an automobile glove compartment.

*   Educational Radio Script and Transcription Exchange. *Radio Program Production Aids: Combining Radio Manual, Radio Glossary, Handbook of Sound Effects.* Cited above as item 669.

1639. Ehrlich, Eugene, and Raymond Hand, Jr., revisers. *NBC Handbook of Pronunciation.* 4th ed. New York: Harper & Row, 1984. 539 pp. ISBN: 0-16-181142-4.

> Almost more than you ever wanted to know about pronunciation is provided in this update with an introduction by Edwin Newman who states that the title could have been *Pronunciation Can Be Fun.*

1640. Ellmore, R. Terry. *The Illustrated Dictionary of Broadcast-CATV-Telecommunications.* Blue Ridge Summit, PA: Tab Books, 1977. 396 pp. ISBN: 0-8306-7950-2.

> Designed for use by broadcast and cable television professionals, instructors, and students, this book is also for anyone with an interest in the vocabulary of an industry. The subjects include acting, advertising, announcing, audience measurement, automation, disc recording, engineering, history, law, magnetic recording, management, music, news, operations, production, programming, regulation, research, sales, sound, statistics, and writing.

1641. Elving, Bruce F. *FM Atlas and Station Directory.* 11th ed. Adolph, MN: FM Atlas Publishing, 1988. 176 pp. ISBN: 0-917170-07-5.

500 Radio Broadcasting

This is a handy reference to the FM stations of the United States, Canada, and Mexico. It lists FM stations both by geographical location and by frequency.

1642. *The Encyclopaedia of Radio and Television.* 2nd ed. London: Odhams Press, 1957. 736 pp.

Produced primarily to provide easy reference to all the major aspects of modern radio and television, this is intended for students, practicing engineers, and radio amateurs. It is arranged alphabetically by term or phrase and has drawings and diagrams to illustrate particular points.

1643. European Broadcasting Union. *Selected Bibliography.* Geneva: The Union, 1967. 2 vols.

Published in both English and French editions, these volumes are the first and only ones in a series planned to eventually cover the whole field of nontechnical broadcasting. Part 1 is confined to educational radio and television while part 2 offers annotations on broadcasting in society.

1644. Fink, Howard. *Canadian National Theatre on the Air, 1925-1961: CBC-CRBC-CNR Radio Drama in English.* Toronto: University of Toronto Press, 1983. 48 pp. plus 25 sheets of microfiche. (The Concordia Radio Drama Project). ISBN: 0-8020-0358-3.

The text puts this descriptive bibliography into perspective and offers historical background and information about the bibliography's preparation. The microfiche sheets include main entries for individual plays, serials, and titles. There are indices of producers, original authors, alphabetical titles, and chronological titles and dates.

1645. Fishman, Joshua A., et al. *Guide to Non-English Language Broadcasting.* Rosslyn, VA: InterAmerica Research Associates, 1982. 115 pp.

Part II of the National Clearinghouse for Bilingual Education publication, *Language Resources in the United States*, this lists radio and television stations that broadcast in a language or languages other than English for any amount of broadcast time, along with their addresses and the names of the broadcasters.

1646. Fletcher, James E., ed. *Broadcast Research Definitions.* Washington: National Association of Broadcasters, 1988. 75 pp. ISBN: 0-89324-039-7.

This is the third edition of *Standard Definitions of Broadcast Research Terms,* first published over 20 years ago. It is designed to reflect the changes that have taken place in the industry during this time and includes terminology, technical jargon, and acronyms.

1647. Ford, Marie, compiler. *Radio Showbook.* Minneapolis: Showmanship Publications, 1945. 42 pp.

A serial publication, this is a directory of syndicated, script, network, and transcribed programs for regional and local sponsors. It includes a section titled "Showmanviews," a concise notation of new releases in the field of syndicated features.

1648. Gauthier, Christiane. *Glossary of Radio Communications.* Ottawa: Information Canada, 1974. 57 pp.

The purpose of this glossary is to provide the employees of the Canadian Department of Communications, especially engineers, electronics technicians, and all those concerned with radio, with a bilingual reference tool

(English-French, French-English). The words and terms are not defined, only translated from one language to the other.

1649. Gleason, William A., ed. *A Glossary of Radio and Television Terms*. New York: Catholic Communications Foundation, 1971. 51 pp.

Illustrated by photographs on nearly every page, this provides brief definitions of terms from A-B rolling to Zoom lens. Two pages at the end list broadcasting information sources such as commercial networks, public broadcasting organizations, governmental agencies, ratings companies, advertising associations, etc.

1650. Godfrey, Donald G., compiler. *A Directory of Broadcast Archives*. Washington: Broadcast Education Association, 1983. 90 pp.

Organized alphabetically by state, this includes in the body of the text data about the contents of and accessibility to the collections that responded to the compiler's questionnaire. There is a brief listing of other known locations for each area, but no detailed information is provided.

1651. Gorder, L.O., ed. *A Dictionary of Radio Terms*. Chicago: Allied Radio Corp., 1941. 36 pp.

Compiled under the direction of the technical staff of Allied Radio Corp., this offers concise definitions of commonly used words in radio, electronics, and television. Drawings and photographs illustrate the text.

1652. Greenfield, Thomas Allen. *Radio: A Reference Guide*. Westport, CT: Greenwood Press, 1989. 172 pp. (American Popular Culture series). ISBN: 0-313-222-762.

Greenfield's purpose, as stated in his preface, is to provide an evaluative survey of available research materials in the field of radio, with the focus on popular radio programming. He divides the book into chapters on networks and station histories, drama, news, music, comedy and variety, sports, women in radio, radio advertising, religious broadcasting, and Armed Forces Radio.

1653. Greet, W. Cabell. *World Words: Recommended Pronunciations*. New York: Columbia University Press, 1944. 402 pp.

Published for the Columbia Broadcasting System, this book is particularly useful to radio announcers. Pronunciation is provided for about twelve thousand names and words. It includes entries pertinent to WW II (battlefields, personnel, etc.), names of important persons, and words that are commonly difficult for broadcasters to pronounce.

1654. Grunwald, Edgar A., ed. *Variety Radio Directory*. New York: Variety, 1937. 1104 pp.

The first edition of an annual publication, this provides a record of events in the field as they become a part of the past. It includes program histories, production aids, federal radio regulations, station and network personnel, the National Association of Broadcasters Code of Ethics, etc. (See item 1700.)

1655. Hamill, Patricia Beall, compiler. *Radio and Television: A Selected Bibliography*. Washington: Government Printing Office, 1960. 46 pp.

Updating the bibliography prepared by Gertrude G. Broderick in 1952 (see item 1619), this lists material under the following categories: General-Historical, Socio-

Psychological, Management, Advertising, Vocational, Program Techniques, Educational Uses, Scripts and Plays, Technical Aspects, Periodicals, and Sources of General Information.

1656. Head, Sydney W., and Lois Beck. *The Bibliography of African Broadcasting: An Annotated Guide*. Philadelphia: Temple University. School of Communications and Theater, 1974. 60 leaves. (Communication Research Reports).

The authors have attempted to list the major books and articles in the field. They also "tried to give guidance as to how to find information on African broadcasting as efficiently as possible."

1657. Higgens, Gavin, ed. *British Broadcasting, 1922-1982: Selected and Annotated Bibliography*. London: BBC Data Publications, 1983. 279 pp. ISBN: 0-946358-14-1.

Intended as a working tool and as an aid for researchers, librarians, broadcasters, and anyone with a general interest in the subject, this contains some 1200 items, arranged alphabetically by author under broad subject headings. It includes books, pamphlets, government (H.M. Stationery Office) publications, and periodical articles along with an index to the listings.

* Hill, George H., and Lenwood Davis. *Religious Broadcasting 1920-1983: A Selectively Annotated Bibliography*. Cited above as item 940.

1658. Hill, Susan M., ed. *Broadcasting Bibliography: A Guide to the Literature of Radio & Television*. 3rd ed. Washington: National Association of Broadcasters, 1989. 74 pp.

Compiled by the staff of the NAB Library and Information Center, this covers materials published on broadcasting fundamentals, business, the law, technology and technique, broadcasting and society, comparative broadcasting, and telecommunications technologies. It includes a list of periodicals on the subject.

1659. Houlgate, Joan, compiler. *British Broadcasting, 1922-1972: A Select Bibliography.* Jubilee edition. London: British Broadcasting Corporation, 1972. 49 pp.

Growing out of the previous bibliographies of British broadcasting published earlier (see items 1617, 1618), this is not a revised edition but is more selective and does not include much of the older and/or less important material. It covers books published in England on radio and television but does not list any titles on engineering aspects of broadcasting.

1660. Hudson, Robert V. *Mass Media: A Chronological Encyclopedia of Television, Radio, Motion Pictures, Magazines, Newspapers, and Books in the United States.* New York: Garland, 1987. 435 pp. (Garland Reference Library of Social Science, 310). ISBN: 0-8240-8695-3.

The author's purpose in compiling this book was to provide one handy, comprehensive reference for historical facts about the American mass media from 135 years before the American Revolution to 1985. Emphasis is on achievements, dates, events, and people. It includes "selected firsts," trends, and an extensive index.

1661. Hurst, Walter E., and Donn Delson. *Delson's Dictionary of Radio & Record Industry Terms.* Thousand Oaks, CA: Bradson Press, 1980. 111 pp. ISBN: 0-9603574-2-4

"The purpose of this dictionary is to define the daily working vocabulary of the industry--specifically those terms pertaining to marketing (advertising, distribution, promotion, and publicity), broadcasting contracts, copyrights, music, and production. Some of the words, terms, and definitions were taken directly from the U.S. Copyright Code" and are marked with an identifying notation.

1662. Jones, Vane A. *North American Radio-TV Station Guide*. 3rd ed. Indianapolis: Howard W. Sams/Bobbs-Merrill, 1966. 128 pp.

Prepared from official FCC information, this lists all AM, FM, and television stations in the United States and its possessions as well as Canada, Cuba, Mexico, and the West Indies. Entries are indexed by geographic location and call letters.

1663. Kaufman, Milton. *Radio Operator's License Q & A Manual*. 11th ed. Indianapolis: Hayden Books, 1989. 483 pp. ISBN: 0-672-48444-7.

Published first in 1949, this revised edition offers complete and current examination preparation for the general radio telephone operator's license, the marine radio operator's permit, the radar endorsement, and the non-governmental technician certification. It includes sample FCC-type examinations for each of these elements.

1664. Kenyon, John Samuel, and Thomas Albert Knott. *A Pronouncing Dictionary of American English*. Springfield, MA: G. & C. Merriam, 1953. 484 pp.

Not intended to be a source book for the study of American dialects, this book nevertheless supplies an important guide for anyone anticipating a career in radio broadcasting. It shows "the pronunciation of cultivated colloquial English in the United States."

1665. Kittross, John M., compiler. *A Bibliography of Theses & Dissertations in Broadcasting: 1920-1973*. Washington: Broadcast Education Association, 1978. 1 vol.

Following analyses by schools, years, and topics, this reference book lists entries by author and provides full title, institution, type of degree, and date. There are key words, titles by year, and topical indices.

* Lichty, Lawrence W. *World and International Broadcasting: A Bibliography*. Cited above as item 1178.

* Lingel, Robert. *Educational Broadcasting: A Bibliography*. Cited above as item 1342.

1666. Litvinenko, A.S.; V.I. Bashenoff, ed. *Dictionary of Radio Terminology in the English, German, French, and Russian Languages*. Moscow: Office of Technical Encyclopaedias and Dictionaries, 1937. 558 pp.

This dictionary is an attempt to give a systematic comparative review of modern radio terminology in four languages. The terms are arranged in four vertical columns according to language. The ones printed in heavy type in alphabetical order and those in different languages placed in the same horizontal row have the same meaning.

* Magne, Lawrence, and Tony Jones, eds. *Passport to World Band Radio*. Cited above as item 1188.

1667. McCavitt, William E., compiler. *Radio and Television: A Selected, Annotated Bibliography*. Metuchen, NJ: Scarecrow Press, 1978. 229 pp. ISBN: 0-8108-1113-8.

Originally covering a time span of 1920 to 1976, this has categories such as history, regulation, organization, programming, research, technical, annuals, periodicals, reference, etc. A supplement was prepared by McCavitt to cover 1977-1981 and a second one was compiled by Peter K. Pringle and Helen H. Clinton for the years 1982-1986 (see item 1677). Both supplements include additions to the original subject categories.

* McClendon, Natalie. *Go Public! The Traveler's Guide to Non-Commercial Radio.* Cited above as item 1349.

1668. McDonald, James R. *The Broadcaster's Dictionary.* Denver, CO: Wind River Books, 1986. 198 pp. ISBN: 0-938-023-04-7.

A dictionary of terms and a directory of associations and governmental agencies are combined in this volume along with data about broadcasting techniques, solutions to problems, and circuits. Appendices include preventive maintenance, trouble shooting, and block diagrams for typical stations.

1669. *Mike and Screen Press Directory.* 2nd ed. New York: Radio-Newsreel-Television Working Press Association, 1955. 215 pp.

Divided into two parts, the first lists the newsmen and their affiliation while the second lists the spokesmen representing federal, state, and municipal governments, as well as those in the United Nations and some leaders in industry. The terms newsmen and spokesmen are appropriate for this publication since very few, if any, women are mentioned.

* Miller, Bobby Ray, compiler and ed. *The UPI Stylebook: A Handbook for Writers and Editors.* Cited above as item 751.

* Murray, John. *The Media Law Dictionary.* Cited above as item 1479.

1670. National Association of Broadcasters. *Awards and Citations in Radio and Television.* Washington: The Association.

   Published as a serial beginning in 1960, this booklet provides a comprehensive list of awards available to persons in the broadcasting industry--specifically radio and television stations, their management and personnel.

* National Broadcasting Corporation. *NBC Handbook of Pronunciation.* Cited above as item 772.

1671. *National Radio Guide.* Milwaukee, WI: WF Innovations, 1990. 125 pp. ISBN: 0-96254-70-0-X.

   The publishers claim this contains a listing of every radio station in every city across the United States and Puerto Rico. Over 10,000 entries in 43 different programming formats are categorized by state and city. The book also includes 15 categories dedicated to ethnic groups as well as a sports section listing all radio stations that broadcast the four major sports in America: baseball, basketball, football, and hockey.

1672. *National Radio Publicity Directory.* 12th ed. New York: Peter Glenn Publications, 1982. 343 pp. ISBN: 0-87314-049-6.

   Revised and published on a regular basis, this describes station formats, topics discussed on the stations, a geographical listing of local, college, and educational stations, and a listing of network and syndicated shows.

1673. O'Drago, Alicia S. *Radio Dial: Radio Station Guide.* Denver, AMP Publishing, 1988. 133 pp. ISBN: 0-929273-00-1.

A reference book that can fit into an automobile glove compartment, this lists over 3,500 AM and FM stations and provides formats and air times. It is alphabetical by state and then by city.

1674. Paulu, Burton, ed. *Radio and Television Bibliography*. Urbana, IL: National Association of Educational Broadcasters, 1952. 129 pp.

Books and magazine articles on the non-technical aspects of broadcasting published between January 1, 1949, and June 30, 1952, are included in this volume. It revises the first NAEB bibliography issued in 1950 and includes all the entries appearing in that one as well as the later material.

1675. Pitts, Michael R. *Radio Soundtracks: A Reference Guide*. 2nd ed. Metuchen, NJ: Scarecrow Press, 1986. 337 pp. ISBN: 0-8108-1875-2.

Information on programs from the late 1920s to the early 1960s available on both tape and records is provided in this updated volume. Entries are often annotated and the cast and/or sponsor noted.

1676. Poteet, G. Howard. *Published Radio, Television, and Film Scripts: A Bibliography*. Troy, NY: Whitston Publishing, 1975. 245 pp. ISBN: 0-87875-063-0.

Concerned only with scripts that have appeared in print, this is the first attempt to index scripts used in the three media. Radio scripts are listed whenever possible by title of the program on which they appeared, and transcripts as well as the scripts themselves are included.

1677. Pringle, Peter K., and Helen H. Clinton. *Radio and Television: A Selected, Annotated Bibliography. Supplement Two,*

1982-1986. Metuchen, NJ: Scarecrow Press, 1989. 237 pp. ISBN: 0-8108-2158-3.

This work is based on bibliographies compiled by William E. McCavitt that covered 1920 to 1976 and 1977 to 1981. (See item 1667.)

1678. Public Service Bureau of the Chicago Tribune. *The Chicago Tribune Radio Book*. Chicago: The Tribune, 1925. 84 pp.

The title page calls this "a listener's handbook, consisting of complete broadcast list, with instructions for selecting, setting up and operating any type of radio receiver--maps, graphs, charts, and logs." One page is devoted to the weekday programming of radio station WGN, and another to its Sunday schedule.

1679. RCA Victor. *Common Words in Radio, Television and Electronics*. Camden, NJ: RCA, 1947. 43 pp.

Selected and defined for non-technical people, this book includes definitions, abbreviations, radio frequencies and organizations as well as illustrations, diagrams and symbols scattered throughout the text.

1680. Roberts, Robert Sydney. *Dictionary of Audio, Radio and Video*. London: Butterworth, 1981. 248 pp. ISBN: 0-408-003339-1.

Going a little further than merely giving a definition of a term, this first defines the term and then offers a brief explanation of the definition in practical terms. There are cross-references for easy use.

1681. Rose, Oscar, ed. *Radio Broadcasting and Television: An Annotated Bibliography* . New York: H.W.Wilson, 1947. 120 pp.

Non-technical books and pamphlets published in English in the United States are included in this volume. Bibliographic data are presented along with short, one-paragraph annotations.

1682. St.John, Robert. *Encyclopedia of Radio and Television Broadcasting (The Man Behind the Microphone)*. 3rd ed. Milwaukee, WI: Cathedral Square Publishing, 1967. 542 pp.

The author states that what this volume has set out to do is to cover the wide range of subjects that are of intense interest to the young broadcaster and to pass on some practical advice on "how to do it." It provides in narrative form the story and techniques of broadcasting and includes reference materials on the National Association of Broadcasters and British Broadcasting Corporation codes, guilds, unions, associations, and periodicals on the subject, plus a pronunciation guide and a dictionary of terms.

1683. Sennitt, Andrew G., ed. *World Radio TV Handbook*. 44th ed. New York: Billboard Publications, 1990. 574 pp.

WRTH is a practical guide to the world's radio and television services and publishes the information in several languages in the same volume. It is a comprehensive, country-by-country listing of long, medium, and short-wave broadcasters by frequency, time, and language. Special features include short-wave receiver test reports, worldwide broadcasts in English, broadcaster addresses and personnel, and maps of principal transmitter sites.

1684. Sharp, Harold S., and Marjorie Z. Sharp, compilers. *Index to Characters in the Performing Arts. Part IV: Radio and*

Television. Metuchen, NJ: Scarecrow Press, 1973. 697 pp. ISBN: 0-8108-0436-7.

As in the other books in this index series, the object is to identify characters with the productions in which they appear. Some data are provided about each with an indication whether they were actual people (Joan Davis, Kay Kyser) or fictitious characters (Dr. Christian, Ralph Krampden). It also states the broadcasting medium (radio, television, or both) and the type of each program (quiz, western, etc.).

1685. Shiers, George. *Bibliography of the History of Electronics*. Metuchen, NJ: Scarecrow Press, 1972. 323 pp. ISBN: 0-8108-0499-9.

While this bibliography lists articles, books and other printed materials associated with the historical aspects of electronics and telecommunications, there is one section dealing only with radio. It contains about 225 entries on the medium published from before the turn of the century to 1971.

* Shore, Peter. *International Radio Stations Guide*. Cited above as item 1223.

* Skolnick, Roger. *A Bibliography of Selected Books and Significant Articles in Foreign and International Broadcasting*. Cited above as item 1224.

1686. Slide, Anthony, ed. *International Film, Radio and Television Journals*. Westport, CT: Greenwood Press, 1985. 428 pp. (Historical Guides to the World's Periodicals and Newspapers). ISBN: 0-313-23759-X.

Entries for more than 200 periodicals provide a general evaluation covering the journal's critical stance and historical background. Information sources and publication history round out each entry. The appendices reference more than one hundred additional periodicals.

1687. Smart, James R., compiler. *Radio Broadcasts in the Library of Congress, 1924-1941*. Washington: Library of Congress, 1982. 149 pp.

Available through the Government Printing Office, this is a catalog of recordings in the collection in two categories: live radio broadcasts between 1924 and 1941 and a number of undated broadcasts. They are listed chronogically with an index of both the programs and the performers.

1688. Sparks, Kenneth R., compiler. *A Bibliography of Doctoral Dissertations in Television and Radio*. 3rd ed. Syracuse, NY: Syracuse University, 1971. 119 pp.

While this began as a term paper for a graduate-level course in communication, it was expanded and revised in order to provide students and others easier access to the most scholarly research in the field. Between 1925 and 1961 approximately 350 dissertations were written, another 100 during the next 2½ years, 430 more in the next 5½ years, and the rate still appears to be increasing (according to the foreword written in 1971).

1689. Sterling, Christopher H. *Electronic Media: A Guide to Trends in Broadcasting and Newer Technologies, 1920-1983*. New York: Praeger, 1984. 337 pp. ISBN: 0-0307-1468-0.

Intended as a handy, single-volume reference, this analyzes quantitative trends in the industry over extended time periods and includes overall growth, ownership, economic factors, training and employment, use patterns, and regulatory aspects.

* Sterling, Christopher H. *Foreign and International Communications Systems: A Survey Bibliography.* Cited above as item 1231.

1690. Sterling, Christopher H. *Mass Communication and Electronic Media: A Survey Bibliography.* Washington: George Washington University. Center for Telecommunications Studies, 1983. 22 pp. (Basic Bibliography No. 2, 9th ed.) (GW Occasional Papers).

    This is an annotated listing of selected current books on the subject published in the United States.

1691. Sterling, Christopher H. *Telecommunications Policy: A Survey Bibliography.* Washington: George Washington University. Center for Telecommunications Studies, 1983. 16 pp. (Basic Bibliography No. 1). (GW Occasional Papers).

    Selected books and documents on U.S. domestic common carrier questions and related information policy are listed.

* Strack, Irene Lydia, ed. *Public Broadcasting Directory, 1987-1988.* Cited above as item 1395.

1692. Stranger, Ralph. *Dictionary of Radio and Television Terms.* London: George Newnes, 1941. 252 pp.

    Designed as a quick reference for radio and television students to help them become familiar with terms in technical books, the author tries to make every explanation as simple as possible. He states that he uses mathematical formulae only where they could not be avoided.

* Terrace, Vincent. *Radio's Golden Years: The Encyclopedia of Radio Programs, 1930-1960.* Cited above as item 262.

1693. Twomey, John E. *Canadian Broadcasting History Resources in English: Critical Mass or Mess?* Toronto: Ryerson Polytechnical Institute, 1978. 1 vol.

The preface states that this was sponsored by the Canadian Broadcasting History Research Project and was designed to discover the size and scope of available materials reflecting Canadian broadcasting history. The data presented reflect resources in the English language; the work on French language broadcasting in Canada is being conducted by a different group.

1694. U.S. Department of the Interior. Office of Education. *Radio Glossary.* 2nd ed. Washington: The Department, 1943. 17 leaves.

Additional terms are included in this new edition along with an updating of some others. In 1948 this volume was revised and combined with the Department's *Radio Manual* and *Handbook of Sound Effects* to create the volume titled *Radio Program Production Aids* (see item 669).

1695. U.S. Federal Communications Commission. *List of Radio Broadcast Stations, Alphabetically by Call Letters.* Washington: The Commission, 1938. 92 pp.

Published annually since 1938, this reference provides call letters, main studio locations, names of licensees, power, frequencies (kc.), and time designations. It includes privately owned stations, network affiliates, and institutionally owned stations.

1696. U.S. Federal Communications Commission. *List of Radio Broadcast Stations by Frequency.* Washington: The Commission, 1937. 66 pp.

The listings in this typewritten booklet provide frequencies, call letters, main studio locations, power, and time designations. It is arranged from 550 kc Regional to 1570 kc Special.

1697. U.S. Federal Communications Commission. *List of Radio Broadcast Stations, by State and City*. Washington: The Commission, 1937. 92 pp.

Similar to the other volumes published by the FCC which list radio stations, this is an annual publication that is arranged alphabetically by state and city and gives call letters, licensees, power, frequencies (kc), and time designations.

1698. U.S. Federal Radio Commission. *Radio Broadcast Stations in the United States*. Washington: Government Printing Office, 1934. 70 pp.

This edition was prepared as of January 1, 1934, and has three lists including all radio broadcast stations that were authorized at that time. They are arranged by call letters, frequencies, and geographical locations.

1699. Unmacht, Robert, ed. *The M Street Radio Directory*. Alexandria, VA: RadioPhiles, Inc., 1989. 1 vol. ISBN: 0-8230-1329-4.

Described on the front cover as "the complete industry guide," this reference book contains comprehensive market data on AM and FM stations in the United States and Canada, program formats, Arbitron and Birch ratings, and information on construction permits and applications, as well as call letters, frequencies, and radio stations by state and city of license.

1700. *Variety Radio Directory.* 4th ed. New York: Variety, 1940. 1087 pp.

"This will undoubtedly be the last volume which has to do with only one type of commercial radio--the type known as 'amplitude modulation' ... In 1941 the broadcasting industry will launch a new kind of transmission, known as 'frequency modulation' to sail the commercial seas alongside the older, present art." Advertisements, articles on research, listings of advertising agencies, program titles, radio stations, trade journals, "professional records," and personnel in the industry constitute the publication. This title was published from 1937 to 1940 (see item 1694).

1701. *Who's Who in Broadcasting.* 2nd ed. Ayr, Eng.: Carrick Publishing, 1985. 210 pp. ISBN: 0-946724-08-3.

About 1,000 individuals involved in British broadcasting are cited in this new edition. The compilers "consciously limited the number of on-air faces and voices in favour of a greater proportion of production staff." Entries include the usual data: education, experience, recreations, and business address.

1702. *Who's Who in Radio: A Quarterly Review of American Broadcasting Personalities.* New York: Radio Publications, 1935. 143 pp.

In addition to providing photographs of radio artists and performers as well as a short paragraph about each of them, this periodical has advertisements by some of the performers and agents giving information on how to contact them for future hiring.

1703. *The Working Press of the Nation.* 1990 ed. Chicago: National Research Bureau, 1989. 3 vols. ISBN: 0-912610-63-8. ISSN: 0084-1323.

Volume 3 of this annual publication is titled *TV and Radio Directory.* It lists more than 10,400 radio and television stations and more than 25,900 local programs by subject. It includes detailed information on power, network affiliation, air time, management, and programming personnel.

1704. Zimmerman, Jane Dorsey. *Radio Pronunciations: A Study of Two Hundred Educated, Non-Professional Radio Speakers.* Morningside Heights, NY: King's Crown Press, 1946. 135 pp.

One purpose of this study was to assemble data on pronunciation used over the radio by a number of prominent, cultured American citizens; another was to compare the pronunciations recorded for these speakers with those of the same words given in a dictionary published in the United States.

AUTHOR INDEX

Aarnes, Hale 1260
Aaron, S.F. 793
Abbot, Waldo 1606
Abel, John D. 289
Ace, Goodman 1
Adair, James R. 2
Adhikarya, Ronny 1055
Advertising Research Fdn 291, 292, 1607
Agnew, Hugh E. 293
Aitken, Hugh G.J. 3
Albert, James A. 1424
Aldington, Toby Low 600, 1057
Alexeyeva, Ludmilla 1058
Alicoate, Jack 1608
Allard, T.J. 1059, 1060
Allen, Fred 4
Allen, Louise C. 601
Allen, Robert C. 871
Allen, Steve 5
Allighan, Garry 6
Allport, Gordon W. 335
Alperowicz, Cynthia 872
Alth, Max 7
Aly, Bower 1425, 1426
American Advertising Museum 8
American Comedy Network 873
American Council for Nationalities Service 1609
American Research Bureau 294
Amin, R.K. 874
Anast, Philip P. 1415
Anderson, Robert Gordon 192
Anderson, Virgil A. 602
Andersson, Donald M. 908
Andrews, Bart 9
Andrews, Cyrus 1610
Andrews, Robert D 10
Angell, James R. 603
Anthony, Edward 229
Anwar, Muhammad 1556
Arbitron Radio 295
Arbitron Ratings Co. 296
Archer, Gleason L. 11, 12
Ardmore, Jane Kesner 55
Armstrong, Ben 875, 876

Arnheim, Rudolf. 13
Arnold, Frank A. 297, 434, 1576
Ashby, A.L. 434
Ashley, Paul P. 1427
Ashmore, Harry S. 1428
Aspinall, Richard 604
Assn of the Junior Leagues of America 605
Atkinson, Carroll 1262, 1263, 1264, 1265, 1266, 1267, 1268, 1269, 1270
Australian Broadcasting Corp. 1061, 1062, 1063, 1064, 1065
Australian Dept of Communications 1067
Australian Dept of Transport & Communications 1067
Avery, Lewis H. 298, 299, 300, 301
Awasthy, G.C. 1068
Axelrod, Donald 963
Aylesworth, Merlin Hall 302, 434

Babe, Robert E. 1407
Bacher, William A. 14
Bachman, John W. 877
Baden, Anne L. 1613
Baehr, Helen 1557
Bailey, George 1313
Bailey, K.V. 1271
Bailey, Norman 878
Bain, Donald 15
Baker, John C. 882, 1414
Baker, W.J. 16
Bakke, Marit 1070
Ball, W. Macmahon 1070
Balon, Robert E. 303
Bannerman, R. LeRoy 17, 18
Banning, William Peck 19
Bannister, Harry 20
Barber, Walter L. 21
Barman, Thomas 22
Barnes, Pat 23
Barnett, Steven 304, 1431
Barnhart, Lyle D. 606, 607
Barnouw, Erik 24, 25, 608, 609, 880
Baron, Mike 1071
Barrass, Bob 305

Barrett, Marvin 610, 611, 612
Barry, David W. 1003
Barsley, Michael 244
Barson, Michael 26
Bartlett, Kenneth G. 1577
Bartlett, Kenneth L. 1272
Baruah, U.L. 1072
Bashenoff, V.I. 1666
Batson, Lawrence D. 598
Baudo, Laura 198
BBC World Service 1091
Beachcroft, T.O. 1073
Beck, Lois 1656
Beckett, Samuel 881
Beckoff, Samuel 613
Bedwell, Raymond T.,Jr. 403
Beerbohm, Max 882
Benét, Stephen Vincent 883
Bennett, Hank 1538
Bennett, Jeremy 1074
Benny, Mary Livingstone 27
Benoit, Philip 479, 780, 781
Bensman, Marvin R. 1432
Benson, Dennis C. 884
Bentley, J. Geoffrey 421
Berg, Cherney 29
Berg, Gertrude 28, 29
Bergendorff, Fred L. 306
Bergreen, Laurence 30
Berle, Milton 31
Berry, Lola 1273
Berry, Tyler 1433
Beveridge, William 1075
Beville, Hugh Malcolm, Jr. 307, 308, 1280
Biagi, Shirley 614
Bickel, Karl A. 615
Bickford, Leland 616
Bilby, Kenneth 32
Bird, Roger 1076
Bird, Win W. 1751
Birnbaum, Jay L. 1623
Bittner, Denise A. 617
Bittner, John R. 33, 34, 35, 617, 1434
Black, Peter 36

Blackburn, Adrian 1077
Blakely, Robert J. 1762
Bland, Michael 618, 619, 620
Blatný, Milan K. 1078
Bliss, Edward, Jr. 37, 621
Bloch, Louis M., Jr. 1277
Block, Mervin 622
Blu, Susan 623
Blume, Dan 1578
Bly, Robert W. 624
Blythe, Cheryl 38
Boemer, Marilyn Lawrence 886
Bogue, Donald J. 309
Bond, C.A. 1615
Book, Albert C. 310
Borie, Marcia 27
Bortz, Paul I. 311
Bouck, Zeh 1579
Boutwell, William Dow 1284
Boyd, Andrew 625
Boyd, Douglas A. 1079
Boyd, James 887
Boyle, Andrew 39
Brack, Hans 1080, 1081
Braden, Waldo W. 1490
Brant, Billy G. 1279
Braun, Everett C. 626
Breckenridge, Gerald 793
Brewer, Fred A. 823
Brickhouse, Jack 40
Briggs, Asa 41, 42
Briggs, Susan 43
Brindze, Ruth 1436
British Broadcasting Corp. 44, 627, 888, 889, 1082, 1083, 1084, 1085, 1086, 1087, 1088, 1089, 1090, 1616, 1617, 1618, 1619
Brix, Dale 863
Broadcast Advertising Bureau 312, 313
Broadcast Financial Management Assn 315
Broadcast Institute of North America 1286
Broadcast Measurement Bureau 317
Broderick, Gertrude G. 1282, 1283, 1620, 1621

Author Index 523

Brokenshire, Norman 47
Brooks, William F. 628
Brosius, Nancy Bancroft 890
Brotman, Stuart N. 322
Broughton, Irv 629
Broussard, E. Joseph 630
Brown, David 48
Brown, Donald E. 631, 1622
Brown, James A. 498
Brown, Ray 323
Brown, Stanley J. 1623
Browne, Donald R. 1094, 1222
Bruner, W. Richard 48
Brunner, Edmund deS. 891
Bryson, Lyman 324, 325
Buckman, Peter 892
Buehler, E.C. 326
Bulman, David 632
Bumpus, Bernard 1095
Buono, Thomas J. 327
Burchfield, Robert 633
Bureau of Agricultural Economics ... 893
Bureau of Labor Statistics ... 328
Burke, J. Frank 1438
Burke, Richard C. 1096, 1284
Burlingame, Roger 49
Burns, George A. 329
Burns, Tom 50
Burrows, A.R. 51
Busby, H.S. 1285
Busby, Linda 634
Buxton, Frank 52, 53

Caldwell, S. Carlton 1292
Callahan, Jennie Waugh 1287
Campbell, Laurence R. 635
Campbell, Robert 54
Canada. Comm. on Broadcasting 1097
Canadian Assn of Broadcasters 330, 1098
Canadian Broadcasting Corp. 1099, 1100
Canadian Radio-TV & Telecommunications ... 331, 332, 1101, 1102, 1159, 1624

Canadian Radio-TV Commission 333, 334, 1103, 1104, 1105
Canadian Royal Commission on Broadcasting 1106
Cantor, Eddie 55
Cantor, Muriel G. 894, 1324
Cantril, Hadley 56, 335
Carl, Larry 724
Carle, Wayne M. 1288
Carlile, John S. 636
Carlisle, Norman V.1581
Carmen, Ruth 637
Carmer, Carl 895, 1034
Carneal, Georgette 57
Carr, Joseph J. 1518, 1539
Carroll, Carroll 58
Carson, David 169
Carter, Alden R. 59
Carter, Boake 60
Cary, Norman D. 310
Cascio, Dominick 878
Cater, Douglass 1289
Cathcart, Rex 1107
Cave, Martin 1108
Chang, Won Ho 1092
Chapman, Allen 793
Chappel, G.A. 638
Chappell, Matthew N. 337
Charnley, Mitchell V. 639
Charters, W.W. 1290
Chase, Francis, Jr. 62
Chase, Gilbert 896
Chatterji, P.C. 1110
Cheen, Bruce Bishop 338
Chernoff, Howard L. 640
Chesmore, Stuart 641
Chester, Edward W. 897
Chester, Giraud 339
Cheydleur, Raymond D. 1625
Childs, Harwood L. 642
Christiansen, Kenneth 1260
Churchill, Allen 63
Cirino, Robert 643
Clark, Dick 64
Clarkson, R.P. 65
Clarricoats, John 1540

524 Radio Broadcasting

Clausse, Roger 1291
Clearinghouse on Development Communication 340
Cleveland Public Schools 1292
Clifford, Martin 644
Clifford, Theresa R. 645, 1401
Clinton, Helen H. 1677
Coase, R.H. 1111
Codding, George A., Jr. 646, 1112
Coddington, Robert H. 647
Codel, Martin 341
Codrescu, Andrew 899
Cogley, John 1435
Cohler, David Keith 648
Cole, Barry 1439
Cole, J.A. 66
Coleman, Howard W. 342
Colletti, Ned 40
Collier, Edwin 726
Collins, A. Frederick 1541
Collins, Philip 67
Columbia Broadcasting System 343, 344, 345, 346, 900, 901, 902, 1440, 1626, 1627
Comm. on Foreign Affairs ... 1114, 1115
Comm. on Foreign Relations ... 1116, 1117, 1118
Comm. on International Relations ... 1119
Comm. on Interstate & Foreign Commerce ... 347, 348
Comm. on Merchant Marine, Radio & Fisheries ... 1141
Comm. on Rules ... 1442
Comm. on the Merchant Marine & Fisheries ... 349, 1443
Commonwealth Broadcasting Assn 1120, 1628
Compaine, Benjamin M. 350
Congress of Industrial Organizations 1629
Connah, Douglas Duff 351
Connery, Robert H. 987
Connors, Tracy Daniel 1630
Contreras, Eduardo 1121
Cook, Joe 239

Coons, John E. 353
Cooper, Isabella M. 1293
Cooper, Louis F. 1445
Corp. for Public Broadcasting 354, 1294, 1295, 1296, 1297
Correll, Charles J. 68
Corwin, Norman 903, 904, 905
Cott, Ted 649
Couglin, Charles E. 69
Coulter, Douglas 906
Coulton, Barbara 70
Council on Radio Journalism 1298, 1582
Cowgill, Rome 650, 728
Cox Broadcasting Corp. 71
Crabb, Richard 72
Crawford, Bill 1140
Creamer, Joseph 651
Crews, Albert 652, 653
Crisell, Andrew 1122
Crocker, Patti 73
Crookes, Philip 1244
Crosby, Bing 74
Crosby, John 654
Crosley, Powel, Jr. 75
Crozier, Mary 355
Culbert, David Holbrook 655
Cullinan, Howell 76
Cunningham, Don R. 387
Cunningham, Mark 377
Curran, Charles 1124
Curtis, Alberta 1299
Cuthbert, Margaret 77
Czitrom, Daniel J. 78

D'Arienzo, Camille 862
Daly, John 656
Daniel, Cuthbert 380, 1274
Darrow, Ben H. 1300, 1301
Dary, David 570
David, Miles 356
Davis, Lenwood 940
Davis, Stephen 1446
Davis, W. Jefferson 1447
Day, Enid 357
De Forest, Lee 79
de Sola Pool, Ithiel 1248

DeFleur, Lois B. 864
DeHaven, Robert 1583
DeLong, Thomas A. 80
Delson, Donn 1661
Denison, Merrill 1302
Dept of Elementary School Principals, MEA 1303
Dept of Elementary School Principals, NEA 1304
DeSoto, Clinton B. 1542, 1543
Dexter, Gerry L. 658, 1544
Diamant, Lincoln 1632
Dick, Ernest J. 1633
Dikshit, Kiranmani A. 907
Dill, Clarence C. 1449
Dimbleby, Jonathan 81
Dimond, Sidney A. 695, 908
Dinwiddie, Melville 909
Dixon, Peter 659, 660
Dizard, Wilson P. 1126
Dobbert, Helga 1212
Dominick, Joseph R. 358
Donahue, Hugh Carter 661
Donahue, M.A. 793
Donovan, William J. 1410
Douglas, Alan 82
Douglas, George H. 83
Douglas, Susan J. 84
Drakakis, John 910
Drake, Galen 85
Drake, Harold L. 662
Dreher, Carl 86
Drinkwater, Jane 1634
Driver, David 87
Drury, Francis K.W. 1635
Dryer, Sherman H. 88
Ducey, Richard F. 289
Dudek, Lee J. 663
Duerr, Edwin 664
Duff, Willis P., Jr. 911
Duffield, J.W. 793
Duggal, K.S. 1127
Dunbar, Janet 665
Duncan, James H., Jr. 89, 359, 360, 361, 1636
Dunham, Franklin 1305

Dunlap, Orrin E., Jr. 90, 91, 92, 362, 363, 666, 1637
Dunn, William J. 93
Dunning, John 94
Durfey, Thomas C. 912
Durham, F. Gayle 667, 1128, 1129
Dygert, Warren B. 293, 364
Dykema, Peter W. 913, 914, 915, 916

Eastman, Susan Tyler 365
Eaton, Walter Prichard 1042
Eberly, Philip K. 917
Eckersley, Peter 1130
Edelman, Jacob Murray 1450
Editors of Broadcasting Magazine 1638
Edmonds, Robert 668
Edmondson, Madeleine 918, 919
Edson, Lee 124
Educational Radio Script & Transcription Exchange 669
Edwards, Frank 95
Eguchi, H. 1131
Ehrlich, Eugene 1639
Eichberg, Robert 96
Eicoff, Al 366
Eiselein, E.B. 1560
Eisenberg, Azriel L. 920
Elkin, Stanley 97
Elliott, Bob 98, 99
Elliott, Philip 694
Ellis, Elmo I. 519, 1594
Ellmore, R. Terry 1640
Elving, Bruce F. 1641
Emeritz, Robert E. 1445
Emery, Walter B. 1132, 1451
Eoyang, Thomas T. 369
Erickson, Don V. 1453
Ermuth, F. 582
Ernst, Morris L. 1454
Erskine, Gladys Shaw 1586
Ethridge, Mark 670
Etkin, Harry A. 671
Etzioni-Halevy, Eva 1133
European Broadcasting Union 370, 371, 1643
Evans, Elwyn 1585

526 Radio Broadcasting

Evans, Jacob A. 372
Evans, James F. 100
Evans, Richard L. 101
Ewbank, Henry L. 672, 673, 674
Ewing, Sam 675

Faenza, Roberto 1134
Fairbanks, Grant 676
Falk, Irving A. 928
Fang, Irving E. 102, 677
Farrell, Nigel 482
Federal Council of the Churches of Christ ... 681
Federal Radio Corp. of Nigeria 1135
Federal Radio Education Committee 1314
Fein, Irving A. 103
Fejes, Fred 1136
Felix, Edgar H. 373
Felton, Felix 921
Ferguson, Max 104
Ferrell, Oliver P. 1137
Ferrier, James A. 912
Fessenden, Helen May 105
Field, Charles Kellog 106
Field, Harry 427
Fink, Howard 1644
Fink, John 107
Firth, Ivan 1586
Fischer, Desmond 1139
Fischer, Henry G. 1552
Fisher, Hal 679
Fishman, Joshua A. 1649
Fisk, George 374
Fitelson, H. William 109
Fitzpatrick, Leo 680
Fletcher, James E. 358, 375, 376, 1646
Floherty, John J. 110, 111
Fly, James Lawrence 681, 1456
Fogg, Walter 616
Fogle, Sonya 1021, 1022
Ford, Ed 112
Ford, Marie 1647
Fornatale, Peter 113
Fowler, Gene 1140

Franklin, O. Thomas 684
Fratrik, Mark R. 289, 377
Frazier, Gross & Clay 378
Frederick, Howard H. 1141
French, Florence Felten 685
Friedersdorf, Burk 114
Friedrich, Carl Joachim 1510
Friendly, Fred W. 115
Frost, S.E., Jr. 1308, 1457
Furlaud, Alice 116
Furlonger, Brian 922

Gaines, J. Raleigh 687
Gair, Wally 490
Gardner, Horace J. 698
Garis, Roger 117
Garland-Compton, Ltd 1309
Garnett, Bernard E. 1561
Garrison, Garnet R. 339
Garver, Robert I. 379
Garvey, Daniel E. 688, 689
Gaudet, Hazel 56, 380
Gauthier, Christiane 1648
Gaver, Jack 118
General Electric ... 690
Giangola, Andrew 691
Gibbons, Edward 119
Gibson, George H. 1310
Gibson, Pauline 1311
Gibson, Stephen W. 1545
Gielgud, Val 120, 121, 122, 923, 924, 925, 926
Gifford, F. 692
Gilbert, Douglas 123
Gillen, David 444
Gilman, Don E. 434
Gilmore, Art 693
Ginsburg, Douglas H. 1458
Giovannoni, David 1312, 1313
Gleason, Marion Norris 1031
Gleason, William A. 1649
Godfrey, Donald G. 1650
Golding, Peter 694
Goldmark, Peter C. 124
Goldsmith, Alfred N. 125
Goode, Kenneth M. 381

Author Index 527

Gorder, L.O. 1651
Gordon, Dorothy 927
Gordon, George N. 928
Gorham, Maurice 1142, 1587
Gosden, Freeman F. 68
Goudy, Elizabeth 69
Gould, Samuel B. 695
Goulding, Ray 98, 99
Grame, Theodore C. 1562
Grandin, Thomas 929
Graves, Harold N., Jr. 1143
Gray, Barry 126
Greenfield, Thomas Allen 1652
Greet, W. Cabell 1653
Grinspan, Mel G. 1314
Grisewood, Frederick 127
Griswold, Clayton T. 930
Grogan, John M. 791
Gross, Ben 128
Gross, Gerald C. 388
Gross, Lynne Schafer 382
Gruenberg, Sidonie Matsner 383, 931
Grundfest, Joseph A. 1459
Grunwald, Edgar A. 1654
Guback, Thomas H. 1144
Guest, Edgar A. 129
Guimary, Donald L. 932
Gunston, David 130
Gunter, Barrie 384
Gurman, Joseph 131
Gutiérrez, Félix F. 1563

Haak, Kees van der 1145
Hackett, Walter 933, 934
Hainline, Gloria 699
Hale, Julian 1146
Hall, Barbara 935
Hall, Camden M. 1427
Hall, Claude 935
Hall, Mark W. 696
Hallman, E.S. 1147
Hallonquist, Tore 483
Hamill, Patricia Beall 1655
Hand, Raymond, Jr. 1639
Harden, Frank 132
Harding, Alfred 385

Harding, Richard 1148
Hardy, David T. 1538
Harlow, Alvin F. 133
Harman, R. Joyce 180
Harmon, Jim 134, 135
Harris, Credo Fitch 136
Harris, Jack W. 164
Harris, Paul 1149, 1150
Harrison, Kate 1151
Harrison, Margaret 1315, 1316
Harwell, Ernie 137
Hasling, John 697
Hasty, Jack 138
Hausman, Carl 478, 780, 781
Haussman, John F., Jr. 1317
Havig, Alan 936
Hawks, Ellison 139
Hayes, John S. 698
Hayes, Vangie 699
Head, Sydney W. 365, 386, 1152, 1153, 1660
Heath, Harry E., Jr. 635
Heighton, Elizabeth J. 387
Hein, Kurt John 1154
Helms, Harry L. 1538
Henderson, Amy 140
Henneke, Ben G. 700
Henry, Robert D. 937
Henry, William E. 1037
Herman, Lewis Helmar 701, 702
Herman, Marguerite Shalett 701, 702
Herring, James M. 388
Hershfield, Harry 112
Herzberg, Max J. 1318
Herzog, Herta 56, 389
Hesse, Jurgen 703
Hettinger, Herman S. 390, 391, 392, 393, 511
Hewitt, John 938
Hiber, Jhan 394, 395
Hickman, Ron 141
Higby, Mary Jane 142
Higgens, Gavin 1657
Higgins, C.S. 939
Higgy, R.D. 1326
Hilbrink, W.R. 14

Hill, Edwin C. 704
Hill, Frank Ernest 396, 397, 1320, 1321
Hill, George H. 940, 1564
Hill, Jonathan 144, 145
Hill, Steven P. 1144
Hill, Susan M. 1658
Hilliard, Robert L. 705, 706
Hilmes, Michele 398
Hind, John 1155
Hindley, H. 1147
Hirshberg, Al 203
Hoffer, Jay 399, 400, 401, 707
Hoffman, William B. 651
Hoffman, William G. 708
Hogan, John V.L. 1460
Hoggart, Richard 1156
Holgate, Jack F. 630
Holloway, Donald F. 941
Holsopple, Curtis R. 709
Holt, Robert T. 1157
Hood, James R. 710
Hood, W. Edmund 1546
Hooker, Jim 402
Hooper, C.E. 337
Hope, Bob 146
Hopf, Howard E. 403
Hornung, J.L. 1588
Hoskins, Colin 444
Hosley, David H. 147, 1565
Hotaling, Burton L. 711
Houlgate, Joan 1659
Howard, Herbert H. 599, 942
Howe, Quincy 712
Howe, Russell Warren 148
Howell, W.J., Jr. 1158
Howkins, John 1159
Huber, Louis J. 943
Hudson, Robert V. 1660
Hughes, Patrick 1163
Hulbert, Claude 713
Hunn, Peter 404
Hunnings, Neville 1159
Hurst, Jack 149
Hurst, Walter E. 1661
Husing, Ted 150, 151
Huth, Arno 1161

Hybels, Saundra 714
Hyde, Stuart W. 715
Hyers, Faith Holmes 405

Ichinohe, H. 1131
Independent Broadcasting Authority 1162, 1163
India Ministry of Information & Broadcasting 1164
Inglis, K.S. 1165
Inman, Elinor 1004
Institute of Radio Engineers 408
International Broadcasting Union 1166
International Communication Agency ... 1167, 1168
International Institute of Intellectual Co-operation 1169
Internationales Zentralinstitut für das Jugend- ... 1322
Irvin, Lee 944, 1323
Isber, Caroline 1324
Ito, Masami 1170

Jackson, Gregory 1589
Jamieson, Don 1171
Jamison, Dean T. 1325, 1391
Jansky, C.M., Jr. 1326
Jedlicka, Daniel A. 177
Jennings, George 1590
Jennings, Ralph M. 1462
Johnson, Joseph S. 718
Johnson, Ray V. 635
Johnson, Walter 299
Joint Communications Corp. 409
Jolly, W.P. 152
Jome, Hiram L. 410
Jones, Carless 945
Jones, J. Morris 1327
Jones, John Paul 631
Jones, Kenneth K. 718
Jones, Louis M. 153
Jones, Tony 1188
Jones, Vane A. 1662
Jones, William K. 411
Jordan, Edward C. 719
Josefsberg, Milt 154

Josephson, Larry 1328
Joske Brothers Co. 412
Juilliard, Ahrgus 9
Julian, Joseph 155

Kaftanov, S.V. 1172
Kahm, Harold S. 1583
Kahn, Frank J. 1463
Kaland, William J. 1566
Kalbfeld, Brad 710
Kaltenborn, H.V. 156, 157, 158
Kansas State Dept of Education 1329
Kaplan, Milton Allen 947
Karr, Harrison M. 720
Karshner, Roger 414
Kasser, Joe 1547
Kassner, Minna F. 1464
Katz, Elihu 1173
Katz, Joan H. 1330
Katzman, Natan 1350
Katzman, Solomon 1350
Kaufman, Milton 1663
Kaufman, Murray 159
Kaufman, Schima 948
Kaufman, William I. 721
Keating, Rex 722
Keats, John 1591
Keegan, Carol 458
Keiller, Garrison 160
Keirstead, Phillip O. 949, 950
Keith, Alice 723, 724
Keith, Michael C. 415, 725, 951
Keliher, Alice V. 161
Keller, Evelyn L. 952
Kendall, Patricia L. 428
Kendrick, Alexander 162
Kenyon, John Samuel 1664
Kerr, Frances Willard 1567
Kerwin, Jerome G. 1465
Kester, Max 726
Khalid, Muhammad 1174
Kievman, Michael S. 942
Kilmer, Bill 727
King, Larry 163
Kingston, Walter Krulevitch 728
Kinscella, Hazel Gertrude 953

Kirby, Edward M. 164
Kirkley, Donald H., Jr. 416
Kirkpatrick, Clifford 417
Kirschner, Allen 729
Kirschner, Linda 729
Kitson, Jack William 822
Kittross, John M. 248, 1466, 1467, 1665
Klages, Karl W. 954
Klein, Lewis 365
Kleiser, Grenville 730
Kneitel, Tom 165
Knight, Ruth Adams 1568
Knitel, H.G. 418
Knott, Thomas Albert 1664
Koch, Howard 166
Koening, Allen E. 419
Konecky, Eugene 420
Koon, Cline M. 1331, 1332, 1333
Kovitz, Roselle 1419
Kozlenko, William 955, 956, 957
Krasnow, Erwin G. 421, 435, 1468
Krause, Joseph M. 415
Krieger, Susan 422
Kris, Ernst 733
Krulevitch, Rome C. 958
Krulevitch, Walter 958
Kuhn, Raymond 1175, 1176
Kumar, Narenda 1334

Labunski, Richard E. 1469, 1470
Lackmann, Ron 167
Laemmar, Jack W. 541
LaGuardia, Robert 959, 960
Laine, Elizabeth 1335
Lambert, Richard S. 1336
Lampell, Millard 961
Landry, Robert J. 168, 423, 732
Lane, Daryl 169
Lange, Mark R. 424
LaPrade, Ernest 962
Larsen, Egon 170
Larson, Raymond D. 1592
Lass, A.H. 963
Laster, Clay 1548
Latham, Jean Lee 964
Laurie, Joe, Jr. 112

Lawrence, Jerome 733
Lawrence, John Shelton 1471
Lawton, Sherman P. 672, 673, 674, 734, 735, 736, 737, 965
Lazarsfeld, Paul F. 425, 426, 427, 428, 429, 430
Le Duc, Don R. 1472, 1473, 1485
Lea, Gordon 966
Leach, Eugene E. 1337
Leach, Frances 1203
Leaming, Barbara 171
Lean, E. Tangye 172
Leatherwood, Dowling 738
Leding, Robert H. 300
Lee, Alfred McClung 967
Lee, Elizabeth Bryant 967
Lee, Robert H. 823
Lee, S. Young 1338
Leinwoll, Stanley 173
Lent, Henry B. 1593
Lent, John A. 1177
Lerner, Mark 1594
LeRoy, David J. 968
LeRoy, Howard S. 1474
Lescarboura, Austin C. 125, 1549
Lessing, Lawrence 174
Levenson, William B. 685, 1339, 1340
Leverton, Garrett H. 969
Levin, Harvey J. 431, 1475
Levin, Murray B. 970
Levine, Carl R. 739
Lewels, Francisco J., Jr. 1569
Lewis, Dorothy 432, 971, 972
Lewis, Peter 973
Lichty, Lawrence W. 175, 1178
Lifset, Reid 1341
Lindsley, Charles Frederick 740
Lingel, Robert 1342
Linney, Romulus 878
Lipscomb, Audre B. 601
Lisann, Maury 1179
Liss, Joseph 974
Litvinenko, A.S. 1666
Liu, Alan P.L. 1180
Lloyd James, Arthur 741
Lodge, Oliver 1550

Logan, John S. 435
Loizeaux, Marie D. 975
Longley, Lawrence D. 1468
Longmate, Norman 742
Lord Simon of Wythenshawe 1181
Lowdermilk, R.R. 1343, 1344, 1405, 1406
Lowell, Maurice 743
Lucas, Peter 176
Luciani, Vince 1551
Lujack, Larry 177
Lumley, Frederick H. 436, 1345
Luther, Sara Fletcher 1182
Luthra, H.R. 1183
Lynch, James M., Jr. 937
Lyons, Eugene 178

MacCabe, Colin 1184
MacDonald, J. Fred 179, 976
Macdonald, Jack 437
MacDonald, R.H. 744
MacFarland, David T. 977, 978
Mackay, Ian K. 1185, 1186, 1187
Mackey, David R. 979
MacLatchy, Josephine 1346
Maclaurin, W. Rupert 180
MacLeish, Archibald 980, 981, 982
MacNeice, Louis 983
MacVane, John 181
Maddison, John 1347
Magne, Lawrence 1188
Maier, Irwin 182
Maloney, Martin J. 802
Mansell, Gerard 1189
Marconi, Degna 183
Marek, George R. 438
Market Facts, Inc. 439
Marks, Hilliard 27
Marsh, C.S. 1348
Martelanc, Tomo 1190
Martin, John T.W. 811, 812
Martin, Pete 74
Martin, Robin B. 421, 440
Marx, Herbert L., Jr. 441
Masani, Mehra 1191
Mastroianni, George A. 827

Author Index 531

Matelski, Marilyn J. 984
Matheson, Hilda 184
Mathur, J.C. 985
May, Derwent 745
Mayer, Martin 442
Mayes, Thorn L. 185
Mayeux, Peter E. 746
Mayorga, Margaret 986
McAnany, Emile G. 1325, 1391
McBride, Mary Margaret 186, 187, 1570
McCavitt, William E. 443, 1192, 1667
McClendon, Natalie 1349
McDonagh, Richard 987
McDonald, James R. 1668
McFadden, Dorothy L. 972
McFadyen, Stuart 444
McGee, William L. 445
McGill, Earle L. 747, 963
McGrath, James B. 1017
McKean, Gil 274
McKinney, Eleanor 988
McLeish, Robert 748
McLuhan, Marshall 188
McMahon, Morgan E. 189, 190, 191
McMahon, Robert Sears 1476
McNair, W.A. 446
McNamee, Graham 192
McNeil, Bill 1193
McNicol, Donald 193
McPhail, Thomas L. 1194
McRae, John 401
McWhinnie, Donald 749
Meany, Anthony B. 447, 448
Melaniphy, Mike 1198
Mendel, Robin 1350
Mendelsohn, Harold 311
Meo, L.D. 1195
Meppen, Adrian J. 858
Merrill, I.R. 1351
Merrill Lynch, Pierce, Fenner & Beane 450
Methold, Kenneth 1352
Metz, Robert 194
Meyer, Ed 132
Mickel, Joseph 989
Mickelson, Sig 1196

Middleton, Glenn Y. 693
Midgley, Ned 451
Migala, Joseph 990
Milam, Lorenzo Wilson 1353, 1354
Miles, Donald W. 750
Miles, J. Robert 1355, 1368
Miller, Bobby Ray 751
Miller, Douglass W. 1577
Miller, Joseph L. 195
Miller, Justin 452
Miller, Merle 1435
Miller, Neville 453
Milligan, Spike 196
Millikan, Robert A. 1356
Mills, Joshua E. 113
Milton, Ralph 991
Minkov, Mikail 752
Minor, Dale 1477
Mitchell, Curtis 197
Moemeka, Andrew A. 1357
Mohanty, Jagannath 1358
Mondesir, Simone 620
Morell, Peter 454
Morgan, Edward P. 753
Morgan, Janet 1156
Morris, James M. 992
Morris, John 754
Morrison, David 304
Morrow, Bruce 198
Mosco, Stephen 1155
Moseley, Sydney 199
Moser, Julius G. 1478
Moss, P.D. 939
Mosse, Baskett 755
Mott, Frank Luther 756
Mourne, William 993
Muggeridge, Douglas 757
Mullan, Bob 566
Muller, Helen M. 1359
Mullick, K.S. 1197
Mullin, Molly Ann 623
Murphy, Jonne 455
Murray, John 1479
Murrow, Edward R. 200
Muscio, Winston T. 1198
Mutual Broadcasting System 456, 457

532 Radio Broadcasting

Myrick, Howard A. 458

Nagler, Frank 758
Namurois, Albert 1199
National Advisory Council on Radio in Education 459, 1360, 1595
National Assn for Better Radio & TV 460
National Assn of Broadcasters 201, 461, 462, 463, 464, 465, 466, 467, 468, 469, 470, 471, 759, 760, 761, 762, 763, 764, 765, 766, 767, 1480, 1481, 1482, 1483, 1596, 1670
National Assn of Broadcasters ... 472, 994, 1484
National Assn of Educational Broadcasters 1361, 1362, 1363
National Assn of Radio & TV Broadcasters 768
National Broadcasting Co. 473, 474, 475, 476, 769, 770, 771, 772, 773, 774, 1364
National Comm. on Education by Radio 1365
National Retail Dry Goods Assn 477
Neff, Walter J. 393
Nelson, Harold L. 1485
Nelson, Lindsey 202, 203
Neurath, Paul 985
New York Academy of Medicine 1366
Newman, Mark 1571
Newsom, Phil 776
Newspaper-Radio Committee 1486
Nichols, John S. 1228
Nicol, John 995
Niggli, Josephina 777
Nippon Hoso Kyokai 1200, 1201
Nisbett, Alec 778, 779
Niven, Harold 1286
Noel, Francis W. 1367
Nordic Council of Ministers 1202
Noriega, Luis Antonio de 1203
Nyhan, Michael J. 1289

Oakes, David 1002
Oboler, Arch 996, 997, 998
O'Brien, Mae 999

O'Brien, P.J. 204
O'Connell, Mary C. 205
O'Donnell, Lewis B. 478, 780, 781
O'Drago, Alicia S. 1673
Oettinger, Mal 1439
Office of the Superintendent of Public Instruction 1597
Olfson, Lewy 1000
Olsson, Harry R., Jr. 1487
O'Neill, Neville 479
Ontario Ministry of Transportation & Communications 1204
Oringel, Robert S. 782
Orlik, Peter B. 783
Ormsby, George W. 1367
Orr, William I. 1553
Osborn, Lynn R. 206
Osgood, Dick 207
O'Shaughnessy, James 434
O'Steen, Anton 1368
Overstreet, Bonaro W. 208
Overstreet, Harry A. 208
Owen, Bill 52, 53

Pack, Richard 1600
Paley, William S. 209, 784, 785, 786, 1488
Palmer, B.J. 480
Palmer, Eric 1553
Paper, Lewis J. 210
Paquin, Lawrence 1001
Parikhal, John 1002
Parker, Bruce 482
Parker, Derek 211
Parker, Donald 634
Parker, Everett C. 1003, 1004
Parker, Lester Ward 1369
Partridge, Simon 1370
Passman, Arnold 1005
Patterson, John M. 621
Paulu, Burton 1205, 1206, 1207, 1208, 1209, 1674
Pawley, Edward 212
Payne, George Henry 787
Pear, T.H. 1006
Pearlman, Donn 1599

Author Index 533

Peatman, John Gray 483
Peck, William A. 484, 788
Pedone, Ronald J. 1338
Pedrick, Gale 789
Peers, Frank W. 1210
Peet, Creighton 790
Pegg, Mark 485
Peigh, Terry D. 486
Pellegrin, Frank E. 487
Pember, Don R. 1489
Pennybacker, John H. 254, 1490
Perry, Armstrong 1371
Perry, Larry 1491
Phillips, David C. 791
Pilgert, Henry P. 1211
Pingree, Suzanne 894
Pirsein, Robert William 1212
Pitts, Michael R. 1675
Ploman, Edward W. 1213
Poindexter, Ray 213, 792
Poling, Daniel A. 1007
Pons, Eugène 1492
Post, Steve 214
Poteet, G. Howard 1676
Potts, John 1214
Powe, Lucas A., Jr. 1493
Powell, Jon T. 490
Power, Leonard 491, 1372, 1373, 1374, 1375, 1376
Practicing Law Institute 1494
Presidential Study Commission 1495
Price, Tom 492
Prigmore, Joan C. 601
Pringle, John 215
Pringle, Peter K. 443, 1677
Prowitt, Marsha O'Bannon 493
Public Service Bureau of the Chicago Tribune 1678
Pusateri, C. Joseph 497

Quaal, Ward L. 498
Quinlan, Sterling 216

Rachford, Helen Fox 796
Radio Amateurs of North America 1554
Radio Corp. of America 217, 1378

Radio Four Seminar 1379
Radio Free Europe ... 1217
Ranson, Jo 1600
Rascoe, Burton 123
Ray, Verne M. 1498
Ray, William B. 1499
RCA Victor 1679
Reck, Franklin M. 794
Redfern, Barrie 795
Reed, Albert A. 1380
Reed, T.H. 1381
Reid, Seerley 519, 1013, 1382, 1383, 1384, 1385, 1386
Reinsch, J. Leonard 518
Reith, John C.W. 219, 1219
Reymer & Gersin Associates 520, 521, 522
Rhymer, Mary Frances 220
Rhyne, Charles S. 1500
Rice, Conrad C. 1581
Rice, Cy 151
Rice, Stuart A. 591
Richard, Pamela 1462
Richardson, David 221
Rider, John R. 1601
Riley, Donald W. 1014
Rivers, William L. 688, 689
Robbins, Irving 1388, 1421
Roberts, Holland D. 796
Roberts, Robert Sydney 1680
Robertson, Milton 1015
Robinson, Ernest H. 797
Robinson, Richard 64
Robinson, Sol 523
Robinson, Thomas Porter 524
Rockwell, Don 222
Rockwell, Vera Cober 685
Rodger, Ian 1016
Roeder, Mary 1389
Rogers, Ralph 798
Rogers, Ralph L. 708
Rogers, Will 223
Rolo, Charles J. 224
Root, Wells 799
Rorty, James 1501
Rose, C.B., Jr. 525

Rose, Oscar 1681
Rosen, Philip T. 526, 1220
Rosenberg, Jack 40
Rosenbloom, Richard S. 527
Ross, Wallace A. 528
Rothafel, Samuel L. 529
Rothel, David 225
Rounds, David 918, 919
Routt, Edd 530, 800, 1017
Rouverol, Jean 1018
Rowan, Ford 1502
Rowland, J. Howard 1019
Rowland, Ruth M. 1621
Rubenstein, Paul Max 802
Ryan, Earl H. 791
Ryan, J. Harold 803
Ryan, Michele 1557

Sackett, Susan 38
Saerchinger, Cesar 226
St. John, Robert 1682
Salisbury, Morse 1326
Sandage, Charles H. 531, 532, 533, 534
Sanders, Ron 1221
Sanger, Elliott 227
Sarnoff, David 228, 535, 804, 805, 1503, 1602
Satterthwaite, N. Doyle 590
Schechter, A.A. 229, 806
Schement, Jorge Reina 1563
Schlosser, Herbert S. 807
Schmeckebier, Laurence F. 230
Schmitz, Charles H. 930
Scholastic Radio Guild 1020
Schroeder, Peter B. 23
Schubert, Paul 232
Schulberg, Bob 536
Schuler, Edgar A. 537
Schutrumpf, E.D. 598
Schutz, David E. 538
Schwartz, Tony 539
Schwoch, James 540
Scupham, John 1390
Seehafer, Gene F. 541
Segal, Paul M. 1041
Seidle, Ronald J. 808

Seldes, George 809
Seldes, Gilbert 542, 543
Seligman, Marjorie 1021, 1022
Selvidge, Barry 1491
Sennitt, Andrew G. 1683
Sergio, Lisa 810
Settel, Irving 233
Sevareid, Eric 234
Seymour, Craig 544
Seymour, Katharine 811, 812
Shane, Ed 1023
Shapiro, Andrew O. 1505
Sharp, Harold S. 1684
Sharp, Marjorie Z. 1684
Shea, Albert A. 995
Sheats, Paul H. 1024
Sherman, Charles 1222
Shiers, George 1685
Shirer, William L. 235
Shively, Gerald D. 1425, 1426
Shore, Peter 1223
Short, K.R.M. 813
Shunaman, Fred 173
Shurick, E.P.J. 236
Siepmann, Charles A. 814, 815, 816, 817
Sieveking, Lance 818
Sill, Jerome 545
Siller, Bob (Robert C.) 819, 820
Silvey, Robert 546
Simmins, G.J.P. 995
Simmons, Steven J. 1506
Singletary, Michael W. 821
Singular, Stephen 237
Sioussat, Helen 1572
Siune, Karen 1069
Skall, Gregg P. 1533
Skelly, Harry J. 1367
Skelt, Barbara 1095
Sklar, Rick 238
Skolnick, Roger 1224
Skornia, Harry J. 822, 823
Skues, Keith 1225
Slager, Myron 131
Slate, Sam J. 239
Slater, Robert 240
Slide, Anthony 241, 824, 1686

Author Index 535

Smart, James R. 1687
Smart, Samuel Chipman 242
Smead, Elmer E. 1507
Smedley, Nick 831
Smeyak, G. Paul 825
Smith, Anthony 547, 826, 1226
Smith, Charles H. 301, 306
Smith, Curt 1025
Smith, F. Leslie 548
Smith, Jeannette Sayre 1510
Smith, Marvin 549
Smith, R. Franklin 243
Smith, V. Jackson 1026
Smythe, Dallas W. 1003
Smythe, Ted C. 827
Snagge, John 244
Snyder, Ross 1004
Sobel, Robert 245
Socolow, A. Walter 1508
Soley, Lawrence C. 828, 1228
Solomon, Richard J. 1248
Sound Broadcasting Society 1229
Spain, Peter L. 1396
Sparks, Kenneth R. 1688
Spearman, Paul D.P. 1504
Special Comm. on Radio & TV ... 1509
Speir, Hans 731
Sperber, A.M. 246
Spicer, Joanna 1145, 1159
Spingarn, Jerome H. 550
Stamberg, Susan 247
Standard Rate & Data Service 551, 552
Stanley, Dave 118
Stanley, Frederick Jackson 626
Stanley, Robert H. 553
Stanton, Frank N. 429, 430
Starch, Daniel 554
Stasheff, Edward 1340
Statistics Canada 555
Stedman, Raymond William 1027
Steinberg, Charles S. 829
Steiner, Peter O. 556
Stephens, Mitchell 830
Sterling, Christopher H. 248, 386, 968, 1231, 1232, 1689, 1690, 1691
Sternberg, Evelyn 1510

Sterner, Alice P. 1392, 1393
Stevenson, Wilf 831
Stewart, Irvin 1394
Stewart, Irwin 511
Stewart, Olivia 1184
Stone, Vernon A. 1603
Stoppard, Tom 1028
Strack, Irene Lydia 1395
Stranger, Ralph 1692
Stuart, Charles 250
Stumpf, Charles K. 251
Stupp, Irene M. 1029
Sturmey, S.G. 558
Stursberg, Peter 252
Subcomm. of the Comm. on Interstate & Foreign Commerce ... 559, 560, 832, 1511, 1512
Subcomm. of the Select Comm. on Small Business 1513
Subcomm. on Activities of Regulatory Agencies ... 1514
Subcom. on Communications & Power ... 1396, 1397, 1555
Subcom. on Communications. Comm. on Commerce, Science ... 561
Subcomm. on Telecommuncations & Finance ... 562, 1398, 1515
Subcomm. on Telecommunications, Consumer Protection ... 563, 1233
Summers, Harrison B. 253, 254, 1516
Summers, Leda P. 564
Summers, Robert E. 254, 1517
Sunter, A. 582
Surlin, Stuart H. 1573
Svennevig, Michael 384
Swaziland Government 565
Swearer, Harvey F. 1518
Swing, Raymond Gram 255, 256, 257

Tannenbaum, Stanley I. 310
Taves, Isabella 1574
Taylor, Glenhall 258
Taylor, Laurie 566
Taylor, Marion Sayle 259
Taylor, Robert 260
Taylor, Sherril W. 1030

536 Radio Broadcasting

Tebbel, John 261, 567
Ted Bolton Associates 568, 569
Teeter, Dwight L., Jr. 1485
Temporary Commission on Alternative Financing ... 140
Terkel, Hal 819
Terrace, Vincent 262
Thomas, Alan 264
Thomas, Bob 265
Thomas, Denis 571
Thomas, Lowell 266, 267, 268, 269
Thomas, Ruth 1234
Thomas, Thomas J. 1401
Thompson, Dorothy 833
Thomson, David Cleghorn 834
Thorne, Sylvia 1031
Tighe, C.R. 1604
Timberg, Bernard 1471
Tolleris, Beatrice K. 572
Tomlinson, John D. 1235
Tooley, Howard 835, 1032
Topping, Malachi C. 175
Tracey, Michael 270
Treadwell, Bill 271
Trethowan, Ian 272
Turnbull, Robert B. 836
Twomey, John E. 1693
Tyler, I. Keith 573, 1019, 1402, 1403, 1404, 1405, 1406, 1422
Tyler, Kingdon S. 837
Tyler, Poyntz 838
Tyler, Tracy Ferris 839, 1407, 1408
Tyson, James L. 1236
Tyson, Levering 1409, 1410, 1411

Ulanov, Barry 273
Ulloth, Dana 714
Underwood, Robert 1412
Unesco 574, 575, 1237
U.S. Dept of Commerce 576
U.S. Dept. of Commerce. Bureau of Navigation ... 1519
U.S. Dept of the Interior 1413
U.S. Dept. of the Interior ... 1414, 1694
U.S. Federal Communications Commission 577, 578, 1520, 1521, 1522, 1523, 1524, 1525, 1526, 1527, 1695, 1696, 1697
U.S. Federal Radio Commission 1528, 1529, 1698
U.S. Federal Trade Commission 579
U.S. Foreign Broadcast Information Service 1238
U.S. House of Representatives 1530
U.S. Information Agency ... 1239, 1240, 1241, 1242
U.S. Office of War Information 840
Unmacht, Robert 1699
Urmston, Mary 1389

Vahl, Rod 1605
Vallee, Rudy 274
Van Doren, Carl 1034
Van Loon, Hendrik Willem 8414
Velia, Ann M. 275
Venmore-Rowland, John 1243
Vernon, William 169
Vervey, Norma Ellen 1035
Vittet-Philippe, Patrick 1244
Von Utfall, Johan 1246
Vyvyan, Richard N. 276

Wagner, Paul H. 842
Walker, E. Jerry 1036
Waller, Judith 581, 1411
Walters, Roger L. 843
Waples, Douglas 844
Ward, John E. 1248
Warner, Harry P. 1531, 1532
Warner, W. Lloyd 1037
Warren, Carl 845
Waters, James F. 277
Watson, K. 582
Watson, Katherine Williams 1038, 1039
Wavell, Stewart 1249
Weaver, J. Clark 846, 847
Weaver, Jackson 132
Weaver, Luther 583, 848
Webster, Bethuel M., Jr. 849
Webster, Lance 306
Wedell, E.G. 584

Author Index

Wedell, George 1173, 1250
Wedlake, G.E.C. 278
Weinberg, Steve 1040
Weir, E. Austin 1251
Weiser, Norman 1041
Weiss, Fredric A. 1017
Welch, Constance 1042
Wentworth, Brandon 279
Wertheim, Arthur Frank 1043
West, Robert 850, 851
West, W.J. 1044, 1045
Westfield, Ernie 280
Westinghouse Broadcasting Co. 1046
Westley, Bruce H. 1415
Wettig, Gerhard 1252
Whan, Forest L. 585, 586
Whetmore, Edward Jay 281
Whippe, Wayne 793
Whipple, James 852
Whitaker-Wilson, Cecil 853
White, Barton C. 588
White, James R. 1047, 1048
White, Llewellyn 589
White, Melvin R. 854, 855, 856, 1049
White, Paul W. 857
White, Ted 819, 858
Whitley, Jack W. 1533
Whitton, John B. 642
Wiebe, G.D. 590
Willey, Malcolm M. 591
Willey, Roy DeVerl 1416
Williams, Albert N. 592
Williams, Arthur 1253
Williams, J. Grenfell 1254
Williams, Marynelle 859
Williams, W.E. 397
Willing, Si 593
Willis, Edgar E. 339, 860, 861, 862
Willis, Frederic A. 1417
Wilson, Charles Morrow 594
Wilson, David 595
Wimer, Arthur 863
Winchell, Walter 282

Windschuttle, Keith 1255
Winfield, Betty Houchin 864
Winn, Conrad 1430
Wisconsin Research Project in School Broadcasting 1418
Wishengrad, Morton 1050
Witherspoon, John 1419
Wober, J.M. 598
Woelfel, Norman 1019, 1386, 1420, 1421, 1422
Wolfe, Charles Hull 599
Wolfe, Charles K. 153
Wolfe, Kenneth M. 1051
Wolfe, Morris 1193
Wolverton, Mike 868
Wood, Clement 283
Wood, Denise E. 1330
Wood, Richard E. 1256
Woodfin, Jane 284
Woodward, Christine 361
Wright, Gene 1052
Writer's Guild of America 1053
Wulfemeyer, K. Tim 867, 868
Wyatt, Frederick 286
Wylie, Max 287, 869, 870

Yamada, Gayle K. 1565
Yates, Raymond Francis 531
Yoder, Andrew R. 1258
Yoffe, Emily 163
Young, Filson 288
Young, Helen Ann 1416
Young, Steve 858
Yugoslav Institute of Journalism 1259

Zacharoff, Lucien 1464
Zeigler, Sherilyn K. 599
Zimmerman, Jane Dorsey 1704
Zimmermann, Ed 1054
Zipf, W.H. 1610
Zollman, Carl 1534
Zuckman, Harvey L. 1535

TITLE INDEX

1938 Radio Annual, The 1608
1957 Iowa Radio-Television Audience Survey, The 586

ABC Achievements and the Implementation of Dix, 1983-85 1061
ABC of Radio, The 461
ABC of the FCC, An 1520
ABC Powers and Functions 1062
ABC's of Radio, The 690
Access to the Air 1423
Accounting Manual for Broadcast Stations 462
Accounting Manual for Broadcasters 315
Across the Dial 1638
Additional Radio Regulations 11496
Addresses at the 39th Annual Convention of the NAB 759
Administration of American Telecommunications Policy 1466
Adult Education Through Radio 1334
Adult Radio 941
Adventures in Radio 77
Advertising Agency and the Broadcasting Medium, The 434
Advertising Agency Looks at Radio, The 479
Advertising and Business Side of Radio, The 451
Advertising By Radio 362
Advertising in Radio and Television Broadcasts 418
Advertising in the Broadcast & Cable Media 387
Advertising Media 293
Advertising on Radio and Television 290
Advertising on Radio and Television 270
African Experiment in Radio Forums for Rural Development 1056
Aids to School Use of Radio 1405
Air Fair 116
Air Law 1474
Air Raid 980

Air-Storming 841
Air Time 808
Air Words 938
Airlanes to English 796
Alien Amateur Radio Operators 1555
All About Amos 'n' Andy 68
All Abut Broadcasting 790
All Children Listen 927
All for Love 893
All-News Radio 949
Allocation of Radio Frequency Spectrum and Its Impact ... 1514
Alternative Financing Option for Public Broadcasting 1400
AM/FM Broadcast Station Planning Guide 671
Amateur Radio Handbook, The 1536
Amateur Radio Operation in the Soviet Union 1128
Amateur Radio, Super Hobby! 1551
Ambassador of Good Will 204
America Handcuffed by Radio C-h-a-i-n-s 447
America's Other Voice 1196
American Broadcasting 175
American Broadcasting and the First Amendment 1493
American Public Radio Qualitative Profile 1261
American Radio 1636
American Radio Industry and Its Latin American Activities 540
American Radio Tenth Anniversary Issue 89
American Radio: A Report on the Broadcasting Industry, The 589
American Radio: Small Market Edition 361
American Scenes 955
American Scriptures 1034
American Story, The 981
American Universities and Colleges That Have Held ... 1262
American vs. British System of Radio Control 326
Americans All--Immigrants All 1327

540 Radio Broadcasting

Analysis of Radio-Listening in Autos, An 346
Analysis of the Radiobroadcasting Activities of Federal ... 1510
Anatomy of Local Radio-TV Copy 788
And Now, Here's Max 104
Announcing 781
Announcing for Radio 727
Annual Report and Accounts (BBC) 1616
Anybody Here from West Virginia? 640
AP Libel Manual 710
Appeal and Public Radio's Music 1313
Appraisal of Radio Broadcasting in the Land-Grant ... 1407
Arkansas Airwaves 213
Armstrong's Fight for FM Broadcasting 1453
ARRL Handbook for the Radio Amateur, The 1537
Art and Science of Radio, The 634
Art of Interviewing for Television, Radio and Film, The 629
Art of Radio, The 749
Art of Radio: A C.B.C. Training Manual, The 1256
Art of Radio Times, The 87
Art of Teaching by Radio 1331
As Good As Any 147
As It Happened 209
Ascertainment of Community Needs by Black-Oriented ... 1573
Associated Press Broadcast News Handbook 710
Attitudes of Rural People Toward Radio Service 893
Attitudes of Rural People Toward Radio Service: A Nation-wide Survey of Farm and Small-Town People 1436
Attitudes to Broadcasting Over the Years 384
Audience 88 354
Audience for Educational Radio, An 1415
Audience Ratings 307
Audio Control Handbook ... 782

Audio History of Commercial Radio 8
Australian Radio 1198
Awards and Citations in Radio and Television 1670

B and T Yearbook, The 1611
B.B.C. from Within, The 1181
B.S. I Love You 31
Backstage at the Mets 203
Bacon's Radio TV Directory 1612
Battle to Control Broadcast News, The 661
BBC and Public Service, The 1184
BBC and the Arts, The 1082
BBC Annual Report and Accounts 1090
BBC Engineering 1922-1972 212
BBC Handbook 1616
BBC Local Radio 1083
BBC: Public Institution and Private World, The 50
BBC: Services Available to Other Broadcasters 1084
BBC: The First Fifty Years, The 41
BBC's Medical Programmes, The 1085
Before Television 258
Beginner's Handbook of Amateur Radio, The 1548
Beginning Broadcast Newswriting 867
Beginning Radio Production 854
Behind the Microphone (1935) 641
Behind the Microphone (1944) 110
Benchmark Television Radio Study ... 1351
Berlin Diary 235
Best Broadcasts of 1938-39 287
Best One-Act Plays of 1940, The 986
Best Radio Plays of 1989 885
Best TV and Radio Commercials 528
Beyond Broadcasting 1472
Bibliography of African Broadcasting, The 1656
Bibliography of CRTC Studies 1624
Bibliography of Doctoral Dissertations in TV and Radio, A 1688
Bibliography of Selected Books and Significant Articles ... 1224

Title Index 541

Bibliography of the History of
 Electronics 1685
Bibliography of Theses & Dissertations
 in Broadcasting, A 1665
Bibliography on Educational
 Broadcasting 1293
Big Broadcast, 1920-1950, The 52
Big Business and Radio 11
Biggest Aspidistra in the World 36
Birth of Broadcasting, The 42
Black Media in America 1564
Black Radio Exclusive 1558
Blacklisting 1435
Blue Book, The 452
Board for International Broadcasting
 Authorization 1119
Board for International Broadcasting,
 RFE and Radio Liberty 1114
Books About Broadcasting 1617
Border Radio 1140
Boston Trade and Distribution Area,
 The 585
Both Sides of the Microphone 698
Breaking into Broadcasting 1599
British Broadcasting (1946) 1073
British Broadcasting (1974) 1226
British Broadcasting, 1922-1972 (1972) 1659
British Broadcasting, 1922-1982 (1983) 1657
British Broadcasting: A Bibliography
 (1954) 1618
British Broadcasting: A Study in
 Monopoly 1111
British Broadcasting and the Danish
 Resistance Movement 1074
British Broadcasting in Transition 1205
British Broadcasting: Programmes and
 Power 1160
British Broadcasting: Radio & TV in
 the UK 1206
British Radio Drama 910
British Radio Drama, 1922-1956 923
Broadcast Advertising 599
Broadcast Advertising and Promotion 306

Broadcast Advertising Handbook 331
Broadcast Advertising in Africa,
 Australia and Oceania 398
Broadcast Advertising in Europe 598
Broadcast Advertising in Latin America 598
Broadcast Advertising: The Fourth
 Dimension 297
Broadcast and Be Damned 264
Broadcast Automation 760
Broadcast/Cable Programming 365
Broadcast Code for Advertising to
 Children 330
Broadcast Communications Dictionary 1636
Broadcast Copywriting 783
Broadcast Copywriting As Process 846
Broadcast Editorializing 832
Broadcast English 627
Broadcast Fairness 1502
Broadcast Financial Journal 314
Broadcast Financial Legal Service
 Guide 327
Broadcast Industry: An Examination of
 Major Issues, The 553
Broadcast Investor 316
Broadcast Journalism, 1979-1981 610
Broadcast Journalism: A Guide for the
 Presentation of ... 648
Broadcast Journalism: An Introduction
 to News Writing 696
Broadcast Journalism: Techniques of
 Radio and TV News 625
Broadcast Law and Regulation 1434
Broadcast Lending 440
Broadcast Management 498
Broadcast News 830
Broadcast News Handbook 750
Broadcast News Manual of Style, A 744
Broadcast News Writing 825
Broadcast Newswriting: A Workbook 868
Broadcast Newswriting As Process 847
Broadcast News Writing, Reporting, and
 Production 858
Broadcast Over Britain 1219
Broadcast Primer 577

542 Radio Broadcasting

Broadcast Programming 365
Broadcast Programs in American Colleges and Universities 1286
Broadcast Rating (1964) 559
Broadcast Ratings (1965) 560
Broadcast Regulation and Joint Ownership of Media 431
Broadcast Regulation and Station Ownership 563
Broadcast Regulation Political Primer 1491
Broadcast Regulation: Selected Cases and Decisions 1432
Broadcast Research Definitions 1646
Broadcast Research Primer 463
Broadcast Station Operating Guide 523
Broadcast Stats 318
Broadcast Word, The 741
Broadcast Writing 688
Broadcast Writing: Principles and Practice 843
Broadcaster 319
Broadcaster and the Librarian, The 1635
Broadcasters, The 21
Broadcasters and the Fairness Doctrine 1515
Broadcasters Can Negotiate Anything 322
Broadcaster's Dictionary, The 1668
Broadcaster's EEO Handbook, A 1623
Broadcasters in a Free Society 807
Broadcaster's Legal Guide for Conducting Contests ... 1424
Broadcaster's Survival Guide, The 1533
Broadcasting (1933) 184
Broadcasting (1966) 1094
Broadcasting (serial) 320
Broadcasting Abroad 1166
Broadcasting: An Introduction 33
Broadcasting: An Introduction to Radio and Television 714
Broadcasting and a Changing Civilisation 797
Broadcasting and Bargaining 419
Broadcasting and Democracy in France 1234
Broadcasting and Democracy in West Germany 1253
Broadcasting and Détente 1252
Broadcasting and Government 1451
Broadcasting and Government Regulation in a Free Society 1437
Broadcasting and Peace 1169
Broadcasting and Politics in Western Europe 1175
Broadcasting and Public Policy 584
Broadcasting and Society, 1818-1939 485
Broadcasting and Telecommunication 34
Broadcasting and the American Public 343
Broadcasting and the Bill of Rights 1480
Broadcasting and the Law 321
Broadcasting and the People 1191
Broadcasting and the Public 254
Broadcasting and the Public: A Case Study of Social Ethics 678
Broadcasting and the Public Interest 1490
Broadcasting Around the World 1192
Broadcasting Bibliography 1658
Broadcasting/Cable Yearbook 1619
Broadcasting Foreign-Language Lessons 1345
Broadcasting from the High Seas 1149
Broadcasting in Africa 1152
Broadcasting in Asia and the Pacific 1177
Broadcasting in Britain 45
Broadcasting in Canada 1147
Broadcasting in Guyana 1221
Broadcasting in India (1965) 1068
Broadcasting in India (1987) 1110
Broadcasting in Ireland 1139
Broadcasting in Japan 1170
Broadcasting in Mexico 1207
Broadcasting in My Time 199
Broadcasting in New Zealand 1185
Broadcasting in Nigeria 1186
Broadcasting in Papua New Guinea 1187

Title Index 543

Broadcasting in Peninsular Malaysia 1055
Broadcasting in Sweden (1970) 1246
Broadcasting in Sweden (1976) 1213
Broadcasting in the Arab World 1790
Broadcasting in the Netherlands 1145
Broadcasting in the Public Interest 769
Broadcasting in the Seventies 1086
Broadcasting in the Third World 1173
Broadcasting in the U.S. 761
Broadcasting: Its New Day 531
Broadcasting Laws 1093
Broadcasting Music 962
Broadcasting Policy and Copyright Law 1430
Broadcasting Primer, A 46
Broadcasting Projects 672
Broadcasting Public Proceedings 994
Broadcasting: Radio and Television 673
Broadcasting Regulation and the New Technologies 1108
Broadcasting Religion 930
Broadcasting Research Methods 358
Broadcasting (Sound and Television) 355
Broadcasting Stations of the World 1238
Broadcasting Strategy for the Future, A 1098
Broadcasting: The Critical Challenges 829
Broadcasting the News 684
Broadcasting to All Homes 770
Broadcasting to Schools 1281
Broadcasting to the Classroom by Universities ... 1263
Broadcasting to the Soviet Union 1179
Broadcasting to the Youth of America 971
Broadcasting: Vision and Sound 596
Broadcasting with Children 1352
Broadcasting without Barriers 646
Building Audiences for Educational Radio Programs 531
Business and Legal Problems of Television and Radio 1487
Business of Radio Broadcasting, The 530
But First, These Messages 588
Buying or Building a Broadcast Station 421

C.A.B. Story, 1926-1976, The 1059
Call Me Lucky 74
Calling CQ 1542
Can You Top This? 112
Canada's Farm Radio Forum 995
Canadian Broadcasting 444
Canadian Broadcasting History Resources in English 1693
Canadian National Theatre on the Air 1644
Canadian Ownership in Broadcasting 333
Canadian Radio Year Book 1099
Capital 336
Career in Newspapers & Broadcasting, A 182
Careers in Radio (1950) 1580
Careers in Radio (1986) 1596
Careers in Radio and Television News 1603
Careers with a Radio Station 1594
Careerscope 6 1591
Cascando, and Other Short Dramatic Pieces 881
Case Studies in Broadcast Management 342
Cases and Materials on Electronic Mass Media 411
Cat's Whisker, The 144
Cavalcade of Broadcasting 197
CBS: Reflections in a Bloodshot Eye 194
Cellular Radio Markets 305
Chain Broadcasting Regulations and Free Speech 1456
Changes in Family Life 1075
Characteristics of Local Media Audiences 323
Charlie Grimm Show, The 61
Chicago Tribune Radio Book, The 1678
Children and Radio Programs 920

544 Radio Broadcasting

Children's Hour, The 886
Children's Programs for Radio Broadcast 1049
Children's Reactions to Radio Adaptations of Juvenile Books 999
Church in the Sky, The 898
Church in the World of Radio-Television, The 877
Churches and the British Broadcasting Corporation, The 1051
Citizen Participation in Broadcast Licensing Before the FCC 1459
Citizens' Groups and Broadcasting 932
Civic Education by Radio 1381
Clandestine Radio Broadcasting 1228
Classification of Educational Radio Research 1274
Clearing the Air 753
Collecting Old Radios and Crystal Sets 7
College Carrier Current 1280
College Radio Handbook, The 1279
College Radio Workshops 1372
Columbia Workshop Plays 906
Commercial Broadcasting 434
Commercial Broadcasting Pioneer 19
Commercial FCC License Handbook 1518
Commercial Radio in Africa 1113
Commercial Radio in Kansas 206
Common Words in Radio, Television and Electronics 1679
Communication Agencies and Social Life 591
Communications Act, 1934 1511
Communications Act of 1934, As Amended, The 1521
Communications and the Law (1962) 1503
Communications and the Law (serial) 1444
Communications by Wire and Radio 1433
Communist International Radio Broadcasting (1976) 1246
Communist International Radio

Broadcasting (1977) 1170
Community Radio: Missing Link? 1309
Comparative Broadcasting Systems 1096
Competition in Radio 571
Compilation of Radio Theses in American Colleges ... 1625
Complete Broadcast Sales Guide, The 401
Complete Shortwave Listener's Handbook, The 1538
Confidential Frequency List 1137
Congress and the Control of Radio Broadcasting 1510
Connections 205
Conqueror of Space, A 57
Constant Voice, The 176
Contact at Sea 231
Contemporary Radio Programming Strategies 977
Continuing Revolution in Communications Technology, The 527
Control of Radio, The 1465
Controlling Broadcasting in Wartime 1510
Controversial Car, The 1046
Controversy on Radio and TV 352
Copywriter's Handbook, The 624
Corporate Plan, 1985-1988 1063
Council on Radio Journalism 1298
Course of Study in Radio and TV Appreciation, A 1392
Court of Missing Heirs 277
Cousin Brucie! 198
Crashing Radio 1604
Craving for Swan, A 899
Creative Broadcasting 823
Criteria for Children's Radio Programs 1019
Critical Issues Report 568
Cross-Cultural Broadcasting 1121
CRTC Ownership 1103
Cuban-American Radio Wars 1141
Cultural Radio Broadcasts 1123
Current Mass Communication Research 1631

Title Index 545

David Sarnoff: A Biography 178
David Sarnoff: Putting Electronics to Work 261
Daytime Radio Broadcasting 1513
Daytime Serials and Iowa Women 564
Debate Handbook on Radio Control and Operation, A 1425
Debate Handbook Supplement on Radio Control and ... 1426
Decade of Radio Advertising, A 390
Decisions of the National Labor Relations Board ... 1448
Deejays, The 1005
Defining and Measuring Radio Audiences 374
Delson's Dictionary of Radio and Record Industry Terms 1661
Developing an Effective Business Plan 544
Developing Information Media in Africa 1125
Development of Radio Education Policies ... 1264
Development of the Control of Advertising on the Air, The 1510
Development of the Top 40 Radio Format, The 978
Dick Gibson Show, The 97
Dictionary of Audio, Radio and Video 1680
Dictionary of Radio and Record Industry Terms 1661
Dictionary of Radio and Television Terms 1692
Dictionary of Radio Terminology in the English, German ... 1666
Dictionary of Radio Terms, A 1651
Dimensions of Broadcast Editorializing 800
Diplomatic Correspondent 22
Directory of Broadcast Archives, A 1650
Directory of Religious Broadcasting, The 875
Directory: Multilingual Broadcasting in Canada 1104
Do You Want to Get into Radio? 1576

Documents in American Telecommunications Policy 1467
Documents of American Broadcasting 1463
Documents of Canadian Broadcasting 1076
Done with Mirrors 138
Don't Let Them Scare You 49
Don't Touch That Dial! 976
Do's and Don'ts of Radio Writing 798
Drama on the Air 979
Due to Circumstances Beyond Our Control 115
Duncan's American Radio 1636
Duncan's Radio Market Guide 359
Dunlap's Radio and Television Almanac 1637

Early Days of Radio Broadcasting 83
Economic Development of Radio, The 558
Economic Study of Standard Broadcasting, An 578
Economic Study of the Radio Industry in the USA, An 369
Economics of the Radio Industry 410
Edgar A. Guest Broadcasting 129
Editorial Integrity in Public Broadcasting 1306
Editorializing on the Air 762
Education by Radio (1932) 1359
Education by Radio (1949) 1291
Education by Radio in American Schools 1265
Education of a Broadcaster, The 20
Education on the Air (1930) 1346
Education on the Air (1959) 1288
Education Tunes in 1409
Educational Aims and Practices of the National ... 1275
Educational AM and FM Radio and Educational ... 1282
Educational Broadcasting 1937 1348
Educational Broadcasting: A Bibliography 1342

546 Radio Broadcasting

Educational Broadcasting: Radio and TV in Education 1358
Educational Program, The 1302
Educational Radio in India 1334
Educational Radio Stations: A Pictorial Review 1365
Educational Television and Radio Amendments of 1969 1396
Education's Own Stations 1315
Edward R. Murrow Heritage, The 864
Edward R. Murrow: The War Years 243
Effective Radio Speaking 708
Eicoff on Broadcast Direct Marketing 366
Electric Evangelism 884
Electric Word, The 232
Electronic Church, The 876
Electronic Colonialism 1194
Electronic Media (1984) 6894
Electronic Media (serial) 367
Electronic Media Management 443
Elements of a Successful Radio Program 298
Empire 210
Empire of the Air, The 368
Employment and Earnings of Radio Artists 328
Employment Outlook in Radio and Television Broadcasting ... 1592
Encyclopaedia of Radio and Television, The 1642
Encyclopedia of Radio and Television Broadcasting 1682
Enterprise in Radio 497
Entertainment Law Reporter 1452
Entrepreneurs of Profit and Pride 1571
Eternal Light, The 1050
Ethnic Broadcasting in the United States 1562
Ethnic Minority Broadcasting 1556
Every Night at Five 247
Everybody's Grandpa 153
Everybody's Music 948
Evolution of the EBU Through Its Statutes, The 1080

Exact Measurements of the Spoken Word 344
Exacting Ear, The 988
Executive's Guide to TV and Radio Appearances 618
Exploring Careers in Broadcast Journalism 1605
External Radio Broadcasting and International Understanding 1190

Fabulous Radio NBD, The 279
Facts Are, The 809
Fair Deal for Radio, A 670
Fair Market Value of Radio Stations 338
Fair Use and Free Inquiry 1471
Fairness Doctrine and the Media, The 1506
Fairness in Broadcasting Act of 1987 1530
Fall of the City, The 982
Fan Mail 266
Farm Broadcasting 879
Father Coughlin's Radio Sermons 69
Father of Radio 79
FCC: The Ups and Downs of Radio-TV Regulation 1499
Fear in the Air 1428
Federal Radio Commission (1929) 1443
Federal Radio Commission (1932) 230
Federal Regulation of the Radio and TV Broadcast ... 1476
Fessenden: Builder of Tomorrow 105
Fifty Fabulous Years, 1900-1950 156
Fifty Years of Japanese Broadcasting 1200
Film and Radio Propaganda in World War II 813
Final Acts of the World Administrative Radio Conference 1138
Financial Analysis of the Private Radio Broadcasting ... 582
Financing for Public Broadcasting 1397
Fine Art of Propaganda, The 967
First 25 Years of RCA, The 217
First 50 Years of Broadcasting 108

Title Index 547

First Amendment Under Siege, The 1469
First Freedom, The 1454
First Quarter-Century of American Broadcasting, The 236
Flick of the Switch, A 189
Floyd Gibbons: Knight of the Air 123
Floyd Gibbons: Your Headline Hunter 119
Flywheel, Shyster, and Flywheel 26
FM Atlas and Station Directory 1641
FM for Education (1944) 1278
FM for Education (1948) 1305
FM Radio in Canada 1101
FM Radio Station Operations Handbook 682
FMedia 683
Foreign and International Communication Systems 1231
Forty Years of Irish Broadcasting 1142
Forums on the Air 1024
Foundations in Broadcasting 860
Four Plays for Radio 1028
Four Years of Network Broadcasting 459
Fourteen Radio Plays 996
Fourth Chime, The 771
Fourth Estate and Radio, The 787
Fred Allen 260
Fred Allen's Radio Comedy 936
Free Company Presents, The 887
Freedom and Responsibility in Broadcasting 353
Freedom of Radio, The 784
Freedom of Speech by Radio and Television 1486
Freedom of the Press 1493
From Approximately Coast to Coast, It's the Bob & Ray Show 98
From Crystal to Color 114
From Ma Perkins to Mary Hartman 959
From Mary Noble to Mary Hartman 918
From Spark to Satellite 173
From the Crossroads 101
From the Third Programme 754
Fundamentals of Radio 719

Fundamentals of Radio Broadcasting 697
Fundamentals of Writing for Radio 650
Funding of Radio Free Europe and Radio Liberty 1116
Funny Men, The 5
Future of Broadcasting, The (1974) 686
Future of Broadcasting, The (1982) 1156
Future of Public Broadcasting, The 1289
Future of Radio and Educational Broadcasting, The 1411

Gas Pipe Networks, The 1277
Gateway to Radio 1586
General Considerations on License Fees for Radio ... 1492
General, The 32
Geographic Distribution of Radio Sets ... 1242
German Radio and Television 1081
German Radio Propaganda 731
Get It on Radio and Television 1634
Getting into Broadcast Journalism 1589
Glossary of Radio and Television Terms, A 1649
Glossary of Radio Communications 1648
Go Ahead, Garrison! 806
Go Public 1349
Golden Age of Wireless, The 42
Golden Throats and Silver Tongues 792
Golden Web, The 24
Golden Years of Broadcasting, The 54
Good Evening: A Professional Memoir 255
Good Evening, Everybody 267
Good Talk 745
Goon Show Scripts, The 196
Grass Roots Radio 722
Great Audience, The 542
Great Ones, The 1566
Great Radio Comedians, The 134
Great Radio Heroes, The 135
Great Radio Personalities in Historic Photographs 241

548 Radio Broadcasting

Groups Tune In, The 396
Guide to CBC Sources at the Public Archives 1633
Guide to Citizen Action in Radio and Television 493
Guide to Non-English Language Broadcasting 1645
Guide to Professional Radio & TV Newscasting 820
Guide to Radio-TV Writing 635
Guide to Understanding and Using Radio Audience Estimates 296

Handbook 1120
Handbook for Amateur Broadcasters 1311
Handbook of Broadcasting 1606
Handbook of Radio Advertising 455
Handbook of Radio and TV Broadcasting 375
Handbook of Radio Drama Techniques 1014
Handbook of Radio Production 608
Handbook of Radio Publicity and Promotion 437
Handbook of Radio Writing 609
Handbook of Sound Effects (1943) 1694
Handbook of Sound Effects (1948) 669
Hard News 1565
Have Tux, Will Travel 146
Head, Heart and Heel 271
Hello America! 226
Hello Everybody, I'm Lindsey Nelson 202
Heralds of False Freedom 1078
Here's Martha Deane 186
Hibernetics 394
Hidden Medium, The 1319
Hip Capitalism 422
History and Development of the ABC 1064
History As You Heard It 268
History Makers 937
History of Broadcasting in Japan, The 1201
History of Broadcasting in the United Kingdom, The 42
History of Broadcasting in the United States, A 24
History of Public Broadcasting, The 1419
History of Radio to 1926 12
History of the Marconi Company 16
Hollywood and Broadcasting 398
Holy Mackerel! 9
Horrorshows 1052
How and Where to Sell Radio Scripts 1029
How Schools Can Use Radio 1364
How Soulful Is "Soul" Radio 1561
How to Announce for Radio and Television 721
How to Audition for Radio 649
How to Be a Ham 1546
How to Break into Radio 1583
How to Build the Radio Audience 351
How to Buy Radio Time 299
How to Enjoy Your Amateur Radio License 1545
How to Get Into Commercials 699
How to Judge a Radio Program 1402
How to Judge a School Broadcast 1386
How to Listen to Music Over the Radio 438
How to Listen to the Radio 583
How to Measure Radio Audiences 301
How to Protect Your Rights in Television and Radio 1462
How to Sell Radio Advertising 593
How to Speak and Write for Radio 723
How to Use Radio 1272
How to Use Radio in the Classroom (Busby, 1941) 1285
How to Use Radio in the Classroom (Woelfel, 1941) 1420
How to Write Broadcast Plays 924
How to Write for Radio (1931) 811
How to Write for Radio (1938) 852
How War Came 256
Human Side of the News, The 704
Humanistic Radio Production 662
Hunt for Tokyo Rose, The 148

Title Index 549

Hysterical Background of Radio 65

I Broadcast the Crisis 157
I Can Tell It Now 48
I Live on Air 229
I Looked and I Listened 128
I Talk As I Like 60
Ideas That Came True 1368
Illustrated Dictionary of Broadcast
  CATV-Telecommunications 1640
Image Builders, The 24
Image of RFE in Poland, The 1217
Images of WGN Radio and Its
  Competitors, The 439
Images of Women 1559
Imperialism, Media and the Good
  Neighbor 1136
Implications of the Radio in Education
  1303
Importance of Radio in Television
  Areas Today, The 406
In Search of Light 37
In the Name of Sanity 257
Incredible Crosby, The 273
Independent Broadcasting 1162
Independent Radio 1071
Index to Characters in the Performing
  Arts 1684
Indian Broadcasting 1183
Indian Experiment in Farm Radio
  Forums, An 985
Information War, The 1477
Innovation of Broadcasting in the Soviet
  Union, The 1144
INS Radio News Manual 716
Inside ABC 216
Inside Radio 407
Intelligent Man's Guide to Broadcast
  Ratings 442
Inter-American Radio Agreement 1461
International Control of
  Radiocommunications 1235
International Film, Radio and
  Television Journals 1686
International Handbook of Broadcasting
  Systems 1220

International Radio Broadcasting 1094
International Radio Listener Discussion
  Panels 1168
International Radio Stations Guide 1223
International Studies of Broadcasting
  1131
International Telecommunications and
  Information Policy 1232
Interpreting FCC Broadcast Rules and
  Regulations 1498
Into the Wind 219
Introduction to Modern Broadcasting
  734
Introduction to Radio and Television
  791
Invasion from Mars, The 56
Inventing American Broadcasting 84
Invention and Innovation in the Radio
  Industry 180
Invisible Resource, The 1475
IRE Book The 1040
Is American Radio Democratic? 1457
Is Your Hat in the Ring? 1481
Issues in Broadcast Regulation 1473
Issues in Broadcasting 827
Issues in International Broadcasting
  1222
It Sounds Impossible 239
Ivory Tower, and Other Radio Plays 997

Jack Benny 27
Jack Benny Show, The 154
Jack Benny: An Intimate Biography 103
Japan's Radio War on Australia 1195
Job of the Radio Announcer, The 717
Journal of Broadcasting 413
Journal of Broadcasting and Electronic
  Media 413
Journalism on the Air 738
Journeys Behind the News 946
Judges and the Judged, The 1435
Just Plain Bill 10

Kaltenborn Edits the News 158
Keep Radio for the People 1438
KOB: Goddard's Magic Mast 275

550 Radio Broadcasting

Ladies and Gentlemen, Easy Aces 1
Lake Wobegon Days 160
Land of the Free, The 987
Larry King 163
Latest Statistics on Radio and
    Television Broadcasting 574
Law of Mass Communications 1485
Law of Radio Broadcasting, The 1508
Law of Radio Communication, The
    1446
Law of the Air 1534
Learn to Write for Broadcasting 713
Legal and Business Problems of
    Television and Radio 1494
Legal Aspects of Radio Broadcasting
    434
Legal Guide to Broadcast Law and
    Regulation 1482
Let Truth Be Told 1189
Let's Broadcast (1939) 1047
Let's Broadcast (1948) 626
Let's Keep Radio Free 453
Libel and the First Amendment 1470
Library and the Radio, The 405
Library on the Air 975
Licenses and Liberty 826
Licensing of Major Broadcast Facilities
    by the FCC 1466
Licensing of Radio Services in the U.S.,
    The (1950) 1450
Licensing of Radio Services in the U.S.,
    The (1980) 1466
Life of a Man, The 283
List of Educational AM and FM Radio
    and ... 1283
List of Radio Broadcast Stations
    Alphabetically by Call ... 1695
List of Radio Broadcast Stations by
    Frequency 1696
List of Radio Broadcast Stations by
    State and City 1697
Listen and Learn 1320
Listen, Hans 833
Listen In 743
Listener Availability and Types of News
    and Music 403

Listener Rules Broadcasting, The 434
Listener Speaks, The 304
Listeners Appraise a College Station
    1299
Listener's Handbook 1595
Listening 592
Listening Habits of Greater Milwaukee
    1947 433
Listening Habits of Oakland
    (California) Pupils 573
Listening Habits of Soviet Citizens to
    VOA 1240
Listening Schools, The 1271
Lists Showing the Ownership of Radio
    ... 334
Little Books on Broadcasting 434
Live Radio Networking for Educational
    Stations 1361
Local Broadcasts to Schools 1394
Local Cooperative Broadcasting 1373
Local Radio 795
Local Radio and Regional Development
    in Europe 1244
Local Radio: Community Education for
    Development 1357
London Calling 1091
Lone Ranger, The 286
Long John Nebel 15
Long Way Home, The 961
Longman Dictionary of Mass Media
    and Communication 1630
Look and Listen 460
Look Now, Pay Later 30
Looking Ahead 228
Lord Haw-Haw & William Joyce 66
Louis MacNeice in the BBC 70
Love in the Afternoon 1054

M Street Radio Directory, The 1699
M.R. DeHaan 2
Ma Perkins, Little Orphan Annie, and
    Heigh Ho, Silver 251
Magazines and Radio Criticism 732
Magic Dials 269
Magic Medium, The 281
Mainly on the Air 882

Title Index 551

Making a Living in Radio 1579
Making Broadcasting Useful 1250
Making It in Radio 1578
Making Money with Co-Op 356
Making the News 694
Man Behind the Mike, The 679
Man of High Fidelity 174
Managing Today's Radio Station 399
Manual of American Dialects 701
Manual of Foreign Dialects 702
Manual of Radio Advertising 487
Manual of Radio News Writing, A 711
Marconi 90
Marconi: Father of Radio 130
Marconi: The Man and His Wireless 152
Mass Communication 25
Mass Communication and Electronic Media 1690
Mass Communication in Developing Countries 1174
Mass Communications Law in a Nutshell 1535
Mass Media: A Chronological Encyclopedia of ... 1660
Mass Media in China 1109
Mass Media Law 1489
Mass News 968
Maverick Inventor 124
Measurement in Radio 436
Media: A New Analysis of the Press, The ... 1255
Media Access 1505
Media and the American Mind 78
Media in America, The 567
Media Law Dictionary, The 1479
Medium and Long-range Economic Planning in Broadcasting Organizations 371
Meet the Russians 1015
MegaRate$ 449
Men and Radio Music 913
Message of Radio, The 804
Method to the Madness, The 873
Microphone and You, The 724
Microphone Memoirs 136

Microphone Technique for Radio Actors 855
Microphones 644
Mighty Music Box, The 80
Mike and Screen Press Directory 1669
Mikes Don't Bite 1572
Minority Broadcasting 1560
Minority Ownership of Broadcast Stations 561
Mister Broadcasting 252
Modern Broadcaster, The 735
Modern Public Affairs Programming 950
Modern Radio 837
Modern Radio Advertising 597
Modern Radio Broadcasting 647
Modern Radio Production 780
Modern Radio Programming 687
Modern Radio Station Practices 718
Modern Stentor: Radio Broadcasting in the U.S., The 302
Modern Stentors: Radio Broadcasters and the Federal Government, The 526
Molders of Opinion 632
Molly and Me 29
Money at the Crossroads 594
Monopoly Steals FM from the People 420
More by Corwin 903
More from Ten to Eight on Radio Four 44
More Solo Readings for Radio and Class Work 1021
Most Contrary Region, The 1107
Motion Pictures and Radio 1335
Municipal Regulations, Taxation and Use of Radio ... 1500
Murray the K Tells It Like It Is, Baby 159
Murrow: His Life and Times 246
Music As Presented by the Radio 914
Music in Radio Broadcasting 896
Music in the Air 917
Music Machine, The 414
Music on the Air 953

552 Radio Broadcasting

Mutual's Second White Paper 456
Mutual's White Paper 457
Muzzled Media 658
My Eyes Are in My Heart 151
My Father, Marconi 183
My Father Was Uncle Wiggily 117
My First 10,000,000 Sponsors 95
My Night People 126
My Time Is Your Time 274

NAB Employee-Employer Relations Bulletin 464
NAB Member Service 465
NAB Radio Code Roster 466
NAB Radio-Television Program Log Recommendations 1484
Nashville's Grand Ole Opry 149
National and International Systems of Broadcasting 1132
National Broadcasting Under Siege 1133
National Educational Radio 1362
National Morale and Radio 775
National Policy for Radio Broadcasting 525
National Radio Broadcasting 349
National Radio Guide 1671
National Radio Publicity Directory 1672
National Survey of Radio and Television Sets 291
NBC and You 473
NBC Handbook of Pronunciation (1964) 772
NBC Handbook of Pronunciation (1984) 1639
NBC Markets 474
NBC Matinee Theatre Presents ... 993
NBC Program Policies and Working Manual 773
NBC Radio and Television Broadcast Standards 774
Network Broadcasting 347
Network School Broadcasts 1382
New Empires 615
New Horizons 1383
New Horizons in Radio (1941) 391

New Horizons in Radio (1971) 511
New Radio Drama 888
News and How to Understand It, The 712
News and Views from National Public Radio 1314
News Broadcasting on Soviet Radio and Television 667
News: Broadcasting's First Responsibility, The 656
News by Radio 639
News for Everyman 655
News in America, The 756
News on the Air 857
News Talk II 614
News War of the Airwaves, The 757
News While It Is News 616
Newswriting for the Electronic Media 689
Nine Radio Plays 964
None of Your Business 58
Nordic Radio and Television via Satellite 1202
Norman Corwin and Radio 17
North American Radio-TV Station Guide 1662
Not So Wild a Dream 234
Not the BBC/IBA 1370
Not to be Broadcast 1436

Oboler Omnibus 998
Occupations in Radio 1577
Of Mikes and Men 284
Off Mike 733
OIRT Review 501
Old Wires and New Waves 133
On a Note of Triumph (1945) 9074
On A Note of Triumph (1986) 18
On the Air 969
On the Air in World War II 181
On the Air: Pioneers of American Broadcasting 140
On the Air: The Story of Radio 111
On the Road with Harden and Weaver 132
On-the-Spot Reporting 938

Once Upon a Time 1038
One Hundred Non-Royalty One-Act
  Plays 956
One Hundred Non-Royalty Radio Plays
  957
One Year of Grace 120
Only the Wind Will Listen 39
Operational Guide for Broadcasting the
  News, An 763
Opportunities in Broadcasting 1584
Opportunities in Radio 1600
Opportunities in Radio and Electronics
  for Returning ... 1602
Order on the Air! 1501
Organization and Operation of
  Broadcast Stations 400
Original Sex and Broadcasting, The
  1353
Orson Welles 171
Orwell: The War Broadcasts 1044
Orwell: The War Commentaries 1045
Our Stake in the Ether 849
Out of the Air 187
Out of the Blue 654
Outlet Story 1894-1984, The 242
Outside Interference 1148
Ownership of Private Broadcasting 332

Pacific Microphone 93
Panic Broadcast, The 166
Paperwork Control in Broadcasting
  Stations 481
Pardon My Accent 76
Passbooks for Career Opportunities
  1598
Passport to World Band Radio 1188
Patterning of Listener Attitudes Toward
  Radio Broadcasts 483
Pay and Conditions of Work of Radio
  Performers, The 385
People in Broadcasting 488
People Look at Radio, The 427
People Speak, The 489
Perry's Broadcast Regulation Political
  Primer 1491
Personal Importance of Public Radio,

The 1312
Persons from Porlock 983
Perspectives on Radio and Television
  548
Pictorial History of Radio, A 233
Pied Piper Broadcasts, The 1031
Pike and Fischer Radio Regulation 1455
Pike and Fischer's Desk Guide to the
  Fairness Doctrine 1445
Pioneers of Wireless 139
Pirate Radio Stations 1258
Playing in the FM Band 214
Plays from Radio 963
Pointers on Radio Writing 777
Poisons, Potions and Profits 454
Polish Radio Broadcasting in the U.S.
  990
Political Broadcast Catechism 1483
Political Use of Radio, The 929
Politics of Broadcast Regulation, The
  1468
Politics of Broadcasting, The (1973) 611
Politics of Broadcasting, The (1985)
  1179
Politics of Canadian Broadcasting, The
  1210
Popular Reactions to Radio
  Broadcasting 434
Portrait of a "Protector" 201
Power Behind the Microphone, The
  1130
Power to Persuade 643
Practical Radio Advertising 393
Practical Radio Writing 812
Prairie Farmer and WLS 100
Present and Impending Applications to
  Education of Radio ... 1360
Press and Television Interests in
  Australian Commercial Radio 1151
Press, Radio and Film in West
  Germany 1211
Press, Radio and World Affairs:
  Australia's Outlook 1070
Press, Radio, Film 1237
Press, Radio, Television, Film in
  Yugoslavia 1259

554 Radio Broadcasting

Pricing the Radio Spectrum 1431
Prime Time 162
Principles and Practices of Network Radio Broadcasting 535
Print, Radio, and Film in a Democracy 844
Prize Plays of Television and Radio, 1956 1053
Problem of the Institutionally Owned Station, The 1326
Problems and Controversies in Television and Radio 822
Problems in Announcing for Radio and Television 606
Problems in College Radio 1260
Producing Radio and Television Programs 739
Production and Direction of Radio Programs 636
Production in Format Radio Handbook 725
Professional Broadcast Announcing 663
Professional Broadcasting 35
Professional Radio Writing 652
Profitable Scriptwriting for TV and Radio 789
Profiting from Radio Ratings 376
Program Patterns for Young Radio Listeners 972
Program Side of Radio, The 1590
Programming Dynamics 1023
Programming for Radio and Television 1026
Programming Radio to Win in the New America 1002
Projects for Radio Speech 674
Promoting Yourself on Television and Radio 620
Pronouncing Dictionary of American English, A 1664
Propaganda by Short Wave 642
Providing for Radio and TV Coverage of House Proceedings 1442
Psychological Impact of Newspaper and Radio Advertisements 425
Psychology of Radio, The 335

Public Arts, The 543
Public Attitudes and Preferences to Radio Programming 409
Public Broadcasting 1398
Public Broadcasting Directory 1395
Public Broadcasting Report 494
Public Broadcasting: The Role of the Federal Govt 1310
Public Interest and the Business of Broadcasting 490
Public Radio and State Governments 1341
Public Radio Handbook 1294
Public Radio Legal Handbook 1401
Public Radio Programming Content by Category ... 1350
Public Radio Stations' Educational Services, 1982-83 1330
Public Radio Stations with Early Experience ... 1377
Public Radio/Telephone Survey 1295
Public School Broadcasting to the Classroom 1266
Public Service Broadcasting: Station WMBD 1374
Public Service Responsibility of Broadcast Licensees 1522
Public Television and Public Radio Awareness ... 1296
Published Radio, Television and Film Scripts 1676
Puget Sounds 221
Pulse of Radio 495
Purchasing a Broadcast Station (1978) 467
Purchasing a Broadcast Station (1979) 496

Qualitative Analysis of Radio Listening in Two ... 532

Radio (1936) 13
Radio (1971) 511
Radio: A Guide to Broadcasting Techniques 1585
Radio: A Reference Guide 1652

Title Index 555

Radio Activities of the Department of Commerce 576
Radio Advertising for Retailers 533
Radio Advertising in Australia 446
Radio Advertising: The Authoritative Handbook 536
Radio Advisory Committees and Audience Preparation 491
Radio Alphabet 1626
Radio Amateur Callbook 1554
Radio Amateur's Hand Book 1541
Radio: America's Star Reporter and Super Salesman 312
Radio and Children (1935) 931
Radio and Children(1984) 872
Radio and Community Development 1379
Radio and Education 1356
Radio and English Teaching 1318
Radio and Its Critics 785
Radio and Its Future 341
Radio and Phonograph Manufacturing Corporations 579
Radio and Poetry 947
Radio and Public Service 432
Radio and Radio Broadcasting 1613
Radio and Records 499
Radio and Retailing in 1943 300
Radio and Television (1952) 613
Radio and Television (1966) 1164
Radio and Television (1976) 170
Radio and Television (serial) 500
Radio and Television: A Selected Annotated Bibliography (1960) 1655
Radio and Television: A Selected Annotated Bibliography (1978) 1667
Radio and Television: A Selected Bibliography (1989) 1677
Radio and Television Acting 664
Radio and Television Announcing 607
Radio and Television Bibliography (1942) 1627
Radio and Television Bibliography (1952, Broderick) 1620
Radio and Television Bibliography (1952, Paulu) 1674
Radio and Television Broadcasting 555
Radio and Television Broadcasting in Eastern Europe 12107
Radio and Television Broadcasting on the European Continent 1208
Radio and Television Commercial, The 310
Radio and Television Communication 740
Radio and Television Continuity Writing 601
Radio and Television Drama 989
Radio and Television in Literacy 1347
Radio and Television in the Service of Education ... 1215
Radio and Television in the Soviet Union 1129
Radio and Television in the USSR 1172
Radio and Television Law 1531
Radio and Television News 631
Radio and Television: Readings in the Mass Media 291
Radio and Television Rights 1532
Radio and Television Sound Effects 836
Radio and Television Stations in Canada 1102
Radio and Television Who's Who 1610
Radio and Television Workshop Manual 908
Radio and Television Writing 869
Radio and the Classroom 1304
Radio and the Farmer 891
Radio and the Law 1478
Radio and the Printed Page 426
Radio and the School 2429
Radio and the Teaching of English 1384
Radio and TV News in Denmark and Norway 1069
Radio and TV Programming 942
Radio Announcer's Handbook, The 700
Radio Announcing 693
Radio As A Career 1588
Radio As a Cultural Agency 839
Radio As a Cultural Force 786

556 Radio Broadcasting

Radio As an Advertising Medium 364
Radio As an Aid in Teaching 1406
Radio Audience for Classical Music, The 309
Radio Audience Measurement (1944) 337
Radio Audience Measurement (1946) 472
Radio Bahá'i, Ecuador 1154
Radio Bibliography 1621
Radio Boys, The 793
Radio Boys Loyalty 793
Radio Boys Under the Sea 793
Radio Boys with the Iceberg Patrol 793
Radio Boys with the Revenue Guards 793
Radio Broadcast Stations in the U.S. 1698
Radio Broadcasting (1927?) 434
Radio Broadcasting (1934) 1441
Radio Broadcasting: A.S.I.C. Class 9114 1216
Radio Broadcasting: An Introduction to the Sound Medium 705
Radio Broadcasting and Television: An Annotated Bibliography 1681
Radio Broadcasting for Retailers 357
Radio Broadcasting: How to Speak Convincingly 730
Radio Broadcasting in Canada 1204
Radio Broadcasting in Communist China 1180
Radio Broadcasting Issues 562
Radio Broadcasting News 10108
Radio Broadcasting Serves Rural Development 1009
Radio Broadcasting to Cuba (1982) 1233
Radio Broadcasting to Cuba (1983) 1117
Radio Broadcasting to Cuba (Radio Marti) (1982) 1115
Radio Broadcasts in the Library of Congress 1687
Radio Business Report 501
Radio Call-ins and Covert Politics 1035

Radio Caroline 1243
Radio Censorship 1516
Radio Classics 878
Radio Classroom, Th291336
Radio Code of Good Practices 764
Radio Collector's Guide 190
Radio Comedy 1043
Radio Communication and Its Import in International Relations 805
Radio Communication Laws of the U.S. ... 1519
Radio Communications Report 502
Radio Continuity Types 736
Radio Copy Book 691
Radio Glossary (1943) 1694
Radio Glossary (1948) 669
Radio Goes to War 224
Radio Guild Plays 1032
Radio Handbook (1941) 835
Radio Handbook (1944) 1629
Radio Handbook (1981) 1552
Radio Handbook for Amateurs and Experimenters, The 1552
Radio Handbook for Extension Workers (1939) 1614
Radio Handbook for Extension Workers (1946) 1615
Radio: How, When and Why to Use It 572
Radio Imagery 329
Radio in 1937 345
Radio in 1985 378
Radio in Advertising 363
Radio in America Today 681
Radio in Australia 1214
Radio in Education 1317
Radio in Education: The Ohio School of the Air ... 1371
Radio in Elementary Education 1416
Radio in Fundamental Education in Undeveloped Areas 1254
Radio in Health Education 1366
Radio in Rural Schools 1315
Radio in Search of Excellence 469
Radio in State and Territorial Educational Depts 1268

Title Index 557

Radio in the Classroom (1938) 1316
Radio in the Classroom (1942) 1418
Radio in the Elementary School 1403
Radio in the High School 1404
Radio in the Schools of Ohio 1385
Radio in the Television Age 113
Radio in Wartime (1942, Dryer) 88
Radio in Wartime (1942, Siepmann) 814
Radio Industry, 218
Radio Is Censored 1464
Radio Is Changing Us 834
Radio Is Yours 550
Radio Journalism (1940) 842
Radio Journalism (1977) 617
Radio Journalism (1980) 752
Radio Law 1447
Radio Law: Practice and Procedure 1449
Radio Listener Panels 380
Radio Listener's Bill of Rights, The 815
Radio Listener's Book of Operas 1010
Radio Listener's Week-end Book 215
Radio Listening and Popular Song Tastes 590
Radio Listening in America 428
Radio Listening Throughout Non-TV America 504
Radio Manual (1937) 1414
Radio Manual (1941) 1001
Radio Manual (1943 1719
Radio Manual (1948) 669
Radio Manufacturers of the 1920's 82
Radio Market Guide 505
Radio Market Trends 567
Radio Markets After the War 408
Radio Markets of the World 598
Radio, Motion Picture, and Reading Interests 1393
Radio Music for Boys and Girls 915
Radio Network Contributions to Education 1269
Radio Networks and the Federal Government 524
Radio News Handbook (1947) 755
Radio News Handbook (1967) 657

Radio News Writing 628
Radio News Writing and Editing 845
Radio News: A Primer for the Smaller Operation 765
Radio Onederland 1225
Radio Only 507
Radio Operator's License Q & A Manual 1663
Radio Ownership and Set Use 508
Radio Papers, The 1354
Radio Personalities 222
Radio Phenomenon in Italy, The 1134
Radio-Play, The 921
Radio Plays 1020
Radio Plays for Children 1039
Radio Plays for Young People 933
Radio Plays from History and Literature 934
Radio Plays of Famous Stories 1000
Radio Power 1146
Radio Preferences of Tenth-Grade Students 517
Radio Production Directing 653
Radio Production Techniques 779
Radio Program Department Handbook 766
Radio Program Production Aids (1943) 1694
Radio Program Production Aids (1948) 669
Radio Program Timelines 492
Radio Programme Production 604
Radio Programming: A Basic Training Manual 991
Radio Programming: Consultancy and Formatics 951
Radio Programming in Action 1030
Radio Programming Profile 509
Radio Programs for Children 1011
Radio Programs in the Public Interest 1012
Radio Programs Intended for Classroom Use 1270
Radio Promotion Handbook 484
Radio Pronunciations 1704
Radio! Radio! 145

558 Radio Broadcasting

Radio Reaches People 510
Radio Realities 680
Radio Reality of Windsor 409
Radio Regulations (1948) 1496
Radio Regulations (1959) 1497
Radio Research 1941 429
Radio Research 1942-1943 430
Radio Retention Guide for Radio and Television Stations 435
Radio Round-ups 131
Radio Rural-Forums in Gujarat 874
Radio Salesmanship 480
Radio Scripts for Practice and Broadcast 856
Radio: Selected A.A.P.S.S. Surveys 511
Radio Showbook 1647
Radio Sketches and How to Write Them 659
Radio Sound Effects 651
Radio Soundtracks 1675
Radio Speech 737
Radio Stars of Today 96
Radio Station, The 415
Radio Station Management 518
Radio Station: Management, Functions, Future, The 545
Radio Station Management News Survey Report 470
Radio Station Operations 424
Radio Station Operations Management and Employee Perspectives 478
Radio Station Transfers 538
Radio Station Treasury 1900-1946 165
Radio Station Turnaround Strategies That Work 402
Radio Stations in the U.S. Broadcasting Foreign Language ... 1609
Radio Stations: Installation, Design and Practice 638
Radio Study 1218
Radio Talk, The 665
Radio Talks to Young People 1007
Radio, Television and American Politics 897
Radio, Television and Motion Pictures 450
Radio, Television and Society 816
Radio, Television and the Administration of Justice 1506
Radio: The Assistant Teacher 1300
Radio--The Conquest of Our Time 810
Radio: The Fifth Estate (1935) 392
Radio: The Fifth Estate (1946) 581
Radio: The Fifth Estate (1971) 511
Radio: The Great Years 211
Radio Theatre 925
Radio Today 1161
Radio Today and Tomorrow 311
Radio Today: The Black Listener 512
Radio Today: The Hispanic Listener 513
Radio Trailblazing 1301
Radio, TV and Cable: a Telecommunications Approach 549
Radio-TV Bibliography 1607
Radio-TV: Perils to Prosperity 448
Radio-TV Times 1135
Radio W.A.R.S.: A Study of the Needs 520
Radio W.A.R.S.: An In-depth Look 521
Radio W.A.R.S.II: How to Push Listeners' 522
Radio Warfare 828
Radio Week 514
Radio Workers 161
Radio Workshop 944
Radio Workshop for Children 1287
Radio Workshop Plays 992
Radio World 515
Radio Writing (1931) 660
Radio Writing (1939) 870
Radio Year-Round 516
Radio, Your Station and You 605
Radiobroadcasting and Higher Education 1510
Radio's Beautiful Day 72
Radio's Best Plays 974
Radio's Conquest of Space 193
Radio's Feminine Touch 313
Radio's Golden Age 53
Radio's Golden Years 262

Title Index 559

Radio's Listening Groups 397
Radio's 100 Men of Science 91
Radio's Past and Future 1356
Radio's Public Service in Time of War 803
Radio's Role in Instruction 1363
Radio's Second Chance 817
Radios: The Golden Age 67
Radioutlook 289
Rape of Radio, The 850
RCA 245
Readings in Radio and Television News 821
Reality on Reels 865
Rebel in Radio 227
Rebel Radio 1155
Recommended Standards for Radio & TV Program Audience Size 393
Reference Shelf for Radio-Television Newsmen 1622
Regulation of Broadcasting 1458
Regulation of Radio and Television Cigarette Advertising 348
Reith Diaries, The 250
Relationship Between Radio Audience Shares and Revenue Shares 360
Religion by Radio 909
Religious Broadcast Management Handbook 912
Religious Broadcasting (1945) 1036
Religious Broadcasting (serial) 519
Religious Broadcasting, 1920-1983 940
Religious Radio 1004
Reluctant Regulators 1439
Re-Marketing of AM Radio 569
Remember Radio 167
Remember When? 63
Report, Canada (1957) 1106
Report, Canada (1965) 1097
Report of a Research into the Attitudes and Habits 417
Report of Radio Activities, 1938-1939 1292
Report of the Advisory Committee on Education by Radio 1413
Report of the Task Force on Women in

Public Broadcasting 1324
Report on Blacklisting 1435
Report on Chain Broadcasting 1523
Report on Radio News Internships 1582
Report on Social and Economic Data Pursuant to the ... 1524
Report to the People, A 1297
Research Guidelines for Programming Decision Makers 295
Resarch Problems in Radio Education 1290
Resource for the Active Community, A 1387
Responses to the White Paper 831
Responsibilities of Broadcasting Licensees and Station ... 1512
Responsibility for Broadcast Matter 1525
Responsive Chord, The 539
Retrospect and Forecast in Radio Education 1410
Review of 1980 CPB Communication Research Findings 458
Review of National Broadcasting Policy 1067
Revised Study of Radio Broadcasting 554
Richard Dimbleby 81
Richard Durham's Destination Freedom 179
Riding the Air Waves with Eric Palmer 1553
Right to Know, The 1495
Right Way to Radio Playwriting, The 926
Rise of the Goldbergs, The 28
Rock, Roll & Remember 64
Rocking America 238
Role of a National Broadcaster in Contemporary Australia 1065
RTNDA Bulletin 801
RTNDA Communicator 801
Rules and Regulations 1528
Rules and Regulations 1529
Rules of the Radio Ratings Game 303
Rural Radio: Programme Formats 907

560 Radio Broadcasting

Sarnoff: An American Success 86
Satellite Broadcasting in Western Europe 1159
Say Good Night, Gracie! 38
Say It Safely 1427
School Broadcasting and the Newsom Report 1390
School Broadcasting in Canada 1336
School Broadcasting in Great Britain 1369
School Broadcasting in India 1334
School Radio Club, The 1323
School Radio in Europe 1322
School Radio-Sound System 1343
School Use of Radio 1332
School-Wide Use of Radio 1421
Schools of the Air and Radio in the High School Curriculum 1375
Script Shop Presents Eleven Radio Plays, The 952
Script-easers: for Radio Commercial Writers 859
Scriptwriting for the Audio-Visual Media 668
Seamless Robe: Broadcasting, A 1124
Selected Bibliography 1643
Selected Radio and Television Criticism 824
Selling and Promoting Radio and Television 372
Serials, The 1027
Serious Music on the Columbia Broadcasting System 900
Seventy Years of International Broadcasting 1095
Shadow in the Cave, The 547
Shall I Listen 288
Shoestring Pirates, The 1077
Short History of Radio Regulation, A 1526
Short Plays for State and Radio 945
Short Radio Plays 943
Shortwave Radio Listening with the Experts 1544
Shortwave Voices of the World 1256
Shut Up and Listen! 1557

Signing On 1193
Simplicity of Radio 75
Sir John Reith 6
Sixty School Broadcasts 1355
Sketches of Life 23
Skills for Radio Broadcasters 709
Small House Half-Way Up in the Next Block, The 220
Small Station Cooperation 1376
Small Station Management and the Control of ... 1510
So Long Until Tomorrow 267
So You Want to Be a Dee Jay After All This 280
So-o-o-o You're Going on the Air 851
Soap Opera, The 894
Soap Opera Evolution, The 984
Soap World 960
Soaps, The 919
Social Stratification of the Radio Audience 308
Socio-economic Aspects of National Communication Systems 1227
Software for Amateur Radio 1547
Solo Readings for Radio and Class Work 1022
Some Interpretations and Conclusions of the Land- ... 1408
Some Public Service Broadcasting 1333
SOS: The Story of Radio-Communication 278
Sound and Fury 62
Sound and Television Broadcasting Stations 1066
Sound and Vision 42
Sound of Wonder, The 169
Sound of Your Life, The 901
Sounds Real 939
Source for Public Service Programming, A 767
Sourcebook on Radio's Role in Development, A 340
Sourcetap 645
Space WARC and the Role of International Satellite Networks 1126

Title Index 561

Spanish-Language Radio in the
  Southwestern U.S. 1563
Sparks Into the USSR 1230
Speaking of Soap Operas 871
Split Screen 272
Spoken Word, The 633
Sportscasting 954
Spot Radio Promotion Handbook 551
Squeezing Profits Out of Ratings 376
Staff Report on the FCC 1466
Stand By for the Ladies 1568
Standard Definitions of Broadcast
  Research Terms 1646
Standards of Good Practice for Radio
  Broadcasters 768
Star-Spangled Radio 164
Starting and Operating Your Own FM
  Radio Station 404
State and Municipal Regulation of
  Radio Communication 1504
Station Policy and Procedures 416
Statistics on Radio and Television,
  1960-1976 575
Stay Tuned 248
Story of Broadcasting, The 51
Story of Cheerio by Himself, The 106
Story of Radio, The 92
Story of WWJ Radio One, The 249
Straight Across the Board 475
Straight Up 1060
Structure and Organization of
  Broadcasting 1198
Struggle for National Broadcasting in
  Canada, The 1251
Studies in the Control of Radio 1510
Study of Future Direction for VOA, A
  1248
Study of Listening Habits 557
Stuff of Radio, The 818
Successful Radio Advertising with
  Sponsor Participation 379
Successful Radio and Television
  Advertising 541
Successful Radio Promotions 471
Successful Television and Radio
  Advertising 541

Successful Women and How They
  Attained Success 1574
Sue 'Em 890
Suggested Standards for College
  Courses in Radio ... 1307
Summary Statistics of CPB-Qualified
  Public Radio ... 1338
Superjock 177
Supplement No. 1 to Study Guide and
  Reference Material ... 1527
Survey of Advertiser and Agency Buying
  Practices 552
Survey of Broadcast Journalism 612
Survey of Jobs in Radio for Girls, A
  1597
Survey of Radio Listeners in Louisiana
  537
Survey of Radio Listenership 565
Survey of Radio Listening in
  Champaign County, A 534
Survey of Research on Children's
  Radio Listening 389
Survey on Degrees and Courses Offered
  in Radio ... 1412
Survey on the Use of Radio As a Retail
  Advertising Medium, A 477
Syntony and Spark 3

Tab Handbook of Radio
  Communications 1539
Take My Life 55
Tales from Far and Near 1013
Talk Radio and the American Dream
  970
Talk Radio Handbook, The 911
Talked to Death 237
Talking on the Radio 666
Talking Points 1087
Talks 902
Talks About Radio 1550
Tangled Tapes 1197
Tape 692
Taps Is Not Enough 895
Task of Broadcasting News, The 600
Teacher and the Radio Program, The
  1399
Teaching Through Radio 1339

562 Radio Broadcasting

Teaching Through Radio and Television 1340
Teaching with Radio 1344
Technique of Broadcast Advertising, The 434
Technique of Radio Production, The 748
Technique of Radio Writing, The 848
Technique of the Sound Studio ... 778
Teens and Taste in Music and Radio 596
Telecommunications: An Introduction to Electronic Media 382
Telecommunications: Economics and Regulation 388
Telecommunications Policy: A Survey Bibliography 1691
Television and Radio (1961) 838
Television and Radio (1978) 339
Television and Radio, 1987 1163
Television and Radio Announcing 715
Television and Radio in American Life 441
Television and Radio in the United Kingdom 1209
Television and Radio News 819
Television News/Radio News 677
Television/Radio Age 570
Television Radio Audience and Religion, The 1003
Telling the Story 1285
Ten Years Before the Mike 150
Thanks for Listening! 40
Theatre Guild on the Air 109
There's Laughter in the Air! 118
They Fly Through the Air with the Greatest of Ease 905
They Listen by the Millions 476
Thirteen by Corwin 903
Thirty Years of Pioneering and Progress in Radio & TV 263
Thirty-Five Year History of Programs Carried on National ... 253
This Business of Radio Programming 935
This Fascinating Radio Business 168

This Is All India Radio 1072
This Is CBS 240
This Is Galen Drake 85
This Is Local Radio 1088
This Is London! 200
This Is Norman Brokenshire 47
This Is the ABC 1165
This Is War! 903
This Is Your Announcer 1593
This Living World 1388
This Thing Called Broadcasting 125
This Was Radio 155
Those Radio Commentators! 102
Those Radio Times 43
Those Vintage Years of Radio 244
Three Way Plays 1048
Time for Reason About Radio 324
To Serve the Public Interest 1276
Tolstoy's War and Peace 889
Touching the Stars 141
Tower in Babel, A 24
Town Meeting Comes to Town 208
Training for Radio 1587
Training the Local Announcer 695
Training the Speaking Voice 602
Treadmill to Oblivion 4
Treasury Star Parade, The 14
Troubled Air, The 1171
Tune in for Education 1321
Tune in for Elizabeth 1570
Tune in Tomorrow 142
Tune In Yesterday 94
Tuned to Baseball 137
Tuning Out Education 1337
TV and Radio: Everybody's Soapbox 482
Two Hundred Meters and Down 1543
Two-Way Radio Dealer 502

Understanding and Using Radio Audience Estimates 294
Understanding Media 188
Understanding Radio 1122
Uninvited Guests 566
United Press Radio News Style Book 776

Title Index 563

United States and the Direct Broadcast Satellite, The 1182
U.S. Broadcasting to the Soviet Union 1058
U.S. International Broadcasting and National Security 1236
Unsound Broadcasting 1229
Untitled, and Other Radio Dramas 904
UPI Stylebook, The 751
Urban Radio Listening in the U.S. 580
Use of Microphones, The 779
Use of Radio Frequencies for Sound and TV Broadcasting in the U.K., The 1057
Use of Radio in Adult Literacy Education, The 1284
Use of Radio in Farm Advisory Work and Farmer Education, The 1033
Use of Radio in Social Development, The 486
Use of the Radio in Leisure Time, The 325
Use of the Radio in Parent Education, The 383
Uses of the Media by the Chicano Movement, The 1569
Using Radio in Sales Promotion 373
Using Radio in the Classroom 1367

Variety of Lives, A 270
Variety Radio Directory (1937) 1654
Variety Radio Directory (1940) 1700
Vietnam: A Reporter's War 922
Vintage Radio 191
VOA Russian Listeners' Panel 1241
Voice and Articulation Drillbook 676
Voice and Personality As Applied to Radio Broadcasting 1006
Voice of America, The 1212
Voice of America at the Crossroads 1245
Voice of Experience, The 259
Voices in the Darkness 172
Voices of the Game 1025

War of Words, The 42

War on the Short Wave 1143
War Propaganda and the Radio 603
WARC-85 1247
Wartime Censorship of Press and Radio 1517
We Now Take You To.... 902
We Stand United 883
Welcome South, Brother 71
Western Tradition, The 1891
WGN: A Pictorial History 107
What About Radio? 381
What Ails Indian Broadcasting 1127
What Do You Think So Far? 1090
What Every Student of Radio Should Know 579
What the Canadian Public Thinks of the CBC 1100
What the New Radio Rules Mean 1440
What, When and How Guide to Broadcast Co-Op, A 445
When Pirates Ruled the Waves 1150
When Radio Writes for War 840
Who Owns the Media? 350
Who Pays for Broadcasting? 434
Who Really Invented Radio? 143
Who Was That Masked Man? 225
Who, What, Why Is Radio? 423
Who's Listening? 546
Who's Who in Broadcasting 1701
Who's Who in Radio 1702
Who's Who: Annual List of Members 1628
Why We Need a New Radio Law 1488
Widening Horizons 1417
Winchell 265
Winchell Exclusive 282
Winning Radio Research 395
Wireless Communication in the United States 185
Wireless Over Thirty Years 276
Wit and Philosophy from the Radio Talks of America's Humorist ... 223
Women and Radio Music 916
Women in Radio 1567
Women in the Media 1575
Word of Mouth 623

564 Radio Broadcasting

Workable Competition in the Radio Broadcasting Industry 556
Workbook for Radio and TV News Editing and Writing 863
Working for Radio 195
Working Press of the Nation, The 1703
World Administrative Radio Conference 1112
World and International Broadcasting: A Bibliography 1178
World at Their Fingertips 1540
World Broadcast Advertising: Four Reports 598
World Broadcasting in the Age of the Satellite 1158
World Broadcasting Systems 1153
World Goes By, The 127
World Radio and Television 1257
World Radio TV Handbook 1683
World Words 1653
Write Broadcast Feature Copy 866
Write If You Get Work 99
Writer's Radio Theater, The 1041
Writing and Reporting Broadcast News 630
Writing Broadcast News 622
Writing for Broadcasting 853
Writing for Radio 758
Writing for Television and Radio 706
Writing for the B.B.C. (1937) 726
Writing for the BBC (1974) 742
Writing for the Broadcast Media 746
Writing for the Media 802
Writing for the Soaps 1018
Writing News for Broadcast 621
Writing Scripts for Television, Radio and Film 862
Writing Television and Radio Programs 861
Writing Television and Radio Scripts 862
Writing the Script 799
WTIC: Radio to Remember 285
Wyxie Wonderland 207

Yale Radio Plays 1042
Years in a Mirror 121
Years of the Locust 122
Your Career in Radio 1580
Your Future in Broadcasting 1601
Your Speaking Voice 720
You're on the Air (1926) 192
You're on the Air (1972) 675
You're On Next! 619

REF/7221/.C37/1991